BRITAIN'S COLD WAR BOMBERS

TIM MCLELLAND

FONTHILL

Fonthill Media Limited
Fonthill Media LLC
www.fonthillmedia.com
office@fonthillmedia.com

First published 2013 in hardback
This paperback edition published 2016

British Library Cataloguing in Publication Data:
A catalogue record for this book is available from the British Library

ISBN 978-1-78155-534-7 paperback
ISBN 978-1-78155-052-6 hardback

Typeset in 10pt on 13pt Sabon
Printed and bound by CPI Group (UK) Ltd, Croydon, CR0 4YY

Contents

Introduction

Aerial warfare embraces a range of roles and capabilities, but since the earliest days of military aviation, there have been three fundamental roles that have remained key to the very existence and development of the warplane. Reconnaissance and air defence are two of these core capabilities, but the other is arguably the most significant: aerial bombing. It is certainly true to say that the concept of destroying enemy assets and territory from the air is a long established one and predates the emergence of the aeroplane. The mighty First World War German Zeppelin airships were undoubtedly the first flying machines that could seriously be described as 'bombers'. However, as the Second World War unfolded, the bomber aircraft developed rapidly and became a pivotal part of the conflict. Ultimately, the bomber was the machine that ended the war, delivering two atomic bombs to the Japanese mainland in 1945.

But while the Second World War was a key point in the history of the bomber aircraft, the years that immediately followed the war were equally significant. The creation of atomic weaponry transformed the bomber into a completely different machine. No longer was the bomber merely a means of engaging in warfare – it was a means of ending warfare or hopefully preventing warfare from beginning.

The term 'bomber' is a description that embraces a broad capability. The popular conception of a bomber is a large, multi-engine aircraft capable of delivering a weighty load of ordnance over a long distance. But there are countless other flying machines designed to fulfil other roles that require smaller weapons loads, shorter range, greater manoeuvrability or other capabilities that are necessary for particular scenarios. For example, the term 'tactical bomber' usually describes an aircraft that carries a smaller bomb load over a shorter distance than a long-range strategic bomber, but it is a bomber nonetheless. There is often a blurred distinction between the definition of terms such as 'tactical' and 'strategic' in any case.

Likewise, there are numerous examples of aircraft designs that have started their in-service lives as fighters or interceptors and gradually developed to embrace a

RF325, the RAF's last operational Lancaster. Retired from the School of Maritime Reconnaissance at St Mawgan in October 1956, it met a sad end in Coley's scrap yard near Hounslow.

Jet power did not immediately create a technical revolution when the concept first emerged. After Britain's first jet aircraft (E.28/39) made its first flight in May 1941, many more years passed before jet power was translated into a practical power source for military aircraft.

Bomber Command entered the postwar era equipped with Lincolns. Although capable of carrying a significant bomb load, the Lincoln was a derivative of the wartime Lancaster and considered obsolete by the late 1940s.

bombing capability. These can often be referred to as 'fighter-bombers', even though the term is often misused and can sometimes describe an aircraft that is merely a small and agile bomber with no practical fighter capability at all. There is also the much used term 'attack aircraft' that may describe aircraft assigned to roles such as close air support, tactical warfare, even nuclear strike, but in realistic terms, all of these exotic epithets embrace one fundamental function: bombing.

Within the confines of just one book, it would be difficult to adequately describe the design, development and operational history of every post-war British aircraft that possessed an ability to carry bombs. The result would be a mere catalogue of many diverse aeroplanes. Conversely, it would be pointless to propose that a book describing Britain's post-war bombers should dwell on only the RAF's V-Force aircraft and the first jet bomber that preceded them.

Left: The three V-Bombers together. In the foreground, a Mk.1 Vulcan accompanied by a Victor and Valiant.

Below: A sight often seen during the 1960s, '70s and '80s. Four Vulcans from the Waddington Wing perform a scramble demonstration. All four aircraft were airborne within two minutes.

The story of the post-war bomber embraces much more than this and must include the Navy's strike aircraft and the smaller tactical aircraft that succeeded the V-Bombers, and also the aircraft which remain in service to this day. It is also important to describe what was perhaps the most seminal event in post-war history when the most ambitious and potentially important bomber programme of all was ultimately cancelled. The story of Britain's post-war bomber programme is long and complex, sometimes exciting and almost ludicrous. But it is undoubtedly fascinating.

CHAPTER ONE
Jet Genesis

During the final years of the Second World War, the basic principles of jet propulsion were carefully explored for the first time, and within a remarkably short period of time, a viable means of powering aircraft was established. The process of developing this knowledge into practical hardware was slow. However, the fundamental concept gradually became accepted as a serious proposition and it was therefore only natural that Britain's aircraft designers would start to consider the ways in which the concept might be turned into something worthwhile.

The Government's Ministry of Supply recognised the potential of the jet engine at a surprisingly early stage and in 1943, while the Second World War was still being fought, the concept of creating a jet-powered warplane was first discussed at an official level. Although it was impossible to project precisely what might be achievable with the new means of propulsion, it seemed likely that jet power would eventually enable military aircraft to deliver greater speed than that which was achievable by propeller propulsion. It was therefore suggested that existing aircraft designs might be improved through the substitution of jet engines.

While this belief certainly held true with respect to potential fighter designs, the same could not be said for bombers of the period. It seemed unlikely that the capabilities of the mighty Avro Lancaster could be improved upon by the introduction of a jet-powered derivative, as the Lancaster was built for range and load-carrying capability rather than speed. However, it did seem reasonable to consider the possibility of creating a future design to replace the Mosquito fighter-bomber, as an aircraft in this category – requiring high speed and manoeuvrability – would probably benefit most from the introduction of jet propulsion.

Britain's aircraft manufacturers looked at the jet engine's potential with a great deal of interest, but with a war to win it was inevitable that much of their attention was devoted to more immediate concerns, not least the continuing production of existing aircraft designs or the pursuance of more conventional developments based on known and trusted propulsion systems. The jet engine was a great idea, although in 1943 there were more important matters to deal with. That said, the proverbial seeds had been sown and the concept of a jet bomber was at least established, even if no practical steps were taken to create one. The idea drifted around the stuffy corridors of Whitehall, but no one had the will to do anything about it. Nonetheless, many miles away from the gloomy offices from where the Ministry of Supply had first raised the subject, the English Electric Company (based in Preston) were investigating the concept of a jet bomber with some enthusiasm.

The company had started to associate itself with jet power, thanks to the acquisition of an order to produce Vampire fighter aircraft on behalf of de Havilland. Acting as a subcontractor, English Electric began work on the diminutive jet fighter during 1944. With a great deal of experience having been gained through the production of Halifax and Hampden bombers for Handley Page, the relatively small English Electric Company – previously better known for the manufacture of tramcars – was becoming increasingly geared towards serious aircraft production.

During July 1944, designer William 'Teddy' Petter was appointed as the company's new chief engineer. Having become a greatly respected designer in this field with Westland, he moved north to Preston, tasked with the responsibility for overseeing new aircraft design proposals for English Electric. Within a matter of months, a new and highly talented design team had been assembled in Preston and while some fairly conventional proposals were investigated, Petter also turned the team's attention to the concept of a jet-powered bomber.

By the end of 1944, the Air Ministry had been considering the jet bomber idea for some time, but had failed to establish precisely what kind of bomber should be created. It seemed likely (almost inevitable, in fact) that the concept would be pursued at some stage, but there was no real enthusiasm within the corridors of Whitehall – perhaps due to the lack of understanding on what the jet engine could offer. In 1944, the idea of abandoning propellers in favour of 'noisy tubes of hot air' seemed to be more of an abstract scientific concept than a serious military application. English Electric took a rather different view and their active interest in the subject – and continual communications with the Air Ministry – finally had some effect. Finally, the Air Staff accepted that there was a case for developing a jet bomber. Although English Electric had been looking at ways to produce a successor to the Mosquito, the Air Ministry expressed its interest in something more ambitious, a 'high-altitude and high-speed bomber' powered by turbojet engines. Neither a Mosquito nor a Lancaster, the jet bomber would be something in between.

This interest in a larger and more substantial machine was probably due to a number of factors. Firstly, it was becoming increasingly evident that the Lancaster was now obsolete and its successor, the Lincoln, was hardly any better.
Therefore, a completely new bomber design would be a good idea, be it jet-powered or otherwise. Likewise, the development of atomic knowhow was a carefully guarded secret, but it was impossible to keep the secret from everyone inside the Air Ministry.

While the RAF soldiered on with Lincolns, the USAF was looking towards jet power. However, SAC possessed a large force of very capable Boeing B-29 bombers, many of which visited the UK on exercises, as illustrated by the 1948 image taken at Scampton. The US leased B-29s to the RAF until Canberras were introduced into service.

Even in the first months of 1945, the concept of an atomic bomb was known to a select few, and this may well have also had an influence on the developing interest in a new jet bomber, even though the Canberra was never designed with atomic warfare in mind.

The Ministry of Supply issued Specification E.3/45 based around this basic concept and Petter's team embarked upon a new company project in order to meet this specification, designated by English Electric as the A1. The Ministry of Supply eventually created three specifications: the B.3/45 for the high-speed and high-altitude bomber; the B.5/47 for a tactical day bomber; and the BPR.31/48 for a photographic reconnaissance version. The Ministry's main specification called for a 'high-speed and high-altitude unarmed bomber' with a nominal cruising speed of 500 knots at 40,000 feet with a ceiling of 50,000 feet.

It was envisaged that only a two-man crew would be needed comprising of a pilot and navigator responsible for additional tasks such as radio and radar operation. A radar bombing system was considered appropriate rather than old-fashioned visual

Many Canberra airframes were used to test new engine variants and models as they emerged. This particular aircraft was employed on trials with Armstrong Siddeley Motors, testing their new Sapphire engine as indicated by the enlarged engine fairings.

bombing: 'The aircraft is to be laid out for bomb aiming by radar and other mechanical vision systems and for the use of guided projectiles.' The stipulation that the aircraft should be unarmed was an indication of the Air Staff's belief that if the aircraft had sufficient speed, altitude and agility, it would not need to be compromised by heavy and cumbersome guns in order to defend itself. This was perhaps an ambitious and unrealistic expectation in 1945, but in this case the Air Staff's optimistic attitude was to be fully justified, even if nobody knew it at the time.

English Electric created a design that met the necessary requirements (or at least showed promise of doing so) and submitted a brochure to the Ministry of Supply in September 1945. The proposed design was the culmination of a great deal of thinking that had originated in Somerset when Petter was with Westland. At that time, he had considered the possibility of creating a relatively small aircraft powered by Metropolitan-Vickers Beryl turbojets (an engine that was eventually developed into the Sapphire).

The idea was never pursued, but when the Air Ministry began shifting its interest from what was almost a fighter-bomber towards a more conventional high-altitude bombing platform, the Beryl engine seemed inadequate for the task. There was some possibility that Rolls-Royce would be developing a new 12,000 lb thrust engine, and although its centrifugal flow system (the type of engine used in the Gloster Meteor) would result in a bulky piece of equipment, it could be accommodated within a large circular fuselage structure. Therefore, Petter and his team worked on a number of design concepts that suited this arrangement, some featuring two of these cumbersome powerplants.

However, the Rolls-Royce engine did not proceed very far, not least because the company was achieving great success with its new axial-flow AJ.65 engine. The new powerplant was capable of delivering 6,000 lb of thrust without the weight and complications of the clumsy centrifugal system. It did not need much imagination to realise that two of the smaller and slimmer AJ.65 engines would be a far better solution. The engines were small enough to be housed either inside or under the wings and the aircraft would also have a degree of additional safety should one engine fail (early jet engines were notoriously unreliable).

Consequently, English Electric dropped the original plan for what was a large and bulky design with a single engine in the fuselage for a more refined design incorporating two engines, each buried in the wing root structure (installing engines in the wing to reduce airflow drag was a new innovation that many British designers embraced at this time). The revised design offered superior fuel consumption figures and this enabled the designers to reduce the aircraft's fuel tankage and enlarge the bomb bay so that a respectable weapons load could be carried. It was predicted that the relatively conservative wing design – essentially straight with a slightly swept leading edge – would enable the bomber to fly at speeds up to 550 mph, although the use of a swept-wing design would have probably increased this figure to 585 mph. However, Petter did not see any advantage in aiming for this higher speed if it meant long delays and rises in cost, both of which would be inevitable if a swept-wing design was pursued.

The concept of swept wings was new in 1945, and although the scientific data (mostly captured from Nazi Germany) seemed to indicate that the idea was sound, it was a radical concept that would require a great deal of time consuming and expensive testing. Instead, it was agreed that more predictable and conventional straight-wing designs should be adopted. It was decided that the two engines should be moved from the wing root some distance so that a wide-track landing gear could be fitted, enabling the main wheels to retract neatly into the deep inner-wing structure. The decision to shift the engines outboard made sense in some respects, but their revised position also meant that streamlined nacelles had to be incorporated into the wing structure. Consequently, almost all of the drag-free advantages of a fully-buried engine were lost. But more significantly, the new engine position also meant that the aircraft would have far less asymmetrical stability should either engine fail. This did not seem to be much of a concern at the time, but it was something that eventually became a significant flaw when the aircraft finally entered service with the RAF.

The Canberra prototype, VN799, pictured during engine tests at Warton. The original rounded tail fin and dorsal fillet are clearly visible.

Despite this, the new wing design was amended and the earlier design's conventional tail and fin structure was retained, creating a simple but surprisingly elegant aircraft that the Air Ministry and Ministry of Supply greeted with great excitement.

The first production contract was issued to English Electric on 7 January 1946 calling for a small fleet of four prototypes. A wooden mock-up was constructed so that the basic construction procedure could be explored and established before production of the actual aircraft got underway. Significantly, English Electric was keen to move away from the traditional practice of building 'by hand' and took advantage of lessons they had learned through the production of aircraft for Handley Page. The aircraft's structure would be largely manufactured by means of production jigs, ensuring that each of the major components was identical. This would be beneficial as primary structures would be interchangeable between aircraft without risk of mismatching due to inaccuracies of building without jigs.

The key structures were the front, centre and rear fuselage sections, the mainplanes (wings) for the early aircraft (which were not to be fitted with anti-icing systems) and later mainplanes for a development-standard engine and anti-icing gear. This production technique was relatively new at the time, but it made good sense and proved invaluable for the company in later years when the same aircraft was produced in many different versions or to replace sections that were either damaged or fatigued. The Rolls-Royce AJ.65 was always the preferred engine for the aircraft, but as English Electric had feared, development and production schedules began to slip. In order to avoid delaying test flights of the new A1 bomber, a pair of 5,000 lb Nene engines were allocated to what eventually became the second prototype. These centrifugal-flow engines required fatter, re-contoured nacelles in order to accommodate their greater bulk. However, the worries over production of the AJ.65 (which became the famous Avon) were soon resolved and the Nene-powered second prototype became little more than a rather expensive precautionary diversion that was ultimately unnecessary.

The first prototype (VN799) was slowly completed at the company's Strand Road factory before being dismantled for transportation to nearby Warton, a former USAAF airfield that English Electric had purchased as a test facility. Meanwhile,

A wintry scene at Binbrook as the first Canberra bombers are delivered to the RAF. A distinctly outdated Lincoln is visible in the background. (*Courtesy BAE Systems*)

the Air Ministry's enthusiasm for the aircraft had grown significantly now that the prototype was nearing completion and its performance capabilities were becoming clearer. On 1 March 1949, a contract was placed for 132 aircraft – quite an achievement for English Electric, especially as the prototype had yet to fly. In fact, the order illustrated not only supreme confidence in the design, but also the growing sense of urgency that was becoming a major concern for Bomber Command and the British Government.

The RAF had barely begun to relinquish its wartime Lancasters and was now faced with only the Avro Lincoln as a direct replacement. The Lincoln was little more than an improved Lancaster and as the Cold War began to unfold, it became abundantly clear that this Second World War-era aircraft would be no credible deterrent against perceived Soviet intentions. The new jet bomber was needed and it was needed fast. Frustratingly, it was at this stage that the Air Ministry had to accept that their plans to equip the A1 with radar-bombing equipment were simply not going to happen. Development of a suitable system (the H2S Mk.9) was dogged with delays and difficulties, and a prevailing sense of urgency finally persuaded the RAF to revert to more traditional solutions.

The A1 bomber's projected radar-equipped nose section was abandoned and the planned arrangement for a two-man crew was changed to incorporate a third crew member who would be responsible for visual bomb aiming. This was by means of a clear nose section incorporating a visual bombing system based on the tried and tested T2 bombsight. The third crew member would have to crawl into the A1's small nose section and lay in a prone position to peer out of a Perspex window in much the same way as the RAF's wartime crew members had done; however, he was afforded the luxury of his own ejection seat, fixed beside the navigator's seat, behind the pilot. The only obvious difficulty would be that the bomb-aimer would have to release himself from the numerous straps and buckles of the ejection seat in order to reach the clear nose section. He would then have to reattach himself to the ejection seat when his work was done. This was hardly an ideal concept and it bore a disturbing similarity to the old-fashioned techniques that the RAF was hoping to leave behind, but it was the best the RAF could hope for in 1949.

Thus, the 'blind bomber' (which would have been the Canberra B.Mk.1) was abandoned before even so much as one example had been built. Perhaps more significantly, the 'tactical day bomber' had now almost seamlessly become a more traditional high-altitude strategic bomber, even though the aircraft did not have the necessary range to handle this role. On 29 April 1949, the first A1 prototype emerged from the flight test shed (Hangar 25) at Warton to make its first engine runs. These tests proceeded smoothly and on 8 May, English Electric's chief test pilot, Roland Beamont, took the aircraft out onto the airfield to begin a series of taxi trials. By the following day, he was able to confidently allow the aircraft to make gentle hops

VX181was the prototype of the Canberra PR.Mk.3, the first variant of the standard bomber design to be developed for photographic reconnaissance duties. (*Courtesy BAE Systems*)

into the air during high-speed runs, one lasting for some 500 yards. However, it was on the auspicious day of Friday 13 May that Beamont finally took VN799 into the air for its first flight. Much to everyone's delight, the flight went well and Beamont reported no major difficulties. Indeed, his only major concern was the performance of the aircraft's rudder controls, which suggested that the rudder hinge might be overbalanced. This minor problem was slowly resolved by reducing the height of the (wooden) rudder horn balance over a series of flights until the original curved fin top slowly changed into the familiar flattered shape applied on all subsequent aircraft.

The second test flight revealed the presence of elevator flutter (self-induced movement that increases in amplitude unless checked) and time was spent modifying the tailplane surfaces until both the rudder and tailplanes functioned perfectly. A 'collar' fairing was introduced behind the pilot's canopy to cure a slight snaking tendency (yawing from side to side) that had also manifested itself on some test flights. But in most respects, the aircraft performed brilliantly and soon exceeded the stipulated 40,000 feet altitude laid down by the Air Ministry. Likewise, the required 450 knots top speed was exceeded by more than 20 knots and it was clear that production aircraft with more powerful engines would be able to offer even greater performance.

Canberras from No. 101 Squadron prepare for 'Jungle King', a major Bomber Command exercise staged in 1953.

For the RAF with its fleet of aged Mosquito, Lancaster and Lincolns, the jet prototype's performance seemed almost eye-watering. The public soon got a taste of just how good the new bomber was when VN799 was cleared to appear at the 1949 SBAC (Society of British Aerospace Companies) Farnborough show. Ironically, English Electric had never displayed any of its products at Farnborough before and they were about to steal the show with a completely new aeroplane that was years ahead of its time. This was just four years after the end of the Second World War and the basic concept of jet power was still a novelty for many. The crowds at Farnborough were accustomed to seeing fighter aircraft performing ever faster and more flamboyant displays every year, but bomber aircraft were something completely different. Bombers were supposed to be big, bulky, heavy and slow, capable of little more than straight flypasts and a few lazy turns for the amusement of the spectators. This perception changed drastically within the first few seconds of Roly Beamont's first performance with VN799.

The aircraft made its first appearance early in the afternoon on 6 September and a great deal of excitement began to build around the show site as Beamont's much-rumoured display grew nearer. The aircraft started up and taxied onto the runway at which stage Beamont was due to switch from a near-empty rear fuel tank onto full tanks. However, a slight delay allowed the port engine to run out of fuel and wind down before the fuel switch was made. Much to his embarrassment, Beamont was obliged to taxi off the runway and request a later display slot while Petter expressed his displeasure at the way in which the new bomber had made such an awkward public debut. But later in the afternoon, the aircraft was back on the runway and the crowds were eager to see what all the fuss was about.

With a mighty roar from its two Avon engines, VN799 thundered along Farnborough's runway and instead of gently easing itself off the runway, it leapt into the air after a run of only 600 yards. This in itself was astonishing, but when Beamont then hauled the aircraft into a tight left-hand turn and returned to sweep past the crowds at a height of just 100 feet, it was clear that the audience was watching something very special. VN799 roared skywards into a near-vertical climb, entered a roll and returned to centre stage in a descending turn at which point Beamont executed a full 360-degree roll as the spectators looked on with astonishment and disbelief. The 6-minute display was one of the most iconic and truly memorable events to have ever occurred at Farnborough and Beamont's performance was the talk of the show. Some of the SBAC Committee members did not know what to

139 Squadron Canberras pictured at Bermuda's Kindley Field during a goodwill visit in the 1950s.

think, but there was a general feeling that the spectacle had been far too flamboyant and that Beamont should tone down his performance for subsequent days.

The Committee's senior test pilot, 'Mutt' Summers, discussed the display with Beamont and he concluded that although the demonstration had seemed almost frightening to some, there was no logical reason to change it. The same breathtaking routine was performed for the remainder of the week and once the show finally ended, English Electric's team returned to Warton with a justifiably proud sense of achievement. They had grabbed world headlines with the show-stopping routine and both they and the RAF were delighted.

Trials with VN799 continued into the winter of 1949, by which stage the Nene-powered second prototype had also been completed. The third prototype followed shortly afterwards on 22 November, flying not from Warton, but from English Electric's factory airfield at Samlesbury where it had been built, a few miles to the north. The fourth machine – which had been fitted with a suitable fuel system – introduced the addition of wingtip-mounted external fuel tanks, which gave the aircraft an additional 500-gallon fuel capacity at the expense of very little drag,

Assorted Canberras pictured at Warton while assigned to trials work. The lead aircraft are B.Mk.6 aircraft and a T.Mk.4 dual-control trainer is in the middle. In the distance is a PR.Mk.3 photo reconnaissance aircraft and a standard B.Mk.2 bomber variant. (*Courtesy BAE Systems*)

Later examples of the Canberra U.Mk.10 were painted in an overall white colour scheme prior to being ferried to Australia for trials work. Most of the U10 fleet was ultimately either destroyed or disposed of in Australia.

although if necessary the tanks could be jettisoned in flight. So successful were these tanks that they became an almost standard fit on every production aircraft.

The first of these production-standard aircraft was VX165 and this aircraft took to the air on 21 April 1950. With tip tanks fitted, the bomb-aimer's clear nose section incorporated and third-crew seat installed, this aircraft also dispensed with the small dorsal fin that had been present on the previous prototypes after test results confirmed that it was unnecessary. Sadly, VX165's contribution to the type's flight test programme was cut short as it crashed on 13 June 1951 after suffering an engine fire. However, the accident was not connected to a design flaw and the test programme continued without delay. By 1951, English Electric's A1 was ready for its customer: the Royal Air Force. As with all British aircraft, the A1 had to be given a name and it was the company's chairman, Sir George Nelson, who decided upon 'Canberra' as a suitable choice.

Keen to foster relations between Britain and the Commonwealth (and with the possibility of export orders), the bomber was named after Australia's capital city on 19 January 1951 at a ceremony attended by the Australian prime minister at Biggin Hill where the first production Canberra (WD929) was placed on show.

It was sad to note that this celebratory event did not include the presence of Petter as he had resigned from English Electric ten months previously and no longer had any association with the company. Despite being a talented designer, Petter did not settle into English Electric's management structure with confidence and his time at Warton was often dogged with disagreements between him and the engineering team at Strand Road. Eventually, he had asked for the two facilities to be separated and his 'go it alone' philosophy did not sit well with English Electric's management. The continual disagreements inevitably meant that he would resign, but his departure was a less than happy one and he actively encouraged members of his team to join him at Folland Aircraft. Some members of the team accepted his offer and it was Freddie Page who subsequently assumed control of the Canberra's design and development, and the creation of the Lighting interceptor that followed it.

Despite the regrettable events at Warton, the Canberra's production continued and on 25 May 1951, Beamont took Canberra B.Mk.2 WD936 to Binbrook in Lincolnshire where he executed another brilliant display that amazed and delighted onlookers, most of whom were associated with the many Lincoln bombers that were scattered around the airfield.

Pictured prior to delivery to the RAF, WF890 joined Bomber Command as a standard B.Mk.2 medium bomber. Some years later, the aircraft was withdrawn and refurbished, re-emerging as a T.Mk.17 ECM trainer.

Above: VX185 was the prototype of the Canberra Mk.5 pathfinder and target-marker variant that was to have joined Bomber Command. The RAF eventually decided that target marking was no longer relevant to postwar bomber operations and the variant was abandoned. (*Courtesy BAE Systems*)

Right: The Canberra T.Mk.4 was a dual-control trainer derivative of the basic Mk.2 airframe. Equipped with an additional seat for an instructor, the aircraft was essentially unchanged apart from the removal of the Plexiglas nose that was no longer required. (*Courtesy BAE Systems*)

Canberra B.Mk.2 WD938 illustrates the black and grey Bomber Command paint scheme that was applied to the first Canberras to enter RAF service. The scheme was short lived and was soon replaced by overall silver, indicative of the type's intended medium-level bombing role.

As they stood beside their obsolete Second World War vintage monsters, they could not fail to be impressed by the sprightly Canberra, rolling and looping high in the skies above the Lincolnshire Wolds. Beamont duly landed and taxied in and handed the aircraft to No. 101 Squadron. This was to become the RAF's first jet bomber squadron, but the Canberra had already made its noisy presence apparent weeks previously when WD951 arrived to join the newly formed Jet Conversion Flight, created to introduce Lincoln pilots to the challenges of jet-powered flight.

As the standard Canberra B2, WD951 was of little use as a hands-on conversion trainer (the dual-control Canberra T4 was still to be produced), a pair of Meteor T7 jets joined the Flight so crews could familiarise themselves with the peculiarities of jet power before embarking on flights in the Canberra. It was quickly established that there were few challenges to be met and training for the fledgling Canberra pilots proved to be straightforward. In the first year of operations at Binbrook, only one significant accident occurred when WD938 ran out of fuel and made a wheels-up landing on the airfield.

The Flight eventually became part of No. 617 Squadron, the second of Binbrook's Canberra units, followed in due course by Nos. 9, 50 and 101 Squadrons. When these units had completed their transition onto the Canberra, Binbrook had almost become an all Canberra base. Despite the station's remote location out in the wilds of Lincolnshire (and the presence of some remaining Lincolns that lingered in service until the Valiant was introduced), Binbrook became a popular destination for countless RAF and other military and Government officials all of whom wanted to witness the world's first jet bomber base in operation.

However, by 1953, attention began to shift to Coningsby where Nos. 15, 44, 57 and 149 Squadrons had been operating Boeing B-29 Washington bombers for a couple of years. In an effort to improve Bomber Command's capabilities, the Washingtons had been leased from the US so that Bomber Command was able to operate an aircraft that had a chance of presenting a serious deterrent to the USSR. The B-29 had the ability to successfully deliver weapons to the heart of the Soviet Union, whereas the RAF's Lincoln had increasingly become an embarrassment, its outward wartime appearance only serving to confirm that the RAF was operating an aircraft that was a decade out of date. The Washington (the adopted British name for the Superfortress) was hardly more advanced, but as a far larger and more powerful machine, it had the ability to fly far and high, and deliver a meaningful bomb load. The Canberra, however, represented a leap into a new era and replacement of the Washingtons gave Coningsby a new bomber that possessed breathtaking speed and agility, and an altitude capability that was (by contemporary standards) astonishing.

On the other hand, it is also true that the Canberra was not, by any standards, a strategic bomber. Designed for a tactical role, it did not have the fuel capacity necessary to fly deep into the heart of the USSR. But as a credible deterrent against the Soviet threat, it was undoubtedly an aircraft to be reckoned with as it had the ability to fly high and fast. Although it was not a threat to the heart of Moscow, it was not an aircraft to be dismissed. If a conflict broke out in Europe, the Canberra would be a very serious threat to any Soviet advance. More importantly for the RAF, it was regarded as a major step towards an even more capable bomber force that would emerge just a few years later when the V-Force came into service. As Coningsby re-equipped with the Canberra, it was unclear to observers that the new jet bomber's stay would be brief and that it would make way for an even more impressive, noisier and deadlier machine.

Scampton was the third RAF base to re-equip with Canberras (during 1953) and Marham duly followed, so that by 1954, Bomber Command could boast a force of sixteen operational Canberra squadrons. The RAF was finally free of its Lincoln, Mosquito and Washingtons and now had a credible force of very capable jet bombers at its disposal. This status also enabled the RAF to begin the task of training crews not only for the Canberra force, but its growing number of aircrew to take on the new V-Force bombers that would be coming into service. No one doubted that the task of operating the new force of strategic bombers would be a major challenge.

Above and below: Canberra T4 WJ867 was operated by the A&AEE and ETPS at Boscombe Down. Unusually, it was painted in a white colour scheme with pale national insignia, similar to that applied to RAF and FAA nuclear-capable aircraft. However, in the case of WJ867, the odd choice of colour scheme has never been explained. (*Courtesy Mike Freer*)

Canberra B2 WD965 joined No. 10 Squadron at Scampton in 1953. In this early photograph, the aircraft has yet to be equipped with wingtip fuel tanks. The early Bomber Command black and grey paint scheme is also applied, although this was soon replaced by overall silver. (*Tony Clarke collection*)

The Canberra squadrons were regarded as an ideal 'stepping stone' towards creating a supply of qualified air and ground crews who were familiar and confident with all aspects of jet bomber operations. The RAF therefore required to train a huge number of crews to fly the Canberra and in order to meet this task, No. 231 Operational Conversion Unit was formed at Bassingbourn. The unit was initially equipped with a variety of aircraft types until the first Canberras were delivered and full-scale training did not get underway until the first Canberra T.Mk.4 dual-control aircraft were delivered in August 1953.

A contract issued in September 1950 covered the first batch of Canberra T.Mk.4 trainers and the first production aircraft (WE188) made its maiden flight on 30 October 1952 before being delivered to Bassingbourn. Unlike many fighter and bomber types from which trainer derivatives are produced, the Canberra T.Mk.4 was almost identical to the 'standard' B2 bomber version. The same fuselage structure and canopy arrangement was utilised; however, instead of a clear nose section for the bombardier, a solid nose was substituted. The student pilot was required to occupy the pilot's seat on the port side of the fuselage while the instructor sat to the right, the

Canberra B2s from No. 231 OCU pictured at El Adem while part of Swifter Flight in 1960. The aircraft were used to investigate the effects of high-speed and low-level flight on aircraft structure and crews. The sun shades provide clear evidence of the Canberra's vulnerability to cockpit overheating while on the ground.

two seats squeezed under the same circular canopy. The navigator's seat in the rear of the cockpit was retained and in order to enable both the student and navigator to reach their positions, the instructor's seat was designed to swivel. It was not the most elegant of arrangements and to describe the T4's cockpit as cramped would be an understatement. That being said, it was a simple and inexpensive means of enabling students to convert onto the Canberra with relative ease. Nonetheless, the OCU's early experience with the Canberra was not entirely trouble free.

Various Canberras had been lost in accidents as a recurring tailplane trim fault took time to identify and cure. Also, there had been losses at the OCU that could not be attributed to this deficiency. After a great deal of investigation, it was established that students were flying into the ground due to a tendency to misread the aircraft's artificial horizon in bad weather conditions or at night. Having become accustomed to the laborious take-off acceleration of piston-engine aircraft, the Canberra's sprightly performance, combined with a misinterpretation of the aircraft's instruments, fooled students into believing that the aircraft was climbing at a higher angle than recommended. As a consequence, the aircraft duly pointed downwards with catastrophic results. It was a simple error that could be resolved through better instruction, but for a period there was a recurrent worry that jet

The Canberra training unit (No. 231 Operational Conversion Unit) based at RAF Bassingbourn assembled a short-lived but hugely popular demonstration team equipped with four Canberra T.Mk.4 trainers. Their display routine included some excellent close formation, rolling manoeuvres and an astonishing vertical bomb break – quite a feat for a jet bomber.

bomber training would not be as straightforward as had been imagined. In fact, the OCU at Bassingbourn succeeded in producing a seemingly endless stream of very capable crews for eighteen years, after which the unit moved to Cottesmore and then to Wyton. When the OCU finally disbanded in 1993, it had trained more than 8,000 Canberra crews in total.

The RAF's re-equipment with Canberras continued at a steady pace with not only the standard B2 bomber variant settling into service, but also the T4 trainer and the PR.Mk.3, a derivative of the bomber variant designed for photographic reconnaissance. Outwardly similar to the B2, the PR3 featured a 14-inch 'plug' in the forward fuselage (behind the cockpit) to enable six cameras to be fitted. Additional fuel was also housed in the fuselage and this gave the PR3 more than 540 gallons of extra capacity, enabling the PR3 to achieve a range of 3,585 miles. By 1954, the B2 had been superseded by the B.Mk.6, fitted with a pair of up-rated Avon Mk.109 engines, each delivering 7,500 lb of thrust. The B6 also introduced a 450-gallon integral fuel tank inside each wing. These improvements (combined with new Maxaret anti-skid braking systems for the landing gear which improved landing performance) gave the Canberra an increased overall speed of a nominal ten knots, but also increased the aircraft's range to 3,400 miles – not bad for an aircraft designed as a tactical bomber.

The Canberra Mk.6 was manufactured by English Electric (at their Samlesbury factory) and also by Short Brothers based in Belfast (the B2 was also built under

Canberra T.Mk.4 WT483 pictured on a former Vulcan dispersal at Cottesmore while serving with No. 231 OCU. The Canberra OCU was based at Cottesmore after moving from Bassingbourn. It subsequently moved to Wyton. (*Tony Clarke collection*)

licence by both Short Brothers and Handley Page). The task of churning out a large fleet of jet bombers was beyond the capacity of English Electric. With the Lightning interceptor taking up an increasing amount of resources, it was inevitable that Canberra B6 production would also be exported to a licence manufacturer. The first production B6 made its first flight on 11 August 1953, followed by the first Shorts-built example in October 1954. In July of that year, the first B6 was delivered to No. 192 Squadron at Binbrook, Lincolnshire. By December, the first examples of the B6 were delivered to the Hemswell Wing, a few miles to the west, followed by the arrival of two squadrons at Waddington.

The whole of Lincolnshire was seemingly reverberating to the sound of Canberra bombers. As the bomber force continued to build up, the Canberra PR3 photographic reconnaissance variant was also treated to the same improvements that had been applied to the B2, the resulting derivative being designated as the PR. Mk.7. By the end of 1955, the RAF proudly boasted a total of thirty-seven operational Canberra squadrons operating a mix of B2 and B6 bombers. Meanwhile, the PR squadrons had a combination of PR3 and PR7s with T4 trainers assigned to the OCU and one or two of these variants assigned to each squadron for continuation training. This was in effect the peak of the Canberra's significance within Bomber Command and as the V-Force slowly began to emerge, the Canberra would gradually be replaced as a high-altitude conventional bomber so that the new nuclear strategic bombers could take over.

It was also at this stage that the Canberra's basic role was re-examined. The RAF was now beginning to accept that the traditional concept of a fast, medium or high-altitude bomber might not necessarily be appropriate when the Soviet Union was rapidly developing interceptors and missiles that could reach the altitudes that RAF bombers had been enjoying. Height no longer meant safety. Both the Canberra and the new V-Force would eventually abandon the quest for altitude and embrace low-level operations amongst the hills and valleys at heights of 500 feet or less. At tree-top level, it was possible to hide from radar and enemy defences. The RAF concluded that the Canberra would be better suited to the low-level environment and with the V-Force slowly assuming the role of a long-range strategic bomber, the Canberra could now embrace the role that it had been designed for: supporting tactical operations at shorter ranges.

It is worth noting that the Canberra had become a rather different aircraft to the one that had first been envisaged. When it was first ordered, the RAF had anticipated a bomber that would be smaller and lighter than the projected 'strategic' V-Bombers that were to follow with a shorter range but a faster speed. But as former VCAS Sir Ralph Cochrane commented, 'There was a tendency to look upon the Canberra as a

No. 27 Squadron operated Canberra bombers only briefly. Unusually, the unit applied red cheat lines to the fuselage and nose sections of their aircraft, together with the squadron's badge.

WK163 was assigned to Napier as a test aircraft for their Scorpion rocket motor. While engaged on trials, the aircraft attained a world record altitude of 70,310 feet on 28 August 1957.

long-range, high-flying bomber and to press for equipment to enable it to undertake this role. At the end, however, it was generally accepted that the Canberra is a short-range tactical bomber, that there is no equipment that will enable it to hit a small target from 45,000 feet, and that it must therefore come down to a height from which it can achieve results.'

This effectively required the Canberra B.Mk.2 to abandon the notion of cruising at 40,000 feet (with a ceiling of 50,000 feet) and shift to operational heights of 15-20,000 feet and a ceiling of 40,000 feet. Likewise, the envisaged 10,000 lb bomb load would be reduced to a maximum of 8,000 lb. Essentially, this meant an aircraft with a more modest performance, but one that was much closer to English Electric's original proposal to create a direct replacement for the Mosquito. Thus, the Canberra had never been a true expression of the RAF's requirement for a truly high-altitude bomber nor had it been a true tactical 'attack bomber' in any real sense – until now.

At this stage, the Canberra B2 was very much a 'traditional' medium-level bomber and had been specifically designed to perform this task. It was not designed to operate at a very low level and could only deliver conventional freefall high-explosive (HE) bombs. If the Canberra was to be operated in the attack (or 'intruder') role, it would have to change considerably. Rather than merely relying on simple modifications to the existing Canberra B2 and B6 bomber design, the RAF issued Operational Requirement OR.302, calling for a development of the standard Canberra model that would be suited to low-level operations as an 'intruder' bomber. The term 'intruder' implied a ground-attack capability and not only as a bomber, but as an attack aircraft through the use of rockets or gun armament.

English Electric proposed the conversion of the existing Canberra Mk.5 prototype that had been built in response to an Air Ministry requirement for a radar-equipped target marker aircraft. Without the original 'blind bomber' Canberra Mk.1 with its own radar equipment, the Canberra Mk.2 was reliant upon visual conditions unless Gee cover was present. (Gee was a wartime vintage radio navigation system comprising of locator beacons that enabled navigation through a triangulation technique.) Bomber Command therefore specified that the Canberra's role was defined as '...bombing in support of the land battle within 250 miles of the front line,' adding that, '...from high altitudes, target identification makes visual day bombing difficult. For accurate bombing therefore, there is a continuing need both by day and by night to be able to mark targets accurately. There will therefore be a requirement for an aircraft to mark visually for a medium-range Canberra force.'

However, the continuing development of a suitable radar system was slow and with the radar-equipped V-Force on the horizon, the target-marker Canberra seemed an expensive luxury. The Canberra B.Mk.5 was therefore dropped and English Electric opted to use the redundant prototype as the basis of what would become the B.Mk.8 intruder variant. For this new Canberra, the forward fuselage behind the cockpit would be removed and a new fighter-type cockpit canopy installed, offset to port with a standard windscreen and a blown perspex canopy.

The original circular 'glasshouse' canopy had always been a controversial choice from the start. It provided the Canberra pilot with good all-round visibility, but it was not optically perfect. A small circular porthole had to be incorporated into the canopy so that the pilot had some clear forward vision through the flat panel. Peering through the porthole was not the most elegant of procedures, but the big bubble canopy was adequate for the Canberra's high-level bombing role. Not so suitable was the canopy's ability to gather and capture heat, which often made conditions for the crew almost intolerable when the aircraft was on the ground in direct sunlight. It was therefore decided that a new intruder Canberra required the fighter-type cockpit arrangement. It was also proposed that the navigator/bomb-aimer's seat should be moved forward and repositioned beside the pilot, inside the fuselage. Oddly, the pilot was to be given an ejection seat, but it was decided that the navigator would rely instead on manual egress through the fuselage door. This was undoubtedly a

The B-57B built under licence in the US by Martin illustrates the revised tandem-seat arrangement for the aircraft's crew devised by the company. Sadly, the same layout was not adopted for any of the RAF's bomber or interdictor variants. (*Courtesy BAE Systems*)

bad decision for an aircraft that was destined to fly low level. And fifty years later, it is still difficult to understand why the 'intruder' Canberra's peculiar arrangement was adopted, especially when it had captured the interest of the USAF. American manufacturer Martin had swiftly devised a superior tandem-seating arrangement for its B-57 derivative.

Why English Electric failed to embrace a similar design is a mystery. Rather more logical, however, was the decision to design a gun pack for the aircraft comprising of four Hispano 20-mm cannon with 520 rounds per gun contained in a fairing that could be attached to the lower fuselage of the Canberra, leaving the forward portion of the bomb bay to be used for other ordnance. Additionally, under-wing hard points would also be installed so that a 1,000 lb freefall bomb could be carried or a Matra rocket launcher plus other weapons. Most importantly, there would be a provision to carry a tactical nuclear bomb internally.

Over a six month period, VX185 was rebuilt and it emerged for its first flight as the prototype B. Mk.(I)8 on 23 July 1954.

Above and below: VX185, the first Canberra B(I).Mk.8 interdictor variant. The all-black paint scheme was peculiar to the prototype and was not adopted by the RAF. (*Courtesy BAE Systems*)

A production contract followed that also included a batch of conversions intended to supplement the main force of new Mk.8 aircraft. The conversions applied to nineteen Canberra Mk.6 aircraft (plus three more that were subsequently ordered) that were modified to carry the new Boulton Paul gun pack with the necessary weapons bay, strengthening and alterations, plus the new wing pylon provisions. The forward fuselage complete with the original 'greenhouse' canopy remained unchanged and as such, these aircraft were designated as the Canberra B.Mk.(I)6 (the 'I' denoting the Intruder role).

The new Canberras were soon deployed to Germany where their modest range was less of an issue.

Just minutes from the East German border, the Canberra was well placed to be called into action. However, the Canberra's range was not an issue that dictated the shift to Germany: it was the lack of space on the UK mainland where the RAF was running out of available airfields that could accommodate the ever-expanding bomber force.

As part of the B(I)8 trials programme, VX185 was flown with the cockpit canopy removed in order to investigate handling and cockpit conditions. Apart from noise and a drop in temperature, the absence of the canopy had no effect on the aircraft or crew. (*Courtesy BAE Systems*)

WT307 was one of the RAF's fleet of Canberra B(I)6 interdictor aircraft delivered to No. 213 Squadron in Germany. The purpose-built gun pod was carried under the fuselage, although it is positioned to the side of the aircraft for this promotional photo. (*Courtesy BAE Systems*)

Moving to Germany therefore made perfect sense as suitable airfields were available and the bomber force would be much closer to its projected area of operations. NATO thinking at this time assumed that a confrontation with the Soviet Union would begin with a huge influx of conventional forces from the East with countless armoured columns progressing across Germany's northern plains. With a perceived numerical inferiority, the West's conventional forces could not hope to contain this kind of attack for more than a few days. Although the Canberra intruders would clearly be called upon to support NATO forces through the delivery of conventional bombs and cannon fire, it was inevitable that the Canberras would deliver tactical nuclear bombs if the advance was not stopped.

Likewise, Britain had adopted a policy of a strategic deterrence and the Canberras would, if needed, act as part of this retaliatory strike capability. The provision of a nuclear capability for RAF Germany's Canberras was made possible through the introduction of 'Project E', an agreement between British and US Governments in 1957 to enable American nuclear weapons to be carried by RAF aircraft. Britain's ability to produce atomic weapons in large numbers was a great challenge due to a woeful lack of resources and money. As the perceived Soviet threat became greater and more serious, it was accepted that the US and UK would have to co-operate if the West had any hope of presenting the USSR with a credible nuclear deterrent. Part of the Project E agreement stated that if a full-scale war should break out, it would probably consist of two phases, one being of comparatively short duration 'characterised by an intensive exchange of atomic blows' and a secondary phase of reduced intensity. Throughout these exchanges, survivability would be a key concern and this implied that the Allied response should be 'conducted with maximum possible speed and effectiveness, and with its weight of effort unwaveringly exerted against the highest priority targets'. This meant that the RAF and USAF would have to operate together with fully co-ordinated strike plans that ensured the best use of resources and avoided 'overlap' wherever possible. It was also stated that the Allied counter air offensive would require 'heavy co-ordinated attacks against airfields, logistic facilities, control centres and command headquarters' and this task would rely heavily upon the RAF's Canberras.

Plans were made to equip the Canberra with a British-designed atomic bomb (Red Beard). However, with development and quantity production taking a great deal of time, the Project E agreement enabled the Canberra to be nuclear capable within a much shorter time scale with only relatively small modifications to the aircraft being necessary to enable the Mk.7 'Thor' weapon to be carried. The Mk.7 bomb was 15 feet long and weighed only 1,650 lb. The Canberra could carry it comfortably, but the bomb bay doors were to be altered in order to accommodate it. Also, baffle plates were fitted so that the bomb bay doors could be safely opened at the higher speeds necessary for release of the American weapon.

The bomb was fitted with a radar altimeter that enabled the weapon to be detonated at around 1,500 feet above the selected target (an 'air burst'), ensuring that the maximum destructive effect was achieved. With Uranium 235 fissionable elements located in the warhead, the amount of material inserted into core could be varied so that different yields might be selected from eight kilotons through to sixty-one kilotons (three times the power of the bomb dropped on Hiroshima). Precisely why the yield might be varied is open to question as there would have been little value in restricting the bomb's destructive power (the higher yields were expected to be used against large targets such as airfields). It seems likely that had the bombs been used in anger, they would all been released at their highest yield setting.

A poor quality (but extremely rare) image of a No. 14 Squadron Canberra B(I)8 on display with a representative selection of armament including its primary weapon, the Mk.28 bomb, visible to the right of the aircraft's nose.

The use of the Mk.7 bomb was undoubtedly an ideal arrangement for the RAF, USAF and NATO. However, there were difficulties to overcome, not least the ways in which America retained control of the weapons. The Canberras were assigned to QRA (Quick Reaction Alert) duties and a number of aircraft were kept at constant readiness for immediate launch should a conflict breakout at short notice. The QRA Canberras were housed in their own alert hangars surrounded by high security fencing and under armed guard. RAF crews were rotated through QRA duty for twenty-four-hour periods on alternate days for a period of two weeks at a time. At least one USAF officer was always present inside the QRA compound so that he could give final authorisation for use of the weapon if ever required. Practice scrambles were often performed although they were usually terminated before reaching engine start. Routine flying training was performed, but nuclear stores were not carried and small inert training rounds were usually used to be dropped on weapon ranges either in Germany (Nordhorn) or in the UK.

The LABS (Low Altitude Bombing System) was employed as the means of delivering the Mk.7 bomb to its target, requiring the Canberra to perform some surprisingly dynamic manoeuvres. From a height of 250 feet and at a speed of 434 knots, the Canberra would be pulled up into a 3.4g climb and the Mk.7 bomb would be released automatically at a predetermined angle (usually around sixty degrees).

If the target was difficult to locate, this meant that no suitable IP (Initial Point) could be used – the IP being a clearly-identifiable point on the track towards the target. Therefore, the Canberra pilot would be obliged to fly directly over the target and release the bomb at an angle of approximately 110 degrees (sometimes referred to as an 'over the shoulder' release). With both types of manoeuvre, the Canberra would eventually be inverted in a descent at approximately 5,500 feet. At this stage, the pilot applied rudder and aileron to turn the aircraft around into an erect descent. If the manoeuvre was executed too soon, the aircraft would be in imminent danger of stalling (speed would be down to around 160 knots). However, if the manoeuvre was left too late, the aircraft would be in a very steep inverted dive from which recovery might be impossible. Consequently, practicing LABS deliveries was an important and regular part of RAFG operations.

The same techniques were also introduced for UK Canberra squadrons although they remained associated only with conventional HE weapons. The RAFG Canberras by comparison were almost exclusively dedicated to the nuclear role, but as part of a NATO agreement, each Canberra squadron was permitted to stand down from their assignment to SACEUR (Supreme Allied Commander Europe) for short periods every year, usually for one month. During this period, the crews had an opportunity to operate the Canberra in the purely national interdictor role for which the Canberra Mk.8 had been designed. Armament Practice Camps were set up for this purpose, normally at RAF Luqa (Malta) with live bomb deliveries and gun firing taking place on ranges in Libya. Nevertheless, the Canberra was also assigned a nuclear role much further afield following the signing of the Baghdad Pact (Cento) Treaty in 1955. As part of this agreement, two Canberra squadrons (Nos. 32 and 73) were deployed to Akrotiri (Cyprus) during 1957 with two more units (Nos. 6 and 249 Squadrons) following a few weeks later from Coningsby.

By this stage, the Canberra had also deployed to the Far East, Nos. 101, 617, 12 and 9 Squadrons having provided detachments in support of Operation Firedog (the Malayan Emergency) from 1955 onwards. No. 45 Squadron based at Tengah in Singapore began re-equipping with Canberras late in 1957. Unfortunately, the Canberra was far from suited to the operational requirements and conditions that were assigned to it in the Far East as the official records of the Malayan campaign indicate.

> They [Canberra] carried half the bomb load of Lincolns and their cruising speed of 250 knots at the optimum bombing height required more elaborate navigational aids and made map reading impracticable and visual bomb aiming difficult. The pilot had a poorer visibility than in a Lincoln and the Canberra could not be flown at night or in close formation and could not be employed in a strafing role. They suffered, in common with all jet aircraft in the tropics, from a serious limitation in their endurance at low

Canberra B.Mk.15 aircraft from No. 45 Squadron pictured at Tengah, Singapore, during 1963.

level, which precluded the possibility of postponing or delaying an air strike once they were airborne. This was a serious disadvantage in the uncertain weather conditions of Malaya, especially in 1958 when Canberras were operating in the northern part of the country, far from their parent base at Tengah, and this was reflected in an increase in the rate of abortive air strikes when they replaced Lincolns.

When flown at their normal speed at low altitude the swirl vanes of Canberra engines suffered badly from metal fatigue in the hot, turbulent air which also made flying conditions difficult for their pilots. For those Canberras that were not fitted with Godfrey air coolers, sun canopies, cooling trolleys and external compressed air supplies had to be employed to combat the danger of loss of body weight through sweating which could amount to as much as 3lb per sortie. Both from the point of view of maintenance and flying conditions, Lincolns were preferable to Canberras in the type of campaign that prevailed in Malaya.

It was somewhat ironic that in this instance the Canberra was found to be inferior to the aircraft that it had been designed to replace, but this odd situation only applied to Malaya. Clearly, the Canberra was ideally suited to other spheres of operation, especially the European theatre. Eventually, the Akrotiri Canberra squadrons were re-equipped with Canberra B.Mk.15 and B.Mk.16 aircraft, these being 'tropicalised'

While assigned to the Microbiological Establishment at Porton Down, but operated from Boscombe Down, WV787 tested the concept of delivering chemical and biological agents by air. It was estimated that in just one flight the aircraft could have released pathogens capable of killing up to thirty-eight million people. Technically at least, this probably makes WV787 potentially the most lethal British bomber by far.

derivatives of the B.6 variant. With these aircraft, the Akrotiri Strike Wing was able to embrace a nuclear capability and Red Beard weapons were assigned to Cyprus for this role. The Wing remained active as a strike/attack force until 1969 when the Canberras were withdrawn and replaced by Vulcans. Most of the RAF's Canberra bomber force was eventually replaced by the Vulcan and as the V-Force (Valiants, Vulcans and Victors) came into service, the Canberra was gradually withdrawn from its pure bomber role. Operations in Germany continued with the nuclear-capable interdictor force continued into the 1970s until the Buccaneer was introduced into service as a direct replacement for the Canberra.

The diminishing need for Canberra bombers might have spelled the end for a less versatile aircraft, but the Canberra remained in RAF service through the 1960s and 1970s. It went on to perform a wide variety of tasks, many of which were very different to the bomber role that the aircraft had been designed for. Most notably, the basic bomber design was developed for photographic reconnaissance operations (the PR3 and PR7). Eventually, the Canberra airframe was redesigned far more extensively to create the Canberra PR.Mk.9 complete with more powerful engines, larger wings and fighter-type cockpit. This was the ultimate expression of the Canberra design, but it had no direct connection with the offensive role for which the original Canberra B2 had been built.

After the Mk.9, the next Canberra derivative to emerge was the U.Mk.10, a specialised pilotless target drone designed to support missile tests that were being conducted at the Woomera range in Australia. Short Brothers were contracted to produce a batch of conversions (from B2 airframes) and the first aircraft was ferried to Woomera in 1959. With 'near miss' telemetry onboard, the aircraft were normally used for tests involving missiles with inert warheads as live tests would have inevitably meant the destruction of the aircraft. The Canberra U.Mk.10 remained in use through the 1960s and a similar variant, the U.Mk.14, was developed for Naval missile trials conducted in Malta during the early 1960s.

The Canberra T.Mk.11 was designed in response to a requirement for a radar trainer to support the RAF's Javelin fighter squadrons. Equipped with the Javelin's radar, the T11 enabled students to practice the art of airborne interception. A batch of eight B2 airframes were converted by Boulton Paul and they joined No. 228 OCU at Leeming in 1959, remaining in service until 1961. The redundant airframes were then transferred to West Raynham where they were assigned to target facilities duties, flying sorties in support of the RAF's Lightning interceptor squadrons and Bloodhound SAM units. From 1965, the T11s were progressively overhauled and the Javelin radar units removed, the bulky nosecone remaining in situ, but with ballast installed to retain the aircraft's centre of gravity. Re-designated as the T.Mk.19, these Canberras joined No. 85 Squadron at Binbrook before returning to West Raynham to join No. 100 Squadron. The final pair of active T.19s was assigned to No. 7 Squadron at St Mawgan and these were retired in 1980. These light and agile Canberras, which had started their lives as B2 bombers, had seen service to the very end of their fatigue lives.

While the Canberra Mk.12 and Mk.14 were export versions, the RAF's Canberra Mk.15 was a direct development of the B6 airframe. With the B6's integral wing tanks, up-rated engines and under-wing pylons, new radio equipment was also installed and an F95 camera fitted in the nose, together with a G45 camera in the starboard wing leading edge. In most respects, the Mk.15 was simply an up-rated Mk.6 intended for operations in the Middle and Far East, and the B.Mk.16 was the designation applied to similarly-modified B.Mk.6(BS) aircraft. The latter variant (assigned only to the Akrotiri Strike Wing) was a relatively short-lived sub-variant of the B6 bomber fitted with Blue Shadow sideways-looking radar. Intended to provide navigational and target fixing information, Blue Shadow proved to be rather disappointing in terms of performance and it was not adopted for widespread use. Its sheer size also required the removal of one of the two rear cockpit ejection seats (the radar gear occupied much of the starboard seat's usual position). If a second navigator and bombardier were carried, they were to carry their own oxygen supply and parachute. The sideways radar system was a useful asset for a while, but as better systems emerged, the notion of equipping more Canberras soon seemed pointless.

The Canberra Mk.17 marked a significant transition away from the Canberra's role as a bomber aircraft and resulted in a specialised ECM (Electronic Counter

Measures) and EW (Electronic Warfare) aircraft, assigned to a joint RAF and Fleet Air Arm squadron dedicated to the provision of ECM/EW training support. A batch of B2 airframes was converted for the role and although no major structural alterations were made to the aircraft, a completely new nose section was installed housing ECM receiver and transmitter gear. Further ECM equipment was installed in the bomb bay and tail cone, and other modifications were made to the aircraft through its service life that continued until 1994 when No. 360 Squadron disbanded. The Canberra proved to be ideal for the EW role, acting as 'electronic enemy' for RAF and NATO aircraft on many routine training missions. Indeed, it was the introduction of the Tornado F3 interceptor and trials with its new radar that took such a heavy toll on 360 Squadron's flying hours. The type's withdrawal had to be brought forward simply because most of the T17 fleet was worn out. But from all of the Canberra's exotic derivatives that gradually emerged, the T17 has to be regarded as one of the most useful.

The last major Canberra derivative to appear was the TT.Mk.18, a specialised target tug variant destined to replace Meteors in RAF and FAA service. By the mid-1960s, Flight Refuelling Ltd had developed a new target and winch system for attachment to Meteor aircraft; however, the small size of the Meteor meant that only one of the new Rushton target packs could be carried. The Canberra was identified as a more suitable aircraft for the Rushton winch and target, and so conversion of a B2 (WJ632) was undertaken by English Electric (now part of BAC). The conversion was successful and a standard conversion programme was applied to twenty-three Canberra B2s, all of which emerged from April 1970 onwards. Designated as the Canberra TT.Mk.18, the target tugs were assigned to the FAA at Yeovilton and to the RAF's No. 7 Squadron at St Mawgan. They proved to be an invaluable asset for the RAF, FAA and the Army (who often relied upon aerial simulations). Although they were ultimately replaced, the choice of a civilian contractor and a fleet of converted business jets suggested to many that the Canberra TT18's final withdrawal was based on cost saving rather than suitability.

The RAF's Canberra fleet had first started to diminish in size when the V-Force gradually came into service. As more and more V-Bombers settled into service, the Canberra's short-range bombing capabilities were no longer required and Bomber Command relinquished its last Canberra during 1961. However, the aircraft remained very much in the offensive bombing and attack business for many more years with units in the Middle and Far East, and, of course, Germany. The Akrotiri Canberras returned home in 1969 with aircraft from Singapore following a year later. It was not until 1972 that the last Canberra B(I)8 was withdrawn from RAF Germany and this was the final year in which the RAF operated the aircraft in its designated bomber role.

But this was not to spell the end for this versatile and sturdy aircraft. Through the introduction of the many specialised training and support variants (and the

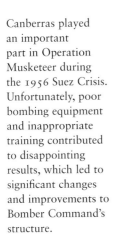

Canberras played an important part in Operation Musketeer during the 1956 Suez Crisis. Unfortunately, poor bombing equipment and inappropriate training contributed to disappointing results, which led to significant changes and improvements to Bomber Command's structure.

continuing reconnaissance role), the Canberra remained in RAF service for many more years and it was not until July 2006 that the last Canberras (reconnaissance-equipped PR.Mk.9 aircraft) were finally withdrawn from use. The Canberra's most deadly role – as a nuclear-equipped strike aircraft based in Germany – had contributed to NATO's strength through the darkest days of the Cold War, but thankfully the aircraft had never been called upon to deliver its apocalyptic load.

In fact, the Canberra's fifty years of active service saw little in terms of 'real' action. It was only during the 1956 Suez Crisis that the Canberra had been brought into action at the very beginning of its long service life. Bomber Command's Canberras were deployed to Malta and Cyprus as part of Operation Musketeer and bombing missions were launched against many targets inside Egypt. With that being said, the Canberra's effectiveness during the crisis as a bomber was a huge disappointment to service chiefs, not because of deficiencies within either the aircraft or its crews, but because of the equipment and support given to the aircraft. With only Gee-H as its main navigational aid, Canberra crews had to rely on traditional map reading to locate their targets, simply because Gee-H was useless without the ground beacons needed to generate homing signals.

Resorting to bombing techniques that had been used in the Second World War was both a frustration and an embarrassment, especially when the Canberra was clearly such a capable aeroplane. The handful of converted Canberra B6(BS) aircraft equipped with Blue Shadow radar were employed during the crisis as target markers

Canberra B(I)8 prototype VX185 pictured at Warton during flight trials in 1954. The unusual offset fighter-type cockpit canopy is clearly visible. (*Courtesy BAE Systems*)

for both the Canberra and Valiant bomber forces that performed attacks in Egypt, but without any up-to-date reconnaissance images of their targets, the Canberra radar operators had nothing to which they could compare their relatively poor radar pictures. Despite this, Bomber Command achieved some satisfactory results, but Suez demonstrated all too graphically that the Canberra's outstanding flying qualities had to be matched by good navigational and bombing equipment, and supported with the necessary target information. It was a lesson that the RAF learned well and as a direct result of Suez, the Canberra and V-Force was supported by a much stronger and practical infrastructure.

The Canberra paved the way for the RAF's V-Force squadrons and gave NATO a fearsome strike capability poised on the USSR's doorstep. Almost as an unexpected bonus, it also provided the RAF with a versatile and reliable aircraft that readily lent itself to a whole range of support and training tasks. It is ironic to note how the majority of the Canberra's long RAF career was occupied by duties that had little to do with the bombing role for which it had been designed and manufactured. After more than half a century of active use, no one could deny that the Canberra had been anything other than an outstanding jet bomber, especially when one considers that it had been the first of its kind.

CHAPTER TWO

Nuclear Knowhow

The story of Britain's post-war bombers is dominated by the creation and operation of the mighty V-Force. It was to be the ultimate expression of nuclear deterrence capable of convincing the Soviet Union that any attempt to launch a nuclear 'first strike' attack on the United Kingdom would result in a reciprocal attack that would lay to waste most of the USSR's main cities and key military installations. Achieving this almost unimaginable destructive capability took many years of planning, huge sums of money and a staggering amount of scientific and engineering knowhow.

Creation of atomic power was an immense achievement in itself, but translating this capacity into military hardware was a completely separate issue that required radical thinking. It might be imagined that when atomic warfare first came to the attention of Britain's military, manufacturing an atomic bomb for the RAF's bomber force would have been an obvious and logical step; however, in 1945 when the Second World War ended, no such assumptions had been made. Atomic power was an entirely new concept and no one made the immediate assumption that an air-launched bomb could be produced, largely because there was no evidence to suggest that such an idea was practical. The test devices produced as part of the famous Manhattan Project were not small, compact and lightweight: they were huge, complicated assemblies requiring careful preparation and attention. No one outside of the secret project imagined that such devices could be neatly fitted into a bomb carcass. The Third Reich had worked long and hard to develop its own atomic bomb, but even though they made some progress towards this achievement, they too had failed to devise a means of turning the theoretical capability into a viable weapon. Nazi Germany believed in rocketry and their V-2 missile undoubtedly represented a theoretical means of getting an atomic bomb into the heart of England, Russia and perhaps the United States.

However, the V-2 was a triumph of concept rather than capability. It could carry a payload of little more than 2,000 lb and often struggled to reach London where its true value was as a weapon of terror rather than one of significant destructive power. Carrying a heavy, cumbersome and complicated atomic 'physics package' was

The 'physics package' (the 'bomb') inside the Blue Danube weapon was somewhat smaller than the casing into which it fitted. Seen here on its mounting, the complicated explosive lens charges can be seen.

far beyond the capabilities of the V-2 and the proposed rockets that were to succeed it. In Britain, there was no such fascination with rockets, nor was there belief that an atomic weapon could be delivered by any form of aerial transport.

Sir Arthur Harris, who had lead Bomber Command through the most pivotal moments of the Second World War, postulated the theory that an 'atomic exploder' device could be manufactured. It was to be disassembled and transported to its destination in secret (either by land or by sea) and then carefully reassembled for detonation. It was not the most practical or reliable means of striking at the enemy, but in theory it would work. The idea lingered for some time, even influencing the choice of detonation site for the British atomic tests when they got underway. But when America – with more than a little British help – turned the clumsy atomic physics packages into deliverable bombs and duly dropped two over Japanese cities, the way forward was dazzlingly clear. The development of smaller nuclear packages was demonstrably possible and British attention moved towards the possibility of creating an air-drop bomb. It was eventually estimated that a functional atomic weapon weighing around 10,000 lb was feasible and this weight was within the lift capabilities of existing bomber designs. This was the point at which the Air Staff began to seriously address the issue of how to create a nuclear bomber.

When the Second World War ended and the dark days of the Cold War slowly unfolded, the existing RAF bomber force comprised of a mixed fleet of relatively speedy and agile Mosquito light bombers and much larger, slower and far less versatile Avro Lincolns. The latter was a long-range bomber and a direct derivative of the wartime Lancaster, albeit with improved performance. A future replacement for the Lincoln was needed and the jet-powered Canberra was a partial solution. The fast, high-flying Canberra represented a major leap forwards in capability for the RAF and when the Canberra was compared to the obsolescent Lincoln, it was only the Canberra's payload and range capability that left it lacking. As a tactical aircraft, the Canberra was an unqualified success, but for a long-range strategic role that would enable Britain to demonstrate a clear ability to strike at the Soviet Union, a larger and more advanced bomber was necessary. The Canberra represented only one step towards the creation of a truly effective bomber force.

As a short-term solution to the RAF's needs, the B-29 Washington came to Britain. The United States agreed to supply the RAF with a fleet of eighty-seven Boeing B-29 Superfortresses during 1950 as part of the post-war Military Assistance Programme. Boasting a range of some 4,000 miles, the B-29 (known as the 'Washington' in RAF service) was an impressive machine that immediately restored the RAF's offensive capabilities. The B-29 was a bomber that could hit the Soviet Union and demonstrate to its country's leaders that Britain had an ability to strike if necessary. Ostensibly assigned to the conventional HE (high explosive) bombing role, the B-29 was nuclear capable – having released both atomic bombs on Japan – but there was no direct plan to use the B-29 in a nuclear role while in RAF service. (Even though it seems likely that plans were made to allow American weapons to be carried if an emergency situation had developed.)

The main purpose of the B-29 was to give the RAF a suitable bomber with which to fill the gap between the existing Lincoln force and the arrival of the new Canberra, and also to demonstrate that the RAF was no longer restricted to the European theatre. The Lincoln's range might have been adequate for a European conflict, but the B-29 had the ability to reach much further including Moscow. The Washingtons were a significant step in improving the RAF's offensive capabilities, but they belonged to America and their loan was only intended to be short lived. Once the Canberra began to enter service, the Washingtons were returned to the US and although the Canberra could never have matched the Washington's load-carrying capability or range, the new jet bomber was fast (astonishingly fast by contemporary standards), high flying and manoeuvrable. It only had a theoretical ability to reach into the USSR, but as a tactical bomber supporting land operations in a European theatre, it was an aircraft that undoubtedly made the Soviet defence chiefs sit up and take notice.

As the Canberra force slowly built up in strength, a far more potent bomber force was being created. Following the British Government's decision to develop a nuclear weapons programme, the Air Staff immediately addressed the issue of how such a weapon would be delivered. After a period of initial discussion, they issued Operational Requirement OR.230, specifying a 'landplane capable of carrying one 10,000 lb bomb to a target 2,000 nm from a base situated anywhere in the world'. The 10,000 lb figure reflected the predicted weight of an atomic bomb, but it was anticipated that the aircraft would also have the capacity to carry a higher load of conventional bombs.

The Air Staff ensured that the new bomber would be capable of carrying whatever weapon the physicists could devise, but they also made sure that if the atomic weapons programme should fail, the RAF would have a long-range bomber with a good load-carrying capability for conventional high-explosive bombs. But despite such conservative precautions, the Air Staff did indulge in some 'blue sky thinking'. Instead of resorting to traditional defensive armament such as turret-mounted machine guns, it was specified that the new bomber should be capable of attaining high altitudes and high speeds – up to 50,000 feet and 500 knots – so that its performance would ensure its invulnerability when flying over enemy defences. But even without the weight of gun turrets, the new bomber would inevitably be a huge and heavy machine that would require significant amounts of runway to get airborne (an all-up weight of around 200,000 lb was assumed). The RAF's existing bomber airfields had mostly been constructed during the Second World War and designed to cater for aircraft such as the Lancaster. Most runways were only 6,000 feet in length (or less) and the prospect of extending Bomber Command's runways by 50 per cent or more was a very unpalatable proposition – often requiring land acquisition, building, demolition and drainage work – that would cost a fortune. Worse still, the existing RAF hangar types would be completely unsuitable as the largest examples were barely capable of accommodating wartime bombers let alone the monstrous machine that OR.230 specified.

The Air Staff soon concluded that OR.230 was not going to be a simple progressive step and that the concept of a high-speed, high-altitude, long-range jet bomber was too ambitious when the RAF had barely begun to embrace the emerging post-war technological possibilities. Also, the country was on the verge of bankruptcy after funding the war against the Axis powers. Even if the OR could be translated into an operational aircraft, its cost would probably be so high that the RAF would only be able to afford a small number of aircraft, therefore making the whole exercise pointless. It was eventually agreed that OR.230 was unnecessarily ambitious and that it should be put on hold and the RAF should take a more practical look at what was truly needed (OR.230 was finally abandoned in September 1952). Essentially, whatever new bomber was designed, it was to carry an atomic bomb and reach

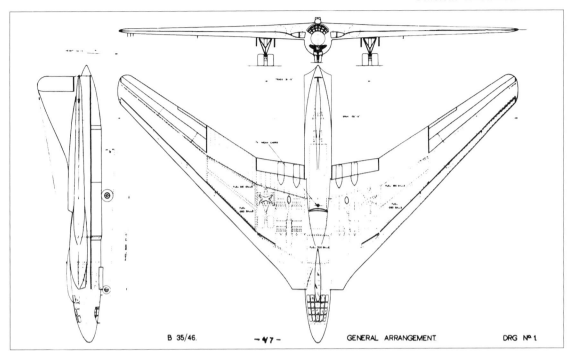

B 35/46. — 47 — GENERAL ARRANGEMENT DRG Nº 1

Various exotic designs were submitted in response to Specification B.35/46, and although the chosen Avro and Handley Page designs are often regarded as the most advanced, some other equally imaginative proposals emerged, including this concept submitted by Armstrong Whitworth.

Moscow. Any range capability beyond that point was a bonus rather than a necessity. The bomber would have to carry a significant bomb load and if an atomic weapon was successfully devised, it would probably be in the 10,000 lb class. Altitude performance and high speed would be necessary so that the aircraft could get through enemy defences to its target. All of this could still be achieved if OR.230's projected range was reduced to around 1,500 nautical miles and the all-up weight dropped correspondingly to around 100,000 lb. A new requirement (OR.229) was therefore issued around these points and this was then translated into Specification B.35/46.

The new project was described concisely by Chief Ministry of Supply representative Stuart Scott-Hall: '...the conclusion had been reached that the long-range bomber, the all-up weight of which would be in the region of 200,000 lb, represented too great an advance in design to be entertained at the present juncture. Considerable research and development would be necessary – including, in all probability, the construction of half-scale flying models.' His recommendation was that '...consideration should be given to the medium-range aircraft, holding the long-range requirements in abeyance for a time'. He proposed a three-phase development.

Firstly, there should be an 'insurance design' which would be a relatively simple aircraft created purely as a direct replacement for the Lincoln which could be developed easily without any risk. Secondly, there would be the medium-range jet bomber and thirdly, the original long-range jet bomber that would still be regarded as a long-term project.

OR.229 was issued on 7 January 1947 and this represented the day on which the Air Staff formally sought its first nuclear bomber. It was also the day on which Governmental authorisation was finally given for the production of the first atomic weapons. Scott-Hall sent letters to Britain's aircraft companies, setting out the terms of the requirement and inviting them to submit tenders. The first letter went to Handley Page with another to Armstrong-Whitworth and further letters went to Avro, Bristol and Shorts the next day. English Electric was notified a few days later. On 24 January, invitations were given to Avro, Armstrong-Whitworth, English Electric and Handley Page to submit formal design tenders meeting the new Specification B.35/46, although Shorts and Vickers-Armstrong also submitted designs at this stage.

On 2 July, a Tender Design Conference was held and it was decided that an order should be placed for the design submitted by Avro, together with an order for a smaller flying model that could investigate the design inexpensively and swiftly. It was also agreed that either the Handley Page or Armstrong-Whitworth design should also be ordered – together with their own respective flying models – but only after further research had been completed on the designs by the Royal Aircraft Establishment in their high-speed wind tunnel at Farnborough. Sir Fredrick Handley Page, with his typical enthusiasm for business, had tried to persuade Scott-Hall to accept his design before the conference. He had sent a letter to Handley Page a few days previously explaining why he had turned down a design similar to Avro's in favour of a crescent wing concept.

However, the RAE felt it prudent to research the concept of a crescent wing before committing to an aircraft design programme and although Avro's submission was almost as unorthodox, the Ministry of Supply gave financial cover to Avro's design in November 1947, followed by similar cover for the Handley Page design the following month. The designs submitted by other companies were dismissed, although the criteria by which they were discounted must have been subjective, there being very little hard scientific fact with which to make decisions. Imaginative proposals had been sent by Armstrong-Whitworth, Bristol and Shorts, and although they might well have had as much potential as others, it was the perceived lack of manufacturing and technical support that led to their abandonment. Likewise, English Electric's surprisingly conventional submission was not taken seriously as the company was already busy with their Canberra and it seemed risky to allocate another major project to an already stretched company. Only the Avro and Handley

Page concepts were adopted for further development although Vickers-Armstrong managed to pluck a late victory from the submission process when Scott-Hall's 'insurance design' was eventually addressed.

A separate specification (B.14/46) was issued for this aircraft on 11 August 1946 and Shorts proposed a design with which to meet it. The design was based on the company's proposed B.35/46 proposal, but in order to produce a more conservative design that would not present any developmental risks, the advanced 'isoclinic' swept wings were replaced by simple straight wings and a non-swept conventional tail unit derived from the wartime Sunderland seaplane. The new design was designated as the S.A.4 and although it was a very simple and straightforward design, it was perhaps too simple for the tastes of some, as indicated by Air Marshal Sir William Dickson:

> As an insurance against the possibility that the firms in question will not be able to solve the aerodynamical problems involved in the production of this new type of bomber [B.35/46] we have asked the Ministry of Supply to build a bomber of conventional design with a reduced performance of not less than 3,350 nm at a height of 40,000 feet and a speed of 435 knots. While this reduced requirement is less than we think to be essential, we cannot afford to have a replacement for the Lincoln that is already obsolescent if not obsolete. To meet our requirements for this 'insurance' bomber, the Ministry of Supply have already placed an order with Shorts. We are not at all happy about this, because from what we know, the Shorts design is very unimaginative and its estimated performance is already dropping below the Air Staff figures I have quoted above. It is probable that the performance will drop still further which is very serious bearing in mind that we do not expect to get even this 'insurance' type into production inside 6-7 years. We also know that since the Ministry of Supply have placed this order, two further designs have been submitted for this 'insurance' specification. From what the Air Staff know these designs are superior to that of Shorts. On the other hand, these two alternative designs are based on a new jet engine which is still on the drawing board, whereas the Shorts design employs an engine which is much further advanced in design.

Within only a few months, the Shorts design had become a subject of heated debate as the Director of Military Aircraft Research commented:

> It has been apparent for some months now that the Short B.14/46 design will not quite meet the performance requirements written by DOR in OR.239 and incorporated by us as the Appendix B in Specification B.14/46. The advisory design conference on this aeroplane was held on 10 July and we are now fairly clear on the extent of the deficiency. I consider that Shorts have made the best job they can of this design and it is no discredit to them that they have fallen a little short on performance.

The fundamental problem that dogged B.14/46 was that the very purpose of the specification was to produce an aircraft that was guaranteed of being designed and manufactured without delay. The only means of ensuring that this aim could be achieved was to reduce the aircraft's performance figures to such an extent that a very simple and conventional design could be built around it. Conversely, a simple and conventional aircraft was therefore capable of only modest performance and it was easy to produce a machine that was in effect too reticent to be of any practical value. This was what Shorts had created, and even though Shorts could hardly be criticised for producing an aircraft that was deliberately designed to under-perform, it took some time for the Ministry of Supply to realise that the venture had been a mistake. However, the two additional designs that had been submitted in response to B.14/46 were still very much on the table. English Electric's design looked promising, but with the Canberra in production, there seemed little point in allocating yet more work to an overstretched company. By contrast, Vickers-Armstrong certainly needed more work and chief designer George Edwards had continued lobbying Ministry officials to re-examine his company's proposal. Eventually, the Principal Director of Technical Development (S. Scott-Hall) stated that:

> In preliminary discussions, Director of Research (Aircraft) and I had agreed that inasmuch as the long-range bomber is by far the most important item in our future programme, we should re-examine the possibility of proceeding with interim types to Specification B.35/46 to take a place in the programme between the Short B.14/46 and the advanced types envisaged, such as the Handley Page crescent wing and the Avro delta wing B.35/46.

In effect, Scott-Hall was advocating an 'insurance-insurance' bomber, a fourth aircraft type that would fit somewhere between the unimaginative Sperrin and the two advanced aircraft that would become the Vulcan and Victor.

Scott-Hall made mention of George Edwards and his influence on the situation: 'We accordingly discussed with Edwards, who considers the difficulties of a delta or crescent wing will be very great. Vickers have now made an examination of such a project and their work fully endorses Edwards' views.' It is not surprising that Vickers supported the views expressed by the company's chief designer, nor is it surprising that Edwards dismissed the Avro and Handley Page designs as being risky. He was, after all, trying to sell his design (the Type 660) to the Ministry and although there was indeed a great deal of risk attached to the outcome of the B.35/46 designs, his position was undoubtedly motivated by good business sense. He revised the company's original submission as follows:

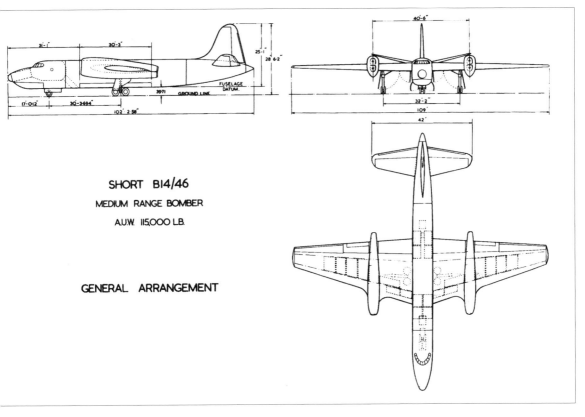

SHORT B14/46

MEDIUM RANGE BOMBER

A.U.W. 115,000 LB

GENERAL ARRANGEMENT

Short's three-view drawing of the Sperrin illustrating the aircraft's functional layout, designed from the outset to be as simple and reliable as possible.

1/ The incorporation of Rolls-Royce Avon or Metropolitan Vickers F.9 Sapphire engines in place of the Napier T.2/46 which was now unlikely to be developed in time for use within the bomber programme.

2/An all-up weight of 115,000 lb and the incorporation of a tandem-wheel main undercarriage that would enable the aircraft to operate from existing RAF runways without any need for strengthening.

3/A total bomb load of 10,000 lb – this being half the total bomb load envisaged for B.35/46 as although the main requirement was for the carriage of a single 10,000 lb (atomic) bomb, it had been specified that the advanced bombers should be capable of carrying up to 20,000 lb of conventional HE ordnance.

4/ The requirement for a jettisonable crew cabin would be dropped.

5/ The removal of all unnecessary equipment such as cloud and collision warning radar.

By early 1948, the Air Ministry had agreed to accept the Vickers-Armstrong proposal and an ITP (Instruction To Proceed) notice was issued in April. The Air Ministry outlined its new position:

> It has been decided that another type of bomber should be built to bridge the gap between the conventional medium-range bomber – the Short B.14/46 – and the two more advanced types which have been ordered from Handley Page and Avro – the B.35/46. Design studies were received from a number of firms and that of Vickers has been judged to be the most promising and a contract is about to be placed for two prototypes of this aircraft. The Vickers medium-range bomber will have a still air range of 3,350 nm carrying a bomb load of 10,000 lb at a speed of about 465 kt and at a height of about 45,000 feet. It will weigh approximately 110,000 lb and this will be distributed on a multi-wheel undercarriage. The aircraft will be powered by four Rolls-Royce Avon engines and will start with an initial sweep-back of 20 degrees on the outer plane with the possibility of increasing this in future to 30 degrees and later 42 degrees. The inner section of the wing is swept back to 42 degrees initially.

This mention of wing sweep was due to Edwards proposing that Type 660 could be developed in due course so that the wing was gradually swept further back to allow performance to increase, effectively comparing the aircraft's performance to the B.35/46 designs. Craftily, Edwards was in effect suggesting that Type 660 could be gradually developed to match the performance of the two aircraft that he had dismissed as 'risky', but his ideas were not of immediate interest to the Air Ministry. The RAF simply wanted their 'interim' bomber as swiftly as possible. But while Vickers prepared to join the ever-growing bomber programme, work was well underway in Belfast where the Sperrin was now being manufactured. Shorts had fixed the aircraft's simple design on the basis of hydraulic analogy tests that had been conducted in the company's seaplane tank at Rochester. Without the luxury of their own wind tunnel, Shorts had often used the facilities at the Royal Aircraft Establishment and National Propulsion Laboratory. However, waiting times for access to these wind tunnels had become so protracted that Shorts elected to learn as much as possible by using fluid dynamic analogy work, taking advantage of their own seaplane test tank.

The result was a rather brutal and solid-looking aircraft with straight wings and tailplanes, a huge Sunderland-style tail and mammoth engine nacelles perched mid-way along the wing's span. By any standards, the Sperrin looked impressive, but at the same time it did not look like the clean, sleek, streamlined type of aircraft that the Air Staff had envisioned. Clearly, the straight wing would never enable the aircraft

The 1951 SBAC show saw VX158 perform for the public, resplendent in the company's specially designed and rather unusual paint scheme, which did nothing to hide the simple and unattractive lines of the bulky machine. The mighty Brabazon is pictured in the background.

to achieve any great speed, but it might have attained a respectable altitude if its engines were capable of delivering enough thrust. But good though the four Avon engines would prove to be, they were housed in pairs, one stacked above the other in fat nacelles that were bound to create a lot of aerodynamic drag. In fact, everything about the Sperrin seemed to suggest drag, but at the same time there was no reason the aircraft could not be completed swiftly. Simplicity was the key to the Sperrin's design and early in 1951, the first aircraft (VX158) was completed while a second prototype and a static test specimen remained under construction.

However, by the time VX158 emerged from the Shorts factory, the Sperrin's fate had been sealed. As performance figured for the Vickers Type 660 became available, it became increasingly clear that this aircraft would be far better suited for the RAF's 'interim bomber' role and the only question had been whether the aircraft could be built quickly enough. Edwards had assured the Ministry of Supply that it would be. Air Vice-Marshal Pelly stated:

At a meeting held at the Ministry of Supply on 11 October [1949] I said that we could do without the B.14/46 for the following reasons. If the long-term planning dates to which the whole of our programme is aimed are still valid, there is every reason to hope that one of the B.35/46 designs will be available in time. We still need one earlier type with which to re-equip Bomber Command, to practice the techniques involved in

When VX158 appeared at the annual SBAC Show at Farnborough, the fantastic paint scheme was replaced with a shiny silver finish. Sadly, the bright colours did little to hide the aircraft's sluggish and unexciting performance.

long-range operations at such high altitudes and to be ready at the same time as the special bomb. Nevertheless, only one type of aircraft would be required and I feel sure that the B.9/48 [The Type 660], in view of its better performance, offers a far better solution to our problem, the only disadvantage being that it is six months behind the B.14/46. Although the B.9/48 is of more advanced design than the B.14/46, the increased knowledge gained lately on swept-back wings and other high-speed complications leads to the belief that no major troubles need to be expected with the B.9/48 and therefore, production of that aircraft could start in 1953 if need be and would, I understand, match up with the production of the special bomb.

The Sperrin was clearly no longer necessary and the Air Staff agreed that it would not be ordered into production. The two prototypes were retained, however, as it would have been costly and wasteful to abandon them. Instead, they were assigned to research work in direct support of the bomber programme and the first aircraft (VX158) took to the air from Aldergrove in the hands of test pilot Tom Brooke-Smith on 10 August 1951. Ironically, this was some three months after the Vickers 660 had made its first flight. Some ten hours of flight time was then conducted before the Sperrin made its public debut at the 1951 SBAC Show at Farnborough. Oddly, Shorts opted to paint the aircraft in an unusual grey, black and red paint scheme that gave the aircraft an appearance of an airliner rather than a bomber, but even with its peculiar coat of colours the Sperrin certainly captured plenty of attention. Its size and bulk combined with a considerable amount of noise made quite an impression on the Farnborough crowds. Nonetheless, even with Brook-Smith's exceptional flying skills, the Sperrin could not hope to match the sprightly displays performed by the Canberra and looked positively old-fashioned when compared to the glittering Vickers 660 prototype that performed in the very same show. Low and relatively fast passes were exciting, but they only served to indicate that the Sperrin was barely capable of anything more flamboyant.

After the Farnborough show, the Sperrin returned to Northern Ireland and on 12 August 1952, the second aircraft took to the air. VX161 was partially dismantled and transported to Aldergrove for reassembly prior to making its first flight as the company airfield at Sydenham did not have a runway long enough for the lumbering Sperrin. Shorts extended the runway at Sydenham at great expense so that trials with both aircraft could be conducted from the airfield, but by the following year both aircraft had moved on. VX158 went to the Royal Aircraft Establishment at

By 1956, Sperrin VX158 was still appearing at the annual Farnborough Show, but by now the aircraft was no longer part of the V-Bomber programme. With enlarged engine fairings, the aircraft was acting as a flying test bed for de Havilland's Gyron jet engine.

An unusual pre-Farnborough publicity photograph showing three of Short's aircraft en route to the show in 1952. Behind the mighty Sperrin is the small and functional Seamew anti-submarine aircraft. In the distance is the unique SB.5 aero-isoclinic wing demonstrator aircraft.

Farnborough to begin radar navigation and bombing trials, taking over from Avro Ashton WB492 that had been assigned to this developmental work.

By the end of 1953, however, the aircraft was back at Sydenham and was placed in temporary storage. The second aircraft (VX161) was not equipped with a radar system, but was to play an important part in the ongoing bomber programme.

In April 1953, it was ferried to RAF Woodbridge in Suffolk, home of the USAF's 20th FBW operating F-84G aircraft. This was the nearest major airfield to the Armament and Instrument Experimental Unit located at nearby Martlesham Heath and on behalf of the Ministry of Supply, the Sperrin was used to carry a variety of bomb carcasses on drop trials over the adjacent Orfordness weapons range. Trails with a variety of bomb casings were necessary as the atomic bomb programme progressed and VX161 carried a number of different 'shapes' aloft to test their aerodynamic characteristics. In addition to the definitive carcass that was used for the RAF's first atomic bomb ('Blue Danube'), the Sperrin dropped a variety of test specimens allocated to the 'Blue Boar' guided bomb programme being pursued by Vickers.

Photographs of the huge Blue Danube bomb are unsurprisingly rare. This AWRE image illustrates the sheer bulk of the weapon that required an equally large aircraft weapons bay to accommodate it.

By the summer of 1956, the aircraft's work was done and was flown back to Sydenham for storage, although it never flew again and was eventually dismantled on site and sold as scrap.

Meanwhile, VX158 had been assigned to engine developmental work, the Sperrin's accessible engine nacelles being ideal for this kind of testing. De Havilland was working on their new Gyron axial-flow turbojet that was expected to deliver an impressive 15,000 lb static thrust. VX158's port lower engine housing was enlarged and modified to house this engine and in July 1955, the aircraft made its first flight with the Gyron installed. It swiftly demonstrated that the single Gyron's power virtually matched the output of the two Avon engines fitted in the starboard nacelle. After a series of tests from de Havilland's airfield at Hatfield, the Sperrin returned to Sydenham to have a second Gyron fitted in the starboard lower engine bay. In June 1956, the aircraft flew with a pair of 20,000 lb Gyron D.Gy.2 engines fitted, the first flight being slightly marred by the loss of an undercarriage door. The stored VX161 was robbed of its landing gear door and duly became a 'Christmas tree' spares source for the remaining flying example. At the 1956 Farnborough show, the appearance of VX158 with its combined power of 53,000 lb was more than enough to attract plenty of attention from both the media and spectators. However, by the following year, the future of the Gyron engine was in doubt, thanks to the cancellation of the Hawker P.1121 as part of the infamous 1957 Defence White Paper. The Gyron was to have powered the P.1121 and with the aircraft gone, the engine was redundant and so was VX158.

De Havilland had purchased the Sperrin from Shorts by this stage and in order to gain some further value from the purchase, the aircraft was assigned to infrared radiation trials. But by 1959, the company no longer had any use for the aircraft and it was scrapped at Hatfield late in 1959. This marked the end of the Sperrin story and it might be assumed that the project had been nothing more than a big mistake. But it is important to bear in mind that the Sperrin was victim of rapid changes. When it had first been ordered, the RAF was desperate to ensure that it would get a jet bomber that would be capable of carrying the first British atomic bomb as soon as they were manufactured. It was accepted from the outset that the Sperrin would not have the range, altitude or speed of the advanced bombers that were being produced by Avro and Handley Page, but it would guarantee that the RAF would at least have a bomber – even if it was not the ideal aircraft that the RAF might have liked.

As the RAF's bomber programme progressed, it soon became clear that the perceived risks with swept-wing design were unfounded and there was therefore no reason to assume that the advanced bombers would not be successfully completed. The only remaining risk was the projected timescale for delivery of these bombers and the Sperrin offered the promise of an in-service bomber at a much earlier date. However, when the Vickers Type 660 emerged as a more capable aircraft and one that could be completed within a surprisingly short timescale, the Sperrin was no longer required. Having been designed to be as simple and functional as possible, it had no real value to the bomber programme. The Sperrin could not have been manufactured with the benefit of hindsight and given the RAF's circumstances, and the Government's circumstances vis-à-vis the Cold War and the Soviet Union, the Sperrin made good sense. Ultimately, the two completed Sperrins performed many useful research tasks, not least the clearance of suitable bomb shapes and some important engine development testing, but also enabled Shorts to develop a four-wheel bogey undercarriage that was later used on the Britannia airliner.

It is also interesting to note that even after the end of the Sperrin project, Shorts maintained a tenuous connection with the original B.35/46 programme. Both Avro and Handley Page designed flying scale models of their proposed bomber designs and Shorts also elected to manufacture a similar scale model of their proposed bomber design that the MoS had declined to accept. Although Shorts were aware that the radical nature of their 'isoclinic' wing design was probably enough to convince officials that the project would never be translated into a viable bomber design, Shorts firmly believed in the advantages of the design and proceeded to manufacture a demonstrator aircraft at their own expense.

Initially, the company had proposed that they should design and build a swept 'isoclinic' wing for attachment to a standard Sperrin fuselage structure, but when the MoS refused to finance the proposal – still believing that the concept was doomed to delay at best or failure at worst – the only affordable option left was to manufacture a flying one-third scale model. The basic premise of the isoclinic wing concept was to create a flying surface that would present the same incidence to the airflow, regardless of the aerodynamic loads being placed upon it. Most wings (especially swept ones) have a tendency to twist under load and this inevitably affects their lift properties. In a tight turn for example, the wing tip lift diminishes while a greater load is applied to the rest of the wing surface and the resulting aeroelastic effect pulls the wing tips towards each other. By moving the wing structure's torsional box further aft, the wing's torsional and flextural axes will coincide so that when the wing flexes, the twisting moment is eliminated. When the wing twists, its incidence is not affected. Turning this theory into a practical design resulted in an unusual swept wing devoid of conventional ailerons. Instead, the aircraft (designated as the S.B.1 by Shorts) featured pivoting outer wings that acted as ailerons when operated in opposition and as elevators when operated in unison (the aircraft had no need for tailplane surfaces).

By 1951, the company had built the bizarre scaled-down model and was launched by winch from Aldergrove on 14 July with Tom Brooke-Smith at the controls. The first flight was successful and further flights were to be performed with air launches, courtesy of a Sturgeon target tug aircraft (a type also manufactured by Shorts). Unfortunately, the Sturgeon's propeller wash had quite an effect on the tiny S.B.1 glider. Despite some heroic attempts to successfully tow the aircraft with the target tug, one particularly unsuccessful launch resulted in the glider hitting the ground with some force, injuring Brooke-Smith and destroying the aircraft. Undaunted, Shorts proceeded to manufacture a second aircraft (the S.B.4 Sherpa) that incorporated a longer fuselage and a pair of Turbomeca Palais turbojets, thereby obviating the risks of further Sturgeon tow launch disasters.

From October 1953, this aircraft conducted a series of highly successful tests flights from Sydenham and Aldergrove. Shorts used the test data to establish that if the S.B.4 had been scaled up to a full-size bomber with 114-feet-span wings, it would have been capable of achieving a speed of Mach 0.87. Also, it would have undoubtedly enjoyed some very impressive range and manoeuvrability properties. But even though Shorts had ably demonstrated that their B.35/46 submission had not been a wild gamble and was in fact a very practical and suitable proposal, the Air Ministry and MoS were no longer interested in the concept. The bomber programme

The rather bizarre Short SB.4 Sherpa G-14-1 pictured en route to the 1953 SBAC Show at Farnborough.

was now proceeding towards the RAF's goal and there was no appetite for drifting off into new and potentially expensive tangents. Thus, the S.B.4 became little more than an interesting footnote to the original story of how the B.35/46 bombers came into being and a hint of what the Air Ministry had turned down.

It could be argued that the Air Ministry and the MoS were foolish to have dismissed the very ambitious (but potentially ideal) proposal that had been put forward by Shorts. However, there was always a continual worry that any design that departed from conventional wisdom might be plagued by delays or failure. It was miraculous that the Ministry officials had the foresight – or at least the sheer nerve – to accept the very ambitious Avro and Handley Page proposals when they did, but the Shorts proposal was just too exotic to seriously contemplate. In complete contrast, the Sperrin had been designed to be as conventional and 'safe' as possible, but quickly became a victim of its own purpose. Devoid of any real speed, range or altitude capability, it was little more than a jet-powered Lincoln and when Vickers-Armstrong offered the possibility of creating something better, it was inevitable that the Sperrin would be dumped.

The Type 660 proposed by Vickers was based on the company's proposed design for the original B.35/46 specification. This had been regarded as a 'safe' design, but one that was incapable of delivering the performance figures that the RAF wanted and therefore dismissed at an early stage. But as the Sperrin's inferior performance

Pictured during a test flight from Sydenham in 1954, the diminutive SB.4 illustrates the unusual swept 'isoclinic' wing that proved to be a very successful concept, and one that may well have contributed to the V-Force programme had the Air Ministry pursued it.

figures slowly sank into the heads of the Ministry officials, the idea of resurrecting the 'safe' Vickers design began to look like an attractive proposition. The Vickers design might not have been capable of meeting the specifications outlined in B.35/46, but it would achieve all that was required by Specification B.14/46. A similar design proposal was also on offer from English Electric, but as the company was heavily committed to production of the Canberra, the prospect of awarding a contract to Vickers was both politically and militarily sensible.

After Vickers had refined the aircraft's design to meet with the Air Ministry's compromised performance figures, the go-ahead for the bomber was given in April 1948. The new specification (B.9/48) was effectively written around the Vickers aircraft. It specified that the aircraft should achieve an altitude of 47,000 feet or more; a cruising speed in excess of 465 knots with a landing speed of 120 knots or less; a take-off run of 1,600 yards or less; and a bomb load of 10,000 lb or 20,000 lb at short range. Endurance was set at a range of 3,350 nm or more. George Edwards was delighted that his lobbying had paid off so handsomely and promised that a prototype would be flying in 1951 with production aircraft available in 1953 and quantity deliveries in 1955. The MoS were suitably satisfied that they now had a suitably capable bomber that did not present any design risks and would therefore be an insurance against the potential failure of the two advanced designs. Moreover, the Vickers Type 660 would also be an insurance against the delay of either advanced aircraft, ensuring that when the first atomic bombs were ready, the RAF would have a bomber to carry them.

Development of the Type 660 design began in earnest and the first components began to emerge from the Vickers-Armstrong factory in 1950. Assembly of the first aircraft was completed at the company's Foxwarren facility, chiefly because the main Weybridge factory was heavily involved with production of Vikings, Vallettas, Varsities and Viscounts. However, Foxwarren was also closer to the company's test airfield at Wisley and after being partially dismantled for road transportation, the prototype 660 was reassembled at Wisley. It was flown from the grass airfield for the first time on 18 May 1951 with test pilot Joseph 'Mutt' Summers at the controls. Summers was due to retire in 1951, but as a seasoned test pilot – most notably of the iconic Spitfire – he did not want to retire until he had flown the latest and most impressive aircraft to have been designed by his employers (Supermarine had by now become part of the Vickers-Armstrong empire). Thanks to a combination of a very substantial workforce and the availability of more research data, production of the first 660 had been as swift as George Edwards had promised. It had also beaten the first Sperrin into the air by some three months, a remarkable achievement by any standards. It took just twenty-seven months from the issuance of the contract to the first flight, after which a further two short flights were made before WB210 was ferried to Hurn Airport at Bournemouth where Vickers had another facility. Hurn offered airspace with far less congestion and also enabled Wisley to be temporarily closed while a concrete runway was laid in preparation for more Valiant testing. Vickers also swiftly bestowed a name upon the new aircraft and although it had been accepted practice to name bombers after British or Commonwealth cities, the name 'Valiant' was chosen for the Type 660. 'Vimy' was also considered in recognition of the other famous Vickers product that had shared the same name.

The chosen name also had an influence on the naming of the two advanced bombers that were to follow. A year later, it was decided by the Air Ministry to adopt alliterative names for both aircraft, creating what then became known as the 'V-Bombers'. There was and still is a great deal of confusion as to what meaning if any was behind the 'V-Force' name. However, there was no meaning at all. The names simply followed from the earlier choice of 'Valiant' for the Type 660. The Valiant's presence in the skies over the south coast drew a lot of attention, not only due to the ear-splitting noise of its four Avon engines, but because of its size, shape and shiny metal finish that was impossible to ignore.

Valiant production at Weybridge. Visible is the wing trailing edge arrangement that accommodated double-slatted flaps and the wing fence aerodynamic modification introduced for production aircraft.

The Valiant's large shoulder-mounted wing was sufficiently thick at its roots to house the engines internally – unlike the clumsy external arrangement chosen for the Sperrin – and the broad inboard chord allowed the design team to restrict wing root thickness to no more than 12 per cent while providing enough space for the engines inside. Space was also available for the huge twin main-wheel landing gear. Vickers opted for a highly unusual twin-wheel tandem layout for the main undercarriage that retracted outwards to lay flat inside the thinner portion of the wing beyond the engine bays. The concept worked well although some years later it encouraged Vickers to adopt a similar arrangement for the TSR2 and the results were far less satisfactory, ultimately contributing towards its cancellation.

The Valiant's wide root chord design enabled a greater acute angle of sweepback to be applied to the inner third of the wing span, raising the critical Mach number (the point at which airflow reaches the speed of sound) in the area where the airflow accelerating around the nose met the wings, thus creating less drag and better stability. The precise angle of sweepback was dictated by the need to locate the wing's aerodynamic centre with the aircraft's centre of gravity. Therefore, the aircraft would enjoy good stability and require a smaller and lighter variable-incidence tailplane positioned high on the tail to clear any effects from the wing's airflow or engine exhaust.

The mean wing sweep angle was twenty degrees, but the inboard section was swept more sharply than outboard where wing tip stalling was to be avoided. The result was a neat 'compound sweep' that was patented by its designer, Elfyn Richards. Apart from a wing fence attached to the upper surface of the outer wing, the Valiant's airframe was remarkably clean and sleek with only the cockpit fairing and lower fuselage bomb-aiming blister emerging from the smooth fuselage. The four engine exhausts were merged into the wing-trailing edges and the intakes were no more than slim rectangular slots containing a row of internal grilles. These were replaced on all subsequent Valiants by larger 'spectacle' intakes with bulged lower surfaces. The intakes provided an increase in air mass flow for the more powerful Avon engines that were fitted to production aircraft. The aircraft's proportions were dictated by various factors. The specified altitude and range were influential, but the projected weight and physical proportions of Britain's first atomic bomb was key. A huge 'backbone' member ran along the top of the fuselage centreline and two right-angled branches formed the main wing spars. These were joined at the centreline and attached to the outer wing spars, heavy channel-section booms extending and tapering towards the wingtips. The main spars were bifurcated and reinforced around the engine bays, while the main keel bean construction also provided the load-carrying roof for the bomb bay. Vickers introduced sculpture milling to manufacture the massive backbone structure and the technique paved the way for engineering employed on successive BAC designs.

A shortage of steel girder sections, largely due to the Korean War, led to the employment of pre-stressed concrete in the construction of the Valiant's main assembly jig pillars. Glass-fibre plastic bonding was also introduced for the production of the various dielectric products such as the huge nose radome and various suppressed aerial panels. Although the aircraft's structure was conventional both in terms of methods and materials used, the Valiant introduced a major innovation in that all electrical systems were employed. The only exception were the hydraulic brake and steering system, but even the pumps for this system were driven by electric motors. The huge H2S radar scanner in the nose inevitably had some influence on the shape of the forward fuselage, as did the need to accommodate a crew of five inside a pressurised cabin. This section of the aircraft was subcontracted to Saunders-Roe and featured a concave diaphragm forward bulkhead with radial stiffening beams and a convex un-stiffened rear shell.

Specification B.35/46 stipulated:

> The complete pressure cabin must be jettisonable. Such a cabin must be provided with parachutes to reduce the falling speed to a value at which the occupants will be unhurt when hitting the ground while strapped to their seats. If such a jettisonable cabin cannot be provided, the seats must be jettisonable.

The Vickers-Armstrong Weybridge factory as the first Valiant B.Mk.1 bombers approach the end of the production line.

The Vickers design team soon found that creating such an escape system was extremely difficult as the space required would have an effect on the design of the whole cabin. Also, the jettison system would require a great deal of time and money to perfect. Consequently, the Valiant's Specification B.9/48 neatly avoided the problem by stating: 'A completely jettisonable cabin is desired. If this is not practicable, arrangements should be made for good emergency escape means for the crew.' Ultimately, the only viable solution was to adopt a compromise with ejection seats for the pilot and co-pilot, but only an escape hatch for the rear crew who would be obliged to bail out in Second World War fashion. The same design impasse was reached with both advanced bomber designs. Although adopting the same escape system as the Valiant, they retained the basic design structure that enabled the whole forward nose section to be detached from the fuselage – in anticipation of an escape system that was never designed.

Tragically, the deficiencies of the Valiant's escape system were demonstrated on 12 January 1952. WB210 had returned to test flying after its glorious debut at the Farnborough show. On this particular day, the aircraft was engaged in engine shutdown, re-lights and noise measurements associated with the V.1000 – a proposed civil transport version of the Valiant that was eventually abandoned. During one re-

With the Sperrin consigned to history and the first Valiant destroyed in a crash, the second Valiant (WB215) became the basis of the fledgling V-Bomber development programme from April 1952.

light, an Avon engine suffered a 'wet' start and a fire broke out inside the wing bay. No fire warning system had been fitted inside the wing bay and by the time the fire was discovered by the crew, it was too late to save the aircraft. The crew believed that the starboard wing was about to burn through and the captain ordered the aircraft to be abandoned. The rear crew successfully bailed out via the fuselage hatch and the two pilots ejected, but the co-pilot was killed when his ejection seat struck the aircraft's fin. Although the accident illustrated that the escape system did not work perfectly, the ejection seats were improved and the Valiant's trouble-free service history confirmed that designing and manufacturing an expensive and time consuming escape capsule would have been pointless. The crash had no great influence of the Valiant's development as it had not been caused by a design or technical flaw.

The second prototype (WB215) was nearing completion at Wisley. Three months after the loss of the first aircraft, WB215 took to the air on 11 April 1952 and flight testing resumed. An order for twenty-five aircraft had been placed, covering five pre-production Type 674 aircraft powered by 9,500 lb Avon RA.14 engines and twenty Type 706 Valiant B.Mk.1 aircraft powered by 10,050 lb Avon RA.28 engines. Production got underway at Weybridge although the workforce was severely stretched and manufacturing space was limited. This led to the termination of Varsity production at Weybridge and the remaining eighty-nine examples of this aircraft were manufactured at Hurn. Valiants would be completed at Weybridge and flown out from the adjacent factory airfield at Brooklands where a meagre 3,600 feet runway was available and long enough to enable the Valiants to make the short hop to nearby Wisley for flight testing. As promised by George Edwards, service deliveries began in 1955 when WP206 arrived at RAF Gaydon in Warwickshire. No. 138 Squadron thus became the first Valiant unit before moving to Wittering, receiving WP213, WP212, WP211 and WP215 in April, followed by the first dual-role reconnaissance and bomber variant in June. The Valiant B(PR)Mk.1 (the Type 710) was the first of a batch of aircraft designed to operate either as a bomber or strategic reconnaissance aircraft, courtesy of a purpose-built reconnaissance crate that could be fitted into the aircraft's bomb bay as required. The crate incorporated eight F96 cameras with 48-inch lenses and four F49 survey cameras, giving the aircraft a horizon-to-horizon coverage capability.

With deliveries of the new Valiant bomber underway, the next step for the V-Force was to introduce the first atomic bomb and successfully mate it with its carrier aircraft. Ballistic trials of various bomb casings had been undertaken using an Avro Lincoln (later casings were dropped from the Sperrin as described previously). The Lincoln had been an appropriate choice. Not only was the aircraft readily available – and the only aircraft suitable for the job – the type would have to be modified to carry operational atomic bombs if the entire V-Bomber programme had failed. During 1948, Lord Tedder suggested to the Chiefs of Staff that the RAF should begin training for the handling and storage of nuclear weapons, and subsequently a committee was established to explore the matter. It was known as the Herod Committee, an acronym of High Explosives Research Operational Distribution, and the first meeting took place on 22 November.

The committee made a number of key decisions on operational activities, including the planning for the acceptance of nuclear weapons at Wittering and Marham. They also agreed that the first in-service bombs should be designed for in-flight fusing, enabling the tube containing the fissile components and corresponding outer layers of the bomb to be inserted after take-off as a safety measure. In November 1951, the Herod Committee specified that the RAF Atomic Weapons School should be located at the first RAF station where nuclear weapons would be stored (Wittering). It was agreed that the Armament Training School should also be based there, after having first considered Honington, which was originally scheduled to be the first Valiant station. The first operational bomber squadron (No. 138) would also be at Wittering, and as it also housed the co-located Valiant Trials Flight, No. 1321, the station was soon at the very heart of the RAF's new V-Force.

The design of the first atomic bombs progressed well, although for some time it was unclear if the bomb would be completed before the first Valiants or vice versa. Doctor Penney commented:

This unusual image of all three V-Bomber types together illustrates that despite the more advanced nature of the Vulcan and Victor, the Valiant was outwardly an equally futuristic design when it first emerged, and was similar in overall size to its V-Force counterparts.

> My philosophy is that the RAF has handled aircraft for a long time and can fly Valiants as soon as they come off the production line. But the Royal Air Force has not yet handled atomic weapons, therefore, we must get some bombs to the RAF at the earliest possible moment, so that the handling and servicing can be practised and fully worked out.

He also added that these first weapons would in effect be the same as more developed versions, but that they might require modifications to the In-Flight Insertion (IFI) cartridge. If these first bombs had to be used, the cartridge might have to be loaded before take-off, rather than in flight.

Infrastructure was designed for the storage of atomic weapons at Wittering, Marham, Honington and Waddington. A bomb depot was to be completed at Barnham in Norfolk. The first of the completed atomic bombs were delivered to the RAF (the Bomber Command Armament School) over the nights of 7 November and 14 November 1953 when a series of convoys arrived at Wittering. Trials with the Valiant were to begin during 1954, but the first aircraft could not be delivered to Wittering until the following year, and so it was not until 15 June that Valiant WP201 arrived. The MoS had formed No. 1321 Flight during 1954 specifically for dropping trials and the unit had completed some bomb delivery and handling training with Vickers at Wisley. It was decided that bombs would only be assigned to operational units so, following the initial drop trials, No. 1321 Flight became C Flight of No. 138 Squadron in February 1956, changing to No. 49 Squadron on 1 May 1956.

The delivery of Valiant WP201 allowed the first ballistic store to be dropped from 12,000 feet at 330 kt over the Orfordness range on 6 July. Progress was satisfactory, but a setback occurred on 29 July when No. 138 Squadron's WP222 crashed shortly after taking-off on a cross-country training flight. The Valiant entered a left-hand turn that continued through 300 degrees until the aircraft impacted three minutes after take-off, killing the entire crew. Subsequent investigations revealed that a runaway actuator had fixed an aileron tab in the 'up' position, causing the uncontrollable roll. Fixing the potentially fatal flaw was simple, but the crash raised more concerns about the ability of aircrew to safely abandon all three V-Bomber types in emergencies. The loss of a second Valiant and a Vulcan in 1956 prompted some serious questions that the Air Staff were obliged to answer. The DCAS replied on 15 October 1956 stating again that when the Valiant, Vulcan and Victor were first conceived, they were to have been fitted with jettisonable cabins that would separate from the aircraft and make a parachute-retarded descent:

As design and development proceeded it became clear that this facility could not be provided, and agreement not to have a jettisonable cabin was reached in the case of the Valiant in June 1948, the Vulcan in May 1949 and the Victor in October 1952. In all three bombers the layout of the cabin, which was operationally very satisfactory, made it impossible, for structural reasons, to produce ejection facilities for aircrew other than the pilots. It was, however, agreed to provide ejector seats for the pilots so that they could remain with the aircraft for longer and help other crew members to escape. Facilities for the other crew members were provided by means of side doors in the Valiant and Victor and through an underneath hatch in the Vulcan, which has virtually no fuselage.

The result of this is that all three bombers and the developments of them will, according to present planning, have ejector seats for the pilots and escape by door or hatch for the three other crew members. A trained crew takes approximately 20 seconds from the time the order to jump is given until the last man leaves the aircraft, but it is important to remember that it is unlikely that the three non-pilot crew members would escape in conditions where high 'g' forces are being applied through battle damage or loss of control, when the aircraft is at low level. On the other hand, when the first Valiant had a fire in the air all live members got out of the aircraft successfully at high altitude - unfortunately, the second pilot was killed by striking the fin.

I have discussed a possible modification plan for the V-Bombers with Mr James Martin (managing director and chief designer of the Martin-Baker ejection seat company) and with the Ministry of Supply, and I am of the opinion that it is certainly not impossible to incorporate ejection facilities for the three non-pilot members of the crew of the V-Bombers, but the implementation of such a policy would naturally raise very grave issues. The first issue is whether or not we would be right to go in for such a policy, and the second is whether we could afford to do so, both in terms of money and effort as well as the delay of the V-Force build-up. A retrospective modification programme would naturally be an immense undertaking but it is not technically impossible, and if we do go in for it we must realise what may be involved. My own view is that we should not attempt to adopt such a policy.

In reality, it was always accepted that in most potentially catastrophic situations, the rear crews would probably have had sufficient time to abandon the aircraft by evacuating through the escape hatch. However, when the V-Force switched to low-level operations, the issue reappeared yet again, but by then it was too late to do much about it. The escape issue might have been addressed more thoroughly if the Air Staff had realised just how long two of the three V-Bomber types would remain in RAF service. At the time, they were expected to be replaced by more advanced bombers (or other delivery systems) within a matter of years and no one could have imagined that they would be in business decades later.

CHAPTER THREE

Grappling with Terror

While the V-Force's aircraft were in production at Orfordness and Jurby, the Blue Danube bomb-dropping trials continued. It soon became evident that the RAE designers had produced a near-perfect ballistic casing for the atomic warhead. In some respects the design was possibly too good, as when the instrumented test specimens were released they often 'flew' beneath the Valiant's rear fuselage before falling clear (each test drop was tracked visually by theodolite). To counter this potentially dangerous tendency, the Valiant was re-equipped with strakes forward of the bomb bay which created an airflow disturbance to push the bomb downwards and away from the fuselage. However, subsequent experience with the Vulcan and Victor confirmed a cleaner bomb release from both types.

Equipped with six Valiant B.Mk.1s, No. 49 Squadron was quickly assigned to Operation Buffalo, which would culminate in the first air drop of a live British nuclear weapon. Two Valiants, W3366 and WZ367, departed for Australia on 5 August 1956. Further training was to have been conducted from Wittering, but poor weather and difficulty in obtaining sufficient weapons-range access meant that the crews could operate more effectively by using the Maralinga and Woomera ranges. The work-up towards Operation Buffalo did not proceed smoothly as a report by Group Capt Menaul, the Commander of the Air Task Group, indicated:

> The Valiants arrived at Edinburgh having completed part of a bombing training programme in the UK. It was planned to complete their training in Australia using the range facilities at Maralinga or Woomera as required. The main reason for the non-completion of training in the UK was the late delivery of aircraft and the lack of flight clearance for certain items of equipment, notably the bombing system, the automatic pilot and the radar altimeter. Unsuitable weather and difficulties in obtaining bombing ranges also added to the delays.
>
> During the training which followed, ten practice 10,000 lb bombs and 60 x 100 lb bombs were dropped in the UK by the two Valiant aircraft. The 10,000 lb bombs were primarily to prove the weapon and aircraft systems and the 100-pounders to prove

A grainy image of an historic aeroplane: Valiant prototype WB210 pictured shortly after its first flight. The original narrow 'letterbox' air intakes can clearly be seen.

the accuracy of the aircraft's bombsight, particularly in the hands of inexperienced crews. On completion of this training programme in the UK, the results of which were not entirely satisfactory, it was decided that the standard obtained, considering the time available, was adequate and the aircraft and crews were prepared to fly out to Australia. Technical defects discovered during the UK training phase were corrected, and modifications to the bombsight sighting head and the Green Satin radar output improved the system and gave considerably better bombing results at a later date. The whole of the training programme in the UK could have been considerably improved if more emphasis had been placed on overseas operations.

Valiant WZ366 took-off from Maralinga airfield with the live nuclear weapon onboard. The crew consisted of Sqn Ldr Flavell (captain), Group Capt Menaul, Flt Lts Ledger and Stacey, Flg Off Spencer and Pilot Off Ford. The aircraft climbed to 38,000 feet in a wide arc, avoiding the range area until it reached the emergency holding area. The bombsight was levelled, contact was established with the air controller on the ground by VHF and HF and the aircraft then descended to 30,000 feet ready to begin the fly-over sequences, using precisely the same drills and procedures as in the concrete and HE drops. At 14:25, the first fly-over, Type A was successfully completed, with all equipment, both in the air and on the ground, working satisfactorily. Types B and C fly-overs were then completed in turn, and by 15:00, all was in readiness for the final Type D fly-over and the release of the nuclear weapon. The final D type fly-over was completed according to plan with all equipment functioning perfectly, and the weapon was released at 15:27. Immediately after release a steep turn to starboard on to a heading of 240 degrees true was executed in order to position the aircraft correctly for the thermal measuring equipment to function. During this turn 1.9g was applied.

The weapon exploded correctly and the aircraft, after observing the formation of the mushroom cloud, set course for base, where it landed at 15:35. The operation had gone smoothly and exactly according to the plans drawn up during training. The bombing error was afterwards assessed at 100 yards overshoot and 40 feet right.

The explosive yield of the Blue Danube bomb had been fixed at forty kilotons. However, for this drop, the figure had been reduced to three kilotons in order to avoid the risks of extensive radioactive fallout, which would have been created if the bomb's barometric fusing had failed and the airburst had in effect become a ground burst. This was mentioned in a report sent to the Secretary of State for Air by Air Marshal Tuttle that read: 'The weapon, a Blue Danube round with modified fusing, in-flight loading and with the yield reduced to 3-4 Kilotons, was dropped from the Valiant aircraft at 30,000 feet. The weapon was set to burst at 500 feet and telemetry confirmed that the burst occurred between 500 and 600 feet. The bomb was aimed visually after a radar-controlled run-up.' This first functional air drop demonstrated to the world that Britain not only possessed nuclear knowhow, but that the RAF now had a practical means of delivering nuclear weapons to their targets.

This demonstration of how atomic weapons could be successfully delivered by the new V-Bombers was another key moment in the creation of a national independent nuclear deterrent. But by this stage, the British Government was turning its attention to what was almost a completely new means of destructive power and Britain was, essentially, a generation behind the US and Soviet Union in terms of nuclear weapon development. The development of the thermonuclear (hydrogen) bomb represented yet another quantum leap in technology which was almost as great as the initial development of atomic weaponry. Although the concept was basically a development of atomic fission – and had been established as a theoretical possibility for almost as long as the atom bomb – the physics involved in the process are rather different.

In simple terms, hydrogen bombs use the energy of a fission bomb in order to compress and heat fusion fuel. In the most common 'Teller-Ulam' design (which accounts for all multi-megaton-yield hydrogen bombs), this is accomplished by placing a fission bomb and fusion fuel (tritium, deuterium or lithium deuteride) in close proximity within a special, radiation-reflecting container. When the fission bomb is detonated, gamma and X-rays emitted at the speed of light first compress the fusion fuel and then heat it to thermonuclear temperatures. The ensuing fusion

A gaggle of Valiants outside the flight test hangar at Wisley in company with some distinctly older Vickers products in the shape of two Vallettas. (*Tony Clarke collection*)

reaction creates enormous numbers of high-speed neutrons, which then can induce fission in materials that normally are not prone to it such as depleted uranium. Each of these components is known as a 'stage' with the fission bomb as the 'primary' and the fusion capsule as the 'secondary'. In large hydrogen bombs, about half of the explosive yield comes from the final fissioning of depleted uranium. By chaining together numerous stages with increasing amounts of fusion fuel, thermonuclear weapons can be made to an almost arbitrary yield.

Just six weeks after the first British atomic test at Monte Bello, the US successfully detonated the first two thermonuclear (hydrogen bomb) devices at Eniwetok, the Soviets following with their own test on 12 August 1953. In 1954, British Prime Minister Anthony Eden said that the hydrogen bomb had 'fundamentally altered the entire problem of defence' and in February 1955, the Government produced a paper that included the following:

> In the Statement on Defence 1954, HM Government set out their views on the effect of atomic weapons on UK policy and on the nature of war. Shortly afterwards, the

US Government released information on the experimental explosion at Eniwetok in November 1952, of a thermonuclear weapon many hundred times more powerful than the atomic bombs which were used at Nagasaki and Hiroshima in 1945. On 1 March 1954, an even more powerful thermonuclear weapon was exploded in the Marshall Islands. There are no technical or scientific limitations on the production of nuclear weapons still more devastating. The US Government have announced that they are proceeding with full-scale production of thermonuclear weapons. The Soviet Government are clearly following the same policy; though we cannot tell when they will have thermonuclear weapons available for operational use. The United Kingdom has the ability to produce such weapons. After fully considering all the implications of this step the Government have thought it their duty to proceed with their development and production. The power of these weapons is such that accuracy of aim assumes less importance; thus attacks can be delivered by aircraft flying at great speed and at great heights. This greatly increases the difficulty of defence. Moreover, other means of delivery can be foreseen which will, in time, present even greater problems.

There is certainly no doubt that when the British scientists returned from the Manhattan Project, they possessed more than a little general knowledge of how a hydrogen bomb might be produced. Theoretical work on the hydrogen bomb appears to have begun in 1951, but early results were evidently disappointing as during 1952, Lord Cherwell, the Prime Minister's chief technical advisor, told Churchill that hydrogen weapons were 'beyond our means'. Despite this initial pessimism, Britain's thermonuclear weapon programme was remarkably successful. The initial decision to manufacture hydrogen bombs was made by a Cabinet Defence Committee on 16 June 1954 and was discussed by the full Cabinet during the following month.

The final Cabinet decision was taken on 26 July when approval was given to the proposal that '...the current programme for the manufacture of atomic weapons should be so adjusted as to allow for the production of thermonuclear bombs'. Churchill stated, 'We could not expect to maintain our influence as a world power unless we possessed the most up-to-date nuclear weapons.' Likewise, the Cabinet agreed that thermonuclear bombs would be more economical than their atomic equivalents and that in moral terms, the decision to manufacture these new weapons would be no worse than accepting what would amount to the indirect support and protection of America's hydrogen bombs. Towards the end of 1955, the Defence Research Policy Committee (DRPC) commented that, 'The earliest possible achievement of a megaton explosion is necessary to demonstrate our ability to make such weapons, as part of the strategic deterrent against war.' In fact, the main reason for the almost frantic development of hydrogen bombs was not directly due to any perceived deterrent policy or any immediate threat – it was simply a response to the growing pressure for an international ban on atmospheric nuclear tests which would

Eight Valiant B.Mk.1 aircraft pose for the media after entering RAF service at Gaydon in Warwickshire, home of the valiant Operational Conversion Unit.

effectively prohibit Britain from testing and eventually manufacturing a hydrogen bomb.

Britain maintained what was perceived to be an even-handed diplomatic position by backing calls for a test ban while maintaining an active developmental programme. Aubrey Jones, the minister responsible for the nuclear tests, said:

> In the absence of international agreement on methods of regulating and limiting nuclear test explosions – and Her Majesty's Government will not cease to pursue every opportunity of seeking such an agreement – the tests which are to take place shortly in the Pacific are, in the opinion of the Government, essential to the defence of the country and the prevention of global war.

Britain was effectively caught up in a race to develop and detonate a hydrogen bomb before being forced to accept a ban on nuclear testing. The DRPC said, '... it is essential that this first series should be planned in such a way as to safeguard the future by obtaining the greatest possible amount of scientific knowledge and

Dramatic view of the Valiant WZ365's upper surfaces. As can be seen, the wing design was relatively simple, comprising of a straight swept leading and trailing edge with a gradually increasing chord towards the inner section. Unlike the Sperrin, the Valiant's engines were comfortably buried inside the wing root, creating less drag.

weapon design experience as the foundation of our megaton weapon development programme.' The committee identified four basic requirements: a megaton warhead for a freefalling bomb; a similar megaton warhead for a powered guided bomb (which eventually became the Blue Steel missile); a smaller and lighter warhead for a medium-range ballistic missile (which was intended to be Blue Streak); and a multi-megaton warhead intended to demonstrate that Britain could match the devices which had been tested by America and the Soviets.

As Britain's scientific knowledge of thermonuclear weaponry was at this stage restricted to theoretical analysis, the DRPC report stated that the most certain way of achieving a megaton explosion in 1957 would be to use a large, pure-fission assembly in a Mk.1 case, surrounded by sufficient fissile material to ensure a megaton yield (a so-called 'boosted' device). The bomb would consequently be big, heavy and extravagant in fissile material, but would work, although it could only be developed into a freefall bomb due to its size and weight. The Government agreed to proceed with a series of test explosions and on 5 June 1956, the Cabinet agreed that the Prime Minister should make a Parliamentary statement about the tests. Two days later, Eden announced to the House of Commons that Britain was to conduct a limited number of test explosions, this time in the megaton range.

The crews of No. 49 Squadron at Wittering began training for Operation Grapple on 1 September 1956 using standard Valiant B.Mk.1s until the first specially modified Grapple aircraft was delivered. Various modifications were made to the Grapple Valiants in order to equip them for their live weapon trials. Most notably they were sprayed with an anti-flash white paint capable of withstanding seventy-two calories of heat energy per square centimetre. The control surfaces were strengthened to withstand the bomb's pressure wave, the flight deck and bomb-aiming positions were fitted with metal anti-flash screens and a number of sensors and cameras installed. Valiant XD818 departed for Christmas Island on 2 March 1957 via Aldergrove, Goose Bay, Namao, Travis and Honolulu as it had not been fitted with underling fuel tanks at this stage. It was followed by XD822, XD823 and XD824 at one-day intervals.

Flown by No. 49 Squadron's CO Wing Commander K. G. Hubbard, XD818 arrived over Christmas Island on 12 March, descending from a familiarisation circuit at 1,500 feet to a rather more spectacular 50 feet for a low-level fly-by over the airfield dispersal area before landing. After a settling-in period, the four Valiant crews began a series of training sorties, establishing a precise bomb-aiming capability and bomb-drop manoeuvres which would be used for each trial. The training was completed by 5 April, despite the unexpected torrential rain which made life in Christmas Island's 'tent city' fairly grim for some time. Two aircraft, XD818 and XD823, were prepared for the first live drop that was designed to test the 'Green Granite Small' warhead. This was a two-stage device weighing 4,200 lb and contained in a lead bismuth casing with a total weight of 10,000 lb. It was a true thermonuclear fusion weapon, the spherical fission primary having a composite U-235 and Pu-239 core with a spherical secondary comprising of U-235 and a U-238 tamper, all packed in lithium deuterate.

Valiant XD818, flown by Wing Cdr Hubbard, was to be the drop aircraft for the first test with XD824 acting as an observer aircraft with a second crew to give them experience of flash and blast from a thermonuclear weapon. The historic two hour and twenty minute sortie took place on 15 May 1957 as reported by Hubbard:

> The aircraft became airborne at 09:00 V-time and all anti-flash screens were in position prior to the aircraft commencing its first run over the target. After one initial run to check telemetry, the Task Force Commander gave clearance for the live run. The bombing run was made at 45,000 feet true, and as Green Satin drift was fluctuating badly, the set was put to Memory on average drift. The bombing run was steady on a course of 203

A magnificent line-up of bombers at Marham with Canberras in the background and five Valiants in the foreground led by XD812, the first dual bomber and tanker derivative.

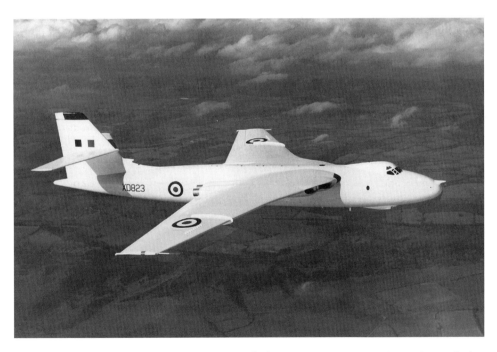

XD823 in 'Grapple' finish. The overall white anti-flash paint gave some protection against radiation absorption. However, the primary means of avoiding blast and radioactive pulse damage was to escape from the detonation area as swiftly as possible.

degrees and the weapon was released at 10:36 W-time. Immediately after release, the aircraft was rolled into the escape manoeuvre, which averaged a turn of 60 degrees bank, excess g 1.8 to 1.9, airspeed Mach 0.76, rolling out on a heading of 073 degrees. The time taken for this turn was 38 sec and at the time of air burst of the weapon, the slant range between aircraft and burst was 8.65 n/ms. Neither crew nor aircraft felt any effect of flash and the air blast reached the aircraft two-and-a-half minutes after release. The effect of the blast was to produce a period of five seconds during which turbulence alike to slight clear air turbulence was experienced. Six minutes after release, all shutters in the aircraft were removed and after one orbit to see the mushroom cloud effect, the aircraft returned to base and made a normal landing.

This rather dry description is typical of most military accounts and it deliberately fails to emphasise the drama of the test, although Hubbard later said that '...it really was a sight of such majesty and grotesque beauty that it defies adequate description'. Nick Wilson, an able seaman onboard HMS *Warrior*, witnessed the explosion from a distance of thirty miles:

I felt my back warming up and experienced the flash, though I had my hands over my face and dark goggles on. Five seconds after the flash we turned round and faced the flash, but it was still bright so I replaced them. There in the sky was a brightly glowing seething ball of fire. This rapidly increased and became more cloudy. Soon it was looking like a very dark ripe apple with a snow-white sauce being poured over it. On the horizon at sea level, a cloud appeared that must have been dust and spray from the island. The whole sight was most beautiful and I was completely filled with emotions.

Although the sight was undoubtedly very impressive, 'Green Granite Small' was not a perfect success. Yielding 0.3 megatons from a predicted yield of up to 1.0 Mt, the lithium deuterate only partly ignited, but the test did at least demonstrate the warhead's potential (and an explosive force 100 times that of the Buffalo air drop). It also provided the opportunity for another airborne test of a live Blue Danube casing. Despite the mixed results, Britain had visibly and audibly entered the thermonuclear age.

The next drop on 31 May was Grapple 2 or 'Orange Herald' that tested Dr Penney's 'fallback' high-yield fission bomb, which was again contained in a Blue Danube casing. The warhead, which was developed into an operational physics package known as 'Green Grass' was, as on the first drop, detonated by barometric means at 8,000 feet and yielded 0.72 Mt. Squadron Leader Roberts, captain of the release aircraft, XD822, was the most experienced Grapple pilot, but the 'Orange Herald' flight nearly ended in disaster as his flight report explains:

A dramatic view of XD812 streaking over the airfield perimeter fence at Teversham. Refuelling probes could be fitted to all RAF Valiants, although they were not always attached. Likewise, the underwing external fuel tanks were a standard fit, but only carried when necessary. (*Tony Clarke collection*)

My crew was detailed to take off at 09:00 on 31 May in variant XD822 to drop Orange Herald on the target area south of Malden Island. The forecast weather for the target area was one- to two-eighths of cumulus, and wind velocity 090 degrees/20 knots at 45,000 feet; conditions at base line. In view of this fuel load was reduced to 5,000 gal in order to give an all-up weight of 99,000 lb immediately after release of the bomb. The crew reached the aircraft at 07:40 and completed cockpit checks by 08:10. AWRE (Atomic Weapons Research Establishment) had connected the bomb batteries by the time the crew entered the aircraft at 08:40, but then the take-off time was delayed on orders from JOC (Joint Operations centre). At 09:00, permission was given to start engines and we were airborne at 09:07. The flight to the RV (radar vector) took 50 min and was uneventful. Good contact on HF and VHF was established and maintained with the appropriate authorities throughout the flight.

The first run over the target was navigation-type and the weather was found to be as forecast. After the first run the remaining black-out shutters were fitted and we went straight round on the initial run. Shortly after completing this, permission was given to carry on with the live run. The run-up was steady and the bomb was released at 10:44, heading 202 degrees, IAS (indicated airspeed) 216, IMN (Indicated Mach Number) 0.75. After a slight pause, I initiated a steep turn to port at 60 degrees bank. At this stage the second pilot should have started to call readings on the sensitive accelerometer, but on this occasion he was silent for a few seconds.

I looked up and saw that the instrument indicated unity. Experience told me to believe the instrument, so disregarding my senses, I increased the backward pressure on the control column. At that instant the second pilot and I realised that the instrument had failed at the time of release; simultaneously, the aircraft stalled, and the bomb aimer, who was making for his seat, returned to the bomb-aimer's well with some force. After regaining control, the manoeuvre was completed in 43 seconds, using the mechanical accelerometer. This instrument might have been referred to earlier had it not been so far from our normal instrument scan. At 53 sec by the navigator's countdown, a bright white flash was seen through chinks in the blackout screens and the coloured glass in the first pilot's panel was lit up.

At 2 min 55 sec after release, the blast waves were felt, first a moderate thump followed a second later by a smaller one. I waited a further two minutes before turning to port to allow the crew to see what had happened. The cloud top at this time appeared to be some 10,000 feet above our flight level and it is a sight which will not easily be forgotten. The symmetry and the colours were most impressive, especially against the dark blue background provided by the sky at that height; as we watched, the upper stem and mushroom head started to glow with a deep peach colour. We then set course for base and landed at 12:47.

The third test, forenamed 'Purple Granite' took place on 19 June. This time, the air drop involved the 'Green Granite Large' warhead, an enlarged version of the 'Green Granite Small' with a total weight of 6,000 lb, excluding the HE. Surprisingly, it was the least successful of the three drops, yielding just 0.2 Mt after being dropped from XD823. The Grapple tests had been useful and spectacular, but they were rather disappointing in terms of results. The situation was summed up at a progress meeting on 16 July when the development of 'Yellow Sun' (codename for what would become the standard freefall megaton weapon for the V-Force) was discussed. While Grapple had been successful in providing data on the performance of two different types of megaton warhead, it had not provided sufficient data to enable a firm decision to be made regarding the warhead to be chosen for Yellow Sun.

On the evidence of the trials, a 'Green Bamboo'-type warhead had been chosen by the Air Staff for use in what would be an interim megaton weapon, pending deliveries of Yellow Sun. Further trials ('Grapple X') were scheduled for November 1957 and No. 49 Squadron was again tasked with the provision of aircraft and crews. This time, the bomb drop at ground zero would be just twenty miles from Christmas

An unusual view of WZ381 while undergoing servicing with Marshalls at Teversham Airport. The fin cap fairing has been removed, revealing the aerial plate inside. The markings of No. 7 Squadron are clearly visible just below. (*Tony Clarke collection*)

Island (instead of nearly 400 miles) to avoid the expense and delays involved in setting up a naval task force to monitor the tests. Valiant XD825, captained by Sqn Ldr B. T. Millett, made the fourth drop on 8 November, the weapon being fitted with a 'Green Granite Small' warhead. This time, however, the scientists were pleasantly surprised at the result when the bomb delivered a yield of 1.8 Mt, the first true British megaton explosion. Sapper Arthur Thomas witnessed the test from Christmas Island: 'Then it happened, the blast, a lightning speed of wind and whistle of trees – a bang – it hit us all unexpectedly, lifting us off our feet and depositing us three to four yards away landing on top of each other in a pile of bodies. We were not told to expect anything of this nature.' The clear success of this drop explains why just one test was made when the Task Force Grapple Air Plan had called for the 'air drop of two thermonuclear weapons with minimum risk to all concerned'.

The records of No. 49 Squadron state that, 'The results were entirely satisfactory, precluding the necessity for any further tests in this particular phase of Operation Grapple.' However, the test programme was far from complete and 'Grapple Y' took

The weathered finish on WZ401 illustrates the early silver paint scheme that was applied to the Valiant fleet. This was swiftly replaced by an overall anti-flash white paint until disruptive camouflage was introduced shortly before the Valiant's premature retirement. (*Tony Clarke collection*)

place during April 1958. Valiant XD824, captained by Sqn Ldr R. M. Bates, made the next (fifth) drop on 28 April. Evidence suggests that the warhead was a 'Green Granite Large' device and the resulting explosion delivered the largest yield of any British nuclear tests, a tremendous 3.0 megatons. This demonstrated that Dr Penney and his scientists could, if necessary, produce weapons which easily matched the destructive power of either the American or Soviet Union's hydrogen bombs. Further tests ('Grapple Z') took place during the summer of 1958 on a faster timescale as Britain slowly moved towards an agreement to end nuclear testing. No. 49 Squadron's records stated that, 'Due to the decision to accelerate the entire dropping programme for political considerations, the intensity of the high-explosive drops in preparation for the nuclear drops has been increased.' These final nuclear detonations took place in September as the squadron's records describe:

> The month of September brought to fruition all the training for Operation Grapple Z with the dropping of two more nuclear weapons by the squadron. On the 2nd, Sqn Ldr G. M. Bailey and crew in Valiant XD822 dropped the first device of the series. This weapon was the first to be dropped by ground-controlled radar. A grandstand aircraft on this occasion, Valiant XD818, was flown by Flt Lt S. O'Connor and crew. On 11th

September, Flt Lt S. O'Connor and crew, in Valiant XD827, dropped a second nuclear device. This weapon was released on a visual attack. Sqn Ldr H. A. Caillard and crew in Valiant XD824 flew as grandstand. Immediately after the second air drop, the aircraft were prepared for the return trip to Wittering.

After the Valiants and crews returned to Wittering, No. 49 Squadron continued training for an anticipated further series of test drops. However, by the end of November 1958, Britain had effectively decided to abandon nuclear testing. The Government later stated that the United Kingdom would no longer carry out further nuclear tests, whether in or above the atmosphere, underwater or underground. Christmas Island was gradually reduced to a minimum holding state and HQ Task Force Grapple was disbanded on 3 June 1960. From 1 December 1958, No. 49 Squadron reverted to a standard bomber role and the Grapple Valiants were de-modified and refitted with the standard radar navigational bombing system. Although the Cabinet decision to manufacture thermonuclear bombs had been taken more than five months previously, Churchill made no reference to this historic date in British history when he said:

The advance of the hydrogen bomb has fundamentally altered the entire problem of defence, and considerations founded even upon the atom bomb have become obsolescent, almost old-fashioned. Immense changes are taking place in military facts and in military thoughts. We have for some time past adopted the principles that safety and even survival must be sought in deterrence rather than defence and this, I believe, is the policy which also guides the United States.

Designed chiefly as a scientific and operational test programme, Operations Buffalo and Grapple had demonstrated to the US that Britain was more than capable of producing thermonuclear weapons which were more efficient than their foreign equivalents. It is hardly surprising, therefore, that relations between America and Britain gradually improved after the first nuclear tests (Operation Buffalo) in 1956 and even survived through the days of the McCarthy period. The Atomic Energy Act, effectively a revision of the infamous McMahon Act, was signed in 1954, permitting the transfer of data concerning the external characteristics of nuclear weapons: size, shape, weight, yield and effects. The US and Britain agreed to co-operate within the terms of this Act in a bilateral agreement signed on 15 June 1955.

However, the real breakthrough came after the huge transatlantic rift that developed during the Suez Crisis. Prime Minister Harold Macmillan and Eisenhower met twice in 1957. During their first meeting in Bermuda during March, agreements were made for the deployment of Thor missiles to the UK which would be under 'dual key' control. Eisenhower commented that this was 'by far the most successful

Valiant WZ402 pictured in 1960. As can be seen, the aircraft's bomb bay was low slung. This made the loading of conventional HE weapons a straightforward operation, but was far from ideal for larger atomic weapons. (*Tony Clarke collection*)

international conference' he had attended since the war. When they met for a second time in Washington during October, revisions were made to the Atomic Energy Act to allow scientific co-operation between 'Great Britain, the United States and other friendly powers'. It was no coincidence that the President's enthusiasm for restoring the 'special relationship' came in the same year that Britain embarked upon the first Grapple tests just months after the first operational hydrogen bombs had entered US service. Britain's thermonuclear advances had been remarkable and the US identified potential advantages for a new co-operative arrangement with Britain.

Another important consideration was the launching of the Soviet Union's Sputnik satellite, which threw into question many assumptions of American technical superiority. It also underlined the possibility that the Soviet Union might eventually be able to deliver nuclear weapons to targets in Europe and the United States by missile. The Suez Crisis had also served to illustrate just how far apart Britain and America were and this possibly served as a catalyst in repairing the faltering 'special relationship'. Finally in 1958, the Agreement for Co-operation on the Uses of Atomic

Energy for Mutual Defence Purposes was signed, enabling both countries to exchange virtually all types of nuclear information. Britain learned a great deal from American expertise in engineering and weapons assembly techniques. Conversely, American officials were amazed at the scientific and technical knowledge Britain possessed, which in many respects was ahead of the Americans. The intimate and totally reciprocal collaboration continued into the 1960s and beyond, long after America could possibly have hoped to derive any further benefits from the co-operation.

A British official illustrated the position in the 1970s when he stated that 'The United States has two laboratories and we have one; they spend five times as much as we do on these establishments; they have conducted some 870 tests – how many of which were really necessary I wouldn't say – and we have conducted 30. That gives, I think, a fair indication of the 'hardware balance' although in the idea end of the business, the relationship is rather more equal.'

The completion of the Grapple tests eventually led to an Air Staff Requirement for a thermonuclear bomb (ASR OR.l136) which was issued on 6 June 1955. It called for a bomb that was not to exceed 50 inches in diameter (and would be made smaller if possible), not to exceed 7,000 lb in weight and was capable of carriage internally by Valiants, Vulcans and Victors for RAF service from 1959. When the Cabinet made their historical decision to proceed with development of hydrogen bombs during June 1954, the meeting agreed that work on the programme should be performed 'as unobtrusively as possible' and that it was 'desirable that costs be concealed as much as possible'. Before them was a memorandum from the Chiefs of Staff that was based on a report by the Working Party on the Operational Use of Atomic Weapons whose members included Sir William Penney, the Deputy Chiefs of Staffs and scientific advisors.

The report concluded that hydrogen bombs would 'go a long way towards overcoming the difficult problems of terminal accuracy simply by delivering a huge explosive force and that only a relatively limited number of bombs would be required, beyond which any increase of stocks would not offer any corresponding military advantage.' The Chiefs of Staff decided (during a meeting on 6 April 1955) to develop, as a first priority, a thermonuclear bomb with a yield of approximately one megaton. ASR OR. 1136 was accepted by the Ministry of Supply on 28 July, leading to the start of development work on the weapon called 'Yellow Sun' and during March 1956, members of the Operational Requirements staff visited Farnborough where drawings and a wooden mock-up of Yellow Sun were prepared. The bomb carcass was 240 inches long, 48 inches in diameter and had small cruciform stabilising fins similar to the Second World War 'Grand Slam' design (larger ones would have had to fold out to enable the weapon to fit into the Valiant's bomb bay).

Unusually, the bomb had a flat nose that was intended to slow the bomb during free fall to increase the weapon's stability. It was also to simplify the requirements of the internal barometric detonation device that would probably be unable to

A well known RAF publicity photograph showing a 214 Squadron Valiant at Marham with a Bloodhound SAM battery in the background. The Bloodhounds were a 'last chance' defence for the V-Force against marauding Soviet bombers.

cope with a terminal velocity exceeded supersonic speeds. The warhead weighed approximately 3,500 lb and the completed weapon had a weight of around 6,500 lb. While Yellow Sun was being developed, a second weapon, Red Beard, was also being developed, primarily as a smaller tactical bomb. This was partly a replacement for the first-generation Blue Danube which, as a relatively crude fission device, delivered a relatively low explosive yield of around twenty kilotons despite weighing a staggering 10,250 lb. However, it was quickly accepted that if the development of these two weapons proceeded smoothly, the warheads would be ready before the bomb bodies being designed to carry them. Therefore, it was proposed that an interim weapon should be manufactured so that the RAF could acquire a thermonuclear capability as soon as possible.

Three warheads – Green Granite, Green Bamboo and Orange Herald – could be made available and incorporated within a standard Blue Danube bomb casing. A report prepared by the RAE in April 1957 described progress with the RAF's hydrogen bomb:

> The Yellow Sun weapon to meet Air Staff Requirement oR.1136 will provide the first
> British bomb having a yield in the megaton range; as such it is the keystone of the

offensive deterrent policy. It is intended for carriage in the V-class bombers and will have a diameter of 48 in and a length of approximately 20 feet. The weight will be about 7,000 lb. The weapon is being designed around the Green Bamboo warhead under development at the Atomic Weapons Research Establishment. The means of making a warhead in this range wholly safe in storage and transport has not been finalised, but all schemes of providing in-flight insertion of some part of the fissile material have been abandoned. Consideration has also been given to the alternative warheads Green Granite and Short Granite, which are being tested at Operation Grapple. Both are fission-fusion-fission types and differ only in that Short Granite is smaller and lighter. Neither warhead requires ENI (External Neutron Initiations). Nuclear safety is ensured by some form of in-flight insertion. Preliminary investigation indicates that if after Grapple Short Granite becomes the preferred warhead, no serious delay should occur, but the Green Granite would require a larger and heavier weapon, so that much of the ballistic and fusing work already well advanced would have to be repeated, and the in-service date would have to be set back at least nine months.

Subsequently, a second Progress Statement issued later in 1957 included the following:

The Operational Requirement OR.1136 Issue 2 calls for the development of a megaton bomb, the type of warhead to be carried not being specified except that it shall be capable of use in both Yellow Sun and Blue Steel. The original requirement was for incorporation of the Green Bamboo warhead and much of the work done has been on the assumption that this warhead will be used. It has, however, been evident for some time that as a result of the Grapple trials another warhead might be preferred, and preliminary investigations were made at an early stage into the problems which would arise if one of the Granite type of warheads were chosen. These have been followed by further work, especially in connection with the possible use of Short Granite. The general position now is that an early decision as to the type of warhead, and information on associated matters such as nuclear safety systems, is essential if development of the weapon is not to be held up.

The revised Operational Requirement stated that Yellow Sun would be carried by the Vulcan and Victor, the earlier requirement for carriage by the Valiant having being cancelled. Despite this decision, many of the Yellow Sun trials were conducted by Valiant aircraft until Vulcans and Victors could be made available. The report continued: 'Yellow Sun is being developed as a fully engineered weapon to meet the requirements of the OR. The provision of an interim megaton weapon only partially meeting these requirements is planned for introduction into service considerably earlier than Yellow Sun.' A paper issued by the MoS in August outlined the indecision that had surrounded the choice of warhead for Yellow Sun:

It is often imagined that the Valiant was somewhat smaller than its more advanced V-Bomber counterparts, but as this image demonstrates, the Valiant was by no means a small aircraft. The Valiant provided the RAF with an excellent AAR capability until the type's untimely withdrawal.

The object was to give the RAF a megaton capability at the earliest possible moment. It was proposed to base the interim weapon on one of the bombs to be dropped in Operation Grapple and it was stated that the date of introduction to the Service of Yellow Sun would not be affected by the interim missile. The results of Operation Grapple were such that none of the rounds dropped was immediately applicable to the interim weapon, but AWRE were satisfied that the principles had been cleared sufficiently for them to offer various alternative warheads to the Air Staff for consideration. The Air Staff, largely on the basis of numbers which could be provided, chose a warhead similar in outside shape to Green Bamboo, but having a yield of half a megaton, known as Green Grass. Throughout the discussions on this interim megaton weapon, the general approach has been that, in the interests of providing a megaton capability to the RAF at the earliest possible moment, the Service is prepared to sacrifice rigorous testing, proofing and clearance of the weapon and to introduce special maintenance procedures in association with AWRE. Furthermore, the Air Staff were willing for the same reason to discount many of the provisions of OR.1136. A reassessment of the Yellow Sun programme has recently been made primarily to examine the possibility of offering an earlier capability to the RAF in view of the successful progress of the development, but also taking into account the desirability of switching over to the Short Granite type of warhead if and when this is cleared by AWRE. This later type of warhead is very desirable because of the smaller amounts of fissile material needed.

After much deliberation, it was agreed that an interim weapon (codenamed 'Violet Club') would be brought into service until the first deliveries of a limited-approval version of Yellow Sun could be made. The Deputy Chief of the Air Staff commented, 'We are anxious to get megaton weapons into service as soon as we can. We most certainly think it worthwhile to have even as few as five by the time the Yellow Suns come along. At the same time, we are anxious to get Yellow Sun as soon as we can because it does not have the serious operational limitations of Violet Club.' On 24 February 1958, the Assistant Chief of the Air Staff wrote to the AOC in C Bomber Command stating that:

I am directed to inform you that the first Violet Club which is now being assembled at Wittering is expected to be completed by the end of the month. A total of five of these weapons will be assembled on Bomber Command stations by July of this year when deliveries of Yellow Sun should commence. Violet Club is still in some degree experimental and it will be subject to a number of serious handling restrictions. The extent of these and their effect on operational readiness are still under discussion with the Ministry of Supply. Until Violet Club has been formally cleared by the Ministry of Supply and it is possible to issue specific instructions on storage, handling and transport, the weapon is to remain exclusively in the custody and under the control of the Atomic Weapons Research Establishment. It is possible that some such arrangement will continue throughout the life of these weapons as it is intended to replace them with Yellow Sun as early as possible. This will be done as soon as sufficient aircraft are modified to carry Yellow Sun. I am to say that the operational limitations of Violet Club, particularly those affecting readiness, are serious. Nevertheless, it provides a megaton deterrent capability several months earlier than would otherwise have been possible.

Although this 'interim' weapon retained the same bomb carcass as its predecessor, Violet Club was a completely different bomb. However, it retained the same ballistics as Blue Danube and could therefore be used with the same bombing equipment, suitably adjusted for the appropriate detonation height. The Bomber Command Armament School (BCAS) Operations Records states that:

...on 28 February, a convoy from AWRE was stuck in a snow-drift at Wansford Hill at 15:00. An officer from this unit was sent to investigate. At 17:00, the vehicle was still unable to be moved. Rations and bedding were sent to the convoy and an officer and a team of airmen were detailed to stand by throughout the night to give help if required. It was not until the following day that vehicles began using the A1. The convoy arrived at the main Guard Room at 12:00. Personnel were sent immediately for a meal. Unloading was commenced at 14:00, when the convoy arrived at BCAS.

This bleak and wintry scene marked the arrival of the first Violet Club bombs and with it the very beginnings of the RAF's thermonuclear capability. By July, a total of five bombs had been completed. Bombs 1 to 4 remained at Wittering where personnel were trained by AWRE staff to install the Green Grass Warhead at the relevant site. Bombs 5, 6, 7, 8 and 11 were despatched to Finningley and 9, 10 and 12 went to Scampton, production of all twelve weapons being completed by the end of 1958. Violet Club was as DCAS commented 'rather delicate' and could only be assembled at the base from where it would be used. Likewise, road transport was limited to relatively short trips from the assembly point to the storage building.

More details of Violet Club were contained in a document issued in July:

In view of the very small number of Violet Clubs being made available to the Service, and the difficulties of clearing the Victor for the carriage of this weapon, it has now been decided to limit its carriage to the Vulcan. Vulcan aircraft modified to carry Yellow Sun are now being returned to service and it is desirable to transfer the warheads from all Violet Clubs to Yellow Suns as soon as possible, and at the same time to redeploy the weapons to Scampton and Finningley.

In November 1958, a further report stated that:

Bomber Command wish to get rid of Violet Clubs as soon as possible, but they are anxious to have a number of Yellow Suns in store before they do this. As the obvious time to change over is at the six-monthly inspections, it is suggested that Violet Clubs should start to phase out at the rate of about one a month from April or May, providing the Yellow Suns are not late.

At the end of 1958, the RAF possessed a force of fifty-four Valiants, ten Victors, and eighteen Vulcans, the Vulcans being capable of carrying the twelve megaton-range Violet Clubs. The remaining V-Force aircraft remained equipped to carry the smaller kiloton-range Blue Danubes.

Although the Valiant was always regarded as the 'poor relation' when compared to the more advanced Vulcan and Victor, it would be unfair to dismiss the aircraft as having been little more than a stopgap. The Valiant proved to be a very reliable and vice-free aircraft that did everything that it had been designed to do. Moreover, it contributed much more to the V-Force that just its bomb-carrying capability. In addition to the facility for photographic reconnaissance, the Valiant was also given

Above and below: Trials were conducted with Valiant WB215 to investigate the possibility of giving the aircraft a RATOG (Rocket-Assisted Take-Off Gear) capability. De Havilland Sprites were successfully used on a number of take-offs, but the RAF never embraced the concept, preferring to develop the more powerful Vulcan and Victor variants that did not require assisted thrust.

an air-to-air refuelling capability from the very outset and by the end of 1956, some eighty Valiants were suitably equipped to receive fuel in flight, theoretically increasing their potential range almost indefinitely. It was also envisaged that all of the V-Force aircraft would ultimately be capable of being employed as receiver aircraft or tankers with the necessary systems being installed or removed as necessary. Early in 1955, Bomber Command stated that no V-Bombers would be designed solely for use as tanker aircraft, but the RAF soon received a dedicated tanker aircraft when the value of aerial refuelling was realised.

The RAF Valiant fleet eventually comprised of a mix of Mk.1 aircraft, some configured for both the bomber and reconnaissance role, and some for the bomber, reconnaissance and tanker roles. Although the tanker refuelling equipment designed for the Valiant was removable, it eventually became a standard fit for many aircraft assigned to No. 214 Squadron. By 1959, the RAF had introduced aerial refuelling into the V-Force's operational posture, enabling the force to boast what truly was a strategic strike capability. The Valiant had reached across the globe thanks to the countless long-range exercises that were performed by the RAF Valiant crews and had even 'gone to war' briefly during 1956, not as a nuclear bomber, but as the carrier of conventional high-explosive weapons.

The Suez Crisis led to the beginning of Operation Musketeer and for Valiant squadrons assigned aircraft to the operations, ferrying a fleet of twenty-four aircraft to RAF Luqa on the island of Malta. Over a six-day period from 31 October to 5 November, the aircraft flew a series of bombing missions against targets in Egypt including airfields at Abu Sueir, Almaza, Cairo West, Fayid, Kabrit, Kasfareet and Luxor. The Valiant crews were excited at the prospect of taking their aircraft into action and doubtless relieved that their first 'real' operation would not be a nuclear one. Indeed, they were briefed to avoid centres of population and concentrate on high-value military targets. Eventually, the RAF delivered 942 tons of explosives during Operation Musketeer, but the experience proved to be a sobering one for Bomber Command.

The Canberra force was unable to function efficiently without its Gee-H beacons and the Valiants, having been designed for a 'radar war' with the USSR, was hardly better suited. Many of the Valiants had yet to receive their fully functional navigation and bombing system equipment and of those that were fully equipped, many were declared unserviceable when they were called upon. The Valiant crews were forced to resort to Second World War-style navigation, bomb-aiming and target marking. The results were disappointing. Operation Musketeer prompted Bomber Command to ensure that the V-Force had reliable all-weather navigation and bombing equipment, and that the V-Force would be capable of operating in any operational environment, not just the skies over the Soviet Union.

A year after Operation Musketeer, the Valiant force was making way for the Vulcan and Victor. With the improved Mk.2 versions of both aircraft also on the way, the

WP204 was the only Valiant to carry the Blue Steel stand-off missile. Assigned to Avro for weapon release trials, the aircraft was suitably modified for the task, although the aircraft's low-slung bomb bay made the task of loading the missile very difficult.

Air Staff addressed the issue of what to do with the Valiants from 1961 onwards. It was agreed that Canberras assigned to NATO's SACEUR could be replaced, the sixty-four Canberras making way for twenty-four Valiants, each equipped with two tactical nuclear bombs. Two squadrons of Valiants would be assigned to aerial refuelling with others assigned to reconnaissance and ECM (Electronic Counter Measures) operations.

Equipped with Mk.28 nuclear bombs – with a yield of up to 100 kilotons – supplied by America as part of 'Project E', the Valiant tactical bomber force soon became NATO's main offensive backbone, operating from their base at Marham, Norfolk. Some miles to the south at RAF Wyton, No. 543 Squadron operated its fleet of Valiants in the strategic reconnaissance role and during July 1964, one of the unit's aircraft (WZ394) was part of a three-aircraft deployment to Rhodesia. During servicing, it was found that the aircraft had a crack in the rear wing spar and was immediately ferried back to the UK for repairs. A month later, WP217 was flying a training sortie at 40,000 feet over Wales with No. 232 OCU when the crew suddenly heard a loud bang followed by a severe shudder that shook through the aircraft. The aircraft was gingerly flown back to Gaydon and as the aircraft was prepared for landing, it was found that the starboard wing flap would not extend. A carefully-executed flapless landing followed and WP217 was towed into its hangar for investigation, its rippled skin and slightly misaligned wings clearly visible to the

Shortly before the Valiant was withdrawn, disruptive camouflage was introduced. This was indicative of the V-Force's shift from high- and medium-level operations to low level – an environment for which the Valiant's structure had not been designed.

crew who had carefully brought the aircraft back to base. The engineers found that the rear wing spar had failed and the starboard flap drive had sheared.

The entire Valiant fleet was immediately examined and it was revealed that many of the Valiants had suffered some cracking within the front and rear wing spars. Vickers worked hard to fix the problem, but the best they could do was to categorise the damage that they found within each Valiant. Those with little or no damage were released for continuing restricted flying pending repairs. Others would be grounded for immediate repairs while the remainder would be grounded and struck off charge. Those that continued flying were confined to a maximum speed of 250 knots, a load of 0.5g and bank angles no greater than thirty degrees. Others were available to fly in only a national emergency, but five were immediately grounded. Vickers then began making plans to repair the aircraft, but when two aircraft were dismantled more thoroughly at St Athan, it became clear that the spar damage was far more severe than expected. On 9 December 1964, the entire Valiant fleet was grounded and the RAF's Valiant force never flew again, the airframes scrapped at their home bases or wherever they had ended their final flights.

It was believed that the primary cause of the Valiant's premature fatigue had been the punishing low-level flight regime that Bomber Command had embraced. Indeed, the RAF and Vickers had investigated this very possibility back in March 1956 when WZ383 was assigned to low-level trails to establish whether the aircraft could be safely operated at heights between 50 feet and 250 feet, and what effect this would have on the aircraft's structure. It had been established that conditions at low level (and at speeds of more than 300 knots) were brutal, but the Valiant could be operated safely, although the aircraft's fatigue life would be drastically reduced. Now that the Valiants had suffered such serious damage, it seemed certain that the V-Force's shift to low-level operations had been the cause... that is until it was revealed that tanker and reconnaissance aircraft appeared to have suffered similar damage.

As these aircraft operated at medium or high altitudes, the low-level punishment could not have been the cause. When damage was found in a Viscount airliner that had employed the same spar alloy material, it seemed likely that it was the alloy (DTD683/RR.77) that was the fundamental cause. But whatever the reason, the RAF suddenly lost its Valiant force almost overnight and only XD816 remained airworthy as this aircraft was re-sparred by Vickers as part of a plan to refit the entire RAF fleet. Bomber Command reluctantly accepted that the cost and time involved in repairing the Valiants in such a drastic fashion would be pointless, especially when the aircraft was due to be retired in five or six years. Although with hindsight, it seems more than likely that if the metal fatigue saga had not arisen, the Valiants would have remained in service for much longer. XD816 remained in use as a test aircraft until 1968 when it made its last public appearances and took part in the ceremonial handover of Bomber and Fighter Commands to the new Strike Command in April of that year.

Mention should also be made of a development of the Valiant that never joined the ranks of the RAF. As part of their early proposals, Vickers drew up plans for a pathfinder and target marker version of the Valiant. Although the new V-Force was not expected to be reliant upon the archaic art of visual bombing, the Air Ministry expressed some interest in the idea, possibly because of the perceived risk that – like the aircraft themselves – the V-Force navigation and bombing equipment might not be developed successfully or at least not swiftly enough. The Air Ministry eventually placed an order for a batch of pathfinder Valiants, but the order was subsequently dropped and replaced by a further batch of standard Mk.1 aircraft when Bomber Command finally accepted that the role of a pathfinder and target marker would not be necessary.

However, the development of this specialised variant enabled Vickers to create a heavily-modified version of the standard Mk.1 bomber and demonstrate just how capable the basic Valiant design could be. Prior to cancellation, the RAF's specification for the pathfinder bomber called for a range of 3,350 nm (this would have been extendable by aerial refuelling), a load of 6,000 lb target indicators and a loiter capability so that the aircraft could operate at low level, searching for its target. Fundamentally, the aircraft was designed to fly fast and low, the designed diving speed being set at 580 knots so the aircraft could egress its target area as swiftly as possible once its marking job had been done. Eventually, the aircraft was refined further still to incorporate all of the Mk.1's capabilities so that it would be

An ejection seat system for the V-Bombers was devised by Martin Baker and tested in a Valiant. The system worked but the Air Ministry believed that its cost was outweighed by the unlikelihood of catastrophic accidents. Thankfully, the Ministry's view ultimately proved to be correct.

able to deliver a maximum bomb load of 41,000 lb over a distance of 4,000 nm. By any standards this would have a phenomenal capability, especially when the specified top speed was also taken into account.

Designing the Valiant specifically for the high speed and low level regime meant that the airframe structure had to be strengthened considerably and this raised the aircraft's all-up weight. However, with powerful Conway engines (delivering 11,500 lb thrust or more), the aircraft would theoretically be capable of carrying the original 10,000 lb bomb load over an astonishing range of 6,000 nm. On 4 September 1953, the prototype Valiant B.Mk.2 WJ954 made its first flight from Wisley. By this time, the order for pathfinder Valiants had been cancelled, but Vickers opted to complete the first aircraft so that it could be used as part of the Valiant test programme. It would also allow Vickers to examine precisely what could be achieved with the Valiant design. The new variant certainly looked impressive with a longer fuselage and a new four-wheel bogey undercarriage that retracted rearwards into streamlined nacelles enabling the internal wing structure to house more fuel. An all-black paint scheme was applied, interrupted only by national insignia and white serial numbers, giving the aircraft a dark and sinister appearance.

The Valiant B.Mk.2 looked the part and when the aircraft was put through its paces it lived up to its appearance. Handling was reported as being excellent and on one low-level flight, it achieved a speed of 552 mph – quite something when

The magnificent Valiant B.Mk.2 at Farnborough in 1954, illustrating the Mk.2 variant's four-wheel bogey undercarriage.

Valiant B2 WJ954 high over Hampshire en route to the SBAC Farnborough show. Although the Valiant B2 was regarded as only a potential pathfinder aircraft, it could have provided the RAF with an excellent and relatively inexpensive low-level bomber had the need for such an aircraft been identified sooner.

The Valiant B2 incorporated a longer fuselage and new main undercarriage units housed in external pods. It was a formidable low-level bomber, and one that could have easily performed the roles that were eventually undertaken by both the Vulcan and Victor.

compared to the Mk.1's speed of 414 mph. WJ954 was eventually assigned to a variety of test duties as part of the Valiant and V-Force trails programme, but it was never adopted for use in any operational sense, the RAF regarding the target marking business as something that should be forgotten. The real irony of the Valiant B.Mk.2 story is that the RAF eventually switched the V-Force to low level operations – the very environment for which the Valiant B.Mk.2 was designed. Although both the Vulcan and Victor successfully operated in the low-level role, the Victor was swiftly shifted to the aerial refuelling role when the Mk.1 Valiant fleet was withdrawn. This was probably a fortunate step as the Victor was far from suited to low-level operations.

With large-span flexible wings, the Victor rode the turbulent low-level air with ease, but the effect on its structure was severe and it is doubtful that the Victor could have operated in the low-level role for long. In total contrast, the Vulcan's sturdy delta wing was tough enough for low-level flight and with additional strengthening proved to be more than resilient to last through the aircraft's operational career. But the Valiant B.Mk.2 was designed for the low-level role and its capacity to deliver a sizeable bomb load over a very respectable distance, combined with an impressive top speed, would have made this aircraft an ideal V-Bomber. Indeed, out of all the V-Bomber designs, the Valiant B.Mk.2 would have been the perfect solution, and had the Air Staff possessed the benefit of hindsight, the Sperrin, Vulcan and Victor might well have never left the drawing boards.

In retrospect, it seems clear that the RAF could have adopted the Valiant Mk.1 and then moved seamlessly onto the far more capable Valiant Mk.2. But, of course, no one had the gift of prophecy and it was impossible to predict that the simple 'insurance' bomber would eventually become a far more suitable aircraft than the aircraft that replaced it. The story of the Valiant is inevitably dogged by the sorry tale of its premature withdrawal. But the Valiant was a hugely successful project. It gave the RAF its first atomic bomber and enabled the RAF to test the delivery of its very first atomic and thermonuclear weapons. It paved the way for two advanced bombers and provided the RAF with a strategic reconnaissance and aerial refuelling capability for many years. The only sorry aspect to the Valiant's story was that it ended all too soon.

CHAPTER FOUR
Chariots of Fire

The history of what undoubtedly became the RAF's most famous post-war bomber aircraft began way back in 1946, but it was not until the following January that serious attention was devoted to it. The company's designers looked at a wide range of potential designs with which to meet the RAF's ambitious new requirement. After a great deal of preliminary investigation, their ideas seemed to gravitate towards some sort of 'flying wing' concept whereby an aircraft's conventional fuselage and tail would be merged into one large flying surface. The idea might have seemed crazy to many (especially in 1947), but the idea was not as radical as some might have imagined.

In Nazi Germany, the concept of all-wing flying machines had been around for some time. A great deal of information had come from Germany since the end of the war and there was a significant amount of aerodynamic data on the potential of tailless designs. Such radical designs has been pursued by Walter and Reimar Horten, ultimately leading to the creation of their H-1 glider and Horten Ho 229 jet bomber, which was about to go into production as the war ended. During the final months of the war, Reimar was working on a six-engine 'Amerika' bomber to carry a hypothetical atomic bomb to New York City, so advanced was the design. Dr. Alexander Lippisch was another leading German designer, famous as the creator of the Messerschmitt Me 163 Komet rocket fighter. He was particularly interested in the potential of all-wing designs and many of his early experimental designs included triangular delta-wing configurations, some of which he succeeded in testing in a supersonic wind tunnel – a facility that only the Third Reich possessed at the time.

As the war ended, Lippisch was working on a revolutionary delta-winged glider known as the DM-1 and when Allied forces captured his factory at Weiner Wald in 1945, the DM-1 glider was transferred to the US together with its talented designer. Back in Britain, it was Armstrong-Whitworth who pioneered research in this field with the construction of an all-wing research glider, the AW.52G, that first flew in March 1945. Two larger designs were subsequently built and Armstrong-Whitworth maintained an interest in the concept for many years even though their work never resulted in an operational aircraft.

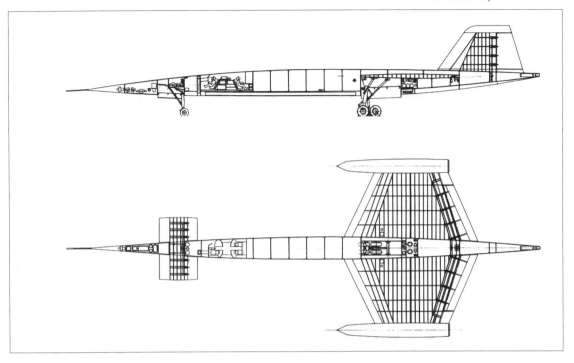

The ambitious Avro 730 promised to deliver an aircraft with phenomenal capabilities both as a bomber and reconnaissance aircraft. It was, however, too advanced, and would have required money and resources that were simply not available. Specification B.35/46 for the V-Bombers represented a more realistic challenge.

Britain's knowledge of flying wing designs was significantly less than that enjoyed by the US, largely because of the way in which so much German data had gone directly to America. The route taken by US forces through liberated Germany meant that almost by accident, the majority of the many scientific and research facilities connected with aviation programmes were stumbled upon by American forces. Therefore, it was not surprising that captured data and artefacts went straight to the US. But co-operation between the US and Britain was on good terms and information slowly drifted across to the UK. Captured German equipment (including many aircraft, which went to Farnborough for evaluation), research data and information recovered via the US, eventually led to the creation of a series of scientific reports that were issued to the UK's aviation companies. The information these reports contained was often radical in nature and almost always new, and it created a great deal of interest that inevitably influenced British thinking from this point onwards. Avro's Bob Lindley made a visit to Germany in 1945 and studied an immense amount of data in person. He subsequently recalled how this visit formed the foundation of what eventually became Avro's new bomber project:

The Operational requirement for the aircraft was put into the Project Office in early 1947. Before we had managed to get very far, the great fuel shortage hit us and the plant was closed down except for a few of us who huddled together in the offices along the front of the main building. If I remember correctly, another upheaval was taking place at the time, and Chadwick was at home suffering from shingles. The performance requirements of the OR were rather startling to people nurtured on Lancasters and Tudors, and the only jet investigations we had made up to that time were for the Tudor 8 and the Brabazon 3 projects, and the latter was designed for a Mach number around 0.7.

The original conception of the delta was not a result of spontaneous inspiration, but was arrived at by what seemed at the time to be an honest design study encompassing a whole series of aircraft, some with tails, some tailless, each type checked for a range of aspect ratios and weights. In retrospect, I shudder to think just how much reliance was placed on the wing weight formula used, but the end product seems to justify the means. The first preliminary study was made for aircraft of aspect ratios not less than four and the result clearly showed that the aircraft required would be tailless and would give a much lower aspect ratio – probably about two. A second investigation covering the lower aspect ratios gave a solution 2.4 which was inevitably a delta wing. I knew that Lippisch had been working on a delta fighter and I had managed to see some reports on his coal-burning ram jet delta in Frankfurt during my trip to Germany in 1945, and the possibility of making use of this configuration for a bomber was most intriguing.

More elaborate checks were made, but only served to confirm the delta configuration. The original arrangement of the aircraft was, of course, somewhat more advanced than that which was finally proposed in the original brochure, in fact I think it would still look advanced today. It had boundary layer suction combined with a movable cockpit so that the pilot could have good vision even when the aircraft was at 30 degrees incidence, and it had a very elaborate arrangement of combined elevator, air brakes and variable area jet pipe nozzle. Just about the time these first drawings were finished Chadwick recovered from his illness. I must say that he was considerably shaken to see the proposal. He had left the project as a sort of jet-propelled Lincoln and returned to find something apparently from a Buck Rogers comic strip in its place. He expressed his doubts very forcibly. I remember going home and sulking all weekend. I was very much in love with my project and couldn't stand the criticism. However, by Monday, he had decided that it had its good points, and from there on he waded in with great enthusiasm and did much to make it a practical aeroplane.

During this period of early development, the aircraft underwent a number of changes. My original proposal was to have five Avons or Sapphires. In the interests of simplicity, we decided to go for a twin-engined version, and for this we required an engine of around 20,000 lb static thrust. Chadwick wrote around the engine industry for proposals for such an engine and the replies were very interesting, ranging from supreme optimism from Armstrong-Siddeley to complete pessimism from Metro-Vickers. I can recall Chadwick taking a 1/48th scale model of this twin engined version up to London. The model was left with Air Marshall Boothman. Chadwick described how Boothman had 'flown' it round the office, presumably making appropriate noises. At this stage we heard of the Olympus, and the four-engined version was investigated and adopted for the brochure. The other feature that was kicked around considerably was the crew accommodation.

The first proposal had the crew compartment inside the wing, with the pilots under two fighter type hoods. Then the requirement for a jettisonable crew compartment was emphasised and we devoted much effort to getting the crew into the minimum nacelle, demountable just aft of the pressure bulkhead, and with a multiple parachute packed into the fairing aft of the canopy. This design was put forward in the brochure. In those days, the radar scanner was installed inside the wing. The first issue of the brochure was finished, I think, in April 1947. After completing this, we produced the drawings for the very beautiful 1/24th scale plastic model. We did some work on a civil version of the aircraft, employing a slightly higher wing loading and operating at a lower height than the bomber project. I remember it made a very attractive transatlantic aircraft. Headwinds didn't seem to worry it too much.

Roy Chadwick has always been traditionally linked to the design of the Vulcan (named after the Roman god of fire), but as Lindley's recollections illustrate, the Vulcan was not a result of some abstract 'eureka' moment over Chadwick's drawing board. The design was the result of a methodical investigation and the solution was radical, initially too radical for Chadwick's experienced eye. But he presided over a large and talented team that included Stuart Davies who had worked with Chadwick to produce the legendary Lancaster. Davies recalled that Chadwick was 'obsessed with the idea of the all-wing aeroplane, so when he came back and found that his lads had finished up with an all-wing aeroplane by accident, this delighted him more than somewhat'. This observation contrasts with Lindley's assertion that Chadwick was reluctant to consider the idea when it was first presented to him and it remains unclear as to when Chadwick had first been confronted with the all-wing idea. But if the bomber's unique shape could ever be credited to any one person in particular, it was probably Bob Lindley who later left Avro and became Vice-President of McDonnell Douglas, overseeing the Mercury space capsule programme and eventually working on the Space Shuttle project.

The Avro design team firmly believed that a 'flying wing' would prove to be the best solution to the Air Staff's demanding requirements both in terms of aerodynamic efficiency and therefore performance, but also in terms of structural integrity. However, Chadwick was also aware that the radical design required imagination and in its present form it would probably be a little too bizarre for the conservative tastes

Following the loss of XA894, a second Vulcan was assigned to engine trials, this time in support of the Concorde programme. As such, XA903 became the last active Vulcan B.Mk.1, remaining in service with the RAE into the 1970s. (*Courtesy Rolls-Royce*)

of the Air Staff. Chadwick feared that when they looked at the proposal, the Air Staff would dismiss it as pure fantasy. However, it was clear that on the basis of the German research and data, the triangular delta wing without any tailplane surfaces was the right one. Consequently, Chadwick and his team made every effort to turn the basics of the design into a more conventional aircraft configuration. But even if the Air Staff could be convinced of the design's merits, the aircraft looked likely to exceed the required maximum all-up weight figure by a considerable margin.

Avro looked at ways in which the wing could be made thinner, but every revision simply pushed the projected weight higher. With the OR's specified cruising speed effectively fixing the basic design configuration, it was clear that the structure's weight would always be too high unless the payload was reduced. It was at this stage that the design team looked more seriously at the possibility of using the aircraft's wing tips to provide longitudinal control, creating vertical surfaces and rudders which could be attached to each wing tip, effectively making any fuselage-mounted fin assembly redundant and thereby saving a great deal of weight and aerodynamic drag. This re-emphasised the original concept of a pure 'flying wing' and with a forty-five degree wing sweep, combined elevators, rudders (elevons), small fins and rudders placed at the wing tips, the gross weight dropped to 137,000 lb. Both Stuart Davies and Robert Lindley believed that they had finally identified the best design configuration. But the team reported that the bomber would still be heavier than they would have liked it to be.

The obvious way to reduce weight would be to make the wing section deeper, but in order to achieve high subsonic speed, the thickness/chord ration had to be kept as low as possible, and so the root chord was increased in order to provide compensation. Further attempts to reduce the wing's span while maintaining the same wing sweep, thickness and overall area, meant that the missing wing space had to be effectively relocated in the space between the wing's trailing edge and fuselage. By March 1947, the design team had followed this process to its logical conclusion and concluded that the relatively simple delta-shaped all-wing design was indeed the logical choice. However, more time was dedicated to the consideration of how the air intakes, radar, crew compartment, fuel tanks, engines, undercarriage and weapon load could be incorporated into the configuration.

Thanks to the deep wing section, all of the necessary equipment could be fitted neatly into an all-wing design including the crew compartment, which resulted in a pair of fighter-type blister canopies for captain and co-pilot. However, the Air Staff's subsequent specification for a jettisonable crew compartment required a fairly radical redesign of the bomber. The crew were to be relocated in a pressurised nacelle that was positioned ahead of the wing leading edge so it could be separated by means of a bulkhead. This effectively destroyed the clean lines of the flying wing configuration and formed the basis of the design that eventually went into production. However, it was with some irony that the plan to provide a jettisonable crew compartment was later abandoned after it was established by Avro, Handley Page and Vickers that the complexity, time delays and overall coast of such a feature would seriously hinder progress on the overall design.

The Air Staff could not afford to run the risk of any significant delays, nor could they risk unnecessary additional costs. Therefore, the capsule proposal had to be dropped in favour of more conventional ejection seats for the two pilots, leaving the rear crew with a ventral escape hatch through which they could – if they were lucky – bail out. Consequently, the extended nose section that became so characteristic of the Avro design was never needed and had the escape capsule proposal been abandoned earlier, the design team could have continued to develop a true flying wing layout. But once the position of the crew compartment had been fixed, the air intakes emerged ahead of the wing leading edge and were positioned each side of the short fuselage section. Each intake was routed through the wing and bifurcated into a pair of vertically-stacked trunks, each feeding an engine with the upper engine exhaust emerging through the wing leading edge a few feet ahead of the lower exhaust.

The huge bomb bay for the 10,000 lb bomb was positioned within the inner section of the wing, but unusually was not positioned on the centreline as has always been the case with previous bomber designs. Avro's radical proposal was to create two identical bomb bays each side of the aircraft's centreline, although there must have been some debate as to the aircraft's predicted handling and trim qualities if a 10,000 lb weapon was dropped asymmetrically. But when further research was conducted in Farnborough's wind tunnels, it was determined that the wing section was still too thick and after much discussion, the Avro team accepted that the thickness/chord ratio would have to be reduced further. This meant that the engines and intakes could no longer be stacked vertically within the available space and they were consequently repositioned in a horizontal side-by-side configuration. This meant that there was now insufficient space to accommodate the twin bomb bays and so a more conventional single bomb bay was relocated to the aircraft's centreline.

The undercarriage was initially envisaged as being similar to that employed by Boeing on their B-47 Stratojet with main centreline-mounted gear and smaller outrigger wheels at the wing tips. However, once the bomb bay had been fixed in a more conventional position, a traditional tricycle undercarriage could be comfortably incorporated into the design which met with Avro's liking for simplicity and ruggedness. Much consideration was also given to the idea of using moveable wing tips in place of traditional ailerons, moving the wing-tip fins slightly inboard in order to accommodate power and drive units. But by September 1947, this concept had been abandoned after concluding that individual elevators could be fitted to the wing's inboard trailing edge with ailerons on the outboard sections, simplicity again being a key aim. This meant that the wing-tip fins could now be replaced by a larger one-piece fin positioned on the centreline, satisfying concerns that the wing-tip fins might not provide sufficient control. It meant that the design weight would again increase, but it was agreed that a more traditional fin section would provide a convenient mount for an equally traditional tail plane unit, should further aerodynamic research indicate one was needed. No one wanted to run the risk of pursuing a complicated design that once fixed required huge effort and expense to change.

It is interesting to note that if a conventional tailplane had ultimately been needed, the bomber would have resembled a scaled-up version on Gloster's distinctive Javelin fighter design. Of course, the similarity was superficial and only temporary as the Avro team opted to remove the large, circular intakes and replace them with horizontal 'letter box' intakes fitted within the extended wing leading edge. This was a move that seemed to make aerodynamic sense, even though little was known about the performance of intakes designed to this configuration. In fact, the horizontal

This famous image illustrates two white-painted Avro 698 prototypes en route to Farnborough accompanied by the red and blue Avro 707s. This created the most magnificent patriotic sight that the Farnborough crowds had ever seen. RAF Thorney Island is visible in the distance.

intakes did eventually create some headaches for Avro as the design entered the test phase.

Chadwick took his proposal to the Air Ministry during the summer of 1947 and successfully convinced them that his 'flying wing' was a viable proposition. Even though Chadwick cannot be credited with either the original concept or eventual design of the Vulcan, it seems likely that without his enthusiasm and persuasive drive, the project would have never been accepted. Tragically, he was killed on 23 August when Avro's Tudor 2 prototype crashed shortly after take-off from the factory airfield at Woodford, the aircraft's aileron control cables having been fixed the wrong way round. The Avro workforce at their Chadderton and Woodford factories were stunned by the loss and feared that the bomber project would collapse without Chadwick's support. Indeed, official interest did begin to diminish, chiefly because there was a belief that Chadwick's loss would inevitably lead to a lack of direction at Avro until a new management structure was established.

William Farren was appointed as Avro's new technical director and as a former director of RAE Farnborough, he had an equally formidable reputation that he immediately used to restore faith in the Avro project. Design of the new bomber resumed under Farren's leadership and slowly developed into what became the Avro Type 698.

J. R. Ewans was a member of Avro's talented design team during this period and in 1951, he prepared a fascinating paper that describes the thinking behind the aircraft's design:

So far as can be ascertained, the idea of using a triangular planform for aircraft wings, now known as the delta wing, was first put forward in 1943 by Professor Lippisch, who will be remembered for his association with the Messerschmitt company. His studies led him to think that this form was most suited for flight at speeds in the region of the speed of sound where conventional designs were already known to be in trouble. By the end of the war, he had a number of delta wing projects in hand, including an un-powered wooden glider intended to explore the low speed properties of the wing. This was by then party built and was later completed under United States orders. The idea of the delta wing was studied by many other aeronautical experts and a strong recommendation for its use was given, for instance, by Professor Von Karman at the 1947 Anglo American Aeronautical Conference. At the time of writing, three British delta aircraft and two American are known to have flown, and it is pretty certain that others are on the way. In the date order of their first flight these are: Consolidated-Vultee XF-92, Avro 707, Boulton Paul PIII, Douglas XF-3D and Fairey FD-1. With the exception of the last named, which is fitted with a small fixed tailplane for the first flights, all the above aircraft are tailless.

The following notes are intended to give a logical explanation of why there is this considerable interest in the delta wing and just what advantages it promises the aircraft designer. But consideration must first be given to the type of aircraft the designer is trying to produce. The delta wing is of value only for very high speed aircraft and at the present stage of engine development, this implies the use of jet engines. When projecting his high speed aircraft, the designer will attempt to produce something carrying the greatest payload over the greatest distance at the highest speed, and for the least expenditure of power (i.e. using the least amount of fuel). This applies to all types of aircraft whether they be bombers in which the payload is bombs, or civil aircraft in which it is passengers or cargo, or fighters in which it is guns and ammunition.

The most fundamental factor determining the ultimate achievement is the height at which the aircraft flies. As height increases, the density of air is reduced so that drag is less; it is possible to fly at a given speed at, say 40,000 feet, for an expenditure of only one quarter of the power required at sea level. The advent of the jet engine has enabled the aircraft designer to get his aircraft up to considerable altitudes and take advantage of the reduced drag, but a new factor is coming in to limit the speed of the aircraft. This is the speed of sound. The speed of sound occupies a fundamental position in the speed

A rare image of the Yellow Sun hydrogen bomb pictured during bomb casing aerodynamic trials at Farnborough. The weapon's flat nose profile gave the weapon a degree of stability during descent.

range of aircraft. It is roughly 760 mph at heights above 36,000 feet. Because the speed of sound is of such importance, aircraft speeds are commonly related to the speed of sound using the term Mach number (the ratio of the speed of an aircraft to the speed of sound at the same height). As an aircraft approached the speed of sound – in fact, for conventional aircraft when a speed of around 70 per cent of the speed of sound (Mach 0.7) is reached, the effects of compressibility become important, for the characteristics of airflow change fundamentally.

There is a very large increase in the air resistance, or drag, and an excessive expenditure becomes necessary to increase the speed any further. For transport and bomber aircraft, the speed at which the drag starts to increase (known as the 'drag rise' Mach number) becomes the maximum cruising speed, because if the aircraft is flown at higher speeds the disproportionately higher thrust required from the engine means excessive fuel consumption and loss of range. At a rather higher Mach number, there will be changes in the stability of the aircraft and in its response to the pilot's control, leading possibly even to the loss of control. In order to progress to higher speeds, it is therefore necessary to design aircraft so as to postpone and/or overcome these effects. We have noted that with an old-fashioned type of aircraft, i.e. that of jet-propelled aircraft current in 1945, the limiting speed in steady cruising flight is likely to be a Mach number of 0.7 (higher speeds have, of course, already been achieved and a number of aircraft have exceeded the speed of sound, but only for short periods by either diving or by use of rocket power).

However, from the knowledge now available, it appears possible, by careful aerodynamic design, to postpone the rise in drag until a Mach number in the region of 0.9 is reached and this figure is likely to be the practical limit of cruising speed for transport aircraft of all types for many years to come. The designer of a civil aircraft, bomber or a long-range fighter will therefore bend all his energies to achieving a Mach number of this order without any change in drag rise. In addition, he must pay attention to the changes in stability or lack of control which might occur in this region, and this will occupy his attention to the same extent as the purely performance aspect of the drag rise. It is quite easy to design a fuselage shape which is relatively immune from Mach number effects. It is the design of wings which is difficult, particularly since a wing that is suitable for high speed must also give satisfactory flying properties at low speeds for take-off and landing.

As air flows past a wing, its speed is increased over the upper surface to a considerable extent and over the lower surface to a lesser extent, so that there is greater suction on the upper surface than on the lower surface. Thus, at whatever speed an aircraft is flying, the speed of the air around the wing will, in fact, be higher. In the case of an aircraft flying at a Mach number of 0.8, the speed of the air around its upper surface may be equal to the speed of sound or may easily exceed it. At this stage, the airflow pattern round the wing will be considerably changed and it is, in fact, this change which gives rise to the drag and stability effects mentioned above. It is essential therefore, to keep the velocity above the wing as little in excess of the speed of the aircraft as possible. There are four ways of improving the behaviour of a wing. They are all different methods of keeping down the air velocities and can all be applied simultaneously: 1) sweep back, 2) thinness, 3) low-wing loading, 4) low-aspect ratio.

1) Sweepback – The amount of sweepback is measured by the angle at by which the tip of the wing lies behind the centreline. The extent of the gains possible from sweepback is very considerable and sweeping back a wing may easily lead to a postponement of the compressibility effects by a Mach number of 0.1.

2) Thinness – Keeping a wing thin leads to a reduction in the amount of air that must be pushed out of the way by the wing, and this helps the passage of the wing through the air. The thickness of a wing is measured by the thickness/chord ratio, which is the maximum depth of the wing divided by its length in the line of flight. In the past, the thickness/chord ratios of aircraft wings have ranged from 21 per cent down to perhaps 12 per cent. Now, values of 10 per cent down to 7 per cent are becoming common.

XA894 performing for the crowds at Farnborough. As signified by the single trail of smoke, the aircraft is only operating under the power of the Olympus test specimen housed in the ventral pod. (*Courtesy Rolls-Royce*)

3) Low-wing loading – The wing loading is the weight of aircraft carried by a unit area of wing, measured in pounds per square foot. Mach number effects are postponed by keeping the wing loading as low as possible, i.e. by supporting the weight of the aircraft with a large wing area. This is particularly important for flight at high altitudes where the low air density puts a premium on keeping the wing loading low. In fact, flight at high altitudes becomes virtually impossible unless this is done.

4) Low-aspect ratio – Aspect ratio is the ratio of the span of a wing to the average chord. For moderate speeds, a high aspect ratio, i.e. a large span relative to the chord, gives greatest efficiency. At high Mach numbers, this consideration is no longer important, in fact, some alleviation of compressibility effects is given by reducing aspect ratio.

There is another reason for choosing a low aspect ratio. One of the disadvantages of sweeping a wing back is that the flying characteristics at low speed become poor. A typical symptom is that the wing tip of a swept wing stalls, giving violent behaviour if the speed is allowed to fall too low. Research has, however, shown that this bad characteristic of swept wings may be overcome relatively easily. Although almost any aspect ratio can be accepted with an un-swept wing, for wings of 45 degrees sweep back, an aspect ratio of little over 3 is the most satisfactory. There is yet a third reason for choosing a low-aspect ratio – the behaviour (as regards stability, etc.) in the high Mach number region. Compressibility effects are minimised and a transition from speeds below that of sound to the speed of sound and above is much more readily accomplished if the aspect ratio is low, say in the order of 2 to 4.

Put the above requirements together and the result is an aircraft highly sweptback with a thin wing, a moderately large wing area and a low aspect ratio. A little consideration of the geometrical properties and possible planform of wings leads to the conclusion that the delta wing is the only form which satisfies these requirements. It possesses high sweepback and low-aspect ratio. The wing area will of necessity be generous for the size of aircraft and, for reasons which will be detailed later, it is easy to build it with a low thickness-chord ratio.

Next, how does the delta planform, indicated from considerations of aerodynamic performance, line up with practical design requirements and, in particular, the over-riding necessity for keeping weight and drag low in order to obtain maximum performance? A preliminary question is whether a tailplane is necessary. From the earliest days of flying, the question has been raised as to whether aircraft can be flown satisfactorily without a tailplane. Confining attention only to the case of the high-speed jet aircraft, each of the functions of a tailplane will be examined in turn in relation to the delta wing aircraft. The functions are:

a) To trim out changes of centre of gravity position according to the load carried and the consumption of fuel. Investigation shows that a control surface at the trailing edge of the wing, provided that the latter has a large root chord (as has the delta), can cater for all but extreme centre of gravity movements.

b) To deal with trim changes due to landing flaps, etc. With the low wing loading associated with the delta wing, take-off and landing speeds are moderate without the use of flaps, and this question does not therefore arise.

c) To deal with loss of stability or control power consequent on distortion of the wing structure at high speed (aerolastic distortion). At very high speeds, all aircraft structures distort to a greater or lesser extent under the high loads imposed, and this distortion alters the aerodynamic form. In extreme cases this leads to loss of stability or control power, making the aircraft dangerous or impossible to fly at high speeds. An aircraft with a high-aspect ratio sweptback wing would need a tailplane to deal with this, but the shape of the delta wing makes it extremely stiff both in bending and in torsion and a tailplane does not appear necessary.

d) To provide for spin recovery. Although this point has not been proved, it is expected that the controls on a delta wing would not be powerful enough to ensure recovery from a fully developed spin. A tailplane appears to be the only way of dealing with the problem. This restriction is of small significance for transport or bomber-type aircraft. It can therefore be concluded that for a delta wing aircraft of the transport type, a tailplane is unnecessary. Its deletion leads immediately to a considerable saving of weight and drag, and to a major gain in performance.

We have now shown that compared with a conventional aircraft, the delta wing aircraft will be simpler by the omission of the following items: the tailplane, the rear fuselage necessary in order to carry the tailplane, wing flaps and other high-lift devices such as the drooped wing leading edge. There is a saving of weight, of design and manufacturing effort, and of maintenance when the aircraft is in service. These economies will have a considerable bearing on the initial cost and the manpower necessary to produce and maintain a number of aircraft. Because of its shape and the large root chord, the delta wing provides a large internal volume in relation to its surface area, even when using the thin sections which, as noted above, are essential for high-speed aircraft. Simple calculations show that for the same wing area, the delta wing has 33 per cent more internal volume than an un-tapered wing, while if the inboard half of the wing only is considered (as this represents a more practical case from the point of view of the aircraft designer), the internal volume of the delta wing is more than twice that of the corresponding tapered wing. It is found that without exceeding a wing thickness of as little as 8 to 10 per cent, it is possible on a moderate-sized delta wing aircraft to bury completely the engines, the undercarriage and sufficient fuel tanks for long range.

The fuselage also has a tendency to disappear into the wing at the root. The result is the attainment of an aircraft consisting only of a wing, a fin and a rudimentary fuselage, representing a degree of aerodynamic cleanliness which has never before been reached. In fairness, it must be pointed out that this is achieved at the expense of a rather larger wing area than usual, but investigation shows that the drag of this area is less than that due to a conglomeration of items such as engine nacelles, tailplane, etc.

From the design point of view, the shape of the delta wing leads to an extremely stiff structure without the use of thick wing skins, and strength becomes the determining feature rather than structural stiffness. This avoids the inefficiency of conventional sweptback wings where the wing has to be made stronger than necessary in order that it shall be stiff enough. Summing up, it can be said that in order to meet the requirements of large loads for a long range at high speed, the high performance transport or military aircraft of the future will cruise at a considerable altitude, at a speed not much below that of sound. The delta wing provides the only satisfactory solution to these requirements for the following reasons:

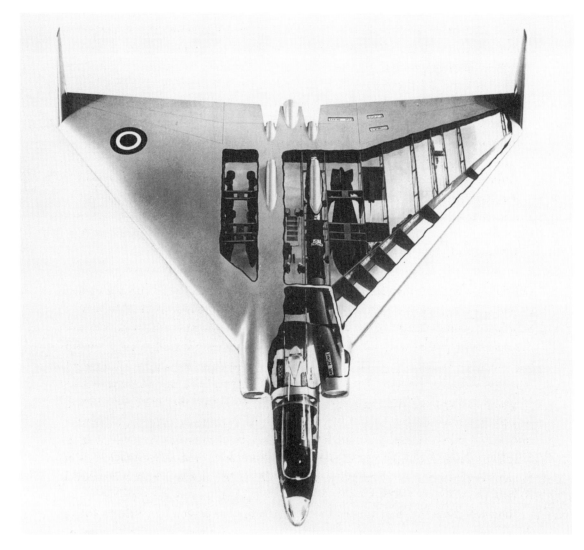

This early model of the 698 illustrates the original plan to incorporate two weapons bays and the circular intakes that were later abandoned. Also visible are the wingtip fin structures that were subsequently dropped in favour of a conventional tail structure.

1) It meets the four features necessary for avoiding the drag rise near the speed of sound, i.e. it is highly sweptback, it can be made very thin, the wing loading is low and the aspect ratio is low.

2) Extensive wind tunnel and flight tests have shown that the low aspect ratio delta wing gives minimum changes in stability and control characteristics at speeds near the speed of sound.

3) In spite of the wing being thin, its internal volume is large so that the engines, undercarriage, fuel and all the necessary equipment can be contained within the wing and a rudimentary fuselage.

4) Adequate control can be obtained by control surfaces on the wing, thus eliminating the need for a conventional tailplane. Together with item No. 3, this leads to a considerable reduction in the drag of the aircraft and, therefore, to high performance.

5) Auxiliary devices such as flaps, nose flaps or slots, and the all-moving tailplane are unnecessary, thereby saving weight and design effort, and simplifying manufacture and maintenance.

6) The delta wing is very stiff and free from distortion troubles.

Official instruction to proceed was given to Avro in January 1948 with permission to build two Avro 698 prototypes. But despite this sign of progress, the Ministry of Supply was still far from confident that the radical new design would work. Without the benefit of present day computer simulations and research, all of Avro's work was based on existing knowledge and although the team's designers were confident that 698 would give the RAF an effective 'medium bomber', the MoS and the Air Ministry had difficult decisions to make. The MoS believed that the only practical way to establish whether Avro and Handley Page's advanced designs would translate into viable bombers would be to test the basic aerodynamic soundness of both aircraft as quickly and cheaply as possible. The only truly reliable way to do this in the late 1940s was to build scaled-down versions of the full-sized designs that could be flown thoroughly before huge resources were poured into the 'real' aircraft.

The MoS requested that three test aircraft should be built to investigate Avro's design, one being a small single-engine aircraft while the second would be a larger twin-engine machine, both incorporating the 698's delta wing design. The third model would be a full-size representation of the bomber, but built as simply and cheaply as possible to explore the aircraft's aerodynamic characteristics. Avro did not like the idea at all as the design and manufacture of three very different aircraft would be a time consuming task that would divert resources and manpower from the design of the actual bomber. Supremely confident in their design, the notion of wasting time on scale models seemed counterproductive. The MoS did not share Avro's confidence and after a great deal of discussion, it was agreed that as a compromise three similar scale models would be built powered by single Derwent jet engines and designed to explore both low-speed handling and high-speed flight.

The MoS issued Specification E.15/48 on 3 November 1948, calling for a simple research aircraft (designated by Avro as the Type 707) with a top speed of 400 knots.

The first Avro 707, VX784, pictured shortly after completion in August 1949.

The Avro team proposed building the 707's wing structure from wood, but eventually it was decided that pressed sheet metal around two supporting spars would give the aircraft sufficient strength for the job, while providing space for internally-housed fuel and test monitoring equipment. The canopy and nose-wheel assemblies for the first aircraft were taken from Gloster Meteor fighters and the main landing gear from the Avro Athena. The sole purpose of the first 707 was to test the all-important wing design. Therefore, the rest of the aircraft was created as simple as possible. The short nose section was manufactured from welded steel tubing covered with light metal alloy skin and removable panels surrounding the single Rolls-Royce Derwent turbojet engine that was positioned below the swept fin and rudder.

The engine intake was faired into the upper fuselage with a bifurcated duct feeding down above the wing spars. There were no powered flying controls and surprisingly no ejection seat, but as a concession towards flight safety, an anti-spin parachute was fitted in a fairing at the base of the fin assembly. Finished in silver with a prototype 'P' marking applied to the nose section (plus national insignia and serials), the first aircraft, VX784, was assembled at Avro's Woodford airfield and subjected to a series of engine trials and short taxiing tests before being dismantled and transported to Boscombe Down in Wiltshire on 26 August 1949 for reassembly. The first flight was scheduled for 3 September, but a steady 20 knot crosswind prevented the aircraft from flying until the next day. Having already completed some short hops at Boscombe Down, test pilot Flight Lieutenant Eric Esler – chief test pilot at the Aeroplane and Armament Experimental Establishment – taxied VX784 onto Boscombe's huge 10,000 feet runway at 19:30 on 4 September.

Esler proceeded to conduct a highly satisfactory twenty minute test flight in the local area. Esler was satisfied with the 707's handling and Avro immediately issued a press release announcing the aircraft's first flight, claiming that the new delta wing design would 'permit controlled flight at and above the speed of sound' and that it would be 'necessary to conduct a vast amount of aerodynamic research over a large range of speeds before application of the new configuration can be made to either civil or military operational aircraft'. In reality, Avro was working on a more direct application and the 707 test aircraft were little more than a means of demonstrating the validity of the bomber's design process that was continuing almost as a separate project. A further two-and-a-half hours of test flying was completed on the 707 before test pilot Esler flew the aircraft directly to Farnborough where it was proudly placed on static display at the 1949 SBAC air show. After spending a few days at Farnborough, Esler flew the aircraft back to Boscombe Down and Avro's flight test team installed test and data recording equipment before commencing on the aircraft's research programme.

The aircraft continued to handle remarkably well and Esler reported that the general handling characteristics were much the same as those found in more conventional aircraft with the possible exception of the take-off run due to the Derwent engine's poor thrust. The test flights proceeded smoothly until 30 September when tragedy struck and VX784 crashed near Blackbushe, killing Esler. The cause of the disaster was never fully explained and at the time of the accident, many cynical observers used the accident to cast doubt upon the delta design and the wisdom of proceeding with the Avro 698 programme. However, investigations suggested that the cause of the crash was not attributable to the delta wing and it was likely the failure of a control circuit that may have locked the air brakes in their open position, causing a low speed stall from which Esler had no means of escape. Work was suspended on the second 707 until further details of the accident were obtained, but despite the tragic loss of Esler, there was great relief that the cause was not that of the aircraft's wing as this would have thrown the project into doubt.

The Avro design team concluded that the second 707 should have an ejection seat fitted. As the first Avro 707A was under construction, it was decided that the most effective solution was to take the nose section from the next 707 being built (designed for high-speed research) and fit it to the new 707 VX790, effectively lengthening the fuselage by some twelve feet.

In response to Esler's findings concerning the lengthy take-off run, a new and longer nose gear assembly from the Hawker P.1052 was installed. The design team believed this would lower the 707's 'unstick' speed, allowing the elevators to become effective at an earlier stage on the take-off run. This simple act was one of the most important contributions that the 707 made to the full-scale 698 development as the bomber's nose gear was lengthened as a direct result of Esler's findings while the design was at

VX790 pictured at the point of touchdown at A&AEE's airfield at Boscombe Down. The 707 required large amounts of runway to get airborne and to land. A brake parachute was fitted in order to improve landing performance.

the drawing-board stage. Wing sweep was increased slightly and the cockpit canopy design was also revised. The 707's wing air brakes were changed – although, rather oddly, not to the same design that had been approved for use on the 698 – and the fuselage air brakes were also altered. However, revisions to the 707 design delayed its completion and it was not until September 1950 that the aircraft was ready to fly.

Emerging from the flight sheds at Avro's Woodford facility, the new 707B VX790 – painted in a bright blue colour scheme – was prepared for its first flight on 5 September. The pilot was Wing Commander R. J. 'Roly' Falk, Avro's recently appointed chief test pilot who had previously worked for Vickers-Armstrong and had also been RAE Farnborough's chief test pilot. After completing a series of pre-flight checks, darkness was beginning to fall over Greater Manchester and so Falk elected to confine the day's activities to a series of hops along the runway. The following day, Falk made a successful first flight of some fifteen minutes in duration. Following completion of the flight, Falk telephoned Avro's managing director (Roy Dobson) and Air Marshall Boothman (Controller of Supplies-Air) in order to obtain permission to immediately fly the aircraft to Farnborough so that it could join the static line-up at the 1950 SBAC show. Arriving at the end of the day's flying, it was a testament to Falk's and Avro's faith in the design that VX790 made its public debut just a few hours after its first flight.

This unusual rear view of VX790 illustrates the simple pop-out air brake mechanism installed in the wing and the simple one-piece trailing edge flap that acted as both ailerons (outboard) and elevators.

With the SBAC show at an end, the aircraft headed north to Woodford and 707B was put to work, eventually attaining a maximum speed of 350 knots during tests. It was found that the air intake was suffering from a degree of air starvation because of the cockpit canopy immediately ahead of it. Modifications had to be made, following tests in the Rolls-Royce wind tunnel at Hucknall, before the flight envelope could be extended further. Ultimately, the intake area was replaced with a completely new NACA Venturi design that proved to be much more efficient. Minor oscillations in the pitching plane were also reported, but after investigation, the cause was found to be out-of-phase movement of the elevators. As the 698 would have powered flying controls, the problem was ignored. Although these minor problems were peculiar to the 707, and therefore only served to distract attention from the 698 programme, the 707B made a significant contribution to the 698's development. A series of flights aimed at investigating trim settings at different engine outputs led to the 698's engine exhausts being 'toed' downwards and outwards in relation to the fuselage to minimise trim changes.

Perhaps most importantly, the 707B served to confirm that there were no fundamental flaws in the wing design. Also, there was no reason not to be fully confident in the 698's continuing development. It was probably just as well as 698 had by now established its own pace and was making good progress completely independent of the concurrent 707 programme. The sprightly 707B impressed test pilot Falk who reported that the aircraft was very stable and did not show any tendency to depart from normal flight characteristics. The aircraft was very manoeuvrable – rolls and loops being performed effortlessly – and Falk repeatedly took the aircraft down to speeds below 100 knots. He also performed angles of attack at around thirty degrees, proving the aircraft showed no inclination to stall at angles that would have been well beyond the limits of contemporary aircraft.

Without cockpit pressurisation, Falk was obliged to cope with conditions at altitude. One particularly florid Avro press release stated that Falk was '...in the habit of taking a surfeit of oxygen for an hour or so before high-altitude flights and then putting-up with discomfort for short periods at upwards of 40,000 feet'. Part of VX790's test programme was conducted from Dunsfold where the aircraft thrilled all pilots who were fortunate to fly it. The aircraft's rate of roll could exceed 200 degrees per second and a pilot even managed to execute an inverted loop, highly impressive for a 1950 design.

VX790 illustrating the modified engine air intake structure that was subsequently dropped in favour of slot intakes within the wing roots as designed for the full-sized 698.

WD280 high above the clouds illustrating the pure delta shape of the wing structure and the scaled down 'letter box' air intakes that were incorporated into the full-size 698 design.

When Air Marshal Boothman had an opportunity to fly the aircraft in September 1951, he was also greatly impressed and immediately issued an instruction that 'twenty-five selected pilots must fly it at once'. After completing around a hundred hours of test flying from Woodford and Dunsfold, the 707B suffered a landing accident and was withdrawn for repair. It was then transferred to Boscombe Down to continue work on other research programmes which had no direct relevance to the Vulcan. However, following the manufacture of the 707B, work continued on the 707A that was still under construction. There was some doubt within the Avro team as to whether there was any point in attributing more resources and time to the third 707 when the 698 programme was so well advanced. Having proved the concept of the delta wing, there clearly was not much that the third aircraft could contribute other than continuing to verify the design of the full-scale aircraft as it progressed.

After having discovered the deficiencies of VX790's air intake and the time consuming modifications, it was finally agreed that the 707A (WD280) should be fitted with 'letter box' intakes similar, but not identical, to those fixed into the design of the 698.

It was now accepted that even if the 707's new intakes highlighted any necessary changes to their design, it would be too late to influence the construction of the 698 prototype. It was precisely the sort of absurd situation that Avro had wanted to avoid from the outset. But the MoS expected their order to be fulfilled and construction of the 707A continued. WD280 was duly completed with new wing-mounted air intakes, new true-to-scale elevators and ailerons, and servo tabs and balances to assist the manual flying controls. Painted in a very unusual salmon pink, the new 707A finally took to the air on 14 July 1951 by which time metal was being cut on the 698 prototype.

As predicted by Avro, despite some ninety-two hours of test flying, WD280 had no direct influence on the design of the 698. Indeed, when Roy Ewans, who became Avro's chief designer, was asked just how much the design team had learned from the 707s, he replied: 'Not a great deal, apart from the reassurance that the thing would fly.' The 707s did yield some useful information at a later stage, however, when a series of flights was conducted to explore buffet boundaries, which required the pilot to apply a heavy amount of g-force at the greatest possible speed and height. It was found that the airframe 'buzzed', a high-frequency vibration, at speeds and heights that would easily be achieved by the 698. After a great deal of investigation, it was finally established that the 707's wing leading edge needed to be modified; the angle of wing sweep was reduced inboard before being increased again outboard, producing a kinked effect that would give the outer wing a greater chord and a mild leading edge droop.

A rare image of WD280 low over Cheshire. The 707 was a simple and austere aircraft, created only to investigate the properties of the delta wing. As can be seen, there was little more to the aircraft other than a basic fuselage and nose structure.

Unusual nose-on view of the Avro 707C illustrating the one-piece plate air brakes that were representative of the system fitted to the full-size 698 prototypes.

WD280 was modified accordingly, but it was too late to make any changes to the prototypes or the initial production 698s as the unusual reverse envelope jigs (in effect a sort of female mould) for the bomber's wing leading edge had been constructed. Consequently, the wing modification had to be retrofitted and sixteen sets of wing leading edges that had been manufactured were destroyed.

Occasionally, the Avro team were obliged to spend time making changes to the 707s in response to developments on the 698, creating a bizarre reversed procedure which clearly should never have been permitted to occur. However, the sad loss of the first 707 led to a mismatch of programme co-ordination from which Avro never fully recovered. With the benefit of hindsight, it could be said that the 707s were an unnecessary and expensive waste of resources, but at the time that they were first ordered, the Ministry of Supply firmly believed that they would save time and money. Despite the controversial nature of the 707 project, a second 707A was ordered in 1952 under Issue Two of Specification E.10/49; however, this was not as part of the 698's development programme. WZ736, painted in a bright orange-yellow scheme, was constructed for the Royal Aircraft Establishment to conduct various trials that were not directly related to Avro's 707 programme. Finally, another 707 was built in the shape of WZ744, an Avro 707C fitted with side-by-side seating under an enlarged fighter-type canopy.

No less than four 707Cs were originally envisaged, two being part of the second issue of E.10/49, to form the basis of a trainer aircraft on which RAF pilots could familiarise themselves with the handling qualities of the delta wing before progressing to the full-scale 698 aircraft. But as the 707 programme continued, it became obvious that the bomber would not suffer from any unusual handling vices and would be perfectly acceptable and safe to conduct the RAF's conversion training on the actual aircraft rather than a scaled-down version. Consequently, three of the 707C aircraft that had yet to be constructed were subsequently cancelled. WZ744 was completed and enjoyed a useful career conducting a variety of tests flights – mostly connected with the development of fly-by-wire electrically-signalled hydraulic flying controls – before being retired to storage at RAF Finningley in 1967.

Construction of the first full-sized Avro 698 airframe began in 1951. The process was delayed by some three months because of a variety of 'last minute' changes that reflected the findings of research data as it emerged. Most significantly, the RAE at Farnborough had been conducting a series of wind tunnel tests. These had predicted a degradation of performance caused by poor distribution of air pressure over the

The Avro 707C incorporated a larger canopy to accommodate side-by-side seating for two pilots. The proposed fleet of 707C dual-control trainers was abandoned by the RAF as the Vulcan's docile handling qualities rendered the 707 unnecessary.

wing surfaces and air intakes. The data suggested that the onset of compressibility drag rise, which effectively capped the 698's maximum speed, would take place at a lower altitude and lower speed than had previously been expected. The RAE's view contradicted Avro's conclusions and the slow pace of the 707 programme meant that no data had emerged from these test flights to support the RAE's findings. But from December 1949 until May 1950, the Avro team worked long and hard to revise the 698's wing shape, moving the thickest section forward to the leading edge, instead of being close to the root chord centre as had been envisaged. The result was a wing root that was almost as deep as the short fuselage to which it was attached, this being some nine feet in diameter. In many respects, it shifted the design back to more of a blended 'flying wing' layout from which the basic design had first emerged.

In addition to the aerodynamic improvements this created, it also enabled Avro to improve the shape, size and efficiency of the air intakes and create internal space for larger engines that were likely to become available in subsequent years. In fact, it was the projected need for more powerful engines that ultimately convinced Avro to revise the wing shape, rather than the theoretical advice from the RAE, which the designers were often tempted to dismiss. A total of 190 draughtsmen were assigned to the 698 together with thousands of engineers both with Avro and various sub-contractors around the country. Companies such as Dowty who produced the multi-wheel bogie undercarriage and Boulton Paul who designed the power controls, produced detailed component designs for the 698 in response to Avro's often vague and constantly changing requirements, long before a proper contract was issued by the MoS.

The 698 slowly took shape at Avro's Chadderton factory where the huge centre section and forward fuselage were manufactured. The massive wings were built at the Woodford factory, the plan being to bring the Chadderton sections to Woodford by road for final assembly prior to flight. Notification of a production contract for an initial batch of twenty-five aircraft was received in June 1952. Avro's delight at this news was tempered by the fact that an equivalent order was also issued to Handley Page for a similar batch of HP.80 bombers. It was assumed that a decision would eventually be made between the Avro and Handley Page designs. However, with the MoS and Air Staff still unconvinced that either aircraft promised any significant advantages or potential deficiencies when compared to the other, there was no enthusiasm to make a final choice between the two, especially when both Chadwick and Handley Page were making such strenuous efforts to convince the Air Staff that their aircraft was the better option.

With a typical twist of British compromise, it seemed that the way forward would be to adopt both aircraft and split the first order for fifty aircraft between the two companies, but no one could be sure that this even-handedness would extend beyond the initial orders. The Avro design team were also somewhat disheartened

Stunning view of the first Avro 698 emphasising the remarkably clean lines of the simple delta wing design.

to learn that Handley Page appeared to be taking the lead, having announced that their HP.80 prototype had been transported to Boscombe Down by road (carefully disguised as a boat) ready for reassembly and a first flight. This encouraged Avro to make even greater efforts to make the 698 ready for a public appearance at the all important 1952 SBAC show. Avro hoped to proudly show their new bomber to the public and thereby convince the Air Staff that the 698 was the right aircraft to purchase in large quantities.

When the prototype's centre section was completed at Chadderton, it was loaded as one piece onto a flatbed trailer ready for transportation through the streets of

Greater Manchester. The seventeen-mile road journey was a particularly challenging task for Avro as the massive inner wing and fuselage section was almost too large to be successfully transported through some narrow Manchester streets. As it was, the route had to be carefully planned and measured with various signs and posts repositioned, and even some street lamps were redesigned so that they could be hinged downwards to enable the huge structure to pass by. The ponderous journey through Manchester was conducted overnight and as the local residents slept in their beds, few people were aware of the carcass of Britain's new strategic bomber passing by outside their windows.

With everything gathered together at Woodford, final assembly of the prototype was completed during August and the aircraft was towed across the airfield to Woodford's flight sheds from where engine running trials began. On 30 August, test pilot Roly Falk taxied the fully functional prototype (VX770) onto Woodford's runway in anticipation of the first flight. Falk backtracked the 698 to the turning circle at the eastern end of the runway and opened up the four Avon engines, releasing the brakes to allow the aircraft to lurch forwards. This first run along the runway provided Falk with an indication of the speed at which the nose wheel would

The Avro 698 prototype VX770 pictured shortly after its maiden flight. Visible on the tail is the historic Avro logo, and the emblem of the Hawker Siddeley Group is applied to the nose.

One of the most famous images of the 698 prototype taken for Avro by Charles Brown. Captured from the rear turret of a Lincoln, VX770 performs for the cameraman high over Hampshire.

unstick. Once satisfied that the aircraft would be capable of safely getting airborne from Woodford's relatively short runway, he concluded that further test runs would be unnecessary.

Rather than risk overheating the wheel brakes, he announced that he was ready to get airborne. He taxied VX770 back to the runway threshold to position for take-off. After a brief interlude while a flock of potentially hazardous seagulls was cleared from the area, the four Rolls-Royce Avon RA.3s were opened up to full power. With a deafening roar, the glossy white-painted bomber lunged forwards, jumping upwards slightly on its nose wheel as the pressure came off the brakes. With a relatively modest combined power of 26,000 lb, the 698 might have been expected to require the full length of Woodford's runway to get airborne, but with no operational equipment or full fuel load onboard, the aircraft was remarkably light. As the aircraft thundered towards the centre of the airfield, Falk gently raised the nose and VX770 lifted cleanly into the air and settled into a steady climb. Much to the delight of the observers scattered around Woodford, the awe-inspiring white delta was airborne.

Falk raised the undercarriage as the aircraft began a steady climb to 10,000 feet where he proceeded to make a series of gentle manoeuvres to establish a feel for the controls and to establish that everything handled as predicted. Once satisfied that the aircraft was not hiding any unpleasant characteristics, Falk completed his preliminary handling evaluation and commenced a long, gentle descent back to Woodford. Just thirty minutes later, the prototype was back in Woodford's airfield circuit and caused a great deal of excitement in the neighbourhood where countless spectators had emerged to see the magnificent spectacle. The noisy departure had only added to the fuss and residents of Woodford stopped in their tracks to marvel at the sight and sound of almost fantastic proportions. No one had seen or heard anything like it before. Falk brought the aircraft back to a respectable approach speed and lowered the undercarriage. It was at this stage that the control tower staff at Woodford noticed something falling from the aircraft's underside. Falk was notified and he reported that everything appeared normal from inside the cockpit and that the undercarriage warning lights were indicating that the landing gear had safely locked in the extended position. However, rather than risk a catastrophe, he decided to hold the aircraft in the airfield circuit while two test pilots got airborne in a Vampire and Avro 707 to make an airborne rendezvous with VX770 in order to examine the aircraft for signs of damage. It did not take much scrutiny to notice that the objects which had fallen from the aircraft were the rear doors attached to the main undercarriage. They had broken free as they emerged face on into the airflow.

Having established that the incident was a minor one, the chase planes cleared the area while Falk brought 698 back onto final approach and gently settled the aircraft onto Woodford's runway before popping the huge brake parachute. Despite the minor problem with the gear doors, the first flight had been a great success and everyone was delighted, not least Falk who commented that the aircraft had been easier to handle than the stately Avro Anson that he had flown many times before. Two more test flights were swiftly made from Woodford over the following days before the aircraft was flown south to Boscombe Down to perform another three hours of initial handling trials. While flying from Boscombe Down, VX770 was able to make the short hop to Farnborough to make daily appearances at the SBAC show as Avro had hoped. It was decided that for security and technical reasons, it would be unwise to land the bomber at Farnborough. Therefore, the gleaming all-white aircraft was flown from Boscombe Down each day to make a series of fly-bys, flanked by the red 707A (flown by Jimmy Nelson) and blue 707B (flown by Jimmy Orrell). This patriotic sight of the huge bomber in company with the diminutive 707s was a magnificent sight which stirred emotions of countless spectators. It brought great satisfaction to the many industry and service chiefs who were present, all of whom were eager to see some tangible results from the protracted and hugely expensive bomber programme. The stirring sight of Avro's formation was proof that Britain's atomic bomb programme was on course.

A total of five displays were completed during the Farnborough week and as there had been no time to reattach the prototype's main undercarriage doors, Avro's

A frame capture from movie footage of VX770 as the aircraft disintegrated over Syerston in 1958. As can be seen, wing structure failure was the cause.

personnel at Boscombe Down made daily checks on the various micro switches and other components in the exposed undercarriage bays. They also made strengthening modifications to equipment where necessary in response to Falk's lively flying display that became increasingly faster and flamboyant each day. After the SBAC show, media interest in the 698 was widespread and everyone with an interest in aviation wanted to know more about the unusual and futuristic bomber prototype. Speculation began to mount as to what name would be applied to the aircraft and following the appearance of the Vickers Valiant, a variety of names were put forward including 'Albion' and (what was probably Avro's most popular choice) 'Avenger'. But the matter was finally resolved when the Chief of the Air Staff announced his preference for a class of 'V-Bombers' which prompted Handley Page to give the name 'Victor' to their design. Of course, Avro's 698 had the hugely appropriate name 'Vulcan' bestowed upon it.

Once the SBAC show appearances had been completed, the undercarriage doors were replaced, some instrument positioning revised and the second pilot's seat was installed in the cockpit. Falk had been heavily involved in the design of the cockpit from the outset, particularly the instrument layout, and it was he who had suggested the installation of a fighter-type control stick rather than the more traditional 'spectacle' wheel that would normally be found in the cockpit of a four-engined bomber. Although there was certainly a case for using more conventional controls,

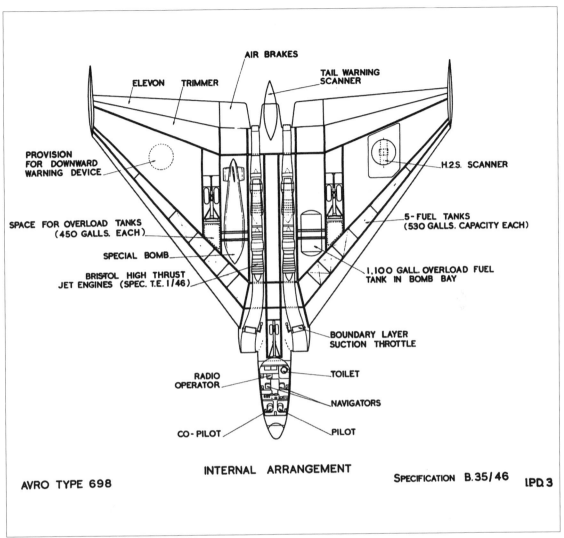

AIR BRAKES

TAIL WARNING
SCANNER

ELEVON   TRIMMER

PROVISION
FOR DOWNWARD
WARNING DEVICE

H.2.S. SCANNER

SPACE FOR OVERLOAD TANKS
(450 GALLS. EACH)

5-FUEL TANKS
(530 GALLS. CAPACITY EACH)

SPECIAL BOMB

1,100 GALL. OVERLOAD FUEL
TANK IN BOMB BAY

BRISTOL HIGH THRUST
JET ENGINES (SPEC. T.E. 1/46)

BOUNDARY LAYER
SUCTION THROTTLE

RADIO
OPERATOR

TOILET

NAVIGATORS

CO-PILOT

PILOT

INTERNAL ARRANGEMENT

AVRO TYPE 698

SPECIFICATION B.35/46   LPD.3

This diagram of the early 698 proposal illustrates how the design was developed. As can be seen, the design originally embraced two weapons bays and the Bristol engines were stacked vertically within the wing structure, fed by two circular air intakes.

Falk was keen to create an environment where the pilot would appreciate the light, fighter-style handling qualities of the Vulcan. The control joystick certainly gave the impression that the Vulcan was not just another cumbersome heavy bomber and possessed a performance capability that outclassed many contemporary fighters. When the second pilot's seat was fitted, there was media speculation that the seat was crammed under the small canopy hood into what was essentially a single-seat cockpit. This was not the case as the 698 had been designed to have seating for two

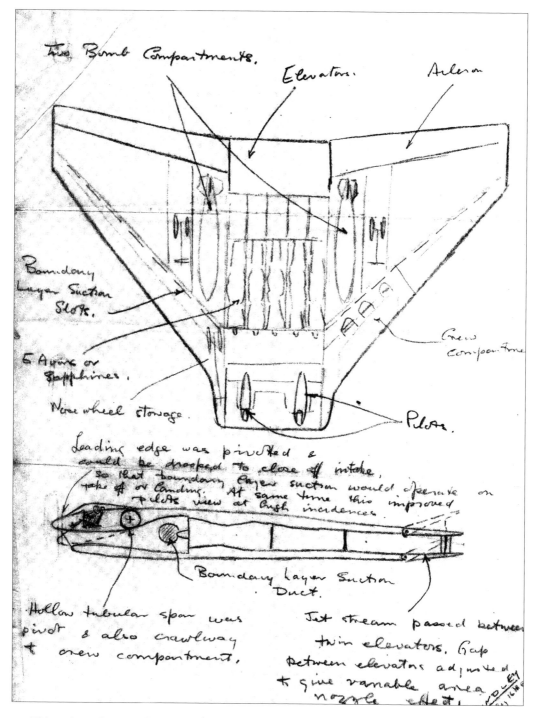

This unique drawing illustrates the earliest design concept that led to the 698. Without a conventional circular nose structure, the entire forward section was to pivot in order to create boundary layer flow for take-off and landing.

Vulcan B.Mk.1 XA894 was assigned to Bristol Siddeley as a trials aircraft for the Olympus engine being developed for the TSR2 programme. The test engine was housed in a ventral pod, fed by a bifurcated intake.

pilots, but for the purposes of the initial test flights, time simply did not allow the second seat to be installed. The Vulcan was never visualised as a one-man bomber, but its astonishing handling qualities were certainly very different from those that had traditionally been associated with aircraft of such size and weight.

Progress after the Farnborough show was encouraging and by the end of January 1953, VX770 had completed thirty-two hours of test flying. The aircraft returned to the factory for modifications to be made including the installation of fuel cells in the wings (until this time only a temporary fuel system had been used and was fitted inside the bomb bay). The cockpit pressurisation system was made operational and the Avon engines were replaced by Armstrong Siddeley Sapphire ASSa.6 models, each rated at 7,500 lb thrust. This gave the Vulcan the same engine power as Handley Page's Victor prototype and enabled the aircraft to reach higher speeds and altitudes. It had been the design team's intention to fit Bristol BE.10 engines, each rated at 11,000 lb, from the start of the flight test programme; however, in the early 1950s, jet engine development was a new science and progress with new engines lagged behind development of the aircraft which required them. The Sapphires made a suitable interim replacement for the Avons and VX770's test programme was resumed in July 1953. By this stage, the second prototype (VX777) was nearing completion and although some initial ground trials of this aircraft were completed with Olympus Mk.99 engines fitted, they had been replaced with 9,750 lb Olympus 100 engines for the second prototype's first flight on 3 September 1953.

In response to emerging data from the 707 programme, VX770's nose wheel leg was extended by a few inches during construction in order to give the aircraft a

Vulcan B.Mk.1A XH502 pictured at Waddington wearing what became the standard Vulcan B1 paint scheme comprising of overall anti-flash white with pale pink/lilac national insignia and serial number.

Many aircraft within the original Vulcan B.Mk.1 fleet were subsequently upgraded to B.Mk.1A standard with ECM gear installed in a bulged tail cone. The air intake fairing on the cone fed cold air into the housing to cool the ECM equipment. Also of note is the nose-high attitude of the Mk.1 Vulcan, thanks to the type's longer nose landing gear leg.

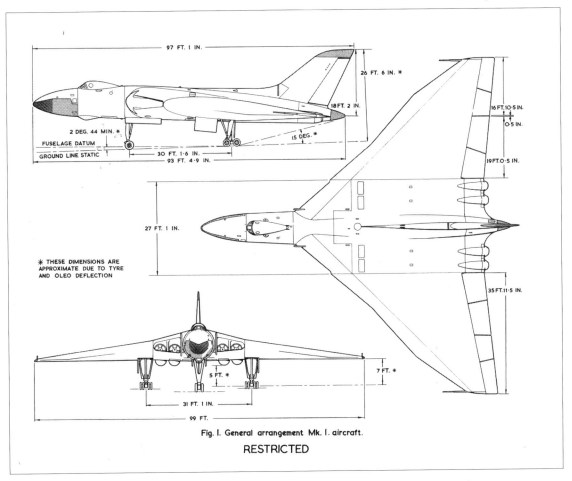

Fig. I. General arrangement Mk. I. aircraft.

RESTRICTED

Vulcan B.Mk.1 dimensions.

three-and-a-half degree angle of incidence in relation to the ground, thereby allowing the aircraft to unstick at a lower speed, thereby using less runway length. This design modification was built into VX777 from the start and rather than relying on a telescoping mechanism to allow the gear to fit into the wheel bay as had been the case with VX770, a one-piece leg was fitted to VX777 together with a correspondingly larger nose wheel bay to accommodate it. As a result, the nose section of VX777 was slightly longer and also included a bombardier's blister under the nose complete with a clear forward panel. Less than a week after its first flight, the second prototype appeared over Farnborough at the 1953 SBAC show. It was at this event that the aircraft participated in what has become one of the most iconic events in British aviation history when VX777 led an enormous 'delta of deltas' formation over Farnborough. The two Vulcan prototypes were flanked by four Avro 707s creating a sight that will never be forgotten by those who were lucky enough to witness it. It was a brilliant demonstration of Britain's emerging military and technological prowess which inevitably made the world's media sit up and take notice.

After Farnborough week, VX777 was delivered to Boscombe Down in preparation for high speed and high-altitude trials, but before they could begin, a series of modifications were made to the Olympus engines together with their control and fuel systems. Almost six months were to pass before flight trials could commence. VX777's troubled beginnings were exacerbated when the aircraft suffered a heavy landing while conducting flight trials at Farnborough. The landing caused significant damage to the airframe that had to be stripped and partially rebuilt. This created yet another delay in the flight test programme, particularly in terms of engine development, and another six months went by before flying could resume, much to the growing frustration of the Avro design team. During the time in which VX777 was laid up, new Olympus 101 engines were installed, each rated at 10,000 lb, and the airframe was structurally reworked using data from a static test specimen that had been constructed. But as VX777 remained grounded, the first prototype remained active on flight trials, achieving as much as possible within the limits of its design.

CHAPTER FIVE
Bigger and Better

When Avro's VX777 resumed flying duties in 1955, the exploration of the high-speed and high-altitude characteristics of the aircraft confirmed the predicted mild buffeting that was expected to occur when pulling 'g' at speeds of Mach 0.8. This problem had been highlighted during the 707's test programme, but only at a fairly late stage. However, with the four 9,000 lb engines, it was not a significant difficulty. With projected improvements in engine thrust likely to result in significantly more powerful engines, the high-altitude buffet would probably be reached with only the slightest application of engine power. This would inevitably lead to problems with bomb-aiming accuracy for operational crews and create a significant risk where the outer wing sections could ultimately fail through fatigue stress.

This potential problem prompted Avro to develop what became known as the Phase Two wing, which eventually emerged with a 'kinked' leading edge that solved the problem. However, because the modification was made at such a late stage in the development programme, the first production Vulcan (XA889) was rapidly nearing completion and was it too late to incorporate the new wing modification. Consequently, while VX777 re-emerged with a revised wing leading edge, the first production Vulcan made its first flight on 4 February 1955 with the original straight wing leading edge installed. Painted silver with national insignia and a striking dark-coloured dielectric radome made from glass-fibre Hycar sandwich, XA889 successfully got airborne a whole twelve months ahead of Handley Page's first production Victor, much to the glee of the Avro team who were very keen to be visibly ahead of Handley Page in terms of development progress.

There was a great deal of doubt as to whether a choice would ultimately be made between the Vulcan and Victor and no one could predict which design would finally receive the most orders. The second production Vulcan (XA890) joined the flight test programme late in 1955 and although it was not fitted with the Phase Two wing, both it and the first production aircraft were eventually retrofitted with the new wing design complete with vortex generators along the upper surface which speeded up boundary layer airflow across the wing. Falk took XA890 to the 1955

An interesting view of VX777 at Woodford, sharing ramp space with a Vulcan B.Mk.1 and an Avro Shackleton MR.Mk.2. The huge aircraft assembly halls can be seen in the distance. (*Courtesy Rolls-Royce*)

SBAC show and once again stole the show, this time by executing a neat barrel roll at a surprisingly low altitude in front of an assembled mass of astonished spectators who had never imagined that they would see a strategic bomber perform such a hair-raising manoeuvre. Sir Arnold Hall, the SBAC president, was just as surprised and immediately forbade Falk from repeating the performance on subsequent show days. Falk confidently explained that the manoeuvre was well within the aircraft's capabilities providing that the roll was kept within a steady 1g throughout the roll, but Hall remained unconvinced. Although he accepted that Falk was right, his main motivation for stopping what would have easily been the daily highlight of the show was that the manoeuvre would ultimately set a bad example to service pilots. In some respects his comments did indeed prove to have some prophetic value as other pilots tried to repeat the manoeuvre – some without the same degree of success – until it was ultimately forbidden by senior industry and RAF chiefs.

On 7 September, Prime Minister Anthony Eden arrived at Farnborough in a CFS Dragonfly helicopter and after watching Falk's Vulcan display was invited onboard and treated to a short flight. During the flight, Eden occupied the co-pilot's seat

Magnificent line-up of nine Vulcans from No. 83 Squadron at their home base at Scampton in Lincolnshire. (*Courtesy Rolls-Royce*)

and briefly took control of the aircraft before Falk returned the bomber to nearby Blackbushe. After the flight, Falk received a hand-written note from Eden thanking him for the flight. In March 1956, the first production Vulcan (XA889) was delivered to Boscombe Down to begin acceptance trials with the RAF. The initial CA (Controller of Aircraft) release was subsequently issued on 28 May as follows:

Tests have been made on the first production Vulcan B.Mk.1 to assess the type for use by the Royal Air Force, in the medium bomber role. The trials programme was completed in 26 sorties, totalling 48 hours 15 minutes flying time. During these tests the aircraft was flown over the full centre of gravity range and at take-off, weights up to a maximum of 165,220 lb. The first production Vulcan XA889 was representative of service aircraft in all respects save those of operational equipment, automatic pilot, the rear crew stations and certain items of cockpit layout. The aircraft incorporated the drooped leading edge outer wing with vortex generators, the longitudinal auto-Mach trimmer, the pitch damper and revised airbrake configuration. These modifications have successfully overcome the unacceptable flying characteristics exhibited by the second prototype in the preliminary assessment carried out by this establishment, and when all stability aids are functioning, the Vulcan has safe and adequate flying qualities for its primary role as a medium bomber.

The CA Release comments contrasted with those made after the A&AEE trials with the second prototype VX777 after which the following report was made:

A preliminary flight assessment has been made on the second prototype Vulcan in 17 sorties totalling 27 flying hours. During these tests the aircraft was flown at a mid-centre of gravity and take-off weights of 119,000 lb and 130,000 lb. The expected operational take-off weight of production aircraft is about 165,000 lb. The expected cruising Mach number is 0.87M (500 knots) and the design Mach number is 0.95M. Above 0.86M, a nose-down change of trim occurred which became pronounced with increase of Mach number towards the limit, making the aircraft difficult to fly accurately and requiring great care on the part of the pilot to avoid exceeding the maximum permitted Mach number. This characteristic is unacceptable; the Firm propose to eliminate it in production aircraft by the introduction of an artificial stability device (a Mach trimmer).

With an increase of Mach number above 0.89, the damping in pitch decreased to an unacceptably low level, particularly near the maximum permitted Mach number, and the aircraft was difficult to fly steadily. The firm propose installing a pitch damper in production aircraft. As tested, the Mach number/buffet characteristics were unacceptable for a high-altitude bomber, but considerable improvement is hoped for with the drooped leading edge and vortex generators. Associated with the buffet were oscillating aileron hinge movements which in these tests imposed severe manoeuvre limitations from considerations of structural safety. Making allowances for the differences in engine thrust and aircraft weight between the aircraft tested and the production version, the performance in terms of attainable altitude, was not outstanding. The likely target height with a 10,000 lb bomb will only be about 43,000 feet with 11,000 lb thrust engines and the high-altitude performance will be poor. The level of performance is considered to be inadequate for an unarmed subsonic bomber, even under cover of darkness. In summary, although the aircraft has certain outstanding features, serious deficiencies are present, particularly in and above the cruising Mach number range, and until these are rectified the Vulcan cannot be considered satisfactory for service use.

Although the report was deliberately concerned with the highlighting of deficiencies, it was clear that the prototype with an unmodified wing was never going to match the performance required by the RAF. But with further refinements and the all-important modification to the wing's leading edge, Avro was confident that the RAF would get the bomber that it needed.

The prototype Avro 698 (VX770) remained active on test flight duties and made an air show appearance at Syerston near Nottingham on 20 September 1958. In front

XM595 returns to its dispersal after completing a training flight. The markings of No. 617 Squadron are visible on the aircraft's tail surfaces and a Blue Steel missile can be seen under the aircraft's bomb bay, the bomb's ventral fin folded upwards. (*Courtesy Rolls-Royce*)

of a crowd of astonished and horrified spectators, the aircraft suddenly disintegrated and smashed into the runway, killing everyone onboard. An investigation revealed that structural failure of the wing had been the cause of the accident, but a more detailed analysis confirmed that the aircraft had been flying outside the safe speed and 'g' flight envelope that had been applied to VX770. The aircraft's structure was clearly not at fault and the accident was attributed to the pilot's failure to keep the aircraft within the safety limits that had been imposed upon it.

In subsequent years there was much discussion over the possibility that the aircraft had been overstressed during test flying prior to the Syerston display and that this may have been the root cause of the aircraft's failure, but no conclusive proof was ever found to substantiate this theory. It remained obvious to Avro that whether the root cause was due to pilot error or damage which had not been identified and rectified, the accident did not indicate any previously undiscovered deficiency in the Vulcan's structural composition. However, the Syerston accident did emphasise that although the Vulcan was an astonishingly manoeuvrable machine, it was often all too easy to forget that it was also a very large and heavy four-engined bomber that was susceptible to aerodynamic stresses as any other comparable machine.

The terrible loss of VX770 and its crew undoubtedly cast a shadow over the bomber project, but with no evidence to attribute the accident to the production-standard Vulcan, deliveries of the Vulcan B.Mk.1 continued. However, even as the aircraft were slowly delivered to their squadrons, Avro and the RAF were already looking towards a second-generation Vulcan based on the promise of greater thrust output from Bristol's Olympus engine series, which continued to benefit from development. By the first half of 1955, sufficient data was available to suggest that the Bristol B.01.6 engine would be capable of delivering 16,000 lb of thrust with the prospect of even more powerful versions of the Olympus becoming available at a later stage. Analysis of the aircraft's structure indicated that with suitable modifications, the Vulcan could accommodate these later power plants within the existing wing framework. However, a Vulcan fitted with these more powerful engines would suffer from the very same high-speed and high-altitude buffet problems for which the Phase Two wing (fitted to the B1) had been designed to counter. Clearly, this wing design would have to be revised yet again and during September 1955, Avro submitted a brochure to the Ministry of Supply describing what would ultimately become the Vulcan B.Mk.2.

Avro had been discussing the possibility of a Vulcan B.Mk.2 with the MoS for some time and having gained a great deal of encouragement from the Ministry, funds had been made available within the company to initiate full-scale development of the new design. Although the revised wing layout was fundamental to the new variant, there were other external differences between the B1 and B2. In many respects, the Vulcan B2 was almost a completely different aircraft both in terms of its overall design and the equipment with which it was fitted. The airframe was re-stressed to a gross weight of over 200,000 lb, which was more than double the figure originally set by Spec. B.35/46. The landing gear was redesigned and strengthened to withstand greater take-off and landing weights. The electrical system was changed to 200V AC and instead of direct-drive 112V generators, each engine was given constant-speed drive and alternators. A gas turbine auxiliary power unit was installed driven by a Rover 2S/150 engine and the flying controls were revised. The ailerons and elevators were replaced by inner and outer elevons – combined ailerons and elevators – each with independent power control units.

The Vulcan B2's new Phase 2C wing design extended the span by 12 feet (to 111 feet) while the thickness/chord ratio changed from 7.92 per cent to 4.25 and the wing area increased from 3,446 square feet to 3,965 square feet. The compound taper of the leading edge was increased further, incorporating a significant concave droop and the wing's trailing edge was also swept rearwards. It is important to note that the creation of the Vulcan B2 was not a simple linear continuation of the Vulcan's development process and had political and military circumstances been different, the B2 may well never have reached the production stage at all.

This image clearly shows the cranked leading edge wing extension fitted to Mk.2 Vulcans. Visible on the aircraft's nose behind the national insignia is the badge of No. 83 Squadron. (*Courtesy Rolls-Royce*)

Governmental discussions on the projected size of the V-Force had been in existence since 1954 and was the subject of much debate. It was not until 31 May 1956 that ministers agreed to proceed with the construction of more Vulcans and Victors, both types being of an improved 'second generation' design. Initially, the plan was to order both types with Rolls-Royce Conway engines as there was little enthusiasm for proceeding with Bristol's Olympus when the Conway was proving to be successful and reliable. The MoS was invited to investigate whether the Olympus engine should be supported only as a civil programme, but Bristol, faced with the cancellation of the Olympus Mk.6, offered to carry all further development costs themselves. Bristol even offered to provide completed engines at the same price as Conways if an order for 200 engines was placed.

It was this act of desperation that ultimately saved the Olympus programme and resulted in hugely successful developments which went on to power not only the Vulcan, but the TSR2 and the magnificent Concorde. Reginald Maudling, Minister of Supply, commented that '...there are at present 99 Vulcans on order and I am proceeding on the assumption that there is no suggestion that this number should be reduced. We have been re-examining the Vulcan programme and it now looks as if the Mk.2 version can be introduced at about the 45th aircraft. This means that 54 Vulcans should be the new and greatly improved Mk.2 version.' Despite this statement, there was a great deal of doubt as to precisely how many medium bombers could be comfortably afforded. Almost inevitably, the Admiralty stepped in and stated that the force should not '...cost so much inside the total resources set aside for defence as to make it impossible to finance the other forces essential to ensure the cohesion of Commonwealth, dependencies and alliances.' Today, the Royal Navy's Trident programme now takes up a significant proportion of modern defence spending and it is clear that the Navy's attitude towards the Vulcan undoubtedly had little to do with sound military thinking and more to do with inter-service rivalry. It was eventually decided that the MBF (Medium Bomber Force) should comprise a frontline strength of 144 aircraft, of which some 104 aircraft would be Mk.2 Vulcans and Victors.

During March 1956, a production contract for a Vulcan B.Mk.2 prototype was placed and a further contract issued in June effectively converted the existing order for the final seventeen B1s into B2s and added eight more machines to the total. Interestingly, these aircraft were covered by Specification B.129P Issue 2 that referred to this new batch of Vulcans as being B(K)Mk.2 versions, which indicates that the aircraft were to have an in-flight refuelling tanker capability. This option was to have been applied to all new V-Bombers and design drawings for a Vulcan in tanker configuration certainly exist amongst Avro's archives, but the proposal was subsequently dropped. It was a quarter of a century later that the Vulcan was finally introduced into the tanker role almost by accident. The second B1 prototype (VX777) was selected for conversion into the B.2 prototype and on 31 August 1957, it made its first flight in the revised configuration. It lacked some of the anticipated changes which would be incorporated into production B2s and acted as an aerodynamic test vehicle for the larger and reshaped wing.

As the B2 development programme continued, Avro received instructions to equip the Vulcan fleet with new ECM (electronic counter-measures) gear, reflecting the ever-increasing capabilities of Soviet forces. This required a fairly radical redesign of the rear fuselage in order to accommodate the bulky equipment that could not realistically be accommodated elsewhere within the Vulcan's airframe. Until this stage in the V-Force's existence, there had been little need for an advanced ECM fit, thanks largely to the Soviet Air Force's notoriously rigid system of fighter control that was well monitored by the West.

Only a limited number of VHF channels were used to control Soviet fighters and the RAF possessed suitable jamming equipment codenamed 'Green Palm' that was deemed more than capable of blocking every frequency with a high-pitched

A No. 44 Squadron Vulcan pictured arriving at RAF Luqa during 1976. Clearly visible is the Terrain Following Radar (TFR) thimble fairing on the aircraft's nose cone. TFR was fitted to almost all of the Vulcan B2 fleet during the early 1970s. (*Courtesy Godfrey Mangion*)

wail. However, developments beyond 1960 suggested that something rather more sophisticated was now required and a tail warning radar (codenamed 'Red Steer') was created. This was to be fitted into the Vulcan together with other ECM equipment including a flat-plate aerial installation (codename 'Red Shrimp') that was accommodated between the starboard jet pipes (and between both sets of jet pipes on some B2s). Although the new ECM fit was intended primarily for the B2, a contract was also received to convert part of the existing B1 fleet to carry the same ECM gear. Aircraft so equipped were re-designated Vulcan B.Mk.1A. Consideration was also given to the rather more ambitious concept of converting the B1 fleet to the full B2 standard, but as the cost of each aircraft conversion was estimated to be roughly two-thirds of the cost of a new-build B2, the idea was too expensive to seriously contemplate. However, some twenty Vulcan B1s from the 1954 contract were eventually converted to B1A standard, together with nine machines from the original 1952 contract.

With VX777 back in the air following modifications, the new Phase 2C-winged Vulcan was displayed at the 1957 Farnborough show where the aircraft's external changes caused more interest, speculation and excitement. After the show, the aircraft was put through a series of aerodynamic trials while a further seven B1s were brought into the B2 development programme ensuring that every aspect of the

Blue Steel trials were conducted from Woodford with live launches taking place over the Woomera range in Australia. Just visible is the camera equipment fairing at the rear of the bombardier's blister trained on the missile round.

redesigned Vulcan could be explored prior to deliveries and entry into service. Early in 1958, XA891 was fitted with the first Olympus 200-series engines, each rated at 16,000 lb. Meanwhile, XA890 was employed on avionics work and XA892 was assigned to weapons research. XA893 was fitted with the B2's electrical system, XA894 was allocated to development of the B2 and B1A ECM fit, while XA899 was also used for avionics research. Vulcan B1 XA903 was later employed as a Blue Steel missile trials aircraft in support of both the Vulcan and Victor Mk.2 programmes. Flight trials with the B2 prototype revealed a 25-30 per cent increase in range over the B1, effectively extending Bomber Command's projected target range by a corresponding amount.

Certainly, the predicted high-speed and high-altitude buffet problem had been prevented and on 4 March 1959, the first production Vulcan B2 (XH533) reached an altitude of 61,500 feet during a test flight. XH533 had made its first flight on 19 August 1958 powered by 16,000 lb Olympus 200s, but was still fitted with the original unmodified tail cone. It is interesting to note that the aircraft made its first flight long before production of Vulcan B1s had been completed – the last B1 made

XH558 was the first Vulcan Mk.2 to enter into RAF service. It was also the last Vulcan to leave RAF service. It is seen here on its delivery flight resplendent in Bomber Command anti-flash white colours.

its first flight during February 1959. Likewise, the second production B2 (XH534) took to the air ahead of the last B1 in January 1959. This was the first aircraft to fly with production-standard Olympus 201s rated at 17,000 lb together with a full ECM fit: it should be noted, however, that the next three aircraft from the production line first flew with unmodified tail cones. As production of the Vulcan B2 got underway, the first seven aircraft, including the prototype, were assigned to flight trials work, XH534 being dispatched to Boscombe Down where the aircraft was used to gain a CA Release issued in May 1960. Finally, on 1 July 1960, XH558 was ferried from Woodford to No. 230 OCU at Waddington, thereby becoming the first Vulcan B.2 to enter RAF service. Ironically, XH558 earned the distinction of becoming the last Vulcan B2 to leave RAF service, thanks to combination of circumstance and good luck. It was the last Vulcan to continue flying more than half a century later.

Vulcan B2 XH559 was delivered during August with XH560, XH561 and XH562 arriving at Waddington before the end of the year. XH557 was loaned to Bristol Siddeley for further engine trials and was eventually fitted with what was to be the ultimate Vulcan power plant, the Olympus 301 engine rated at 20,000 lb thrust. Two engines of this standard were fitted, one in each of the port nacelles, flying for the first time in this configuration on 19 May 1961. Although these immensely powerful engines required a greatly increased amount of intake airflow when compared with the early Vulcan B1 powerplants, the first production Vulcan B2s retained the same air intakes as the B1. However, on later aircraft, the lower lip of the intake was deepened (starting with XH557) and all subsequent B2s were manufactured accordingly to accommodate the increased airflow mass. XH557 was later fitted with a standard complement of four Olympus 301s before entering RAF service. Approximately half the Vulcan B2 fleet was completed or retrofitted to this standard while the remainder continued to operate with 17,000 lb Olympus 201s.

The Vulcans fitted with the more powerful engines were sometimes informally referred to as the 'B2A' variant. There is no evidence to suggest that this designation was ever officially applied either by Avro or the RAF and this dubious designation appears to have been no more than convenient slang that has gradually drifted into widespread use. Although continued Vulcan production naturally enabled the RAF to form more squadrons, official policy dictated that the B2s should first be delivered to an established unit, which would then transfer its B1s to newly converted squadrons. Consequently, the crews of B Flight of No. 230 OCU went on to No. 83 Squadron at Scampton where transition to the Vulcan B2 began in November 1960. On 1 April 1961, No. 27 Squadron formed at Scampton on the B2 and the Scampton Wing was completed in September 1961 when No. 617 Squadron (the legendary 'Dambusters') started their conversion from B1s onto B2s. Waddington standardised on the B1A variant with No. 44 Squadron forming on 10 August 1960 using aircraft that had previously been operated by No. 83 Squadron (the first B1A being delivered to No. 44 in January 1961). No. 101 Squadron relocated from Finningley during June and No. 50 Squadron formed on 1 August (using former No. 617 Squadron aircraft). The Vulcan OCU then relocated to Finningley where it was divided into A Flight with Vulcan B1 and B1As, and B Flight with Vulcan B2s.

Finningley also provided a home for the Bomber Command Development Unit that operated a mixed fleet of Vulcans, Valiants and Victors for various trials work. The second Vulcan B2 Wing was then established at Coningsby where No. 9 Squadron formed on 1 March 1962 followed by No. 12 Squadron on 1 July and No. 35 Squadron on 1 December. The Wing later moved to Cottesmore in November 1964 and the last production Vulcan B2 (XM657, the final Vulcan to be manufactured) was delivered there on 15 January 1965 when it joined No. 35 Squadron. Following the initial order for twenty-five B2s, a further contract had been issued for an additional twenty-four aircraft followed by a final order for another forty machines. The final Vulcan B1A conversion was XH503, which was delivered to Waddington in March 1963, after which the remaining B1s were either withdrawn from use or transferred to the OCU and the Bomber Command Development Unit at Finningley. From 1966,

XL318 was dismantled after being withdrawn from service and transported by road to the RAF Museum at Hendon. The process involved removing the Vulcan's nose section and revealing the bulkhead that was originally designed to separate the section as part of a proposed escape capsule concept that was never adopted. (*Courtesy Bruce Woodruff*)

the Waddington Wing converted to Vulcan B2s, completing the transition at the end of 1967. At this stage, the OCU then relinquished its remaining B1 aircraft and the RAF finally standardised on the Vulcan B2 from 1968 onwards. Just a handful of Mk.1 Vulcans remained active on test duties, the very last machine being XA903 that continued flying on engine development work with Rolls-Royce until 1 March 1979 when it was grounded and subsequently scrapped at Farnborough.

The US's once lukewarm military relationship with Britain shifted considerably when it finally accepted that Britain had both the knowledge and capacity to create a viable nuclear bomber force, even though there were insufficient resources to build a nuclear arsenal of any great size. An agreement was therefore made to supply the RAF with American atomic weapons as a stopgap measure, until sufficient British-made bombs could be completed to render Britain's deterrent posture fully effective. For political reasons, the US could not hand weapons to Britain and so the American bombs would be kept in USAF custody on RAF bases from where they would be released to the RAF in a wartime emergency. The detailed agreements made in London included references to the general concept of Allied atomic air operations stating that in a general war, atomic weapons would be used from the outset. At this stage, there was no question of a graduated response to Soviet aggression. It was established that if an atomic war began, it would probably begin with an initial phase characterised by an intensive exchange of atomic blows, followed by a subsequent exchange of 'indeterminate duration' at a 'reduced atomic intensity'.

The 'Brief Plan of Action' stated that the Allied counter air offensive would begin with heavy co-ordinated attacks against airfields, logistic facilities, control centres and command headquarters. It was hoped that in creating a contraction of forces, surviving enemy aircraft would concentrate on remaining airfields enabling SAC and Bomber Command to exploit the vulnerability of such concentrations. In January 1956, the British defence minister Duncan Sandys wrote to Charles Wilson, his American counterpart, with a detailed set of proposals. The reply from Wilson was positive and agreed that arrangements should be made to furnish the RAF with US atomic bombs in the event of war and to co-ordinate an atomic strike. It was therefore planned that the USAF and RAF forces could effectively operate as one decisive power. However, Wilson also added that, 'the provisions of United States legislation must govern and that the United States cannot engage in a commitment to transfer custody of such weapons to the Royal Air Force other than by Presidential decision in strict accordance with his constitutional and legislative authority'. The supply of American atomic bombs (Project E) was discussed in detail by President Eisenhower and Prime Minister Macmillan when they met at the Bermuda Conference in March 1957.

The 1956 Suez Crisis had been a turning point for Anglo-American relations and the Bermuda meeting marked a significant improvement in mutual confidence between the two countries. After the conference, Eisenhower outlined his views stating that:

> The United States Government welcome the agreement to co-ordinate the strike plans of the United States and United Kingdom bomber forces, and to store United States nuclear weapons on RAF airfields under United States custody for release subject to decision by the President in an emergency. We understand that for the present at least these weapons will be in the kiloton range. The United Kingdom forces could obviously play a much more effective part in joint strikes if the United States weapons made available to them in emergency were in the megaton range, and it is suggested that this possibility might be examined at the appropriate time.

America's decision to co-operate with Britain and supply the UK with weapons was a well-kept secret at the time as the president indicated in his communication to Macmillan that:

XH558 pictured at Kinloss after withdrawal from operational service. Stripped bare, she is ready to receive a new paint scheme for a second lease of life as an air show performer.

> With respect to the item 'Nuclear bomb release gear for RAF bombers', I agree, of course, that you shall probably have to make some statement in order to prevent speculation in the press that might prove not only inaccurate but damaging. However, as I explained to you verbally, the United States would prefer not to be a party to a public statement which might give rise to demands upon us by other Governments where we should not be in a position to meet the requests. Consequently, I suggest the possible adequacy of a unilateral statement by yourself or by the British Defence Minister to the effect that Canberras are now being equipped to carry atomic bombs.

In fact, Project E covered the supply of atomic bombs not only to the RAF's Canberra tactical bomber force, but also to the V-Force. An Air Ministry meeting in August 1956 reported that the US Government had not given any indication of the numbers of weapons to be supplied, nor were they likely to, but it was believed to be almost certain that the numbers would exceed any delivery capacity that the UK was ever capable of developing. Records do not indicate when the first E weapons arrived in the UK, but US transport flights began towards the end of 1958 and both Honington and Waddington received the first suitably modified bombers in October of that year. Approval was given for modifications to be made to seventy-two aircraft at Honington, Waddington and Marham to carry American Mk.5 (6,000 lb) bombs (and subsequently the Mk.7, Mk.15/39 and Mk.28). Nos. 90 and 57 Squadrons at Honington equipped with Valiants and Victors respectively were the first units to be assigned to Project E during the spring of 1959. These were followed by Nos.148, 207 and 214 Squadrons (with Valiants) at Marham and No. 83 Squadron (operating Vulcan B1s) at Waddington. In 1960, No. 7 Squadron (flying Valiants) and No. 55 Squadron (with Victors) at Honington together with No. 44 Squadron (operating Vulcan B1s) at Waddington joined Project E. Finally, Nos. 101 and 50 Squadrons (both flying Vulcan B1s) at Waddington were assigned in 1961.

The supply of American bombs enabled Bomber Command to equip the V-Force with significant numbers of atomic weapons at an earlier date than would ever have been possible with British weapons. Had the US weapons not been supplied, there would have been an absurd situation in which the RAF possessed more bombers than bombs for quite some time. However, Project E was a less than perfect solution to Britain's early problems, chiefly because of American restrictions on the deployment of the weapons. The E weapons could not be distributed throughout Bomber Command nor could they be dispersed to remote sites from which clutches of V-Bombers would operate during wartime in order to evade enemy attack. Project E was essentially a political gesture that served to convince the USSR that Britain's growing fleet of strategic bombers was not merely a bluff. Consequently, Project E was relatively short-lived and the decision to start a phase-out was taken on 7 July 1960. America was reluctant to disclose how many nuclear bombs were stored at RAF bases and they were equally ambiguous when revealing the nominal yield of each weapon. Eventually, it was established that the bombs were largely of a type that would deliver only half the yield which they had previously been thought to possess. This meant that once British equivalents were available, the greater flexibility they afforded would also be married to a much greater destructive capability. Valiants assigned to Supreme Allied Commander Europe (Saceur) and RAF Germany's Canberras would continue to carry E weapons for some time, but in a matter of months the Vulcan squadrons no longer had any association with American weaponry.

Throughout the story of the Vulcan's development, many other vital projects were being pursued in an effort to ensure that Britain could retain a credible deterrent capability. The concept of guided nuclear missiles had already been established and by 1954, the Air Staff had issued OR.1132, calling for a propelled air-to-surface missile for the V-Force. Capable of being launched at up to 100 nm from its target, the missile would rely on the parent aircraft's NBS system for aiming and would use Green Satin Doppler equipment to determine ground speed and drift, and to provide an accurate heading reference. Responsibility for the weapon, named Blue

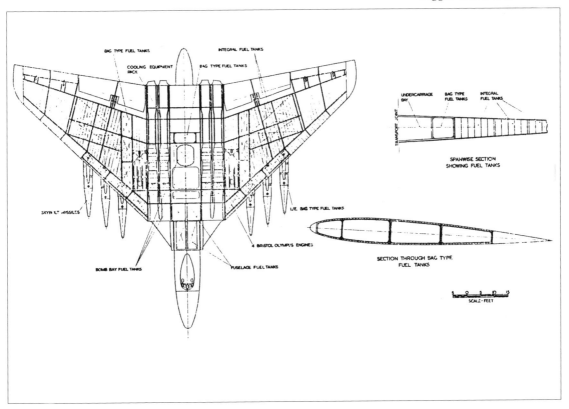

A tantalising glimpse of what might have been. A drawing of the proposed Vulcan Mk.6 designed for longer range with greater fuel capacity and a complement of six Skybolt missiles, enabling the aircraft to maintain a round-the-clock airborne alert capability.

Steel, was divided between the MoS and Avro's Weapons Research Division, which had completed a design study for a stand-off bomb. This resulted in a development contract being awarded in March 1956.

Tests of a two-fifths-scale model of the guided bomb were conducted in 1957-58, a series of drops being made from Valiant WP204 over the Aberporth range off the Welsh coast. Designing Blue Steel was time consuming and extremely difficult, not least because the entire programme represented a move into completely unknown territory as far as technical knowledge was concerned. In essence, Blue Steel was an aeroplane and Avro treated the missile as such. Some thirty-five feet long with small delta foreplanes, rear-mounted thirteen-feet-span wings and vertical fins, it was powered by a hydrogen peroxide and kerosene Armstrong Siddeley Stentor rocket motor. Guided by inertial navigation and with automatic flight control and trajectory decision-making, the missile manoeuvred at supersonic speeds before delivering a one megaton ('Red Snow') warhead to its target. The all-up weight of the bomb was

An image from a test firing of a Blue Steel round over Woomera. At this point, the missile has just been released, and after a few seconds, the missile's Stentor rocket will ignite, powering the missile into a climb.

about 17,000 lb which included 400 gallons of high-test peroxide (HTP) fuel and eighty gallons of kerosene.

After release at 40,000 feet, the bomb would freefall to 32,000 feet at which stage the motor would ignite and the missile climb to 59,000 feet where speed would increase to Mach 2.3. The missile would then cruise-climb to 70,500 feet where the engine would burn out and a steady dive towards the target would begin. Bearing this very complicated system in mind and that Avro had no previous experience of designing and manufacturing guided missiles, it was not surprising that the development programme timescale began to slip, especially when the MoS were unable to supply a Valiant test-bed aircraft on time. The Air Staff's hope that Blue Steel would be operational by 1960 was quickly discounted, despite the fact that they were already looking for a missile that could fly up to ten times further. In May 1958, Air Staff Requirement OR.1159 called for an extended-range air-to-surface guided missile, stating that:

> By 1963, it is expected that the Russian SAGW (surface-to-air guided weapons) and the fighter defences will be so improved and expanded that the V-Bombers, even with Blue Steel and RCM, will find it increasingly difficult to penetrate to many of their objectives. In order to maintain an effective deterrent during the period commencing

with the decline in effectiveness of Blue Steel and continuing during the build-up of the RAF ballistic missile force, it will be necessary to introduce a replacement for Blue Steel having a range for attacking targets from launching points outside the enemy defence perimeter. It is envisaged that V-Bombers equipped with this missile should be able to supplement the ballistic missile deterrent for several years. Missile range of 600 nautical miles will be acceptable as an initial operational capability but a range of 1,000 nm is desirable.

Duncan Sandys, who was then the Minister of Aviation, recognised that it would be foolish to distract Avro's efforts to get Blue Steel into service by adding the complication of long-range Blue Steel development. Therefore, the subsequent cancellation of both Blue Streak and Blue Steel Mk.2 enabled Avro, the RAE and the Royal Radar Establishment to concentrate on getting Blue Steel Mk.1 into service at the earliest opportunity. On 28 April 1961, the current Minister of Aviation, Peter Thorneycroft, reported that:

> Blue Steel was accepted as a requirement in January 1956. It was then thought that the first delivery of missiles would be made to the RAF in 1961/2. By the end of 1960, however, it had become apparent (owing to delays in the development programme) that the number of trial firings that could be expected by early 1962 would not be sufficient to enable the first deliveries of missiles to the RAF to be approved for normal operational use. It is, however, expected that by mid-1962, the functioning and safety of the weapon (including its warhead) will have been sufficiently improved to enable the missile to be used in an emergency, if required, thus providing a deterrent capability. Further trials will continue during the succeeding months to enable approval to be given for normal operational carriage and use of the missile.

He also added that the delays in the programme were due to '...detailed engineering faults and problems which are a normal part of the development process and may be expected to continue'. An order was placed for fifty-seven missiles made up of a unit establishment of forty-eight operational rounds plus four backing rounds and four proof rounds. Additionally, there would be sixteen training rounds, ten of which would be manufactured from light alloy and six with steel carcasses. During 1959, Vulcan B.1 XA903 joined the Blue Steel programme and a variety of full-sized missile test bodies, mostly powered by de Havilland Double Spectre engines, were dropped from both the Valiant and Vulcan. Most of the later test flights were made over the Woomera range in Australia where two Vulcan B2s (XH538 and XH539) were employed on test drop and monitoring duties.

Blue Steel was perpetually dogged by a series of relatively minor problems which led to increasing frustration on behalf of the Air Staff. Avro was accused of poor

Blue Steel inert training rounds were often painted overall blue. Also visible is the ECM aerial plate fitting over the starboard engine jet pipes. These were common to all Vulcan B2s with some aircraft having a second plate on the port side.

management and of wasting time on projected plans for a long-range Blue Steel when it should have devoted all of its efforts to completion of Blue Steel Mk.1. Avro simply suffered from a combination of initial over-optimism shared by the Air Staff and a range of new technical problems which, as an aircraft manufacturer, the company had never before encountered. Considering that the typical development period for a conventional military aircraft could be anything up to ten years, it was perhaps unrealistic to expect a system as complicated as Blue Steel to be completed in a significantly shorter timescale. The Minister of Aviation also said in 1961 that:

> Blue Steel was a fully navigated cruise-type missile with a range of 100 nm designed for launching from Mk.2 Victors and Vulcans. It was intended to provide the main deterrent weapon between the time when bombers equipped with freefalling bombs were likely to become less effective against enemy defences, and the introduction of Skybolt which would replace it. Its cost was currently estimated at £60 million for R&D and £21 million for production; of this total, some £44 million had been spent or committed. Trial firings had proved disappointing in some respects, but it appeared that the difficulties were caused by teething troubles rather than by any basic fault that might

invalidate the concept of the weapon. Further trials were proceeding at Woomera and it should be possible to make a comprehensive review towards the end of the year.

Early in 1962, the project's progress was evaluated and the Cabinet Defence Committee learned that the firing of W. IOOA rounds, closely representative of the final production version, was about to start. By August or September, enough preliminary information would be available from launchings to enable the Air Ministry to assume an emergency capability. Finally, in July 1962, a production-model Blue Steel was successfully fired after being air-launched from a Vulcan over Woomera. On 25 July, the Minister of Aviation, now Julian Amery, wrote to the Air Minister stating:

> I am glad to be able to inform you that Sir George Gardner (Controller of Aircraft, Ministry of Aviation) has today forwarded to DCAS a CA Release for Blue Steel to be carried on Vulcan Aircraft, complete with its operational warhead, in a national emergency. The clearance does not specifically authorise the launching of the missile because the required trials to prove the safety of the systems are not yet complete. However, no difficulties have been experienced up to date which affect the safety after launch and we are confident that further trials will provide the necessary proof. We expect to issue the operational launch clearance in December 1962. We have issued the Present Clearance on the understanding that, should a national crisis occur which warrants the carriage of the operational Blue Steel with its warhead, limitations as to its use could be overridden. In effect this means that you could declare an operational capability with Blue Steel as soon as you consider that you are in a position to do so.

The first unit to be declared operational on Blue Steel was No. 617 Squadron at Scampton. A great deal of time was spent discussing when the RAF should officially declare that the squadron had an operational capability as Bomber Command wanted to arrange a press facility to show the Blue Steel system to the public. It was feared that a premature display of Blue Steel might lead to embarrassing questions as to the true extent of the RAF's capability at the time. Therefore the date of the press day was continually delayed until 14 February 1963, by which time the squadron was fully operational with at least six missiles available. Unfortunately, the Skybolt programme had been cancelled and the press were more concerned with plans for the V-Force's future than the event being celebrated at Scampton. However, Nos. 17 and 83 Squadrons subsequently re-equipped with Blue Steels at Scampton followed by No. 139 Squadron on Victors at Wittering, their conversion beginning in October 1963, followed by No. 100 Squadron. On 21 August, an Air Ministry Nuclear Weapon Clearance for the use of Blue Steel on Quick Reaction Alert (QRA) standby was issued, although the weapons were to be unarmed and unshelled except in an

XM605 out in the cold at CFB Goose bay. The RAF's Vulcan crews regularly flew long-range flights to and from Canada. Goose Bay was regularly used as a base from where low-level flying exercises could be conducted, taking advantage of the vast areas of uninhabited land across Labrador.

emergency. Clearance for a fully armed and fuelled Blue Steel on QRA was finally issued on 16 April 1964.

The final delivery of the last of Handley Page's Victor B2s in 1962 represented the culmination of Britain's long-established plans to equip the RAF with a fully effective nuclear deterrent. By 1961, with a combined force of 144 Valiants, Victor B1s and B2s, and Vulcan B1s and B2s, Bomber Command possessed awesome striking power beyond anything imaginable during the Second World War. The first generation twenty-kiloton Blue Danube fission weapon was gradually withdrawn during 1960, Red Beard temporarily replacing it as the RAF's preferred fission weapon. Red Beard was essentially a tactical bomb, however, developed into Mk.1 (fifteen kiloton) and Mk.2 (twenty-five kiloton) versions to be carried by RAF and Fleet Air Arm tactical strike aircraft – Canberra, Scimitar, Sea Vixen and Buccaneer – although Valiants, Vulcans and Victors were capable of carrying the weapon. It was a potential 'second strike' bomb that could have been used for repeat attacks following a first strike with megaton-class weapons (assuming there was a need for a second strike after the first exchange).

The Yellow Sun Mk.1 with a yield of 500 kilotons was superseded by Yellow Sun Mk.2 beginning in February 1962, initial stocks going to Waddington. The Red

As part of the Olympus development programme, Rolls-Royce employed a Vulcan B2 as a flying test bed for the more powerful 300 series engine. One such powerplant is fitted in the outboard port bay of this aircraft as indicated by the slightly larger engine exhaust shroud. (*Courtesy Rolls-Royce*)

Snow warhead, which was also fitted to Blue Steel, was manufactured to deliver one of three different yields and it is likely that both the Blue Steel and Yellow Sun warheads were largely of the one megaton variety, the remainder being 500 kiloton. For much of the 1960s, the Yellow Sun Mk.2 became the standard freefall nuclear weapon for the Vulcan squadrons while the Scampton Wing concentrated on Blue Steel operations. The Government's unease at the prospect of relying on fixed-site ballistic missiles, which could take at least fifteen minutes to prepare for launching, prompted a search for a more suitable nuclear delivery system to replace Blue Steel towards the end of the 1960s. The difficulties and costs associated with the production of Blue Steel Mk.1 effectively killed off the Mk.2 project before it started. With the Thor missile system as a stopgap, Britain seemed destined to rely upon developing the far more advanced Blue Streak missile as the country's main nuclear deterrent for the late 1960s, though the system (similar in concept to Thor) was likely to be obsolete before it entered service.

It was at this stage that Britain again looked towards America where the Douglas GAM-87A Skybolt missile was being developed. This air-launched nuclear-tipped guided bomb was to be capable of delivering a sizeable warhead from a range in excess of 1,000 miles, far beyond the capabilities of Blue Steel. In essence, it was everything that the Air Staff had wanted from Blue Steel Mk.2. Talks with the US president at Camp David suggested that there would be no American objection to the

This post-Falklands image was taken at Waddington to illustrate the range of weaponry that the Vulcan was cleared to carry. In addition to freefall and laser-guided 1,000 lb and 2,000 lb bombs, Shrike missiles can be seen to the left and Martel ASMs to the right, with the huge Blue Steel missile in the centre. Not shown is the WE.177 tactical nuclear bomb and the Yellow Sun freefall weapon.

British purchase of Skybolts and it was also indicated that the sea-launched Polaris might also be made available should Britain be interested. The ever-increasing cost of the Blue Streak programme and the pressing fears that the weapon would be highly vulnerable to Soviet attack led to the conclusion that an updated V-Force equipped with Skybolts would be a cheaper and more credible option than relying on another non-mobile IRBM.

Consequently, Blue Streak was abandoned. Skybolt was originally designed in response to a USAF requirement for an air-launched strategic-range nuclear missile to be carried by SAC Boeing B-52s and Convair B-58s. It was established that development of the weapon would be completed to enable the first Skybolts to enter RAF service in 1966, although a new carrier for the weapons would probably be required by 1970 as the Vulcans and Victors would reach the end of their useful life at that time. Macmillan was keen to place a provisional order for 100 Skybolts, but the chancellor was rather more cautious, not least because the missile was only just beginning development.

However, following the meeting between Macmillan and Eisenhower in March 1960, a minute was issued by the US Government which stated:

> In a desire to be of assistance in improving and extending the effective life of the V-Bomber force, the United States, subject only to United States priorities, is prepared to provide Skybolt missiles minus warheads to the United Kingdom on a reimbursable basis in 1965 or thereafter. Since Skybolt is still in the early stages of development, this offer is necessarily dependent on the successful and timely completion of its development programme.

The minute also made mention of the emerging Polaris submarine-launched missile programme, stating that:

> As the United Kingdom is aware, the United States is offering at the current NATO Defence Ministers meeting to make mobile Polaris missiles minus warheads available from US production to NATO countries in order to meet Saceur's requirements for MRBM's (medium-range ballistic missiles). The United States is also offering to assist joint European production of Polaris if our preference for United States production proves unacceptable.

Given that Britain and France were the only NATO countries outside the US with a nuclear capability – and therefore the only countries able to operate the missiles – this offer was of particular significance to Britain who effectively had the luxury of a choice between two weapon systems. However, Britain continued to pursue the Skybolt project, even though American concerns over the possible success of the development programme were being expressed as early as 1961. With more than 150,000 component parts, some 60,000 of which had to function perfectly in order to launch the missile, Skybolt was a very complex piece of hardware. The first live launches in 1962 ended in failure and the US Secretary of Defense advised his British counterparts that, although they did not believe Skybolt was a technical failure, they did believe that continuing the programme would be a waste of money in view of the emergence of other delivery systems at the time such as Hound Dog and Minuteman. It was pointed out that the Skybolt missile was essentially a research programme when Britain first requested it rather than a production weapon. Consequently, the path would be open for Britain to continue development of Skybolt in association with a scaled-down American effort or to develop Skybolt in isolation, albeit by using American technology.

The only other available would be to adopt the Hound Dog missile or to participate in a multilateral force of sea-launched Polaris missiles under the terms being offered in March 1960. The Hound Dog option was quickly discounted as the weapon could

XJ783 from the Akrotiri Strike Wing, pictured during a stopover at RAF Luqa, Malta. (*Courtesy Godfrey Mangion*)

not be carried by V-Bombers and the Ministry of Defence (MoD) concluded that the options for Britain were to acquire Polaris; complete Skybolt in America; complete Skybolt in the UK; or produce a ballistic weapon in co-operation with France. It had already been agreed that the V-Force dispersal concept – whereby the bombers would leave their home bases in a wartime emergency and relocate in groups of four or two to thirty-six dispersal airfields scattered around the UK – would not be a credible option for very long without improvement. The increasing sophistication of Soviet forces meant that bombers on the ground would be at risk from attack. The best alternative to a dispersal policy would be to mount a continuous airborne alert with Skybolt-equipped bombers maintaining a round-the-clock airborne presence immune from attack. It was an expensive and technically difficult concept, but one that America was pursuing at the time. If Skybolt was abandoned, Britain would have to choose one of two expensive alternatives: either adopt an Anglo-French ballistic missile system, which would mean accepting all the disadvantages of Blue Streak again, or buy the Polaris missiles and a submarine fleet from which to launch them.

When Prime Minister Macmillan met President Kennedy at Nassau in the Bahamas during December 1962, Macmillan pressed Kennedy to continue with the Skybolt programme, but as a post-talk report stated, Kennedy, who was fairly ambivalent towards British interests, wanted to abandon the project:

The President and the Prime Minister reviewed the development programme for the Skybolt missile. The President explained that it was no longer expected that this very complex weapon system would be completed within the cost estimate or the timescale which were projected when the programme was begun. The President informed the Prime Minister that for this reason, and because of the availability to the United States of alternative weapon systems, he had decided to cancel plans for the production of Skybolt by the United States. Nevertheless, recognising the importance of the Skybolt programme for the United Kingdom, and recalling that the purpose of the offer of Skybolt in 1960 had been to assist in improving and extending the effective life of the British V-Bombers, the President expressed his readiness to continue with the development of the missile as a joint enterprise between the United States and the United Kingdom, with each country bearing equal shares of the future cost of completing development, after which the United Kingdom would be able to place a production order to meet its requirements.

This was a very generous offer to Britain, bearing in mind that Kennedy had little practical reason to provide further funds for the Skybolt programme and was not a great believer in the 'special relationship'. Macmillan recognised the value of Kennedy's offer, but the continuing doubts over technical difficulties, rising costs and delays in the delivery timescale prompted him to decline the opportunity to divert more financial responsibility on to Britain. Likewise, Macmillan could not accept Hound Dog because of the time and expense which would be involved in modifying the Vulcan and Victor to carry it. Instead, he opted for Polaris and Kennedy agreed that America would provide Polaris missiles, minus warheads, for British submarines. Consequently, Skybolt was officially cancelled by America on 31 December 1962 a few days after a test round had made a perfect launch from a B-52 over the Eglin weapons range. As far as the RAF was concerned, the programme officially ended on 3 January 1963 and having abandoned Skybolt in favour of Polaris, the future of the RAF's nuclear force had been sealed. The British airborne nuclear deterrent was to be transformed into a seaborne system.

The choice of Polaris did not immediately spell the end of the V-Force. Developing and manufacturing the missiles – and the submarines required to launch it – would require years of development before they became available. Therefore, the V-Force would have to remain viable for the time being and the Air Staff turned their attention to ways in which Bomber Command could maintain a credible nuclear deterrent until the end of the 1960s. The Air Staff concluded that beyond the mid-1960s, improvements in Russian air defences would mean it would be practically impossible to penetrate Soviet airspace at high level. The V-Force would have to attack at low level if it was to survive. Soviet radar systems had been geared towards the detection of high-flying bombers and although the range and sensitivity of their equipment was continuing to improve, radar detection was not effective at heights of

A sight only seen very rarely: the Vulcan's bomb bay loaded with a full load of twenty-one live 1,000 lb HE bombs.

around 3,000 feet or lower where radar returns merged with other forms of ground-generated clutter. However, if the V-Force was prepared to attack at a low altitude of 500 feet or less, the Soviet radar systems would probably be unable to detect them. Fears were naturally expressed that the V-Bombers would not be capable of performing a low-level penetration role, bearing in mind that they were designed for high-altitude operations. However, the BCDU at Finningley pioneered a series of test flights to prove that low-level sorties could be conducted safely and a Vulcan and Victor were sent to Libya to perform a series of ultra-low flights over the desert to demonstrate the capability further still. In any case, the Valiants that had been assigned to SACEUR had already begun low-level operations without experiencing significant problems (serious problems were to be encountered later).

The Vulcan B1A squadrons at Waddington (Nos. 44, 50 and 101), Victor B.1A squadrons at Honington (Nos. 55 and 57) and Cottesmore (Nos. 10 and 15) were assigned to low-level operations in March 1963. Training flights were normally made at 1,000 feet, a conservative figure aimed at preserving aircraft fatigue life, but every third sortie was flown at 500 feet. The Mk.2 Victors and Vulcans assumed a low-level role as of 1 May 1964. Blue Steel also had to be amended as outlined in a revised version of the original Operational Requirement: 'The Air Staff requires the further development of the Blue Steel missile to enable it to be launched from Mk.2 V-Bombers flying at the lowest possible level in the height band 250-1,000 feet.'

XM603 preparing to depart from RAF Luqa for the long flight home to RAF Waddington. XM603 was used as a trails aircraft for the Vulcan K2 tanker programme and remained at Woodford after withdrawal from use. Although Woodford has now closed, the aircraft is expected to be retained on site as a museum exhibit. (*Courtesy Godfrey Mangion*)

After a further series of trials in the UK and at Woomera, the Blue Steel missile was found to be readily capable of being launched at low level. After release, its motor was ignited and Blue Steel comfortably zoom-climbed to 17,000 feet before beginning a terminal descent to its target. Having been designed for high-altitude launch and then having had new operational profiles developed around it, Blue Steel entered RAF service primarily as a low-level weapon, requiring a completely different training programme to the one that had first been envisaged. The V-Force's main nuclear weapon, Yellow Sun Mk.2, was incapable of low-level delivery. Bombers assigned to Yellow Sun delivery were trained to make low-level penetrations followed by brief pop-up ascents to medium altitude from where the bomb could be released. This was a far from ideal situation and the Air Staff accepted that a completely new weapon would be required to suit the low-level delivery environment. Joint Naval/Air Staff Requirement NASR.1177 gave the details:

> Because of envisaged enemy counter measures and the need to change aircraft approach and delivery tactics, the existing British nuclear bombs Yellow Sun, Blue Steel and

Red Beard will be unsuitable as primary weapons beyond 1975. Moreover, with the cancellation of Skybolt as the planned replacement for Yellow Sun and the introduction of Polaris unlikely to become effective before 1970, an urgent need exists for a new bomb to maintain the United Kingdom independent deterrent during the interim period and as a supplementary capability thereafter. By 1966, the manned bomber aircraft may survive enemy defences in the European theatre and deliver a successful strike only by flying at high speed at very low level. Yellow Sun and Blue Steel are designed for release at medium/high altitude where the delivery aircraft and/or bomb is vulnerable to interception, while Red Beard cannot withstand the low-level flight environment, is limited in method of fusing and delivery, and possesses some undesirable safety restrictions when held at readiness in an operational state. Early replacement is essential. The replacement bomb must be multi-purpose by design. It must satisfy joint Naval and Air Staff requirements for carriage and delivery in current medium-bomber aircraft and planned high-performance aircraft, to exploit fully their low-level strike capability against strategic and tactical, hard and soft targets, with corresponding different warhead yields. Research and development studies show clearly that such a bomb can be produced fully within the timescale. However, to maintain an effective United Kingdom nuclear deterrent during development of the Polaris weapon system, priority is given to production of the high-yield version for the RAF medium bomber force.

This design, which became the WE.177 bomb, was to be used as a laydown weapon, either by ballistic/loft mode or by retarded (parachute) delivery. It was also to be as small and light as possible. The type B version was not to exceed 1,000 lb (it weighed 950 lb while WE.177A weighed 600 lb). The A and B designations referred to different yields of 200 kilotons and 400 kilotons. They were 144 inches long and had a carcass diameter of 16.5 inches and a tail-fin span of 24 inches. Deliveries of the WE.177A began in September 1966 and trials were conducted with a Vulcan B2 at Cottesmore. The WE.177C was a 10 kiloton naval derivative of the same weapon carried by Buccaneers and Sea Harriers until the weapon was withdrawn in 1992. The aircraft in the amended low-level Vulcan and Victor force were modified with an updated ECM fit, sidescan radar, roller maps, ground position indicator equipment and terrain-following radar. The all-white, anti-flash paint was replaced on their upper surfaces by a disruptive grey/green camouflage, the first aircraft so finished being Vulcan XH505 that emerged from Hawker Siddeley Aviation's Bitteswell plant on 24 March 1964.

Therefore, the V-Force was assigned to high-low-high delivery profiles with a low-level phase of up to 1,000 nm in the extreme case (for training sorties this would normally be 350-500 nm). All-weather operations were practiced and the height of the low-level phase of an operational sortie would be left to the discretion of the aircraft captain: in poor visibility conditions this might be 1,000 feet, but in good

Air show performances provided an opportunity for the public to see the Vulcan at close quarters. This particular aircraft is pictured during a low fly-by with the bomb bay doors open, revealing the capacious weapons bay and additional fuel tank suspended inside. Unusually, the landing gear is also extended.

weather it could be as low as an incredible fifty feet. For delivery of Yellow Sun, and possibly of Red Beard if required for a second strike, the captain would fly a pop-up manoeuvre to 12,000 feet. Consequently, the unmistakable shape and sound of Valiants, Vulcans and Victors became a regular part of rural life in the UK. The V-Force crews would descend from above the clouds and thunder over Britain's hills and valleys at 500 feet or lower in specific low-flying areas much to the surprise of those who lived underneath the new low-level air corridor that was set-up for V-Force training.

The Vulcan's long and distinguished service career began to draw towards an end during the early months of 1982. Although the aircraft's key role had ended in 1970 when Britain's independent nuclear deterrent had shifted to the Royal Navy, the Vulcan soldiered on, tasked with tactical strike duties armed with the WE.177 bomb. No longer at the forefront of the country's offensive capabilities, the Vulcan was often regarded as a redundant relic of the Cold War and destined for a well-earned retirement. In fact, the Vulcan played a key part in the RAF's offensive capabilities. Still very much in the nuclear delivery business, the Vulcan squadrons – distributed between Scampton and Waddington – also had a conventional bombing capability and with their arsenal of WE.177s, the Vulcan force presented the East with a formidable presence. It was to assume a pseudo-tactical role that fitted neatly between the Navy's Polaris long-range strike missiles and RAF Germany's tactical strike Buccaneers (later replaced by Phantoms and Jaguars). Additionally, a handful of Vulcans were modified to undertake a maritime radar reconnaissance role, enabling the Victors which were performing that task to be withdrawn and converted into refuelling tanker aircraft.

Vulcan accidents were extremely rare, although some mishaps did occur, such as the loss of XM576 that veered off the runway after making an asymmetric approach during May 1965. It was written off and scrapped.

In order to disable Argentine anti-aircraft radar systems, the RAF's Black Buck Vulcans were equipped with AGM-45 Shrike missiles, two of which could be carried on each wing pylon.

More than twenty years elapsed before any prospect of a replacement for the Vulcan's capabilities finally emerged. Finally, during the early months of 1982, the end of the Vulcan's long story was in sight. The first Panavia Tornado bombers were delivered to the RAF and the process of replacing the Vulcan could begin. During April, the first Tornado to carry No. 9 Squadron's unit markings appeared at Waddington, ceremoniously placed adjacent to one of the squadron's Vulcans that they were now dispensing with. The Vulcan units at Scampton slowly wound down their operations, the aircraft gradually disappearing to museums, other RAF stations (for crash and rescue training) or to end their days being dismantled for scrap. Even No. 27 Squadron's reconnaissance Vulcans flew their last missions and with only the surviving Vulcans at Waddington, it would be only a matter of weeks before the mighty Vulcan would be replaced in its entirely by the Tornado. But while the steady progress to retirement was taking place, events were unfolding thousands of miles away in the South Atlantic that would have a remarkable last minute effect on the Vulcan's story.

The story of the Vulcan's vital contribution to the Falklands conflict is well known. It was also ironic that the only occasion on which the Vulcan was ever called upon to release bombs in anger was one that came in the very last weeks of the aircraft's service life. It was also ironic that having been designed as a nuclear bomber, the Vulcan was pressed into action as a conventional HE bomber. But then, it could be argued that the Vulcan had been 'in use' continually, performing the very role for which it was designed as a deterrent asset. Had the Vulcan ever been called upon to release nuclear weapons in anger, then deterrence would demonstrably have failed and with it the Vulcan. The fact that the Vulcan never did deliver its deadly load into the Soviet Union illustrates that the Vulcan, and the V-Force as a whole, was an unqualified success.

The Falklands War also caused the Vulcan's scheduled withdrawal to be delayed, especially when the RAF's Victor refuelling tanker fleet was so heavily overworked. The Victors were heavily committed to the Falklands and although the conversion of VC10s into tankers was by now under way, there was a short term requirement for more tankers. While the USAF were supporting RAF operations in the UK with their Boeing KC-135 tankers, it was decided to swiftly convert a number of Hercules and Vulcan aircraft into single point refuelling tankers. The initial proposal sent to British Aerospace at Woodford was to install a hose drum unit (HDU) in the aft section of the Vulcan's bomb bay, the Vulcan then being designated B(K).2. However, this idea was dropped, mainly because of the resulting proximity of the receiver to the tanker aircraft. It was felt that for safety reasons the HDU should be placed as far aft as possible to provide adequate separation between the tanker and receiver. The ECM bay was identified as being a suitable location – the internal equipment being unnecessary for tanker operations – and this would also allow an additional fuel tank to be installed in the bomb bay.

An aerial image of Port Stanley's runway after the first Vulcan strike. The all-important bomb crater can be seen, almost perfectly placed on the runway, rendering the runway useless for Argentinean fast jet operations.

Just seven weeks after the tanker conversion programme had begun on 18 June, the first converted aircraft made its initial flight. An interim CA release was granted on 23 June and the first aircraft was delivered to the RAF on the same day. Although greatly valued, the Vulcan K.2 did not enjoy a particularly long career with the RAF as although the Vulcan proved to be an excellent tanker aircraft, the hose drum units had been out of production for some time. The Mk.17 HDUs fitted to the Vulcans had been allocated to VC10s which were being converted to tankers. As the VC10s were slowly completed, the HDUs were removed from the Vulcans, starting with XJ825 on 4 May 1983. Finally, on 31 March 1984, No. 50 Squadron, the last operational Vulcan unit, disbanded at Waddington, leaving their fleet of six K.2s and three B.2s to be delivered to museums and fire dumps. The MoD decided to retain XL426 on a temporary basis for air display appearances and this aircraft was ultimately replaced by XH558, which had been withdrawn for fire training at Marham. This Vulcan continued to fly purely for air show demonstrations until 1992 when the Ministry of Defence reluctantly accepted that the support infrastructure necessary to keep the aircraft flying would soon be unavailable and it was offered for sale.

Right: The V-Force regularly practised its dispersal techniques with groups of four or two aircraft flying out to designated dispersal sites. Four aircraft are seen here on RAF Finningley's Operational Readiness Platform (ORP). Finningley's ORP was the only such installation to feed onto the runway from the right-hand side.

Below: Having earned the distinction of flying the longest bombing mission in the history of British military aviation, XM607 is now on public display outside RAF Waddington in Lincolnshire. Sadly, there seems to be no prospect of housing this historic aircraft indoors. (*Courtesy Mike Freer*)

After the conclusion of Operation Corporate, four of the participating Vulcans made a formation flight around parts of the UK, led by the now famous XM607. To the rear is XM597, the Black Buck aircraft that made an unplanned stay in Brazil.

On 23 March 1993, the aircraft made the very last RAF Vulcan flight, making the short journey from Waddington to its new and private owners at Bruntingthorpe in Leicestershire. This was not to be the end of the Vulcan story. On 18 October 2007, the mighty Vulcan took to the air yet again after a successful charity campaign succeeded in getting XH558 restored to flying condition. Thanks to generous public support, the aircraft continued to appear at air shows across the UK beyond 2012 – the Vulcan's sixtieth year. Few people could have imagined back in 1952 that the RAF's new strategic nuclear bomber would become an icon of public affection, but the Vulcan's size, sound and sheer presence was enough to make this particular bomber much more than a warplane. It was and is a shining example of British scientific knowhow and ingenuous engineering skill. Also, it was undoubtedly beautiful.

CHAPTER SIX

Victor Ludorum

The Handley Page Victor was the last of the three V-Bomber types to enter RAF service and the last to be withdrawn decades later. It might be imagined that the Victor was something of a latecomer to the V-Bomber story, but history records that the original design for this aircraft was created before the others. It was during 1945 that Sir Fredrick Handley Page first turned his attention to the RAF's post-war requirements and the possibility of creating a new bomber. He had learned of English Electric's plans to build a new jet-powered tactical bomber (the Canberra) as a projected replacement for the beloved wartime Mosquito. Sir Fredrick concluded that a replacement for the Avro Lincoln would probably also be sought in due course and on 14 June, he issued a memorandum to his design team (Messrs. Stafford, Radcliffe and Lee) requesting that they investigate the possibility of producing a new jet bomber. Sir Fredrick specified two types of bomber, one being a 60,000 lb machine powered by two Avon engines while the other would be a 100,000 lb aircraft with four such engines.

Drawing upon experience with the company's HP.75 Manx tailless research aircraft, he also suggested that both aircraft should feature forty-degree swept wings. The diminutive Manx aircraft had been built in 1943 in order to explore research data produced by Dr Gustav Victor Lachmann, a former Luftwaffe pilot who had become chief designer for both Schneider and Albatros companies before joining Handley Page in 1929. Although living and working in England, he never applied for naturalisation and was interned on the Isle of Man during the Second World War. His knowledge and skills were not forgotten and in 1943, permission was given for Lachmann to communicate with his former employers and the swept-wing Manx aircraft was a direct result of this arrangement. Lachmann's deputy at Handley Page (Godfrey Lee) went to Germany in 1945 as part of an Allied intelligence mission designed to investigate the huge quantities of captured Nazi research data and aircraft hardware that had been gathered as the Allies moved across Germany.

Lee discussed a variety of design concepts with aerodynamicists at the Volkenrode experimental establishment and learned a great deal about swept-wing design. Lee

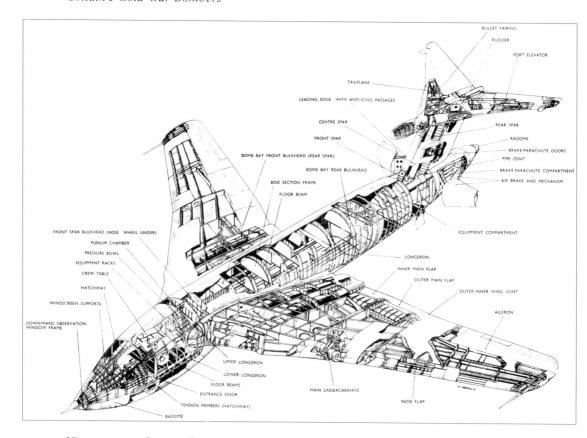

Victor cutaway diagram illustrating the internal structure of the airframe and the interior of the weapons bay and crew compartment.

returned to England with great enthusiasm and new knowledge, but soon feel ill with pneumonia forcing him into hospital. During his stay there, he devised an ambitious fifty-ton and fifty-seat jet airliner that the company eventually designated as the HP.72. Lee later admitted that the design was rather clumsy and that it would not have translated into a viable airliner. However, the designation was retained as a convenient 'cover' for a military design based on Sir Fredrick's request memorandum for new bomber proposals. The result was a 90,000 lb bomber with an alternative transport role powered by four Avon engines. The HP.72A featured straight swept wings, wingtip-mounted rudders, a small swept fin and a swept tailplane. This became the basis for a more detailed proposal that was eventually renamed as the HP.80 and Handley Page duly sent a basic proposal document to Stuart Scott-Hall, the Government's Principle Director of Technical Development.

At this stage, the Air Staff were looking at ideas for new bomber designs and the overly-ambitious OR.230 bomber concept was being considered. It is difficult to

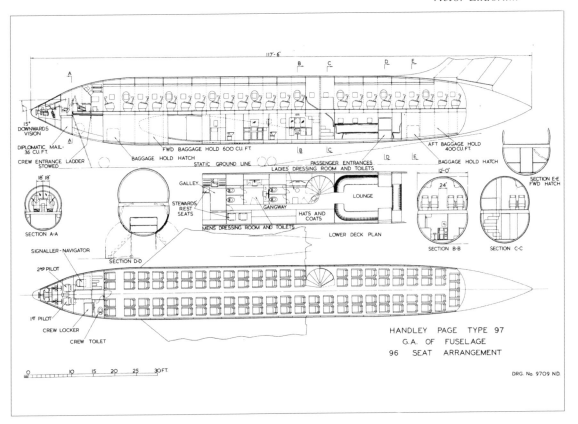

Many developments of the Victor were proposed, but none progressed beyond the concept stage. The HP.97 illustrated was a proposed airliner design that embraced the overall design of the Victor's fuselage and tail, and retained the Victor's crescent wing. Like similar proposed developments of Avro's Vulcan, it received little interest from potential buyers.

establish how much influence Handley Page had on this process, but it is known that the RAF's Director of Operational requirements visited Handley Page's Cricklewood factory in July 1946. Also, a number of MoS research staff followed a few weeks later to discuss the new H2S Mk.9 radar that was being proposed for whatever new bomber was pursued. This bulky piece of equipment would inevitably affect the overall design of the bomber that carried it and undoubtedly affected Handley Page's development of the basic HP.80 design. However, the most fundamental change to the original HP.80 layout was the wing. The design was swiftly changed from a relatively simple swept design into an unusual progressive sweep that reduced in degree towards the wingtips. This new innovation – soon referred to as the 'crescent wing' – was created in order to offer a compromise solution to the conflicting needs for stability and control at both high and low speeds. The inner swept wing surfaces were better suited to high-speed flight, but the less swept outer portions of the wing would reduce the risk of tip stall problems and provide better low-speed stability. Designer Godfrey Lee explained in some detail his reasons for adopting the crescent wing for the HP.80:

No layout or design formula is the best for all specifications. The Victor specification called for long range with an appreciable load, a high cruising Mach number and a high cruising altitude. It appeared from this that the required characteristics were: a moderate or large aspect ratio in order to get long range and high cruising altitude; a high sweepback to permit a reasonable thickness/chord ratio on the wing and yet to enable the specified high Critical Mach Number to be obtained. To combine these desiderata, however, is unfortunately inimical to good stalling behaviour because such a wing is liable to tip stall. The term 'tip stall' means that when a wing is brought to a high incidence the stall begins at or near the tips. This is bad on a swept wing since loss of lift on the rearward-disposed tips leads to a nose-up pitching moment or a self-stalling tendency and the usual wing dropping danger with a tip stall… The crescent wing is a working compromise between the requirements for performance and for good tip stalling. Otherwise, the choice is between high sweep and low aspect ratio, or moderate aspect ratio with moderate or small sweep and correspondingly thin wings. In the crescent wing the aspect ratio is as large as necessary for performance and high sweep is obtained over the centre wing, permitting a good thickness/chord ratio which is important structurally and for stowage reasons. By reducing the tip sweep, the tip stall problem is eased and the design penalty – a thin outer wing – is not too severe. It was for these reasons that we started work on a wing whose sweep varied with span…

Typical of early wing tunnel evidence in favour of the crescent wing were tests on an ordinary straight wing of 45 degrees leading edge sweepback and a crescent wing with leading edge sweeps of fifty degrees at the root, forty degrees at the middle section and thirty degrees at the tip. The tests showed the superiority of the crescent layout over the straight wing in that the stability near the stall was always better in the crescent case. Another point was that as well as better tip stalling properties, the crescent wing actually had a higher root sweep than the straight wing. Despite the reduced sweep at the tips, the highly swept root does not want to stall so there remains, even for the crescent wing, a tip stall tendency. This can be brought within reasonable bounds by the careful choice of wing section, particularly camber. The wing/fuselage junction may in some cases be arranged so that it tends to promote a stall at the root. Aerodynamically there is nothing very special about the stability and control of the crescent wing for flight cases where the flow is un-separated, i.e. not near the stall. It acts very much like a straight swept wing having about the same average sweep. It is important, however, that the tip sweep is not reduced too much as otherwise there may be a loss or even a reversal of aileron control at high Mach number. On the other hand, a loss of tip sweep is beneficial for aileron power at low Mach number and especially near the stall. Sweepback has a profound effect on the dynamic stability of an aircraft; that is to say, the manoeuvre margin is largely influenced by sweep when, as always the case in practice, the wing is flexible. Here again the crescent wing offers a useful compromise solution. Just as aerodynamically at the stall, the crescent formula permits the use of a root with more sweep than would otherwise be possible, so it does aerolastically. The reduced outer sweep is beneficial in itself and the crescent planform leads to a favourable twist over the centre wing.

Lee also explained the choice of the Victor's wing shape in relation to other potential solutions:

The Victor specification called for a long-range aircraft carrying a good load, having a high critical Mach number and a high cruising altitude. There are currently three different solutions to this problem: the high aspect ratio layout with engines usually installed in external pods, favoured by the Americans and especially by the Boeing company; the delta layout and the crescent planform. Assuming that the critical mach number is equal in all cases considered, the value of the lift/drag ratio that can be obtained follows from the way in which all remaining problems are solved. With regard to tip stall, the engine nacelles help the podded layout because, apparently, they direct the air in a direction more or less parallel to the chord. They reduce the local angle of incidence near the tip at high angles of attack and the engine supports act partly as 'fences'. In a typical podded layout, the outer nacelles are quite near the tip. The delta layout gets over its stall problems by using its lower aspect ratio. The stalling behaviour of the crescent wing has already been discussed. It may be concluded that, approximately, the total drag of the delta is some 10 per cent higher than for the other two layouts.

No proper weight estimate can be made, but it is possible to consider weight trends. The podded wing has small thickness and torque box area, but has very good weight relief due to the engine disposition, small wing area and unbroken structure. The delta wing has large thickness and torque box area, but small engine weight relief and much the largest gross area and a high rib weight. From this it would be expected that the delta wing weight would be highest. The crescent wing has moderate thickness, moderate torque box area and moderate wing surface area combined with small weight relief. The fuselage weight for the podded aircraft is probably largest because the undercarriage has to be stowed in it. The delta fuselage weight is probably the lightest because it is a small one. The weight of the delta tail should be the lightest since there is no tailplane. Combining all of the above tendencies, it may be concluded that none of the layouts appears to have a marked advantage. The crescent wing and the podded aeroplane have a fairly similar weight distribution; the delta weight distribution is different and what it loses on the wing it gains on the fuselage and the tail. A 10 per cent improvement in lift/drag ratio (as produced by the crescent wing) does not perhaps at first seem very much. But at long ranges where the useful load may be quite small – only 5 or 10 per cent of the all-up weight – then 10 per cent of the fuel adds 50 or 100 per cent more to the load that can be carried. Thus, for a long-range aeroplane, an extra 10 per cent on lift/drag ratio is undoubtedly worthwhile.

Lee's conclusions were undoubtedly correct and the HP.80 represented the best solution to meet the Air Staff's rather less ambitious B.35/46 specification that emerged in early 1947. At the time, there was no guarantee that the proposed layout would translate into an effective bomber aircraft. While Avro firmly believed that their delta design was the most promising solution, the Air Staff and the scientists at Farnborough were unable or unwilling to pinpoint any significant advantages or disadvantages attributable to either the Avro aircraft or Handley Page's. Meanwhile, Vickers had concluded that both designs were too ambitious and proceeded to produce their conventional Type 880 (Valiant). However, there was a stark contrast between Handley Page's bomber and the competing design produced by Avro.

Avro's delta wing enjoyed a low aspect ratio – the ratio of the span to the chord – which was offset by a very large wing area. A more conventional swept wing is likely to stall first at the tips leading to an unstable pitching problem caused by the wing tip's position aft of the aircraft's centre of gravity. The HP.80's crescent wing featured a greater sweep towards the wing root, meaning that the inner wing was likely to stall first, creating a much more stable situation. Likewise, as Lee explained, the sweep wing tips are well aft of the wing root, which means that the outer wing's lift can create a tendency to twist. By contrast, the crescent wing brought the outer wing's lift further forward, thereby lessening the tendency to twist.

Handley Page's wing design required a thin outer section and a much thicker inboard section which enabled the design team to bury the four engines and main undercarriage units inside the wing root. Naturally, this created a streamlined and drag-free arrangement, but the massive air intakes either side of the fuselage created a significant loss of standing thrust – the air flow concentrated itself at the outer corner of the intake – and this was only restored when the aircraft began to roll forward on its take-off run. Lee later commented that '…perhaps we were the only firm brave enough or daft enough to do it'. But despite some minor difficulties, Handley Page believed that the crescent wing was a much better choice than Avro's delta wing. The Avro bomber would not be able to attain the same altitude although it was accepted that as more powerful engines became available, the shortfall could be made up. On the other hand, the HP.80 was unlikely to be capable of carrying a significantly larger bomb load, although this was not a major consideration for the Air Ministry. The new bomber was to be created almost exclusively for the carriage of a single 10,000 lb atomic bomb and conventional high explosive capacity was regarded as a secondary consideration, albeit a very important one.

Victor K.Mk.1A XH651 began its service career as a standard bomber before becoming one of the first batch of aerial tanker conversions, equipped only with wing-mounted refuelling pods. Later aircraft also carried a bomb bay-mounted HDU. (*Courtesy Handley Page Association*)

After Specification B.35/46 was issued, the MoS and Air Ministry were soon in possession of a number of design proposals that were submitted in response. The Avro and Handley Page designs were identified as being the most promising even though they were also the most ambitious. It seemed inevitable that a choice would ultimately be made between one or the other, but the decision simply never came. Both had great potential and there was no logical reason for abandoning either. In the traditions of typical British compromise – and with industrial policy firmly in mind – the Air Staff finally agreed to order both aircraft into production. While Avro developed its aircraft, Handley Page continued work on its HP .80 design. The basic proportions of the aircraft were largely dictated by two factors. The most obvious was the size and weight of the 10,000 lb atomic bomb that was the aircraft's raison d'être. The second was the H2S Mk.9 radar that was being developed as a replacement for the wartime vintage H2S radar. The new equipment promised to deliver more than twice the accuracy of the old H2S, but its scanner was some six feet in width, designed to rotate on a horizontal axis under the HP.80's nose. This, together with the bomb, dictated the aircraft's overall size.

As a precaution against possible delays in developing the new radar system, a visual bomb-aiming position was incorporated into the nose, although access to the glazed panels was only possible through a cramped gap between the pilot and co-pilot's seats. Initially, a rear crew member was to have been housed in a separate pressurised cabin at the rear of the new bomber's fuselage, tasked with the control of electronic countermeasures equipment. Access to and from the position was to have been achieved by means of a tunnel (in much the same way as the Convair B-36 was configured), but the sheer size and bulk of the atomic bomb indicated that there would be insufficient room for a tunnel to run through the bomb bay. The idea was finally dropped in favour of a rearwards-facing 'Red Steer' radar scanner that was remotely operated from the flight deck. The main crew cabin was designed to be pressurised, but a great deal of effort was devoted to escape systems for the crew. In the late 1940s, little information was available on the practicality of bailing out from an aircraft at 50,000 feet. Therefore, it seemed logical to create a system that enabled the entire crew cabin to be jettisoned in an emergency, breaking away from the bomber's fuselage to descend by parachute. The crew members remaining attached to specially-designed seats which could withstand a high impact of up to 25g.

Handley Page invested a great deal of time and money on the concept and in theory it would have worked well. Fins were to be deployed to stabilise the ejected compartment and huge braking parachutes to slow the cabin's descent, the final shock of impact being absorbed by the collapse of the nose radar compartment and the special seats. However, the escape system was complicated and expensive, and after some initial model trials (and plans to conduct test drops from a Lincoln bomber) the idea was dropped in favour of conventional ejection seats for the pilot and co-pilot. The three rear crew members, situated behind the pilots in a slightly raised, rearwards-facing compartment, did not have the luxury of ejection seats, even though Martin Baker successfully demonstrated that seats could be fitted. The Air Ministry concluded that the complexity and cost of seats for the rear crew was outweighed by the very slim possibility they would ever be required. It was believed that the pilots would be capable of maintaining control of the aircraft in an emergency until the rear crew had escaped from their seats and bailed out through the crew door on the port side of the forward fuselage. History demonstrated that although ejection seats for all the crew would have been an ideal solution, the Air Staff's thinking was sound with hardly any catastrophic incidents occurring through the bomber's service career. The only evidence of the initial escape capsule concept was to be found in the finalised structure of the aircraft, the crew compartment being attached to the main fuselage by four large bolts where the explosive releases would have been fitted.

Handley Page received an ITP (Instruction to Proceed) on 1 January 1948 and serious design work got underway. Almost immediately, the early design drawings were changed in order to abandon the unusual wingtip-mounted fins that had first been proposed. Sir Fredrick Handley Page feared that asymmetric shock waves on

The Handley Page HP.88 VX330 pictured at Brough, prior to being transported to Carnaby for its maiden flight. (*Courtesy BAE Systems*)

the fins might cause the aircraft to yaw and so a conventional and heavier centrally-mounted tail unit was substituted. Initially, the tailplanes were to be positioned low on the fin structure, but they were later shifted to the top of the fin in order to avoid the aircraft's jet efflux and the wing's slipstream. An all-moving tailplane was proposed, but this was changed to a fixed section incorporating conventional elevators, thereby eliminating the need for the ailerons to act in unison to create pitch control. The huge tailplane structure was virtually identical in size to the main wings of a Hunter fighter.

In order to explore the characteristics of the HP.80's design, Handley Page chose to construct an unpowered flying scale model of the aircraft designated as the HP.87. The one-third-scale radio-controlled glider promised to give the design team plenty of useful data, but on its first flight it crashed and was written-off. Subsequently, it was agreed that a more ambitious model would be constructed. This was the HP.88, a simple aircraft that would be jet powered. It was designed almost exclusively to investigate the flying characteristics of the new crescent wing layout (and to a lesser extend the tailplane layout). The most inexpensive solution was to attach the scaled-down wings to the fuselage of a Supermarine Attacker, although this was later substituted for a Supermarine 510. With Handley Page's Cricklewood factory already extremely busy, the project was handed to General Aircraft Ltd at Feltham, a company that was then taken over by Blackburn. The unique HP.88 (VX330) was finally completed at Brough and after a series of engine runs and taxi trials, it was dismantled and transported to Carnaby where a huge wartime-era runway was available.

The aircraft made its first short flight on 21 June 1951 in the hands of Blackburn's chief test pilot G. R. I. Parker. The concept of producing a flying scale model made good sense, but in practice the project was expensive and time consuming. Supporting the HP.88 inevitably drew resources away from the full-scale HP.80 and both projects continued to progress independently of each other, so much so that when the HP.80's wing was revised in shape – with the outer leading edge 'king' moving inboard and the wing root reshaped – the smaller HP.88 remained unmodified and so the two aircraft bore little resemblance to each other.

The HP.88 was a troublesome aircraft from the outset. Test pilot Parker reported that the aircraft suffered from pitch instability so that even a small bump of turbulence would cause the aircraft to enter into a series of porpoising oscillations which became more serious as speeds increased. The problem was solved by attaching a light alloy angle bracket to the upper surface of the tailplane's leading edge. With a second strip added to the underside, the aircraft was stable at speeds of up to 430 knots. With the handling problem largely solved, the aircraft was flown to Stansted to conduct a series of airspeed calibration flights before being prepared to appear at the 1951 SBAC Show. The first of these flights was made on 26 August and after returning to Stansted, Handley Page's test pilot Duggie Bloomfield positioned VX330 for a fast, straight run over the airfield at 300 feet. Suddenly, the aircraft began to pitch up and down and then broke up over the airfield, completely disintegrating before Bloomfield had time to bail out. The aircraft had flown a total of only fourteen hours and although it had provided some useful information for Handley Page, there was no appetite for building another, especially as development of the full-scale HP.80 was making good progress.

As mentioned previously, the full-scale HP.80 design was revised following wind tunnel tests at Farnborough where it was discovered that the aircraft's critical Mach number – the speed at which drag begins to increase rapidly – was around Mach 0.8 instead of the expected 0.875. The outer wing chord was increased by 20 per cent and the outer 'kink' was moved inboard. Leading edge slats (referred to at the time as 'nose flaps') were introduced in order to resolve the wing tip stalling issues and the tailplane was given dihedral in order to effectively increase the fin area. On 28 April 1948, the Ministry of Supply awarded Handley Page a contract to build two HP.80 prototypes, both powered by Metropolitan-Vickers F.9 engines (this later became the Sapphire). Construction began at Cricklewood and in the new experimental shop at Park Street in early 1951. The first aircraft was to be a simple 'flying shell' aerodynamic test vehicle while the second would be a fully equipped version. With no clear advantages between Avro's and Handley Page's designs, a production order was placed in 1952 for twenty-five Avro 698s and twenty-five HP.80s.

Handley Page introduced many new manufacturing techniques during the programme and seriously considered using a honeycomb sandwich construction with stress-bearing skins separated by a honeycomb material such as Dufaylite, held together by adhesive. Research eventually revealed that the preferred adhesive (Araldite) lost some of its strength in high humidity conditions and so the idea was subsequently dropped although it demonstrated how Handley Page were considering manufacturing techniques which would later become a routine part of aerospace technology. The basic concept of sandwich construction did survive, however, and the HP.80 incorporated a great deal of construction which comprised of light alloy sheet which was spot-welded to a light alloy corrugated core. This saved a great deal of weight as conventional stringers were not necessary and the sandwich could easily be riveted or bolted to wing ribs or fuselage frames. The process required more than 500,000 individual spot-welds per aircraft and each one was X-rayed in order that stringent quality control was ensured.

The fuselage was manufactured in three main sections comprising of the front, centre and rear portions to which the tail unit and wings were attached. The central wing spar box was well forward of the aircraft's centre of gravity that ensured that the bomb bay needed only to carry the weight of the bomb load. The bomb load would then be attached to four girders anchored to heavy box frames. The two bomb doors retracted inwards, the bomb bay being some five feet longer than the equivalent bay in Avro's 698. It also enjoyed twice the capacity of 698's bomb bay and while the massive Boeing B-52 could carry a 34,000 lb bomb load, the HP.80 could, if necessary, lift a staggering forty-eight 1,000 lb HE bombs.

Construction of the aircraft was divided into a multitude of small components, contrasting with Avro's preference for a smaller number of larger components. Handley Page's approach enabled different parts of the aircraft to be manufactured at their Cricklewood factory and at the Colney Street and Park Street facilities attached to Radlett airfield in Hertfordshire. Final assembly was set up at Radlett and the prototype's first flight was planned to take place there. However, the MoS decided that the new bomber should be afforded the safety of a 10,000 feet runway at Boscombe Down and the first HP.80 was partially dismantled and transported to Wiltshire by road. The task was far from simple. Secrecy was paramount and a great deal of planning was required with numerous surveys necessary to ensure that the huge load could be transported safely, especially through troublesome areas such as the roundabouts on the North Circular Road. Even scale models were built to explore the best methods of getting the HP.80 through Greater London's road network, eventually leading to various sections of the route being 'modified' by bulldozer. Seven trial runs were performed, culminating in a 'dress rehearsal' using a wooden mock-up on a Queen Mary trailer. Finally, the genuine aircraft departed from Radlett on 25 May, heavily disguised with tarpaulins, complete with a bogus ship name *Geleypandhy Southampton* painted on the load's side. No one ventured to explain why the anagram of 'Handley Page' had been spelled incorrectly.

After an overnight stop at the start of the Great West Road, the convoy arrived at Boscombe Down on the morning of 25 May after another delay caused by one of the route's bulldozers that had broken down blocking the route. Some manual spadework finally cleared the convoy's path and after a truncated six-hour journey, the aircraft was ready for reassembly. Handley Page's team wryly pointed out that the HP.80 would be capable of flying back to Radlett in as many minutes. Reassembly of the prototype was delayed when it was discovered that the absence of radar equipment in the nose had shifted the aircraft's centre of gravity beyond its aft limit. Half a ton of scrap iron plates were procured and bolted under the flight deck's pressurised floor to restore balance and a similar 'fix' was incorporated into the second aircraft. A 42-inch fuselage stretch combined with the installed radar equipment was subsequently incorporated into later aircraft. Work continued with great urgency, Handley Page's team being eager to beat Avro to the first flight stage and in order to ensure that the aircraft was able to appear at the 1950 SBAC Show.

There was still no assurance of further orders and there was always a possibility that the MoS might favour Avro's design if Handley Page could not get the HP.80 into the air and demonstrate its abilities at the earliest opportunity. But more difficulties were to emerge and tragedy hit the programme when a fire broke out during hydraulic tests. A number of the test team were covered with burning hydraulic fluid and Eddie Eyles died in hospital a few days later. The accident was a major setback and it was compounded further still when the powered flying controls failed to function correctly, creating another delay of some six weeks. By this stage, Avro's 698 had made its first flight and the opportunity to appear at Farnborough had gone.

Finally, after a long and troublesome development programme and many months of frantic preparation, the first prototype HP.80 (WB771) made its first taxi run a week before Christmas.

Faster runs were then conducted, but Handley Page's chief test pilot, Squadron Leader Hedley George Hazelden, was unable to attempt short hops into the air due to heavy rain. Hazelden had spent a great deal of time learning to handle the Sapphire engines in a Hastings test bed aircraft – and by flying a Sapphire-engined Canberra – but the weather delays enabled him to spend more time becoming accustomed to HP.80's systems. On Christmas Eve, the weather at Boscombe Down had improved. Designers Godfrey Lee and Charles Joy swiftly drove down to Wiltshire from Radlett arriving at Boscombe Down as Hazelden began to start up WB771. He described the ensuing events:

Right: 1. Sixty years after the Vulcan first flew, XH558 is still flying. In civilian hands, the mighty bomber is pictured approaching the former RAF Finningley where the aircraft now resides as it did forty years ago.

Below: 2. Magnificent colour image from the 1950s showing three Canberra B.Mk.2 aircraft early in the type's service life. Like many early Canberras, the aircraft are finished in an overall sprayed silver paint scheme that was soon replaced by camouflage.

3. The Canberra TT.Mk.18 was a direct replacement for the elderly Meteor TT.20, operated by both the RAF and FAA. Former RAF Canberra B2 aircraft were converted for the specialist role during the early 1970s. These Canberras were usually equipped with underwing Rushton target pods (as illustrated) or occasionally flown 'clean' as radar tracking targets.

4. The former world altitude record holder WK163 ended its military career with the Royal Aircraft Establishment, engaged on a variety of equipment trials. It was sold to a private buyer and remains airworthy in the UK on the civilian register. (*Courtesy Mike Freer*)

Above: 5. Skybolt AGM trials were conducted both in the US and in the UK at Avro's Woodford facility. The Vulcan was well suited to the Skybolt thanks to its strong structure and high undercarriage. Sadly, the missile was not suited to the aircraft due to its visual navigational alignment requirements.

Right: 6. A rare photograph of the Vulcan delivering its maximum load of 21 x 1,000 lb HE bombs over the Jurby Range off the Isle of Man.

7. XM648 wearing the markings of No. 9 Squadron pictured returning to its home base at Waddington. The station's nuclear bomb storage area can be seen in the distance. (*Courtesy Terry Senior*)

8. XM652 was the first Vulcan to be painted in wraparound disruptive camouflage. Only a handful of aircraft were camouflaged in this fashion for participation in Red Flag exercises in the US. (*Courtesy Terry Senior*)

9. XJ825 pictured during a deployment to RAF Coningsby while repairs were made to the runway at No. 50 Squadron's home base at Waddington. Just visible is the sensor wire extending from the Hose Drum Unit. The sensor was linked to a light in the cockpit alerting the pilot when contact with the ground was made. (*Courtesy Terry Senior*)

10. Vulcan K.Mk.2 XL445 with landing gear down and air brakes extended. The patched paintwork on the tail indicates a number of changes between different Vulcan squadrons towards the end of the aircraft's service life. (*Courtesy Terry Senior*)

11. The RAF's last Vulcan, XH558, low over the Norfolk countryside. As of 2012, the aircraft was still airworthy, much to the delight of Vulcan fans across the country.

12. XH558 on its landing run at RAF Waddington, air brakes deployed.

13. Remarkably, even in 2012, the stirring sight and sound of a Vulcan returning to Finningley was still to be found on many summer weekend afternoons. More than forty years after XH558 first operated from the airfield with the RAF's 230 OCU, it remains here in the very same hangar, now part of Doncaster-Sheffield Airport.

14. Rare colour image of a Victor B.Mk.2 pictured with its Blue Steel missile. The aircraft wears the markings of No. 139 (Jamaica) Squadron that was based at RAF Wittering.

15. XL191 was one of numerous Victor B2 aircraft that were stored at Hawker Siddeley's Woodford facility after withdrawal from their strategic strike role. Most were subsequently refurbished and modified for further service as refuelling tankers. This aircraft retains the Wittering Wing markings on its tail. (*Courtesy Richard Muir collection*)

16. Although designed as a bomber, the Victor became an equally important asset as a refuelling tanker. Ironically, by the 1970s, the Victor was a vital part of the RAF's fighter operations, supporting many air defence missions, particularly the short-legged Lightning that required Victor support for almost every sortie.

17. A Victor pilot's view of a refuelling rendezvous, the refuelling probe plugged into the hose basket from the lead Victor. The 'traffic lights' on the open HDU fairing enabled refuelling manoeuvres to be undertaken in complete radio silence if necessary. (*Courtesy Richard Muir collection*)

18. Even after conversion to refuelling tanker standard, the Victor retained its futuristic sleek lines. Some aircraft, including this example, eventually had the bombardier's glazed panels replaced by cheaper and more simple metal sheeting when repairs were undertaken.

21. The Fleet Air Arm was keen to show its new Scimitars to the public at every opportunity. Successive SBAC Farnborough shows included displays by numerous Scimitars, often in large formations, as illustrated by this three-ship flypast with 'everything down'.

22. A rare colour image of a pre-production NA.39 trials aircraft ready to be launched by catapult. Note the raised engine exhaust blast plate behind the aircraft.

Opposite above: 19. XH672 was the last Victor to fly in RAF service making its last flight on 30 April 1993 with Handley Page's Victor test pilot Johnny Allam onboard for this last historic flight.

Opposite below: 20. The final time that a Victor got airborne was during May 2009 when XM715 was subjected to strong winds during a high-speed ground run at Bruntingthorpe. The flight was unintentional and short, but certainly made the headlines. (*Courtesy James Vaitkevicius*)

23. A Buccaneer wearing the all-grey paint scheme applied to only a few RAF Buccaneers shortly before retirement. Airflow stains can be seen behind the wing vortex generators and the wing-fold mechanism is also partly visible. The mechanism blanking plates were often removed on RAF Buccaneers during later years.

24. 809 Naval Air Squadron Buccaneer S2Bs resting in the rain at Yeovilton in July 1972. (*Courtesy Mike Freer*)

25. A Buccaneer up close as a 208 Squadron S2 approaches the camera with landing gear extended.

26. The MoD(PE) utilised a number of Buccaneers for trials work and a small number of aircraft were manufactured specifically for the RAE. XW988 is resplendent in a bizarre yellow and green paint scheme designed to aid visual and photographic tracking. The aircraft was mostly used for weapons trials at West Freugh.

27. To mark the end of Buccaneer operations, the RAF repainted some aircraft in the markings of former Buccaneer units. It generously reapplied Fleet Air Arm colours to one of its aircraft even though this particular Buccaneer had never served with the Royal Navy.

28. A final farewell four-ship for the media shortly before the Buccaneer's retirement. The lead aircraft wears an overall grey paint scheme applied to only a few aircraft shortly before the Buccaneer's withdrawal, although it retains 'Sky Pirate' artwork, indicative of its participation in Operation Desert Storm.

29. The first TSR2 XR219 pictured at Weybridge as it neared completion. Once completed, the aircraft was partially dismantled and transported to Boscombe Down for its first flight. (*Courtesy BAE Systems*)

30. XR219 pictured at Boscombe Down undergoing preparations for a test flight. Just visible is the partially open starboard airbrake. A control mechanism fault caused a risk of damage to the airbrakes and they were fixed to only partially close until repairs could be made. (*Courtesy BAE Systems*)

Left: 31. The mighty TSR2 thunders skywards during a wintry day at Boscombe Down. Thanks to a combination of high lift devices and lots of engine thrust, the TSR2 required only modest amounts of runway to get airborne. (*Courtesy BAE Systems*)

Below: 32. XR222 now resides at the Imperial War Museum, Duxford. It is a composite airframe that comprises of parts cannibalised from a number of TSR2 airframes. Although largely complete when withdrawn from the BAC production line, the aircraft was far from airworthy. (*Courtesy BAE Systems*)

33. A rare colour image of XR219 trailing her brake parachute after returning to Boscombe Down. TSR2's short-field capability was a fundamental part of the design that was built in at the insistence of the Air Ministry from the outset. (*Courtesy BAE Systems*)

34. The TSR2 was designed to achieve short take-offs and landings so it could operate from unprepared surfaces dispersed across Europe. However, it is doubtful whether the aircraft could have practically been operated in such circumstances. A nuclear bomber inevitably requires services and support, and the short-field requirement was probably an aspiration that would not have translated into a practical capability. (*Courtesy BAE Systems*)

35. XR220, the second TSR2, was prepared for flight at Boscombe Down in the weeks prior to the project's cancellation. A last minute fault delayed its first flight by a few hours, but by the time the flight had been rescheduled, the programme had been cancelled. Despite being minutes away from flying, XR220 never took to the air. (*Courtesy BAE Systems*)

36 and 37. When the Government imposed a 10 kiloton yield limit on tactical weapons, the RAF looked at ways in which the TSR2 could carry more than one WE.177 weapon. Two WE.177A bombs could be neatly fitted in tandem inside the TSR2's bomb bay (as illustrated). However, the more powerful WE.177B was longer and could only be accommodated in a side-by-side arrangement, necessitating a redesign of the bomb bay doors to incorporate bulges to fit around the bomb's fins. (*Courtesy BAE Systems*)

38. The JP233 runway denial weapons dispenser was designed specifically for RAF Tornado operations. It was put to use during the early stages of Operation Desert Storm and although it was very effective, it required aircrew to fly directly into target areas at low level. The arrival of stand-off precision munitions soon led to JP233's withdrawal. (*Courtesy BAE Systems*)

39. The Tornado's RB.199 engine was developed specifically for the aircraft as a joint project between Rolls-Royce, MTU and FiatAvio. With a nominal thrust of some 16,400 lb (with reheat), the engine is reliable and light, although many technical issues dogged the engine during the first years of operational use.

40. Unlike the bomber aircraft that preceded it, the Tornado does not incorporate a bomb bay. Weapons are attached to pylons under the aircraft's fuselage and wings, the latter pylons being designed to swivel in relation to the swing-wing position.

41. View from the cockpit during a low-level mission. Visible are the swing-wing fuselage gloves and the heat-stained engine thrust reverser buckets. Also visible is the retracted bolt-on refuelling probe in its housing on the starboard side of the nose. (*Courtesy RAF*)

42. Over the waters of Loch Ness, a Tornado GR.Mk.4 flanked by a GR.Mk.4A aircraft, indentified by the small sensor plate visible on the fuselage side below the cockpit, linked to the TIRRS (Tornado Infra-Red Reconnaissance System). After shifting to medium-level operations and new 'bolt-on' reconnaissance systems, TIRRS is no longer used and the specialised Mk.4A aircraft are used routinely within the main attack fleet.

43. Out over the Donna Nook range, the Tornado demonstrates its self-defence flare capability. The Vinten 2300 system comprises of two dispenser units under the Tornado's fuselage, each housing fifty-five two-flare cartridges. The flares provide a useful decoy measure against incoming infra-red missiles.

Above: **46.** Suitably decorated as the latest incarnation of 'McRobert's Reply'– first applied to one of the unit's wartime Stirling bombers – a Tornado from No. 15 Squadron leaps skywards, wings fully swept. (*Courtesy RAF*)

Right: **47.** ZH588 (DA2) made its first flight on 6 April 1994 with Chris Yeo as pilot. On this fifty-minute flight, the aircraft attained a top speed of 287 mph and an altitude of 10,000 feet. It was painted black in 2000 when 490 pressure transducers were fitted over the airframe as part of the test programme. (*Courtesy Geoff Lee, Eurofighter*)

Opposite above: **44.** RAF Tornado operations with the Storm Shadow cruise missile began in 2001. With a range of more than 150 miles, the weapon is a 'fire and forget' system that relies upon GPS positioning and an infra-red camera contained in its nose. (*Courtesy Geoff Lee/RAF*)

Opposite below: **45.** Marham Wing Tornado GR4s from Nos. 2, 9, 13 and 32 Squadrons. Various representative weapon loads are carried, including freefall 1,000 lb HE bombs, laser-guided bombs, Storm Shadow and ALARM. (*Courtesy RAF*)

48. A pre-Farnborough publicity image showing ZH588 (DA2) in formation with DA4 (ZH590) and the first Typhoon, DA1 98+29. (*Courtesy Eurofighter*)

Above and opposite above: **49 and 50.** RAF's No. 11 Squadron deployed its Typhoons to the US for the first time in 2008. At Nellis AFB in Nevada, they participated in a NATO 'Green Flag' exercise operating in an offensive role. As part of the exercise, the Typhoons were armed with Enhanced Paveway II laser-guided bombs together with a Litening III designator pod. The deployment served to illustrate the Typhoon's excellent all-round capabilities and its outstanding performance in the air-to-ground role. (*Courtesy Geoff Lee, Planefocus*)

51. The RAF celebrated the introduction of the Typhoon into service with its first nine-ship Typhoon formation during November 2006. Aircraft were drawn from No. 29(R) Squadron, No. 17(R) Squadron and No. 3 (F) Squadron, the three resident Typhoon units at Coningsby. (*Courtesy Geoff Lee, Planefocus*)

Left: 52. Test aircraft IPA3 is pictured during the intensive weapons trials programme carrying a mix of AMRAAMs (Advanced Medium-Range Air-to-Air Missile), IRIS-T AAMs and Paveway II laser-guided bombs. (*Courtesy Eurofighter*)

Below: 53. A Typhoon from No. 6 Squadron pictured during an overseas deployment to Malaysia as part of Exercise Bersama Lima during 2011. No. 6 Squadron will move to Lossiemouth in due course, joined by the Typhoons of No. 1(F) Squadron and a third Typhoon unit yet to form. (*Courtesy Geoff Lee, Planefocus*)

Right: **54.** A Typhoon from No. 3(F) Squadron over the desert during a visit to the 2009 Dubai Air Show. (*Courtesy Katsuhiko Tokunaga/Eurofighter*)

Below: **55.** An atmospheric image of a Typhoon from No. 3 Squadron returning to Coningsby on a wintry evening. The main runway once supported the mighty Vulcans of the V-Force and was scheduled to accommodate the TSR2 and F-111. Decades later it is Coningsby's Typhoons that fulfil the RAF's offensive tasks.

56. The first British F-35 was ZM135 pictured here departing Lockheed's Fort Worth facility en route to Eglin AFB for testing and evaluation. The UK took delivery of the first aircraft during July 2012. (*Courtesy Lockheed Martin*)

57. Testing of the F-35 is being conducted both at Edwards AFB (illustrated) and Eglin AFB. Further British testing and evaluation will be completed at Boscombe Down after which the F-35 will enter service, Lossiemouth or Marham being the likely bases. (*Courtesy Lockheed Martin*)

58. The British Government's troubled F-35 procurement saga finally favoured the STOVL F-35B variant (illustrated) that will be capable of operating from Britain's new aircraft carriers without need for conventional catapult and arrester gear. Whether the choice of this more complex and expensive F-35 derivative was a good decision remains to be seen. (*Courtesy Lockheed Martin*)

59. Only one RAF Buccaneer flew with the large external fuel tanks manufactured for South African export aircraft. Although flown and cleared for use, the RAF never purchased the larger tanks.

60. Buccaneers were used to support the Tornado programme, this particular aircraft fitted with the Tornado GR1's radar system. Some commentators argued with the latter aircraft's systems, the Buccaneer would perform superior to the Tornado.

61. Canberra T4 WT480 pictured at Cottesmore while serving with No. 231 OCU. The light grey paint scheme with stick-on day glow orange patches was standard for a time. However, a number of OCU aircraft were repainted in training-style red, white and grey colours as can be seen on WT483 to the left of the picture. (*Courtesy Tony Clarke collection*)

Victor WB771 pictured during a promotional photographic sortie, with legendary cameraman Charles E. Brown capturing images of the aircraft from the tail turret of an Avro Lincoln.

The Victor was on the apron and in company with Mr. Bennet, my flight observer. I climbed aboard. This was the thing we had waited for! Cockpit checks were completed, engines were started and I taxied to the runway. Conditions were perfect with a light breeze straight down the runway, bright sunshine though a few woolly cumulus clouds and visibility up to 20 miles in the crisp December air. I locked my radio on to transmit so that all we said could be heard on the ground. In a matter of seconds we would know if the Victor would fly. I opened the engines to fairly low power and released the brakes. The aircraft rolled up the runway, rapidly gaining speed. I pulled the control column back and the nose wheel leg left the ground. So far so good. I held the Victor like that for a few seconds. The rumbling of the wheels ceased and I knew we were off. I kept close to the runway, still gaining speed for a few more vital seconds and then I knew it was all right. An imperceptible movement of the control column and the ground started

The beautiful all-silver Victor prototype WB771 captured on film high over Hertfordshire in 1953.

to fall away as we climbed. Smoothly, effortlessly, the Victor had slid into its natural element. By doing so it had just become an aeroplane instead of just the expression in metal of so many drawings and hieroglyphics on paper. Whatever happened now we all knew it would fly. After a few minutes in the air my thoughts turned to landing. I had got the Victor up there, now could I get it back again? I tried reducing speed to see how it would behave at a suitable speed for the approach. Once more it was all right and coming in on a long, straight approach, I headed for the runway. Lower and lower we came until the beginning of the runway was only a few feet below the wheels. I throttled right back and in a few seconds the wheels started rumbling again and we were down. The Victor had come back to Earth as smoothly as it had left. We had a comfortable flight together with no anxieties.

The first seventeen-minute flight was a great success and Hazelden's comments failed to mention that he performed a complete airfield circuit followed by an overshot before repositioning for a long final approach. He later added that, '...it was all so effortless ... it is difficult to see why we were so apprehensive'. The initial take-off had used just 1,500 feet of Boscombe's massive runway. This was only a quarter of the runway length available at Radlett and demonstrated how ridiculously

Arriving at the SBAC Farnborough show, Victor WB771 flares for touchdown, the prototype Avro Vulcan visible in the distance.

overcautious the MoS decision had been to transport the Victor at huge expense to Boscombe Down. Despite this, Radlett's runway was extended and until work was completed, the prototype remained at Boscombe Down to continue test flying.

It was on 2 January 1953 that the Air Council finally agreed, after fourteen previous discussions, to name the HP.80 'Victor' as one of the new trio of V-Bombers. Of course, Handley Page's Gustav Victor Lachmann was delighted at the choice! Flight testing proceeded smoothly, the only major incident occurred when the main landing gear mechanism failed to function correctly and all sixteen tyres on the main units burst on landing. Hazelden also made the short flight back to Radlett in order to demonstrate the aircraft to the assembled Handley Page staff and on 25 February, the aircraft returned to Hertfordshire for good, courtesy of Radlett's newly-extended 6,910 feet runway. Testing then resumed at Radlett and proceeded smoothly apart from when one of WB771's main landing gears skipped on touchdown, jamming in the vertical position. Hazelden was obliged to carefully land the aircraft on the aircraft's rear tyres and Handley Page subsequently fixed rotation dampers to the bogies in order to solve the problem. Although personnel at Radlett became familiar with the Victor's sleek shape, it was not until June that the aircraft appeared before the public at a Royal Aeronautical Society Garden party.

Its first major public appearance was at the 1953 Queen's Coronation review of the RAF at Odiham on 15 July when the aircraft joined the huge flypast over the airfield. The Chief of the Air Staff, Air Chief Marshal Sir John Baker, was treated to a flight in the aircraft shortly afterwards and was greatly impressed with the aircraft, only expressing concern for the relatively poor visibility from the flight deck. He was delighted by Hazelden's demonstration of the Victor's hands-off landing capability that was possible due to the aircraft's high-set tail. The tail remained clear of any ground effect upon landing where a lower-set tail would produce a pitch-down movement. Handley Page believed that this might be a useful benefit for service pilots, but Boscombe Down's test pilots subsequently concluded that it was 'of no particular advantage'. When the Victor's tail unit was later shortened and wing slats removed, this unusual capability was lost in any case.

After completing more test flying and a number of VIP flights, WB771 was temporarily withdrawn from use and painted in a striking black scheme complete with red cheat line and silver wings (a paint scheme devised by Sir Fredrick Handley Page). Resplendent in its smart new colours, WB771 was flown to Farnborough to appear at the 1953 SBAC show where the aircraft captured everyone's imagination and enthusiasm.

Although the audience did not know it, the first of the demonstration flights was performed on just three engines after an igniter plug failed on take-off. Following a week in the public eye, the Victor returned to Radlett and by 15 October, Hazelden had flown the aircraft to 50,000 feet without encountering any difficulties. He extended the aircraft's speed envelope to Mach 0.83 and then Mach 0.91 at which speed he observed only a small nose-down trim change. Rather more concerning was a loud noise inside the cabin above Mach 0.75 which he described as sounding between a flute and an underground train. The cause was eventually traced to the air conditioning system and in order to cure the problem, the ramp intakes on the aircraft's nose were fitted with 'nostril' scoops and (later) vortex generators. Hazelden's only other concern was a tendency to roll on take-off, but this was found to be due to poor aileron movement that was easily fixed.

Such was Handley Page's confidence in the aircraft that by February 1954, the Victor was routinely flying at high-subsonic speeds. On one flight, test pilot John Allam inadvertently almost broke the sound barrier and attained Mach 0.98 resulting in visible skin buckling on the tailplane structure. As a short term fix, the second prototype's tailplane was fitted to WB771 so that the damaged structure could be repaired and attached to the second aircraft, WB775.

Once refitted, another twenty-four hours of test flying was completed before the aircraft was ferried to Cranfield to conduct speed calibration flights. The resident College of Aeronautics had suitably advanced ground-based calibration equipment

The second Victor (WB775) was also painted in the same black and silver paint scheme with a red cheat line that had been applied to the prototype. Sir Fredrick Handley Page devised the colour scheme specifically for Farnborough appearances. (*Courtesy Handley Page Association*)

for such measurements. Hazelden completed the first flights here, but after being assigned to a presentation at Woodley for 14 July, he handed the day's test flight to his deputy Ronald Ecclestone, a former RAE test pilot. Ecclestone conducted the first test runs over the airfield without any difficulty, but as WB771 ran in at speed to begin another calibration pass, the aircraft's tailplane suddenly sheared off from the fin structure. With no pitch control, the aircraft tipped forwards and ploughed into the ground, disintegrating and bursting into a huge ball of flames. Ecclestone and his crew were killed instantly and onlookers watched in horror as the severed tailplane fluttered down to land near the burning wreckage.

As the Cranfield test flights were being calibrated, film evidence of the accident was available and this enabled the investigation team to determine that fatigue cracks in three fin-mounted bolt holes had allowed the securing bolts to shear, thereby releasing the tailplane. The cure for this catastrophic failure was simple: an additional bolt was added to subsequent aircraft, spreading the tailplane's load. However, this detailed structural analysis led to the production-standard Victor's tail height being reduced by 15 inches. The second prototype (WB775) was partially modified with additional metal skins added to the fin having made its first flight on 11 September. It was this aircraft that assumed all of the continuing test and evaluation work which WB771 had begun before its tragic loss.

By 1955, the second Victor (WB775) had been repainted in a striking blue colour scheme. Clearly visible in this image is the wing leading edge 'nose flap' slat system that was eventually abandoned in the Mk.2 variant.

The production-standard Victor B.Mk.1 was essentially similar to the prototypes, but these aircraft featured the revised fin design and slightly longer fuselage that had been stretched by 42 inches. The crew door was repositioned to avoid the risk of crews hitting the engine intakes during bailing out; additional cockpit windows were installed; the tailplane bullet fairing was reshaped (the leading-edge intake and filler being removed); and vortex generators were attached to the outer wing upper surfaces. The first production Victor was XA917 and this made its first flight on 1 February 1965, completing a fifteen minute test flight in the hands of Johnny Allam. Powered by four Sapphire Mk.202 engines each rated at 11,000 lb, this aircraft became the world's largest aircraft to break the sound barrier when on 1 June 1957, Allam 'inadvertently' exceeded Mach 1.0 in a gentle dive initiated at 40,000 feet during a test flight from RAF Gaydon. The double sonic bang rattled across a wide area from Banbury to Watford and flight test observer Paul Langston, sitting in one of the rear crew seats, earned himself the distinction of becoming the first man to break the sound barrier backwards!

XA917 flew a long series of development flights from Radlett while WB775 went to Suffolk to conduct bomb dropping trials over Orfordness, carrying dummy

Handley Page Victor B.Mk.1 bombers under construction at the manufacturer's Colney Street factory. More than twelve examples can be seen in the picture in various stages of manufacture.

representations of the huge Blue Danube atomic bomb for which the aircraft had been designed to deliver. The next aircraft (XA918) was assigned to wing flutter tests and XA919 was retained as a 'conference airframe' for ground investigations and did not fly until 13 March 1957. When Handley Page completed its new assembly hall at Colney Street, a further two aircraft (XA920 and XA921) joined the first three to celebrate its official opening by Minister of Supply, Reginald Maudling. Unlike the first four aircraft which had been painted in an overall silver finish, XA921 was completed in a gloss white paint scheme. This was a standard finish that was eventually applied to all V-Bombers, designed to reflect heat and radiation from atomic devices as they exploded.

When Boscombe Down's test pilots got their hands on the Victor for detailed evaluation, they identified a number of deficits which they deemed unsuitable for RAF operations. Like Avro's Vulcan, the Victor enjoyed very responsive controls, but the pilots at the Aeroplane & Armament Experimental Establishment (A&AEE) requested that the light feel of the controls should be 'heavied up' for service use in order to avoid the temptation to overstress the aircraft.

Some of the A&AEE's findings were quite discouraging:

The overall layout of the cockpit fell far short of the standard required in this class of aircraft. Generally, there appeared to be no logical grouping of associated controls and indicators and in certain aspects the layout was haphazard. The layout of the power control switch panel was illogical and dangerous. Some of the indicators and controls for primary services could only be operated by the first pilot and several warning and monitoring devices were not visible to both pilots, making it impossible for either pilot to relax completely at any time. The extreme discomfort of the pilot's stations was severely criticised and will result in a lowering of efficiency and morale during only average-length sorties. In conditions of poor visibility the restricted view was inadequate for the circuit and landing, and concern was felt for possible external windscreen reflections during night flying. It is essential that these major criticisms be rectified before the aircraft can be considered acceptable for Service use.

Although the A&AEE was clearly not satisfied with the aircraft, Handley Page's team were relieved to learn that there were no major flaws in the overall design of the aircraft and that it performed well under all circumstances. The various issues were slowly fixed, but deliveries to the RAF were some two years late. The Initial Release to Service, issued on 29 July 1957, stipulated that the aircraft be restricted to daytime operations in 'temperate climes' and other limitations were also imposed until suitable modifications could be made. The first aircraft delivered to the RAF was XA931 (the fifteenth production aircraft) and this Victor arrived at RAF Gaydon on 28 November 1957, joining the fledgling Victor conversion unit, No. 232 OCU. More Victors followed including two aircraft (XA924 and XA925) which were fitted with Yellow Aster radar as part of the RAF's plan to equip a radar reconnaissance squadron with Victors.

The first operational Victor squadron was No. 10 Squadron that received its first aircraft (XA935) at RAF Cottesmore on 9 April 1958.

Once fully equipped, No. 15 Squadron was formed at Cottesmore and by the end of 1958, the V-Force was well established with seven operational Valiant squadrons, three Vulcan squadrons and two Victor squadrons. The Blue Danube atomic bomb was integrated into service and early deliveries of the far more powerful Yellow Sun thermonuclear hydrogen bomb were beginning. The RAF possessed more destructive power than it had ever done before, but in order to maintain its ability to strike at the heart of the Soviet Union, further developments were necessary. Until the late 1950s, the Soviet system of rigid fighter control required little effort to overcome its effectiveness. A simple piece of jamming equipment (Green Palm) was enough to jam the system with a high-pitched wail. But the Soviets continued to improve their technology and it became clear that a more advanced Electronic Countermeasures (ECM) system would be needed for the V-Force. Rather than rely on a dedicated ECM jamming aircraft, new ECM equipment was fitted to both the Vulcan and Victor fleets, the Victors receiving Red Street radar jammers and a passive radar warning receiver system. This was sufficient to ensure that the RAF's bombers could

Right: Victor B.Mk.1s from No. 10 Squadron pictured in their hangar at RAF Cottesmore. The limited size of the RAF's standard hangars ultimately dictated the overall dimensions of the V-Bombers.

Below: A publicity image of the first Victor B.Mk.1 aircraft delivered to No. 10 Squadron at RAF Cottesmore in September 1958. Most of these aircraft remained active with this unit over the next decade.

deliver their deadly weapons to targets with precision and efficiency without any significant risk of interception.

The establishment of the RAF's V-Force gradually persuaded America to shift its official policy towards the United Kingdom with regard to the sharing of nuclear technology. Having maintained some distance from Britain, America believed that the UK was inevitably at risk from Soviet invasion and the seemingly endless series of spy allegations only served to harden America's position further still. Despite good relations between British prime ministers and American presidents, the US played no part in Britain's efforts to 'go it alone' in developing both an operational atomic bomb and a more powerful hydrogen bomb. Now that Britain had demonstrated that it had both the weapons and means to deliver them, the US changed its attitude. America was clearly not going to enjoy a nuclear monopoly and its best means of defence would be to support Britain in defending the West. In a remarkable volte-face, the US agreed to supply Britain with atomic weapons to act as a stopgap measure until more supplies of British-built bombs could be completed. Likewise, plans were made to integrate operations between America's Strategic Air Command and the RAF's Bomber Command, creating a co-ordinated plan of attack so that potential targets were assured of destruction and that pointless and dangerous overlapping was eliminated.

The supply of American bombs (Project E) culminated in the first transport flights arriving in the UK during 1958 and as part of this process, the Victor force at Honington, comprising of Nos. 90 and 57 Squadrons, was duly equipped to carry American Mk.5 and Mk.7 bombs followed by No. 55 Squadron at a later stage. This arrangement was less than ideal as the weapons remained under American control. This meant that the bombs could not accompany the Victor or the other V-Bombers to their designated dispersal sites from which they would operate in the event of a war. An essential part of the V-Force plan was to disperse the bombers away from their home bases in groups of four or two, so that the aircraft would be difficult to detect and destroy. The difficulties of distributing bombs which were under American control suggested that Project E was largely symbolic rather than practical and it was short-lived ending in 1960. However, as deliveries of British bombs had been slow – initially there were more bombers than bombs – it enabled the RAF to build up its effectiveness and enter the Sixties as a powerful strike force.

Armed with three atomic bomber types, a dispersal plan that kept the bombers mobile and less vulnerable to attack, and British atomic/thermonuclear bombs backed by an American supply of nuclear weapons, Britain found itself playing a vital part in the new concept of deterrence and Mutually Assured Destruction. It is also fair to say that the V-Force enjoyed a significance far in excess of its actual size. Although dwarfed by the resources available to Strategic Air Command, the RAF's capabilities were second to none and having engaged in joint planning with SAC, the V-Force

Underside view of a Victor B1 landing at Cottesmore. This view illustrates the Victor's wing trailing edge flaps that were designed to extend rearwards and downwards, suspended from tracks in the upper surface of the wing trailing edge.

was in effect an integral part of the West's strike capability. Britain's geographic position implied that the V-Force could reach the heart of the Soviet Union well in advance of America's bombers and it was, therefore, a very serious deterrent which the Soviets understood and, as revealed in recent years, respected greatly.

The Victor's story reached a pivotal stage when production of a second-generation Victor began. Almost as soon as the Victor Mk.1 had been initiated, it had been accepted that growing Soviet capabilities would soon require the V-Force to increase its effectiveness. The bombers would need to fly higher and further. As a relatively small firm, Handley Page had invested a huge proportion of its resources in the creation of the Victor and the company was keen to maximise its investment by continuing to produce the Victor Mk.1. However, the Air Staff wanted a more capable aircraft that they anticipated would be equipped with more powerful Sapphire engines. After a variety of design changes and proposals were considered, the Air Staff finally agreed to order the Victor Phase 2A (a compromise solution between two other variants offered by Handley Page) equipped with Conway Co.11 engines each rated at 17,250 lb. The engine chosen for the new Victor was physically

Victor B.Mk.1 XA918 pictured getting airborne from Radlett whilst assigned to Sideways Looking Radar (SLR) trials with Handley Page. (*Courtesy Handley Page Association*)

larger than the Sapphire, but Handley Page was able to retain the existing engine bay rib design that avoided the cost and delays of creating a completely new centre-section. The Conways required deeper intake ducts to cater for the increased air flow mass and this placed a greater load on the wing spar. In order to relieve stress on the spars, each engine was surrounded by reinforced 'spectacle' fittings forged from 6-foot square slabs of alloy.

Trials with the new Conway engine were troublesome, the powerplant's susceptibility to surging being a major problem for some time. Some two years were required to solve all of the engine's problems, a number of which were resolved by modifying the aircraft's intakes with additional vertical splitter plates installed to smooth the swirling air flow before it entered the engines. The more powerful engines also required a greater wing area, up to 2,600 square feet, so that the Victor retained a good degree of manoeuvrability at the greater altitudes which the

Conways would be able to attain. Increasing the wing span to 120 feet could not be achieved by simply extending the wing tips as this would have shifted the aircraft's centre of gravity beyond its aft limit. Consequently, the new wing incorporated an additional 3 feet 6 inches at each wing tip and a 'stretch' of 18 inches at each wing root. The aircraft's electrical system was changed from DC to constant-frequency AC and an auxiliary power unit fitted to give the aircraft a self-start capability. With a much greater all-up weight, some 223,000 lb with external fuel tanks, the new Victor Mk.2 would be capable of reaching an impressive 60,000 feet. On the other hand, the aircraft would be slightly slower than the Victor B.Mk.1 as the aircraft suffered from buffeting at speeds beyond Mach 0.92. But despite this slight deficit, the second-generation Victor was undoubtedly a far more capable aircraft than its predecessor.

The prototype Victor B.Mk.2 was converted from XH668, an existing B1 airframe, and made its first post-conversion flight on 20 February 1959. After a short series of handling and systems tests at Radlett, the aircraft was sent to Boscombe Down for some 'Preview Handling' flights. On 20 August, the aircraft departed on one such flight that was intended to explore the wing buffet boundary at 52,000 feet in a series of tight turns at speeds of up to Mach 0.94. The flight was monitored infrequently on radar and at 11.37 the aircraft disappeared from radar coverage, appearing briefly as a series of multiple targets. The aircraft had been lost somewhere in the Irish Sea and thoughts turned to the troublesome tailplane unit. A thorough search of the area eventually traced XH668 to a site in St Bride's Bay, some 400 feet deep. Almost 600,000 pieces of wreckage were eventually recovered and the cause of the accident was traced to a missing pitot tube on the starboard wing tip. It was concluded that the tube had become loosened by the test flight's buffeting and this had allowed both the Mach trimmer system and stall detector to become disabled, causing the aircraft to enter into a nose-down descent with the wing slats deployed. A simple collet had caused the catastrophic accident and the loss of five lives.

Handley Page assigned XH669 to the B2 development programme with XH670 joining it by November. Progress was satisfactory and by September 1960, the Victor B2 was ready to make its public debut and XH669 appeared before the crowds at Farnborough. The first Victor B.Mk.2 joined RAF Bomber Command on 2 November 1961, joining the newly formed Victor B2 Trials Unit at Cottesmore. This unit eventually became a Flight of No. 232 OCU, most of which remained at Gaydon, but with space at a premium at that base, B2 operations were concentrated at Cottesmore. The first operational Victor B2 unit was No. 139 Squadron that formed at Wittering on 1 February 1962 followed by No. 100 Squadron on 1 May.

Both of the Wittering-based Victor B2 units were primarily armed with the Avro Blue Steel stand-off missile, a weapon that had been developed as part of the RAF's efforts to maintain the V-Force's capabilities.

Avro Blue Steel missile undergoing engine tests, with the Stentor rocket motors pictured in full, noisy flow. (*Courtesy Rolls-Royce*)

Victors pictured on the Operational Readiness Platform (ORP) at Wittering. When this photograph was taken, Wittering retained its fighter-style ORP, but this was soon replaced by a new V-Bomber ORP complete with individual tracks for four aircraft and quick-release service attachments. (*Courtesy Handley Page Association*)

With Soviet defences continually improving, a stand-off bomb that could be launched some distance from the target would enable the bomber to evade known enemy defences and ensure that the bomb stood a greater chance of reaching its target. Blue Danube and Yellow Sun – the thermonuclear weapon that replaced the early Blue Danube atomic bomb – were formidable weapons, but as freefall bombs, they both required the vulnerable bomber to fly over the target at high level. Clearly, this was a risky business when fighter and missile defences would inevitably be protecting each target.

The solution was Blue Steel, a huge flying bomb that was carried in a recess under the Vulcan and Victor's bomb bay. Equipped with its own propulsion and navigation system, the bomb had a nominal range of some 100 nm and after a short period of operations in freefall bombing, the new Victor B2 squadrons were both assigned to Blue Steel. While the Victors were undoubtedly first-class bombers, they were less than ideal launch platforms for the Blue Steel weapon. The Victor's bomb bay doors were particularly low slung and far too low to the ground to enable the missile to be towed easily under the aircraft for loading. A more serious note, the missile was far from reliable. It required HTP (High Test Peroxide) fuel and this volatile mixture required extremely careful handling. It had a capacity to spontaneously combust with catastrophic results and huge water troughs were constructed next to the Blue Steel facilities so that weapons or personnel could be quickly doused if a fuel fire broke out.

The weapon's guidance system and engine were not entirely reliable either. It was believed that many Blue Steels might have failed to launch successfully if ever called upon and such failures would have required the bomber to drop the weapon in freefall. (The very delivery technique that the missile was created to avoid.) Blue Steel was an excellent concept, albeit one that was flawed by development problems and cost. Although the RAF accepted it as a useful part of the V-Force, something better was undoubtedly required and Blue Steel was in effect a stopgap weapon, destined to maintain the V-Force's credibility as freefall bombs made way for guided weapons.

Britain looked towards America for a more effective standoff missile system. The new GAM-87A Skybolt with a range of some 1,000 miles looked like a good solution to the RAF's requirements.

Unfortunately, the Skybolt's development was troubled by endless failures and delays, and after a dark period of uncertainty, the US decided to abandon the project. This left Britain without an effective delivery system to replace the Blue Steel bomb that was coming into RAF service. Although America offered the Skybolt system to Britain for further development, Britain's Government did not have sufficient confidence in the project to risk continuing alone. After more discussions, it was agreed that America's only practical alternative was the Polaris submarine-launched missile system that could be fitted with British nuclear warheads. Britain accepted

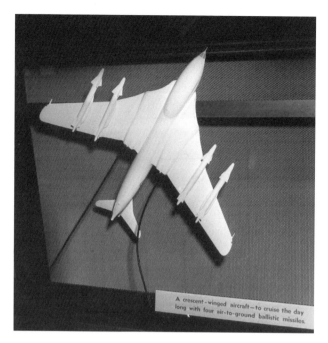

A crescent-winged aircraft—to cruise the day long with four air-to-ground ballistic missiles.

Various proposals were drawn up by Handley Page to convince the RAF that the Victor could carry Skybolt missiles. However, the Victor's low-slung and flexible wing structure was entirely unsuitable for the huge missile. If Skybolt had been adopted for the V-Force, it seems inevitable that only the Vulcan would have carried it.

this offer and the entire V-Force concept was effectively abandoned. The long-term future of the Valiant, Vulcan and Victor appeared to be in jeopardy...

However, even though the future of Britain's INT (Independent Nuclear Deterrent) had been secured, the more immediate future required the V-Force to continue maintaining its viability. The Blue Steel system, although far from perfect, provided an effective means of reaching targets deep in the heart of the Soviet Union. When combined with an existing arsenal of freefall weapons, the V-Bombers represented a very powerful force to be reckoned with. But Soviet defensive capabilities were growing and the Air Staff concluded that by the mid-1960s, it would be practically impossible to penetrate Soviet airspace at high level. This meant that even Blue Steel could no longer be relied upon as a guaranteed means of destroying targets. The only practical solution would be to attack targets from low level at heights of 500 feet or less where Soviet radar was less capable of locating individual targets.

The V-Bombers had been designed to fly at high level and there was great concern that switching to low-level operations would not be possible with aircraft that were not specifically designed for such a demanding flight regime. Flight trials performed by the Bomber Command Development Unit at Finningley indicated that the three bomber types could operate successfully in the punishing low-level conditions and the Valiant fleet – part of which was eventually assigned to NATO's Supreme Allied Commander Europe – had demonstrated this. Consequently, Vulcan

A rare picture of the Yellow Sun Mk.1 thermonuclear bomb, seen alongside a Victor B.Mk.1. This particular weapon is an inert casing used by the RAE for release clearance trails.

squadrons switched to low level followed by Victor squadrons in early 1964. The Blue Steel missile was reconfigured so that both the Vulcan and Victor could launch the weapon from low level after which it zoom climbed to altitude before making its terminal descent towards the target.

Plans to develop a Blue Steel Mk.2 were abandoned (the cost and complexity of the proposal proved to be too high) and the freefall Yellow Sun bomb delivery profile was also amended.

The bomber crews performed a swift 'pop-up' climb to release the weapon before returning to low level. Ultimately, a new nuclear weapon was created for the Vulcan and Victor, and although it had first been designed for the abandoned TSR2 project, the WE.177 was designed for low-level 'laydown' delivery. This became the standard weapon for both the Vulcan and Victor fleet and remained in use for many years after the RAF finally relinquished the responsibility for providing Britain's nuclear deterrent during 1969.

The handover of the nuclear QRA (Quick Reaction Alert) to the Royal Navy's submarines took place at 00:01 on 1 July 1969, but by this stage the Victor squadrons had relinquished their Blue Steel and laydown nuclear role. With the first generation

Mk.1 aircraft replaced by the Mk.2, No. 100 Squadron at Wittering disbanded on 1 October followed by No. 139 Squadron on 31 December 1968. Their Mk.2 Victors were placed in storage, thereby ending the Victor's role as a strategic bomber. However, the Victor's story was far from complete.

During 1954, one of No. 543 Squadron's Valiants was found to be suffering from metal fatigue with significant cracks being found in the aircraft's wing spar. A few weeks later, another Valiant crew suffered what was almost a catastrophic incident when a wing spar broke in flight. Inspections revealed that half of the Valiant fleet was affected by metal fatigue and most aircraft were immediately grounded with only a few Valiants restored to limited operational standard in order to meet NATO commitments. By the end of 1954, the Air Staff had reluctantly accepted that a combination of punishing low-level operations, combined with an unsuitable choice of metal alloy used in the aircraft's construction, meant that the Valiant would have to be withdrawn from RAF service with immediate effect.

For strategic reconnaissance operations, this decision was not a major blow as plans had been made to assign Victors to this role and the first Victor SR.Mk.2 aircraft – with reconnaissance equipment installed in the aircraft's bomb bay – joined No. 543 Squadron at Wyton in 1965. By 1966, the squadron was back to full strength with a fleet of specialised Victors. However, the vital aerial refuelling role had also been lost with the withdrawal of the Valiant and this had a major effect on RAF operations. Thankfully, the importance of aerial refuelling was self-evident and plans had been put in place to develop a refuelling tanker variant of the Victor back in 1962, taking advantage of the surplus Victor B1 aircraft which were no longer required when the more capable B.Mk.2 was introduced. Trials aircraft, XA918, was first fitted with hose and drogue refuelling units in 1964 and the premature withdrawal of the Valiant fleet prompted the Air Staff to hasten the conversion of surplus Victors for tanker operations. Initially, some six B1A Victors were swiftly fitted with wing-mounted refuelling pods and the first B(K)1A (XH620) was completed in April 1965.

No. 55 Squadron reformed at Marham in May 1965 as a combined bomber and tanker unit. In November of that year, the first dedicated tanker variant of the Victor made its first flight. This aircraft (XA397) had not only the two wing-mounted refuelling pods, but also a third unit mounted in the rear fuselage together with two 15,300 lb fuel tanks in the bomb bay. The Victor K.Mk.1 entered RAF service on 14 February 1966 with No. 57 Squadron at Marham. Further tanker conversions followed and by 1966, the Valiant's sorry demise had been successfully rectified thanks to the availability of the versatile Victor.

However, the Mk.1 Victor was slowly reaching the end of its useful life and a long term solution to the RAF's tanker requirements was necessary. The final withdrawal of the Blue Steel-equipped Victor B2 fleet at Wittering offered a potential solution.

The more powerful and capable and 'younger' Victor B2 was an obvious choice for tanker conversion and following withdrawal from the bomber role, the Victors were temporarily stored pending conversion to the tanker role. Unfortunately, the punishing low-level bomber role had taken quite a toll on the Victors. Although the Vulcan's rigid delta wing layout was largely unaffected by low-level turbulence, the Victor's long, slender wing was routinely subjected to continual flexing. When the B2 fleet was inspected, it was revealed that the aircraft's wing spars were suffering from fatigue cracks in the lower boom forgings to which the wings were attached. Fixing the cracks became a major part of the tanker conversion programme and as the once mighty Handley Page company was by now in extreme financial difficulty, the conversion programme was handed to Avro (now part of the Hawker Siddeley Group), the company that had been Handley Page's competitors for so many years. Without the conversion contract there was no future for Handley Page and the company went into liquidation in August 1969. Sir Fredrick must surely have turned in his grave. The Victors were ferried to Avro's airfield at Woodford and the first K.Mk.2 tanker emerged in 1972, making its first flight on 1 March.

As with the earlier Mk.1 tankers, the K.Mk.2 was essentially a stripped-down bomber with wing-mounted refuelling pods, a third HDU (Hose Drum Unit) in the rear fuselage and additional fuel tanks. The only other significant modification was the shortening of the Mk.2's wing span – 1.5 feet being removed from each tip – in order to reduce the wing's tendency to flex and an overall strengthening of the airframe in order to equip the aircraft for approximately fourteen years of operations in the tanker role. In fact, the Victor K2 went on to serve the RAF for twenty years after entering service in May 1974. As some of the Victors were judged to be beyond economic repair, the SR.Mk.2 aircraft assigned to strategic reconnaissance were withdrawn so that these could be added to the pool of available airframes (a squadron of Vulcans was reformed to take on the Victor's reconnaissance role). Eventually and largely as a result of cost considerations, a fleet of only twenty-four Victor K.Mk.2 tankers was completed. These were assigned to Nos. 55 and 57 Squadrons at Marham with a handful of aircraft serving with No. 232 OCU from time to time.

The older and less capable Mk.1 tankers soldiered on in diminishing numbers until late 1976 when the remaining aircraft were retired. The Conway-powered Victor K2 with an impressive range, altitude capability and excellent fuel capacity was a remarkably successful tanker aircraft that the RAF was loathe to part with. It was only the airframe's structural life that eventually forced the RAF to retire the Victors in favour of converted VC10 airliners. As a vitally important component of the RAF's order of battle, the Victors provided refuelling support for all of the RAF's offensive and defensive aircraft and often provided additional support for other NATO forces during exercises and deployments.

The Victor's flight deck was fairly spacious when compared to the Vulcan. In contrast to the Vulcan's seating arrangement, the Victor's pilot and co-pilot were placed slightly below the level of the rear crew. The central instrument console could be hinged upwards to allow access to the nose compartment, although such access was rarely needed for tanker operations.

In 1982, the Victor was called upon to participate in Operation Black Buck, supporting the RAF attack missions mounted as part of the campaign to retake the Falkland Islands which had been invaded by Argentina. For the first such mission – at the time the longest bombing mission in military history – the Victors provided the vital tanker support to enable a Vulcan to reach the Falklands and deliver a payload of twenty-one 1,000 lb bombs and return to Ascension Island. Although the Vulcan and its crews rightly received a great deal of acclaim for their exploits during the Falklands campaign, little credit was given to the Victor tankers and their crews. They tirelessly supported the attack missions and also enabled the RAF's transport aircraft to deliver goods to Ascension Island directly from the UK. British-based refuelling tanker operations were largely suspended during the conflict and USAF tankers were temporarily assigned to the support of operations in the UK so that the Victor fleet could deploy south. Without the Victor, it was unlikely that the RAF could have provided any worthwhile contribution to the campaign. As a direct result of the growing need for more post-conflict tanker support, particularly the new requirement for transport links to the Falklands, a number of Vulcans were hastily converted into single-point tankers in order to supplement the Victor fleet/ However,

A Victor releasing its full load of thirty-five 1,000 lb HE bombs. The Victor's impressive conventional bomb-carrying capability was a useful asset, but the aircraft's primary role was the delivery of a single atomic bomb.

the Victors with their greater fuel capacity and a three-point refuelling hose system, remained at the core of the RAF's tanker capability.

The Victor squadrons were once again called into action in December 1990 when four aircraft deployed to Muharraq (Bahrain) on 14 December. Eventually, eight aircraft were based there as part of Britain's contribution to the Gulf War.

By the time the Victors returned to Marham in March 1991, they had completed 299 combat support missions totalling 870 hours. Subsequently, Victors were deployed to Akrotiri as part of Operation Warden (protecting Kurdish communities in Iraq) and to Muharraq in 1992 as part of Operation Jural supporting Tornado missions over Iraq. This deployment marked the end of the Victor's operational career and when the aircraft returned to Marham in September 1993, their use to the RAF effectively came to an end. The last RAF unit (No. 55 Squadron) disbanded on 15 October and a trio of Victors – XH672, XL231 and XL161 – flew over the airfield in formation to mark the squadron's disbandment, the end of Victor operations and a sad farewell to the mighty V-Force. On 30 November, Victor XH672 was ferried to Shawbury minus its refuelling pods and underwing fuel tanks in preparation for dismantlement and road transportation to RAF Cosford where the aircraft is now part of the Cold War Museum.

The magnificent Victor was undoubtedly a supremely capable aircraft and one which Britain's aerospace industry can justifiably be proud of. It exceeded all of the requirements that were expected of it and provided the RAF with an effective bomber with which nuclear weapons could be delivered deep into Soviet territory. The Victor also had an outstanding capacity for delivering conventional HE bombs and demonstrated an excellent capability as a strategic reconnaissance platform. The Victor also became a refuelling tanker and it was in this role that the Victor served for so many years with great distinction. By any standards, the Victor certainly provided Britain with value for money. Of course, it could be argued that in some respects the Victor was perhaps over-capable and that the Valiant – particularly in its Mk.2 version that was abandoned – could have formed the basis of the RAF's V-Force without need to devote vast sums of money and resources to the creation of both the Vulcan and Victor. But at the time when the V-Force concept was devised, no one could predict what, if any, bomber design would prove to be successful.

It is only with hindsight that the notion of manufacturing three different designs to tackle one specific role seems rather absurd. It can also be argued that the Victor was perhaps less than ideal for the RAF's bomber requirements as the aircraft was unsuited to the punishing low-level role. It was similarly unsuitable for both the Blue Steel missile and the abandoned Skybolt, but these were requirements that came into being long after the Victor had been commissioned. On the other hand, it was perhaps a matter of good fortune that the Victor was in existence when the Valiant was prematurely retired. Without the Victor, the RAF would have struggled to provide refuelling support and this deficit would have hampered the RAF's capabilities for many years. The availability of the Victor was certainly fortuitous and it enabled the Victor to take on a completely new role after successfully serving as part of the V-Force. Although the Victor's service career turned out very differently from that imagined by Sir Fredrick Handley Page and Gustav Victor Lachmann, there is no doubt that the Victor was a successful and very impressive machine.

CHAPTER SEVEN
The Cutting Edge

During the early stages of the Cold War, the Soviet's naval forces were rapidly expanding and developing. The threat that they presented to the West was of increasing concern, particularly the new Sverdlov-class cruisers – huge 17,000-ton warships bristling with armament. Not only were they big and brutal, they demonstrated the Soviet's ability and intention to become a global force, extending Soviet influence to every part of the world. Britain's Royal Navy had a serious interest in these cruisers and the Admiralty turned its attention to ways in which they might be countered if necessary.

In 1953, the Navy possessed an impressive fleet of warships including carriers. It was inevitable that the means of countering the Sverdlovs was to create an aircraft that was tailor-made to achieve this task. Missile technology was still in its infancy and there was no practical means of producing a ship-launched, anti-ship guided weapon of any great accuracy, range or destructive power. The only practical means of destroying the Sverdlovs would therefore be by air using an attack aircraft capable of achieving high speed, but capable of flying at ultra low level to evade enemy radar, skimming the sea surface at heights of 100 feet or lower. But reaching the target would be only part of the battle. Knocking out a huge warship with conventional high explosive bombs or relatively unsophisticated missiles would be an incredibly difficult task when the Sverdlovs were so heavily defended. But the emergence of atomic weaponry changed everything. With an atomic bomb there would be no need to reach the target, nor to attack it with any great accuracy. An atomic bomb could be thrown at the ship from a comfortable distance, confident that the power of the weapon's explosive yield would ensure utter destruction.

The Fleet Air Arm's first post-war jet bomber was a fighter. The aircraft evolved from a bizarre project that began as a direct result of the poor performance of the earliest jet engines. With only a meagre power output, aircraft designers were obliged to keep aircraft weights as low as possible. Landing gear was an obvious choice for attention, being big, bulky and heavy by nature. Various schemes were investigated that offered alternatives to the usual arrangement undercarriage legs,

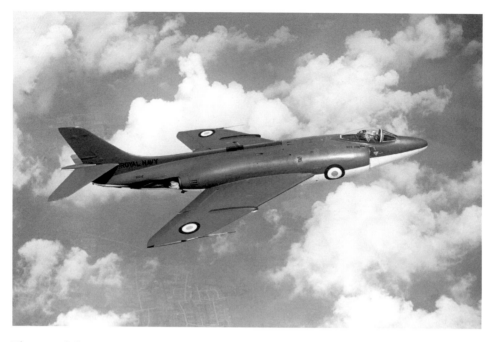

The second Supermarine N113 prototype WT859, illustrating the original dihedral tailplane configuration that was soon changed prior to series production.

wheels and door fairings. The concept of using retractable skids was examined and Germany had embraced this concept during the Second World War, in particular the revolutionary Arado Ar 234 *Blitz* jet bomber. The French also looked at the idea and produced the Barouder, a small fighter that used a trolley for take-off and relied on a skid for landing.

However, Britain's main interest was driven by the Navy. With carrier operations firmly in mind, it was proposed that a rubber landing surface could be developed, enabling aircraft to land without wheels or skids. In retrospect, the idea seems ludicrous, but trials were conducted both on land and at sea using Vampire jet fighters. The first landings were often spectacularly poor, but once suitable techniques had been learned, the landings became almost routine and it was proved that the system could work. The problem was that deck landings would damage the aircraft unless some sort of undercarriage was fitted and this defeated the whole object of the exercise. Likewise, the landing system did not take into account the difficulties of recovering the aircraft and preparing it for launch by catapult. Most importantly, it was accepted that advances in jet engine design would enable engines to develop more thrust. Therefore, future jet aircraft could operate with conventional landing gear and the idea was eventually forgotten. However, the original concept was very much alive.

Supermarine created an aircraft that was designed specifically for flexible deck landings. The Supermarine Type 505 featured a flat lower fuselage incorporating two Avon engines, perfectly suited for the task of settling comfortably onto a rubber deck. With swept wing design at an early stage, the 505 featured straight wings and incorporated a 'butterfly' V-tail that saved some airframe weight. When the Admiralty abandoned the flexible deck scheme in 1947, Supermarine opted to continue development of the 505, but with a conventional landing gear housed within a slightly thicker wing surface. The overall dimensions were increased to enable the aircraft to fly at lower landing speeds. This also enabled Supermarine to use the existing Attacker fighter fuselage as the basic core of the new aircraft's structure, although the resulting aircraft (Type 508) bore little resemblance to the earlier design. The Admiralty adopted this design under Specification N.9/47 and three prototypes were ordered. One was to be fitted with the new 30-mm cannon and radar ranging equipment and cameras were also included to enable the aircraft to undertake both the fighter and reconnaissance roles.

The first of these aircraft (VX133) was transported by road to Boscombe Down from where it made its first flight on 31 August 1951 with test pilot Mike Lithgow at the controls. A short series of test flights swiftly ensued so that the aircraft could complete the ten flying hours necessary to enable VX133 to appear at the 1951 SBAC Farnborough show. It duly appeared at the event and Lithgow performed a sedate series of manoeuvres for the assembled spectators, mindful that the aircraft had hardly been tested. After Farnborough, 508 was returned to test flying and on 5 December, Lithgow was flying the aircraft at low altitude when the aircraft began to shake violently. The aircraft then began to pitch up violently and Lithgow disengaged elevator power in an attempt to restore control. Unfortunately, this act made things far worse and he blacked out as the g-forces became intolerable, eventually reaching 11g. When he regained consciousness he was at 11,000 feet in an upward vertical roll. He finally managed to regain control of the aircraft and carefully returned to Chilbolton, the aircraft looking distinctly worse for wear with both pitot probes having been torn away.

Supermarine's design team assumed that the undercarriage had accidentally extended during the flight and this had been the cause of the sudden uncontrollability. The aircraft was carefully examined for damage and the undercarriage was modified to ensure that no such accident would happen again. Alarmingly, the same fault occurred a few flights later; however, the modified undercarriage stayed retracted, indicating that accidental extension of the gear had not been the cause at all. The aircraft was observed from the ground when the loss of control occurred and this enabled Supermarine to establish that it was aileron flutter that was causing the issue. The installation of power controls soon overcame this problem. In all other respects, the Type 508 performed well and the next aircraft was completed a year later flying for the first time in August 1952.

Supermarine Type 529 VX136 pictured during a public demonstration at the 1952 SBAC Farnborough show. The prototype Valiant is visible in the background.

VX136 incorporated a number of design changes – including cannon armament – and the aircraft was re-designated as the Type 529.

The two Type 529 aircraft were both found to be prone to flutter problems and this limited the scope of the test programme, but they did provide Supermarine with much data. As the heaviest and most powerful aircraft to have flown with the Fleet Air Arm, they also enabled the Navy's carrier crews to learn a lot about ship-borne operations. Also, they undoubtedly helped the Navy prepare for the future and inevitably influenced Admiralty thinking on future projects. The third of the new jets was re-designated yet again, this time as the Type 525. In this case, the reasons for the change of designation were immediately obvious as VX138 incorporated redesigned swept wings and a conventional cruciform tail layout with a swept fin and tailplanes. In effect, it was a completely different aeroplane although it retained the 529's fuselage, cockpit and modified landing gear. Supermarine had gleaned enough knowledge to adopt swept wings and by redesigning the 529, they believed that the aircraft would demonstrate a marked improvement in terms of maximum speed.

Mike Lithgow successfully flew VX138 for the first time on 27 April 1954. Although the aircraft performed well, there was some disappointment with the more powerful Avon RA7 engines, each delivering 7,500 lb of thrust, as speed did not improve significantly. It was a problem that US manufacturers also experienced and the solution was the adoption of the area rule principle whereby the aircraft's frontal cross-section is contoured to enable a constant section to be presented to the airflow. This meant reshaping the fuselage so that the middle portions were tapered inwards in order to compensate for the additional cross-section of the wings. The result is the 'Coke bottle' effect that can be seen on many post-war and contemporary aircraft. Unmodified, the Type 525 was still an impressive performer and was capable of reaching Mach 1 in a shallow dive. Dive brakes were incorporated into the 525's airframe and attention was directed towards the aircraft's low-speed handling. In addition to powerful double-slotted flaps, the wings also featured full span leading edge slats. Most significantly, Supermarine also developed a BLC (Boundary Layer Control) blowing system for the 525. This enabled high-pressure air to be bled from the engines and directed through thin slots in front of the trailing edge flap leading edges. This served to smooth the airflow over the flap where it would otherwise have become turbulent creating drag. The BLC system reduced the 525's landing speed by 18 mph and the lower angle of attack that resulted gave the 525's pilot a slower approach speed and a better forward view – assets that were vitally important for carrier operations.

Sadly, the 525's existence was short as it was destroyed in July 1955 when it entered an uncontrollable spin during a test flight. However, it was a useful step towards the ultimate development of this series of aircraft and on 19 January 1956, the first Type 544 made its maiden flight, once again in the hands of Mike Lithgow. This aircraft was a direct development of the earlier 525, but with a re-contoured fuselage and other refinements. It was in effect the prototype for what became the Scimitar – the production variant that went into Fleet Air Arm service.

The sleek Supermarine Type 525 takes to the runway at Farnborough during September 1954, ready to begin a thrilling high-speed demonstration.

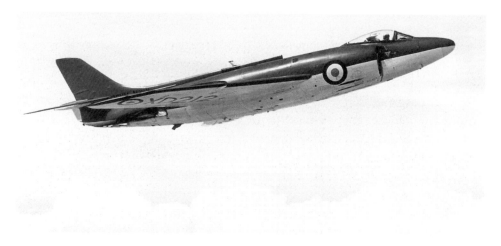

The first production Supermarine Scimitar, XD212, resplendent in FAA dark grey and white colours. The revised tailplane angle can be seen.

By the time the Type 544 emerged, the Navy's requirements had changed, and although the Scimitar was almost always referred to as a fighter and designated as such, it was a bomber. The Navy required a low-level, high-speed attack aircraft capable of delivering the first generation atomic bomb that would soon be available and the Scimitar was identified as being the most suitable aircraft for this role. The Scimitar's robust construction would be ideal for the punishing low-level environment and the aircraft's high speed would be useful for post-attack egress. Although the Admiralty proposed the aircraft should be capable of fulfilling fighter, reconnaissance and conventional bombing roles, the Scimitar was therefore expected to realise the low-level nuclear strike role even before it entered FAA service.

The first examples of the 544 revealed some troublesome handling issues that resulted in fairly significant changes to the aircraft's outward appearance. The wing leading edge was redesigned to incorporate notches while fences were fitted to the upper wing surface. Together, these modifications cured a recurrent pitch up problem that was caused by high-speed air separation over the wing surfaces. The aircraft's tailplanes were also redesigned to help overcome this problem and the prototype's ten-degree dihedral attachments were changed to ten-degree anhedral. After a lengthy test and trials programme, the first production Scimitar F.Mk.1 (XD212) took to the air on 11 January 1957. By August of that year, No. 700X Flight had been formed at RNAS Ford to start acceptance and operational development of the new aircraft type. In FAA service, the Scimitar proved to be a versatile aircraft that was suited to a variety of roles. Armed with Sidewinder AAMs and Aden cannon, the aircraft was a useful if unremarkable fighter and reconnaissance platform, but as an attack aircraft, it was a far more practical aircraft.

An excellent 'action' shot of a Scimitar getting airborne. The carrier's catapult attachment strop can be seen falling away underneath the aircraft.

Although designated as a fighter, the Scimitar was almost exclusively assigned to the attack role. As illustrated, AAMs were occasionally carried, but generally only as a self-defence measure.

No. 807 Naval Air Squadron applies a very appropriate scimitar motif to the tails of its aircraft, as seen on this Scimitar F.Mk.1 about to take the wire on HMS *Victorious*. Small practice bombs can be seen attached to the outer wing pylons.

With AGM-45 Bullpup ASMs, conventional HE bombs and rocket projectiles, the Scimitar was perfectly suited to the low-level environment thanks to its tough construction. Most importantly, it could carry the Red Beard tactical nuclear bomb and LABS (Low Altitude Bombing System) 'toss' manoeuvres were swiftly developed to enable the Scimitar to be used in the nuclear strike role. A great deal of the Scimitar's operational activity was centred on this role and many training sorties were frequently conducted so that the LABS technique could be perfected and practiced. Small practice bombs were usually carried for LABS training although dummy Red Beard rounds were also used occasionally. Live Red Beard weapons were rarely carried as the weapon was notoriously delicate and far from suitable for routine carriage. When Red Beard weapons were carried by the Scimitar, catapult launches were only made if the carrier was in range of a land base as all recoveries with Red Beard weapons were made conventionally on land. The Scimitar's frontline service with the FAA was relatively short, largely due to the Navy's general dissatisfaction with the Scimitar's serviceability and safety record. In-flight difficulties became common and hydraulic failures, engine fires and other problems were compounded by numerous landing accidents, eventually resulting in thirty-nine of the whole fleet of seventy-six Scimitars being written off.

Set against a glittering sea, the huge bulk of a Scimitar streaks over the stern of HMS *Victorious*, tail hook extended.

Although an effective attack aircraft, the Scimitar was soon replaced by the Buccaneer. Scimitars remained active in second-line roles, however, especially as refuelling tankers, often operating in direct support of the Buccaneers that had replaced them in frontline service. The underwing refuelling hose and drogue pod can be seen here under the starboard wing.

Above and below: The Scimitar earned a reputation for unreliability and temperamental performance thanks to a number of accidents, including many landing accidents onboard carriers. In fact, the aircraft performed well, but FAA training was at the time unsuited to fast jets and often included very little carrier landing practice. Little wonder that accidents ensued.

Although unremarkable by contemporary standards, the Scimitar was a big and heavy warplane. Both air and ground crews took some time to become accustomed to the Scimitar's size and bulk. Arguably, even the FAA's command structure was ill prepared to take on the Scimitar. (*Courtesy Terry Goulding*)

However, most of the Scimitar's deficiencies were not attributable to the aircraft as most were due to the Navy's poor logistical support and flying training procedures. Pilots flew carrier launches and recoveries all too infrequently and it was their lack of experience that often contributed to so many Scimitar mishaps. The single-seat Scimitar was also a difficult aircraft to operate and the Navy soon had their eyes set on a much more capable two-man bomber: the illustrious Blackburn Buccaneer.

When the Buccaneer began to enter FAA service, the Scimitar was soon made redundant although a number remained in service on second-line duties. The woeful lack of power from the Buccaneer S1's Gyron Junior engines effectively prohibited heavy carrier launches and the Scimitar became a useful asset 'topping up' Buccaneers with fuel after launch. The Scimitar was a short-lived chapter in the Fleet Air Arm's post-war history, but nonetheless an important one. It was the first of a new generation of heavy, powerful high-performance carrier aircraft and paved the way for even more capable aircraft that followed. As a fighter, it was unremarkable. However, when the Navy opted to adopt the Sea Vixen as its new fleet fighter, the rigged Scimitar was a perfect solution for the Navy's requirement for a fast, low-flying attack platform. But its capabilities were limited and the Navy was already looking towards its longer-term requirements long before the first Supermarine 544 took to the skies.

So it was that Naval Staff Requirement 39 was issued in 1952 calling for a low-level and high-speed (Mach 0.85) attack aircraft for carrier operation capable of delivering conventional and nuclear weaponry. The requirement was detailed and

Magnificent and moody, the Scimitar set against a seascape sunset. Despite its size, the Scimitar's wings could be folded to enable the aircraft to be accommodated in standard aircraft carrier lifts. (*Courtesy Terry Goulding*)

specific describing an aircraft that would be capable of carrying a bomb load of up to 4,000 lb, but compatible with the Navy's carrier decks and deck lifts that dictated overall dimensions of no more than 51 feet in length and 20 feet in span. Maximum take-off weight would be 45,000 lb, maximum landing weight would be 35,000 lb and compatibility with British catapult and arrestor systems would be necessary. Long range was also stipulated (more than 400 nm) and the aircraft would also be expected to 'double-up' as a carrier-borne refuelling tanker.

This was quite a bold requirement for 1952 and a number of equally daring design submissions emerged during 1953. Among these was Armstrong Whitworth's AW.168, which was probably one of the most conservative of the NA.39 design proposals. With swept wings and engines mounted in fairings under each wing, the design looked similar to Sud Aviation's Vautour, but in order to meet the Navy's carrier requirements, the design was to feature wing boundary layer control (BLC) 'blowing' in order to increase lift and lower carrier approach speed. Additionally, it was proposed that the engines should be fitted with exhaust scoops which would deflect thrust downwards at forty-five degrees, enabling slower approaches and improved launch characteristics. However, despite these exotic innovations, the overall design did not offer any promise of particularly high-speed or a good low-level performance and in many respects the AW.168 was an obsolescent design.

Westland's submission was potentially more promising, but it was the design offered

Resplendent in smart naval colours and panels of bright red (applied for test flying), this pre-production Buccaneer S1 carried a Red Beard test specimen in its weapons bay. When the bulky weapon was fitted, the rotating bay door was often fixed in the open position.

by Shorts that was undoubtedly the most radical featuring their new 'isoclinic' wing design. This swept wing abandoned the concept of conventional ailerons and opted for complete outer sections of the wing surface, pivoted to create directional control. With an offset fighter-type canopy and no horizontal tail surfaces, the design was bizarre and probably too exotic for the Admiralty, even though the isoclinic wing concept was subsequently demonstrated by Shorts and acknowledged as a sound concept.

However, interest in the various design concepts slowly gravitated towards the B.103 that was submitted by Blackburn, a Yorkshire-based company with a long tradition of naval aircraft design. Their B.103 was relatively conventional in layout when compared to some of the competing proposals, but it appeared to offer both speed and durability without the risks associated with the other design proposals that may well have led to delays or failure. Blackburn opted for a swept wing design with a generous amount of wing area combined with twin engines, one mounted on each side of the fuselage. Initially, the aircraft was to have been powered by a pair of Bristol Siddeley Sapphire turbojets, but when de Havilland began development of a scaled-down version of its Gyron engines, this powerplant – the Gyron Junior Mk.101 – was chosen, even though it offered 3,000 lb less thrust than the 11,000 lb Sapphire. The reason for this seemingly odd choice was one of weight as Blackburn's designers were eager to keep the aircraft as light as possible both in order to meet the projected performance figures and also to meet the Navy's carrier take-off and landing weight requirements. Unfortunately, the choice of the Gyron subsequently proved to be one that Blackburn may well have regretted. However, even with the 8,000 lb Gyron, the task of creating an aircraft within the Navy's criteria was quite a challenge. Having barely moved on from the Second World War, many Fleet Air Army chiefs were accustomed to smaller, lighter piston-engine aircraft. The concept of a huge jet-powered atomic bomber was one that they could barely imagine and it is to the Admiralty's credit that they had the foresight to seek such an aircraft at the time.

Blackburn's designers subsequently commented with glee that one Naval official specified that the new aircraft should include handholds at the wing tips so that deck crews could bring the aircraft to a halt if it was in danger of over-running. Needless to say, Blackburn explained that an aircraft of the B.103's size and weight was not going to be the kind of aeroplane that could be man-handled! Even with relatively small engines and intelligent engineering design, the aircraft was large and extremely heavy, but Blackburn embraced the new concept of BLC wing 'blowing' that was being developed by the NACA in the US. Boundary Layer Control was a fascinating concept whereby high pressure air bled from the engine could be directed through a series of ducts to thin slots placed across the wing leading edge upper surface. This feed of air would then run across the wing surface and 'smooth' the airflow when it became disrupted at slow speed. The result of this smoothing technique was the creation of more lift and would enable the aircraft to fly at a slower speed. The downside to this concept was that some 10 per cent of each engine's mass flow would be directed to the BLC system, decreasing the thrust of the already-modest engines further still. However, BLC offered a good solution to Blackburn's aims and with drooped ailerons – i.e. each aileron deflected simultaneously – the aircraft would effectively have full-span flaps, bringing landing speed down by at least 17 knots. The BLC system would also act as an anti-icing system without any further design effort being necessary. The only potential difficulty with the proposal seemed to be the predicted trim change when the flap was selected. Blackburn's solution was once again a bold one and the BLC system was simply extended to the tailplane surfaces and a flap system incorporated.

From the outset, the NA.39 design was intended to be a nuclear bomber. Its primary means of destroying its designated targets, particularly the Sverdlovs, would be an atomic bomb. After the Blackburn B.103 was selected for development, the initial design was drawn up around the carriage of Green Cheese: an air-launched guided bomb that was being developed by Fairey for carriage by their Gannet Anti-Submarine Warfare (ASW) aircraft. Green Cheese was to have been used by the Gannet, Blackburn B.103 and the RAF's Valiants, but the task of producing a missile capable of being launched from three very different aircraft types proved to be a challenge. The design of this weapon began as a glide bomb with small wings

Buccaneer S1 aircraft from No. 809 Naval Air Squadron pictured at Lossiemouth. The all-white anti-flash paint scheme lasted for only a few years and soon gave way to more standard naval camouflage.

and an atomic warhead, but Fairey eventually abandoned this concept in favour of a powered version with a rocket motor. Another version had fixed wings for the Valiant and another with pop-out wings for carriage by the Gannet and B.103. However, the weapon was not suitable for the Gannet as it was too heavy. Even if its weight could be reduced, it would still not fit into the Gannet's weapons bay with the bay doors closed.

Consequently, the Admiralty eventually dropped the proposal to equip Gannets with Green Cheese, leaving Fairey to continue development of a weapon that could no longer be carried by their own aircraft. The missile would have a semi-active radar seeker, but would be initially directed by data supplied from the B.103's radar. Once launched, the missile's own seeker would make the weapon vulnerable to detection. Therefore, it was proposed that a 'jinking' system would be introduced to steer the missile on a weaving trajectory while heading towards its target. Hitting the water at an angle of forty degrees, the missile radome would shear off and an angled internal surface would steer the missile upwards to detonate under the ship. This required the radar seeker to be configured so that the missile did not hit the ship, but impacted in the water ahead of it. This led to a great deal of development work – including test drops made by RAF Washington bombers – and the combination of delays and cost increases led to the cancellation of the project in 1956.

As an alternative, a more conventional freefall bomb was selected in the shape of Red Beard, a small tactical weapon with an atomic warhead providing an explosive yield of up to 25 kilotons. With no guidance system, the bomb would be released on a free trajectory. Instead of being dropped from level flight, it would be thrown towards the target in a 'toss' manoeuvre. The launch aircraft would enter a steady climb during which the bomb would be released towards its target while the aircraft turned away and out of reach of the bomb's effects. Partly as a result of the initial plans to carry Green Cheese, the B.103 was developed to incorporate a revolving bomb door system so that the Red Beard bomb could be housed in a specially-contoured carriage unit within the weapons bay allowing the bay to be opened at relatively high speed. This revolutionary design enabled the aircraft to operate at high speed with the weapons bay open. It also enabled weapons to be loaded easily, the rotating door being held at ninety degrees while weapons were attached. Conventional bombs would also be easily carried in the bay and a reconnaissance pack was also designed that could be fitted into the bay as required.

Another significant aspect of the Blackburn B.103's design was the incorporation of area rule principles. This was another relatively new concept at the time, embracing the notion that an aircraft's aerodynamic efficiency could be improved by keeping the aircraft's frontal cross-section the same throughout the airframe. The result of this thinking was the now-familiar 'Coke bottle' effect with a bulged rear fuselage and 'waisted' centre fuselage that became accepted as a standard part of combat aircraft design. The area ruling principle changed the shape of the B.103 considerably, but it did reduce the aircraft's drag at high speed. Also, as an indirect benefit, the fatter rear fuselage provided more internal space for avionic equipment. In order to meet the stringent requirements of the Navy's carrier deck lifts, Blackburn also incorporated some fairly drastic measures to enable the aircraft to be folded down in size when not in use. The wings were designed to hinge upwards in traditional naval fashion, but the nose section forward of the cockpit was also designed to hinge, the entire radome section pivoting backwards so that the unit faced rearwards.

Even more ingenious was the creation of huge speed brakes in the form of two petal devices attached to the extreme rear fuselage. When closed, they formed a streamlined rear fuselage, but when required they opened horizontally to provide extremely effective aerodynamic braking. At the same time, they effectively reduced the aircraft's overall length and when opened fully on the ground a 4-foot reduction in length was achieved. These devices enabled the B.103 to fit comfortably onto the Navy's carrier lifts and when combined with an under-fuselage tail hook and very sturdy landing gear, it was clear that the Navy was to get a very serious piece of kit perfectly designed for the maritime environment. Perhaps most significantly, Blackburn recognised the need for structural strength in an aircraft that would be purpose-designed for continual operation at low level. It was envisaged that the

Pictured at the moment of take-off, a Buccaneer S.Mk.1 roars away from the deck of HMS *Ark Royal*. The Buccaneer S1's Gyron Junior engines were adequate for routine operations, but lacked sufficient power for 'hot and high' deployments.

aircraft should be capable of achieving at least 3,000 hours of operational flight, a figure that seems surprisingly modest when compared to modern aircraft, but the need to operate at wave-top height would inevitably take a disproportionately high toll on the aircraft's strength. Constant airframe stress would require an extremely tough aircraft and in order to achieve this, Blackburn employed a system of milling components from solid blocks of aluminium alloy (even the huge wing sections were cut from solid aluminium). As if this was not enough to ensure structural strength, steel was used in areas where durability was critical and the result was an aeroplane which its crews often proudly described as 'tough as old boots'. Indeed, the aircraft was to last and to take a huge amount of punishment.

When the B.103 was accepted for a development contract in July 1955, it was decided that a fleet of twenty development airframes would be built. This was quite a departure from normal British practice of manufacturing perhaps only a couple of prototypes. It might be argued that this decision reflected a lack of certainty in the aircraft's capabilities. However, it was probably the Admiralty's sense of urgency and a desire to get the aircraft into operational service as swiftly as possible. Despite a variety of fairly radical design innovations, the B.103 was fairly conventional in terms of overall layout. Blackburn certainly took a bold step in taking on the creation of a high-speed nuclear bomber when their most recent product had been the lumbering piston-powered Beverley transporter. The company's factory airfield at Brough on the banks on the river Humber had become scattered with examples of this mighty twin-finned transport aircraft. On the other hand, the comparatively small and sleek B.103 – which became more commonly referred to as the NA.39 in relation to the original naval requirement – did not become a familiar sight here. As Brough was a small site with a modest runway, Blackburn opted to export all flight testing of the new aircraft to Holme on Spalding Moor, a former wartime RAF airfield with hangar facilities and substantial bomber runways.

As each development aircraft reached completion, it was partially dismantled and transported by road to Holme where it would be reassembled and assigned to the test programme. However, Ministry officials dictated that the first flight of the new aircraft should be conducted from the Royal Aircraft Establishment's airfield at Thurleigh, even though there was no logical reason why this was necessary. The first aircraft (XK486) was completed at Brough early in 1958 and a series of engine runs was completed before the aircraft was partially dismantled and transported to RAE Bedford, shrouded under tarpaulins in order to keep the aircraft away from public scrutiny. After reassembly at Thurleigh, the aircraft emerged in a striking blue and white paint scheme complete with national insignia of non-standard size, designed to confuse any attempt at establishing the aircraft's precise proportions. It later transpired that these attempts to thwart espionage achieved very little and both British and Soviet observers established the aircraft's size and its likely capabilities.

In April 1958, the aircraft was ready to conduct taxi trials and on 30 April, test pilot Derek Whitehead took XK486 into the air for the first time, completing a short test flight of just under forty minutes which he described as very satisfactory. Further test flights were then conducted and introduced the BLC system that worked successfully. On 9 July, Whitehead flew the aircraft from Thurleigh over to Blackburn's test facility at Holme on Spalding Moor. Just three years had elapsed since the contract had been awarded to Blackburn and the new strike aircraft was ready to begin its test flight programme.

The second and third development aircraft were designed purely as aerodynamic test aircraft and these aircraft made their first flights from Holme. The third example, XK488, spent much of its time at de Havilland's airfield at Hatfield where it was assigned to trials of the Gyron Junior engine's performance. Pure aerodynamic performance was explored by the two aircraft at Home and representative deck landing equipment was installed on the airfield so that carrier approaches could be investigated. Arrester gear was also installed, although catapult launch trials were conducted at the RAE's facility at Thurleigh. From the fourth aircraft onwards, attention moved to avionics and weapons, and these aircraft incorporated some subtle design alterations such as the nose contours changing significantly to incorporate radar gear. Later aircraft also introduced what was to become the standard Fleet Air

A rare photograph of a white-painted Buccaneer S.Mk.1 carrying the purpose-built reconnaissance rack that could be fitted inside the aircraft's rotating bomb bay. (*Courtesy Tony Clarke collection*)

Arm paint scheme for the aircraft with white undersides and dark grey upper surfaces instead of the garish blue that had been previously applied. XK489 introduced naval features such as the wing folding mechanism and arrestor hook, and after making its first flight in January 1959, it transferred to RAE Bedford via A&AEE Boscombe Down to commence catapult launch trials and arrested landings. This aircraft also tested the revolving weapons bay door design and it was demonstrated to be effective throughout the aircraft's projected speed range. The NA.39 made its public debut as a staid exhibit at the Paris Air Show in 1959. The aircraft then made its British debut at Farnborough in September of that year, although it was operated from Boscombe Down so closer public scrutiny was not possible. No mention was made of the aircraft's nuclear capability nor was any reference made to its intended targets. On the ground, the rather odd-looking bomber gave every impression of being relatively insignificant. But first impressions can, of course, be highly deceptive...

Sea trials were particularly important. XK489 and XK523 were assigned to the carrier HMS *Victorious* during 1959 although the start of the trials was delayed by the crash of XK490 on 12 October. The aircraft was flying from Boscombe Down on test with a US Navy pilot and an observer from Blackburn occupying the rear seat. The aircraft crashed in the New Forest and although both crew members ejected, they were both killed as the aircraft was inverted at the moment of ejection. Investigations caused delays to the test programme, but it was soon established that the accident had not been due to a design or technical error. The aircraft had been flying too slow and had stalled at a low altitude from where there was insufficient height to recover. The tragic accident cast a shadow of gloom over the NA.39 programme, but by January, the project had resumed its enthusiastic pace and carrier trials began in Lyme Bay.

Derek Whitehead performed the first carrier landing in XK523 and X489 followed from Holme on Spalding Moor two days later. Some thirty-one flights were made during the trials, often in very poor weather conditions and at various all-up weights. No significant problems were encountered although some changes were made to the aircraft's landing gear and tail hook as a direct result. The trials demonstrated that the aircraft operated easily from the carrier deck and could be accommodated by the carrier's deck lift. With the carrier trials complete, the main test programme continued and on 4 April 1960, the first true production-standard aircraft made its first flight. XK524 incorporated many design changes which resulted from the flight trials and completion of the aircraft was consequently delayed. The next aircraft (XK525) flew just three months later and was fitted with a complete navigation and weapons system. By the end of 1960, three more aircraft were flying and after some time at Boscombe Down, they contributed towards the completion of CA (Controller Aircraft) Release in July 1961 at which stage the aircraft was officially cleared for service use.

In celebration of this milestone, the Admiralty sought a suitable name for the new aircraft and on 26 August, it was formally named 'Buccaneer' in recognition of its maritime and combative role. The name also perpetuated the tradition of alliteration that had become popular with British aircraft manufacturers. Thus, the first production aircraft was to be designated as the Blackburn Buccaneer S.Mk.1, the 'S' designation indicating nuclear capability. The 'S' designation had been applied to the Westland Wyvern although there is scarce documentation to explain why 'A' could not have been used to designate an attack capability in this instance. Likewise, the RAF did not subsequently embrace the 'S' designation for its nuclear bombers, opting to use 'B' or 'G' (indicative of only 'Ground Attack'). It would seem therefore that the 'S' designation was purely a naval innovation that was applied to the Buccaneer and never used again. Testing continued at Boscombe Down, the manufacturer's site at Holme and further testing was conducted from West Freugh where many weapons release trials were conducted. On 5 October 1960, another catastrophe occurred when XK486 performed a test flight from Holme. Thanks to the failure of its artificial horizon, the aircraft crashed while flying at low level at Market Weighton. Both crew members ejected safely, but the crash was another setback that caused yet more delays to an urgent schedule. (The CA Release had been scheduled for the following April.)

In 1961, the Buccaneer finally joined the ranks of the Royal Navy and No. 700Z Flight was formed at RNAS Lossiemouth in Scotland. The Navy's Intensive Flying Trials Unit (IFTU) received some of the later development aircraft that were close to production standard. All twenty of development aircraft had joined the test programme by the end of 1961 – two having subsequently been lost – and the final six aircraft were in effect completed to S.Mk.1 standard. A third aircraft was sadly lost on 31 August 1961 when XK529 was assigned to HMS *Hermes* for a series of deck launches and recoveries conducted in Lyme Bay. The crew, both from Boscombe Down's C Squadron, were killed in what was established to be an accident caused by human error rather than technical fault. No. 700Z Flight was formed on 7 March 1961 and its first aircraft arrived in May in the shape of two Meteor T7s followed by four Hunter T8s, all assigned to training. It was not until August that the first Buccaneers arrived. By the end of the year, six Buccaneers from the development fleet were stationed at the unit with 'LM' tail codes (designating Lossiemouth as home base) and nose codes 680 through to 685. Unusually, XK534 was not delivered to Lossiemouth in the standard dark grey and white paint finish. It arrived at the base sporting an eye-catching overall white finish. This seemingly bizarre paint scheme was introduced by the Navy in recognition of the aircraft's nuclear role, the specially-manufactured white paint designed to reflect radiation and heat. It was subsequently applied to all new Fleet Air Arm Buccaneers and RAF's nuclear bombers too, but abandoned in favour of more traditional camouflage just three years later.

No. 700Z Flight was commanded by Lieutenant Commander A. J. Leahy, the former commander of No. 738 Squadron operating Sea Hawks. Transitioning to the Buccaneer was quite a step for the pilots and at the time only one FAA pilot had any prior experience on the type having been assigned to the Blackburn trials team. The aim of the new unit was as quoted by Leahy '...to get as many hours with the Buccaneer as possible' and this task was achieved only through a careful process of training. No dual-control Buccaneers were built – the Fleet Air Arm traditionally did not allocate funds to such concepts – and any pilot transitioning to the aircraft effectively made his first solo on his first flight. The Hunters assigned to the unit enabled some flights to be performed with instructors flying alongside the Buccaneer to talk new pilots through initial handling, but there was no doubt that the lack of a 'twin stick' Buccaneer was a hurdle that could have been avoided. Thankfully, the Buccaneer's handling qualities were good and even though initial flying on the type was always done with great trepidation, no major accidents occurred during the process.

For the 1962 Farnborough SBAC show, No. 700Z Flight formed a four-aircraft display team. The crowds were thrilled by the fast and manoeuvrable jet that looked sleek and powerful in flight in contrast to its rather bulky and heavy appearance when on the ground. The 700Z pilots performed an impressive display that put the new Buccaneer through its paces, indeed the unit worked the aircraft very hard at all times. During one display rehearsal, one aircraft landed with damaged tail fin and flaps, emphasising that even a tough machine like the Buccaneer could be overstressed. The unit's intensive flying involved a huge number of flying hours in all flight regimes, weather conditions and day and night operations. The unit concluded that the Buccaneer was reliable, handled very well and performed admirably with an impressive top speed, an excellent ride at low level and a very useful carrier approach speed that was ten knots slower than other contemporary FAA types. Ground crews also reported that the aircraft was easy to maintain and it was therefore no surprise that the Navy swiftly introduced the first operational squadron, this being No. 801 Naval Air Squadron that formed on 17 July 1962.

Once equipped with early-production Buccaneer S1 aircraft, this unit made the Buccaneer's first carrier deployment in February 1963 when a four-week cruise was completed on HMS *Ark Royal*. A year later, the unit deployed again, this time on HMS *Victorious* for a cruise to the Far East. They also contributed to a British show of force when a potential conflict was developing between Nairobi and neighbouring Tanganyika. Already, the Buccaneer was at the forefront of Britain's worldwide naval influence.

The third unit to form, also at Lossiemouth, was No. 809 NAS from the remains of 700Z Flight in January 1963. This unit became the Buccaneer's shore-based training unit, eventually acquiring a fleet of fourteen aircraft and a gaggle of Hunter trainers. It was renumbered as No. 736 NAS in 1965. Finally, No. 800 NAS formed on 18 March 1964 embarking on HMS *Eagle* for the first time in December. This unit enjoyed a great deal of operational activity beginning in 1965 when HMS *Eagle* was sent to Aden and the unit's Buccaneers were assigned to reconnaissance and over-flight duties in the region. The unit then participated in similar activities off the coast of Rhodesia when it declared independence and many long-duration flights were conducted, often requiring in-flight refuelling from FAA Scimitar and Sea Vixen tankers. In flight refuelling capability was built in to the Buccaneer's design from the outset and some of the first development aircraft had incorporated a retractable refuelling probe on the aircraft's forward fuselage. Unfortunately, the probe was less than ideal and a series of test flights revealed that the probe was not suitable for safe in-flight refuelling. The test pilots reporting that the probe was difficult to line up with the tanker's hose basket. Investigations indicated that the cause of instability was the probe's relatively close proximity to the Buccaneer's fuselage, which also raised concerns that airflow into the engine intake could also be disturbed. Although a series of 'fixes' was attempted, the ultimate solution was to abandon the retractable probe in favour of a much larger 'bolt-on' probe that could be positioned ahead of the cockpit windscreen, offset to starboard to aid forward vision and sufficiently high to avoid any risk of engine air intake disruption. This system worked perfectly and the simple bolt-on system was adopted for service use.

The Buccaneer was also designed to have a refuelling tanker capability and Blackburn looked at various schemes to develop a refuelling pack that could be

An interesting image of a Buccaneer S1 just seconds after the aircraft had accelerated away from an aborted landing (known as a 'bolter'). The air brakes are still partially open and the Gyron Junior engines are working hard to provide sufficient thrust, both for forward thrust and the BLC system.

fitted into the Buccaneer's weapons bay in much the same way as the developed reconnaissance pack. The plan was eventually dropped in favour of a more simple provision for a standard Flight Refuelling Mk.20 pod that could be attached to a wing pylon when required and this system was used successfully throughout the Buccaneer's service life. The Buccaneer's tanker and receiver capability was recognised as a vital asset, especially when many Buccaneer operations were affected by the aircraft's relatively poor take-off performance. The Buccaneer S1 relied on the Gyron Junior, an engine that was barely sufficient to give the Buccaneer the power that it required. Carrier launches at high weights – especially in hot conditions – were often impossible and tanker-configured aircraft were often needed to 'top up' Buccaneers once they got into the air. In September 1964, this led to a unit being formed at Lossiemouth specifically for the purpose of supporting Buccaneer operations that were hampered by the Gyron's meagre performance. No. 800B Flight was equipped with tanker-configured Scimitars and the unit routinely assigned its Scimitars to deployed Buccaneer squadrons so that HMS *Eagle* was able to launch Buccaneers with full weapons loads, even in the least favourable conditions. With a reduced fuel load, the Buccaneer could safely get airborne to be topped up with fuel from a Scimitar before embarking on its assigned mission. The concept worked well, but illustrated the absurdity of fitting the modest Gyron Junior engine to the hefty Buccaneer.

CHAPTER EIGHT
Piratical Perfection

Although the Buccaneer was recognised as a highly potent warplane, it was also clear that it was underpowered. Its lack of power was observed when it was required to carry a heavy fuel load for endurance/range and was often laden with ordnance carried in the weapons bay or from the four wing pylons. The need for BLC blowing exacerbated the problems further still, but once safely into the air, the Buccaneer S1 was a fast and stable platform that enabled the FAA pilots to press home attacks with great accuracy. It enjoyed the capability to approach targets from long distances at ultra low level without undue fatigue being caused to either the aircraft or its crew.

As planned, the Buccaneer's primary weapon was the 2,000 lb Red Beard atomic bomb and inert 'shapes' were regularly carried for training sorties. These were occasionally released during practice 'loft' manoeuvres, although smaller practice bombs were more often used for this kind of training. Conventional freefall 1,000 lb bombs were also commonly carried (eight in all) and 2-inch rocket projectiles were also employed, eventually replaced by the SNEB rocket pod, each containing eighteen 68-mm projectiles. The Bullpup ASM was also introduced from 1965. Additionally, reconnaissance profiles were regularly exercised with the purpose-built reconnaissance pack being fitted as necessary. The pack contained six F95 cameras together with a flash crate, although Gloworm rockets were generally carried on wing hard points for illumination of night targets. By any standards, the Buccaneer was a major step forward from the less capable Scimitar. The Navy were greatly impressed by its capabilities, so much so that many officials within the Admiralty firmly believed that the aircraft should also have been acquired by the RAF.

The RAF became embroiled in the long saga of the TSR2 strike aircraft that was designed to replace Canberras in the tactical strike role. It was obvious to everyone – not least Britain's politicians – that the Buccaneer fulfilled the RAF's needs and that a huge amount of money and resources could be saved by adopting it for RAF operations instead of the endlessly delayed and hideously expensive TSR2. The RAF resolutely refused to even consider the concept, claiming that the Buccaneer

Line-up of Buccaneer S1s at Yeovilton in 1964, wings folded and canopy hoods open.

did not have TSR2's range, speed or short field performance that was deemed to be vital for the land-based tactical strike role. In some respects this was true. However, Blackburn had already been looking at ways in which the Buccaneer's performance could be improved and a developed version of the aircraft would undoubtedly have been entirely suitable for the RAF's requirements. But inter-service rivalry was intense and the RAF had no desire to express interest in what was a purpose-built naval aircraft. So much so that their stated requirements became increasingly advanced that the Buccaneer stood no chance of meeting them. This is not to imply that the RAF's position was less credible than the Navy from where a great deal of pressure to buy the Buccaneer came.

The main advocate of the Buccaneer was Lord Louis Mountbatten. He insisted that the RAF should abandon the TSR2 and buy the Buccaneer on the grounds that a joint RAF/FAA design would save the country a huge amount of money. But his position was slightly dishonest in that his main motive for promoting the virtues of Buccaneer was to ensure that treasury money was not wasted on TSR2, so that defence resources might be more readily available for new aircraft carriers. Even

NA39 trials aircraft pictured together at Holme-on-Spalding Moor. Clearly evident are the carefully-designed national insignia, all with different sizes and positions in order to thwart attempts at intelligence gathering.

so, it was clear that the RAF had no truly plausible reason to dismiss Buccaneer as being inferior; however, the RAF remained resolutely against the aircraft – for the time being.

Blackburn recognised the Gyron Junior's deficiencies and consideration of alternative engines had been continuing for some time. There was hope that the Gyron could be developed to produce more thrust, but there were also other powerplants emerging, some of which held great promise. The most significant was the Rolls-Royce Spey turbofan that was in production for the Trident airliner. Rolls-Royce believed that a military version of the engine could be produced that would deliver 11,3080 lb of thrust for only a marginal increase in weight over the Gyron Junior. Two Speys would therefore offer almost 7,000 lb of additional thrust and would require very little modification to the Buccaneer airframe other than enlarged intakes to cater for the greater airflow mass required and larger exhaust jet pipes. Therefore, it was no surprise that Blackburn adopted the Spey as the basis for what became the Buccaneer S.Mk.2. Even before the Mk.1 had entered service, Blackburn announced in January 1962 that a production order for the Buccaneer Mk.2 had been placed. The historic name of Blackburn then disappeared in 1963 when the company became part of the Hawker Siddeley Group and British Aerospace many years later.

The Buccaneer Mk.2 airframe was designed as a minimal-change derivate of the Mk.1 machine, the most significant alteration being the engine intakes. Aircraft from the Mk.1 development batch could have been allocated for conversion to Mk.2 standard, but the Admiralty's eagerness to get the first-generation aircraft into service meant that Blackburn simply could not afford to divert aircraft from the Mk.1 programme. Eventually, XK526 was withdrawn for conversion and it emerged to make its first flight as a Buccaneer Mk.2 on 17 May 1963, flown by Derek Whitehead from Holme on Spalding Moor. XK527 followed a similar path and flew for the first time on 19 August and only a year later, production Mk.2 aircraft were nearing completion on the Brough production line, the first production aircraft taking to the air on 5 June 1964.

Development of the Mk.2 was relatively trouble free and straightforward as the aircraft retained most of the Mk.1 variant's handling characteristics, apart from a superior performance. The Spey engine was recognised as a tough and reliable powerplant that enabled the Buccaneer to operate without any great regard for thrust limitations. Fundamentally, it removed any concerns over the loss of thrust caused by air being bled from the engines for the BLC system and the system was redesigned to take advantage of the Spey's higher mass flow, knocking another eight knots off the necessary launch speed and two knots off the landing speed. It also bestowed a much better land-based take-off and landing performance which was obviously useful for the Fleet Air Arm, but far more relevant to the RAF where interest in the aircraft was officially shunned in favour of the TSR2.

In April 1965, No. 700B Flight formed at Lossiemouth to introduce the Buccaneer Mk.2 into service and the aircraft was subjected to the same intensive flying trials that had been applied to the Mk.1. The trials were completed far more rapidly with much of the handling and weapons delivery testing being little more than a duplication of lessons learned on the Mk.1. The A&AEE conducted deck landing trials on HMS *Ark Royal* before 700B Flight made its first carrier landing with the Mk.2 on HMS *Centaur* on 29 July 1963. Three Buccaneers were also deployed to the US for hot weather trials and additional carrier compatibility exercises. XN974 earned a claim to fame by completing a spectacular return journey to the UK by flying directly from Goose Bay, Canada, to Lossiemouth without in-flight refuelling. This mammoth 1,950 mile flight was, and still is, quite an achievement for a twin-engine, jet-powered attack aircraft.

No. 700B Flight disbanded in September 1965 to make way for the first operational squadron, this being No. 801 NAS that relinquished its less capable Mk.1 aircraft and reformed at Lossiemouth on 14 October 1965. The Navy's delight was scarcely concealed and after inviting the media to marvel at the new aircraft's abilities, it was

Holme-on-Spalding Moor and a magnificent line-up of the NA39 Buccaneer test fleet. The gradual development of the aircraft's nose profile can be seen here, transitioning from the prototype's test instrumentation boom through to a dielectric radome nose cone on XK525.

noted that the Mk.2 had entered service in less than thirty months from the type's first flight, indicating just how trouble free the transition from the earlier Mk.1 had been. To emphasise the new variant's significance, XN980 was flown over Trafalgar Square on 18 October to mark the 160th anniversary of the historical Battle of Trafalgar. This was to illustrate to illustrate to the country at large, and countries further afield, that the Navy now possessed a supremely powerful strike asset. The RAF was still steadfastly set against the Buccaneer, even though they had lost all hope of acquiring the mighty TSR2. Instead, the RAF had pinned its future strike capability on the American F-111K and the Admiralty's, particularly Mountbatten's, efforts to persuade the Government to effectively force the Buccaneer onto the RAF had failed. Much to the Navy's huge disappointment, the Labour Government opted to abandon the plan for a new generation of aircraft carriers during 1966 – the Navy's main motivation for promoting the Buccaneer as a suitable RAF choice – and it therefore became clear that the Navy's carrier force would gradually wind down until the last carrier was withdrawn from use in the mid-1970s.

This inescapable fact meant that the new Buccaneer Mk.2 would be destined to enjoy only a relatively short service life with the Navy of little more than ten years.

The design staff at Brough worked hard to convince the RAF that the Buccaneer would be a good alternative to TSR2 and even proposed a new derivative that would have become the Buccaneer Mk.3 had it been ordered into production. Based on modifications made for the Buccaneer S.Mk.50 export version created for the South African Air Force, the P.145 would have featured larger 430 imperial gallon external fuel tanks, rocket packs for take-off assistance and a four-wheel bogey landing gear to cater for the RAF's short/rough field performance requirement. The Mk.3 could not hope to meet the RAF's Mach Two speed requirement, but the manufacturer and many governmental and service officials questioned whether this speed performance was strictly necessary. Despite all this, the RAF remained disinterested and Defence Minister Healey strived to give the RAF the aircraft that they wanted: the F-111K. Healey later remarked that one of his greatest regrets was having failed to persuade the RAF to buy the Buccaneer in preference to the TSR2 or the F-111K. Ironically, the F-111K order was subsequently cancelled as a result of Britain's growing economic problems – and partly due to delays in development of the F-111 aircraft – leaving the RAF's procurement plans in tatters. Having lost the all important TSR2, the prospect of a fleet of F-111 aircraft had been regarded as a more preferable solution. However, when this plan was also axed, the RAF was effectively forced to embrace a much troubled Anglo-French project that promised to deliver a swing-wing strike aircraft that matched the F-111's capabilities. When the Anglo French Variable Geometry aircraft was also abandoned – largely as a result of France's growing reluctance to pursue a joint project that would compete with its own indigenous export efforts – the RAF was left with no other option than to buy the Buccaneer, the aircraft that had been dismissed and scorned for so long.

During May 1966, No. 801 Squadron embarked on HMS *Victorious* for a three-week cruise through the Mediterranean enabling the Buccaneer Mk.2 to operate in its designated environment for the first time. The deployment was a great success and when HMS *Victorious* returned to UK waters, a Buccaneer was launched on a simulated strike mission against the RAF's facilities on Gibraltar. The aircraft launched from its position in the Irish Sea, performed a low-level attack on the airfield at Gibraltar and returned to HMS *Victorious* in the Irish Sea after a trip of some 2,300 miles. HMS *Victorious* then took the Buccaneers to the Far East and 801 Squadron became involved in the British withdrawal from Aden, flying show of strength missions in the area before sailing home. This was the last cruise performed by HMS *Victorious* as although the carrier was scheduled for eventual withdrawal, a fire broke out on the vessel during a refit in November 1967. It was decided that the cost of completing repairs would outweigh the advantages of keeping the carrier in service for a limited period and was therefore scrapped in 1969. No. 801 Squadron was duly reassigned to HMS *Hermes* but completed only one cruise before disbandment on 21 July 1970.

XK528 pictured during weapon release trials. A dummy WE.177 bomb can be seen just milliseconds after release from the weapons bay. The wingtip fairings contain cameras used to film the weapon releases.

The second frontline Buccaneer S.Mk.2 unit was No. 809 NAS that reformed during January 1966. Assigned to HMS *Hermes*, the unit was soon participating in the serious business of flying show of strength missions around the Gibraltar region after Spain's imposition of airspace restrictions around the British outpost. HMS *Hermes* was scheduled to follow HMS *Victorious* into retirement and No. 809 NAS transferred to Yeovilton for a fifteen month stay from February 1968. It was then deployed to HMS *Ark Royal*, remaining with this ship until it too was decommissioned. It was thus the very last FAA Buccaneer squadron disbanding in December 1978. The Fleet Air Arm's early experience with the Buccaneer S.Mk.2 was undoubtedly satisfactory and the aircraft performed well without any serious vices emerging. It was June 1966 when the first of the type was lost. XN979 from No. 801 Squadron crashed off the Lizard during a training sortie mounted from HMS *Victorious*. The aircraft's wreckage was recovered from a great depth and analysed; however, experts at Boscombe Down believed that pilot error had been the cause and that catapult launch procedures had not been followed.

In order to prove their point, XV153 was launched on 6 October 1966 with an A&AEE pilot at the controls, determined to prove their pilot error theory. With grim success, the aircraft crashed only twenty seconds after launch, but investigations made by Hawker Siddeley revealed that the true cause was an uncontrolled tendency to pitch up and stall thanks to aerodynamic loads imposed by particular combinations of underwing stores and external fuel tanks. The remedy was to redesign the fairing between the wing-mounted 'slipper' fuel tank and the wing, improving BLC efficiency at the expense of slightly greater drag. The tailplane position indicator was improved and a new attitude display was incorporated into the cockpit instrument display. Changes were also made to launch procedures and pilots would no longer select the undercarriage retraction switch until after launch. The set procedure had been for the landing gear to be selected 'up' so that when the aircraft became airborne, solenoid switches would trip as soon as the landing gear oleos became extended, enabling the gear to be retracted at the earliest possible moment. The various changes solved most of the recognised launch risks, but it is fair to say that with certain external loads and in particular take-off conditions, the Buccaneer could be a handful when it left the carrier.

The third of the Fleet Air Arm's frontline Buccaneer units to form was No. 800 NAS, a squadron that transitioned from the S.Mk.1 onto the later variant early in 1967, before embarking on HMS *Eagle*. No. 736 NAS was also reequipped with the Buccaneer S.Mk.2 and became the shore-based Buccaneer training unit for the type, stationed at Lossiemouth and operated a mixed fleet of Mk.1 and Mk.2 aircraft into the 1970s. Shortly after, 800 NAS re-equipped with the Buccaneer S.Mk.2. The unit was called to action in the strangest of circumstances when an oil tanker went aground in the South Western Approaches off Land's End. The *Torrey Canyon* began to break up and its load of crude oil began to spill into the Atlantic causing a grave environmental hazard. Although such disasters are now almost commonplace, the *Torrey Canyon* incident was an international event back in 1967 and no one was entirely sure how the oil spill could be dealt with. It was decided that the most effective solution was to bomb the vessel by air, causing it to break up as swiftly as possible and enabling the huge load of oil to be released in one manageable spill that could theoretically be set alight and burned. The Fleet Air Arm's Buccaneers were selected as the primary means of bombing the ship – this was precisely the type of target that the Buccaneer was designed to attack – and on 28 March, eight aircraft from 736 and 800 Squadrons flew from Lossiemouth and delivered their 1,000 lb high explosive bombs onto the ship.

Some forty-two bombs were dropped on 'academic' twenty-degree dive attacks and thirty bombs hit the ship. The *Torrey Canyon*'s load of crude oil did not burn and a further two attack missions were performed backed up by Hunters and Sea Vixens armed with napalm weapons. These bombing runs also failed to burn most of the oil. The exercise was successful from the Navy's point of view, but the *Torrey Canyon* incident was a perfect example of how not to deal with an oil spillage at sea. After the incident, 800 NAS deployed to HMS *Eagle* and set off on a cruise to the Far East, eventually participating in the British withdrawal from Aden. The unit also spent some time on shore, not least during 1968 when HMS *Eagle* was refitted and

Two early-production Buccaneer S.Mk.1s streak past HMS *Eagle*. This image clearly illustrates the Buccaneer's area ruled fuselage with a large bulge visible in line with the wing's trailing edge. This bulge countered the sudden loss of frontal area, thereby reducing drag.

modified to handle the new Phantom fighter-bombers that were due to enter FAA service. More than eighty touch and go 'bolter' landings were made by the Phantom, but the Government decided that the full costs of equipping HMS *Eagle* for Phantom operations was prohibitive and so the carrier was withdrawn in January 1972. This effectively ended 800 Squadron's existence and the unit disbanded on 23 February.

The last of the Navy's Buccaneer S.Mk.2 units to form was No. 803 NAS that operated from Lossiemouth on 3 July 1967. Unlike other units, 303 was not a routine operational or training squadron and conducted weapons trials and avionics tests, eventually developing standard delivery tactics for FAA squadrons. In addition to the primary nuclear role with Red Beard, the Buccaneer eventually embraced the use of conventional freefalls bombs, Bullpup missiles, rockets and Martel ASMs. By the time that Martel came into regular use, the crude and temperamental Red Beard atomic bomb had been replaced by the WE.177A, a weapon of slimmer proportions that required a new weapons bay fairing to be designed so that the bomb could be carried and delivered at high speed. However, the Buccaneer's primary nuclear role became a less important feature of day-to-day training as the Buccaneer's range of potential targets grew and the operational squadrons devoted most of their time to delivery tactics that were peculiar to more conventional weapons. The decision to

Above and below: Underside view of Buccaneer S2 XN976 showing the Bullpup ASM and the SNEB rocket pod, both being standard fits for many FAA Buccaneer operations during the 1960s. Also visible is the open air brake and the recessed tail hook. XN976 underwent 'tropical' trials at NAS Pensacola and flew further trials onboard the USS *Lexington*. It subsequently became part of the RAF's Buccaneer fleet. (*Courtesy Tony Coles collection*)

accept Martel was taken in September 1966 even though it was obvious the new missile would take years to develop, by which stage the Buccaneer would be due for withdrawal from FAA service.

Martel was created in two distinct forms, one being a TV-guided weapon that featured a camera in the missile's nose. The Buccaneer observer could control the missile by means of a television screen and joystick fitted in the Buccaneer's rear cockpit and although the system worked well, it was reliant upon careful control, good weather and daylight. Martel was also developed in an anti-radar version, a seeker on the missile's nose being designed to home in on radar emissions giving the Buccaneer an effective radar suppression capability. While the Martel's development was underway, the Navy's Buccaneers were modified to carry it and in addition to new controls for the rear cockpit, new weapons pylons were manufactured and the Buccaneer's outer wing panels were modified so that they could each accommodate two Martels. The strengthened wings with new pylons would also enable the Buccaneer to carry triple ejector racks so that six 1,000 lb bombs could be carried under each wing, but although this weapons fit was successfully tested, it was not introduced into regular service. Modified aircraft were re-designated as the Buccaneer S.Mk.2D while a batch of upgraded aircraft without Martel capability were designated as the Buccaneer S.Mk.2C. The Navy achieved Martel capability in late 1973 by which stage and with great irony the RAF had already attained a similar capability.

With both TSR2 and the F-111K unavailable, the RAF expected, or at least hoped, that the AFVG would finally give the RAF the 'Canberra replacement' it had been waiting for. Sadly, AFVG was doomed to failure almost from the outset, hampered

Martel trials aircraft at Holme-on-Spalding Moor. Anti-radiation missiles are attached to the aircraft's underwing pylons for release trials. The IR and TV-guided versions of the Martel became a major part of both FAA and RAF Buccaneer operations from the 1970s onwards.

by France's inability to allow politics to prevail over commercial interest. But by the time that AFVG was finally abandoned, it was becoming clear that the RAF no longer needed the type of aircraft that it had been hoping to acquire. TSR2 had become a long-range, supersonic tactical bomber with strategic capability, but by the late 1960s, Britain was gradually withdrawing from many of its global commitments and strategic bombing was to become a thing of the past as the Navy assumed control of Britain's independent nuclear deterrent in the shape of Polaris. There was little doubt that the long-anticipated Canberra replacement no longer needed to have supersonic capability nor did it need global reach. A truly tactical design was necessary and despite the RAF's dogged determination to avoid it, the Buccaneer was the obvious solution. In its improved Mk.2 form, the Buccaneer would give the RAF a fast (but not supersonic) tactical bomber with a nuclear capability, outstanding low-level stability, a very respectable conventional weapons capability and impressive range. Buccaneer ticked all the boxes, but most importantly it was the only option left available to the RAF. With the greatest of reluctance, it was agreed that the RAF would finally accept the aircraft that it had fought so hard to dismiss for so long.

A batch of twenty-six aircraft was ordered during July 1968 and it was anticipated that the Royal Navy's aircraft would be transferred to the RAF as the FAA carrier force wound down. In 1969, the first RAF crews began training with the Navy's 736 NAS at Lossiemouth. A number of Buccaneer S.Mk.1 aircraft were brought back from retirement in order to provide the unit with sufficient airframes for their new task even though there was never any plan to equip the RAF with Mk.1 aircraft. However, the Buccaneer Mk.1 was soon to be withdrawn completely following a series of events that began in 1970. On 1 December, XN951 crashed while operating in the airfield circuit at Lossiemouth. One engine surged and with only low speed and little height, the aircraft had to be abandoned. Just one week later, XN968 suffered a catastrophic engine turbine failure that forced the crew to eject although the observer was killed due to a malfunction in the ejection sequence. The incidents led to a careful examination of the remaining S.Mk.1 aircraft and their Gyron engines and it was revealed that the powerplants were in very poor condition. It was immediately decided to withdraw the remaining aircraft and the last S.Mk.1 was retired in January 1971.

The RAF designated Honington as their new Buccaneer base. As the first aircraft were completed at Brough, they were transported to Holme on Spalding Moor for flight testing before being delivered to the airfield in Suffolk (some examples moving temporarily to Boscombe Down for clearance trials). The RAF's S.Mk.2B was similar to the Navy's aircraft although some changes were made to the electrical system and the fuselage air brakes were redesigned to avoid metal-to-metal contact. The plan to give the RAF's aircraft additional range through the employment of larger external tanks was dropped as an economy measure, although trials were conducted

Line-up of shiny new Buccaneers. No. 15 Squadron reforms on the type at RAF Laarbruch, enabling the Canberra B(I)8 to be retired from the nuclear-strike role.

at Holme. The first such flight provided some moments of tension as the aircraft was found to be very reluctant to 'unstick' at take-off speed. The reason for this anomaly was the shift in the aircraft's centre of gravity. The longer tanks had been balanced by heavy rocket packs fitted in the rear fuselage of the South African export examples for which the tanks had originally been developed. Former FAA Buccaneers were gradually transferred to the RAF and these were designated as Buccaneer S.Mk.2A, creating a mixed RAF/FAA fleet of four Buccaneer variants all of which were outwardly similar. To confuse matters further still, some Martel-capable FAA aircraft without some of the RAF's modifications were informally designated as 'interim S.Mk.2B' variants.

XV350 was the first new-build Buccaneer to be delivered to the RAF and after being officially handed over on 1 January 1969, made its first flight on 11 February from Holme. In contrast to the Navy's dull, grey-painted aircraft, the new RAF machine was finished in glossy polyurethane grey and green disruptive camouflage with light grey undersides. Despite being the RAF's first machine, it was destined to remain in use as a test airframe, based at Holme, Boscombe Down and other experimental establishments. No. 12 Squadron, a former Vulcan unit, became the first RAF Buccaneer squadron and reformed on 1 October 1969. Four aircraft, former Navy machines, arrived at Honington that day to equip the unit. Assigned to the maritime strike role, 12 Squadron was not truly representative of the RAF's plans to utilise the Buccaneer as a tactical strike aircraft. Instead, the unit was essentially created to assume the anti-ship role that the Navy would soon relinquish when the dwindling carrier force was finally phased out. It was not until 1 October 1970 that the first of the RAF's true tactical strike units was formed on the Buccaneer when No. 15 Squadron stood up at Honington. With new-build aircraft, the unit moved to Laarbruch, Germany, three months later to start the task of replacing the nuclear-capable Canberra interdictors that remained in service, some being assigned to alert status.

Unlike No. 12 Squadron, the new Germany-based unit – together with No. 16 Squadron that reformed during June 1972 – was dedicated to the overland strike role armed with the WE.177 tactical nuclear bomb, one of which could be carried inside the Buccaneer's weapons bay. Delivery profiles similar to those employed by the Navy were developed although the weapon was designed to be delivered by lay-down mode with deployable parachutes to retard the weapon so that the release aircraft had sufficient time to clear the target area. Consequently, the Navy's loft manoeuvre was practiced less frequently as it would be regarded only as a secondary means of delivery. It is unclear whether a single weapon was to be carried as routine, but the weapons bay could be modified to carry two bombs side by side if necessary. The new RAFG Buccaneer squadrons regularly practiced the low-level, lay-down delivery technique on RAF Germany's Nordhorn weapons range using 4 lb practice bombs, although loft delivery profiles were also used. The standard 'varitoss' technique was to climb from low level at an angle of sixty degrees, the bomb released automatically by the onboard computer's timing mechanism. Once released, the aircraft was rolled through 150 degrees and turned back towards the horizon to escape.

Toss bombing manoeuvres were regularly practiced at the Vliehors range on the Netherlands coast, although RAFG Buccaneers often ventured further afield and many weapons release profiles, both nuclear and conventional, were practiced on British ranges at Holbeach, Wainfleet, Theddlethorpe and Donna Nook. Holidaymakers on Mablethorpe's beaches became accustomed to the sight and sound of Buccaneers making their dive attacks, aimed at the weapons range targets a couple of miles distant. The RAF's Buccaneers had a nominal range of 500 miles and this was more than adequate for missions which in wartime would have been flown from Laarbruch. External drop tanks could be carried to extend range further still, but there was no perceived need for longer missions. Therefore air-to-air refuelling was not practised and RAFG Buccaneers were not fitted with bolt-on refuelling probes. Most visits to UK ranges were dictated by weather conditions in

Germany where heavy cloud, fog and rain could be more severe than in the UK. The Buccaneer's range made the use of UK ranges perfectly acceptable and a typical sortie could be mounted to Laarbruch without a refuelling stopover. During the 1970s, the restrictions on flying over Germany were relatively few and training missions were almost always conducted at heights of 500 feet or 250 feet in designated low flying areas. The only significant concerns were the presence of other NATO aircraft in the same region operating from their own respective bases.

As the planned withdrawal of the Navy's carrier force grew closer, the FAA Buccaneer squadrons disbanded until only 809 Squadron remained in business, operating from the sole remaining carrier HMS *Ark Royal*. The task of training the first RAF Buccaneer crews had been undertaken by the Navy but now that the emphasis had shifted to RAF operations, the remaining requirement for naval Buccaneer training was to be handled by the RAF. The RAF's Buccaneer Operational Conversion Unit (237 OCU) was formed at Honington on 1 March 1971. With the Buccaneer force slowly expanding here, the remaining FAA unit at Lossiemouth (809 NAS) moved south to consolidate all of the UK Buccaneer operations at one base. For the first time since the type's entry into service, Lossiemouth was devoid of Buccaneers. The OCU was equipped with a mixed fleet of Buccaneers and twin-seat Hunters, most of which were modified to incorporate Buccaneer instrumentation so that student pilots could familiarise themselves with the Buccaneer's layout. In Germany, No. 16 Squadron joined 15 Squadron to maintain the RAF's commitments to NATO within Germany. In addition to their primary nuclear role with the WE.177 bomb, the RAFG Buccaneers were also equipped with conventional freefall bombs and SNEB rocket pods, together with the BL755 cluster bomb unit that came into use during the 1970s.

Most RAFG Buccaneers were capable of carrying the Martel, but this was essentially a maritime weapon and was used only by No. 12 Squadron and 809 NAS. The ability to carry triple ejector racks for conventional bombs was never taken up – even though it would have given the Buccaneer an ability to deliver sixteen 1,000 lb HE bombs – nor was the opportunity to adopt larger external fuel tanks. However, most Buccaneers were progressively upgraded to incorporate an integral 425 imperial gallon fuel tank that was attached to the weapons bay door. It resulted in a pronounced bulge that made the aircraft appear more ungainly than it already did. However, with only a marginal increase in drag, the bomb bay door tank was an ingenious innovation that gave the Buccaneer a total ferry range with bomb bay, door and wing tanks of a staggering 2,300 nautical miles. On 1 July 1974, a fourth RAF squadron stood up and No. 208 Squadron began operations from Honington, although their designated area of wartime deployment was Norway where the aircraft were assigned to Saceur's AFNORTH reinforcement plan. In the overland attack role, 208 Squadron's Buccaneers were equipped with conventional HE bombs together with the WE.177 nuclear store and by 1983, the unit had joined No. 12 Squadron switching to the maritime attack role.

A fifth and final squadron was to follow when additional Buccaneers became available following the decommissioning of No. 809 NAS. This unit remained in business until HMS *Ark Royal* was retired in 1978. By December of that year, the unit's Buccaneers had been withdrawn to RAF St Athan where they were placed in short-term storage, pending further use by the RAF. The Fleet Air Arm bid farewell to its much loved Buccaneer with little fuss or fanfare, undoubtedly embittered by the way in which the Navy's global power had been so summarily dismantled by the Government. The supreme irony of the way in which the Navy had lost its carriers and Buccaneers to the service that had poured so much scorn on the very same aircraft was almost too much to bear for many senior naval officials. In complete contrast, the RAF found itself with a very potent and adaptable aircraft that had been accepted into service with the greatest of reluctance. However, as the Buccaneer settled into service, it became abundantly clear that the aircraft was a huge asset and even the most grudging of the RAF's chiefs were obliged to admit this.

The availability of more former FAA Buccaneers enabled No. 216 Squadron to reform on the type on 1 July 1979. Assigned to the same SACLANT maritime role, 216 Squadron was to be the first Buccaneer unit to employ the Paveway LGB (Laser Guided Bomb) system that had been adopted by the RAF. With a Pave Spike laser designator pod attached under the Buccaneer's port wing, the Martel-capable aircraft could be linked to the system so that an image of the intended target could be designated by the aircraft's navigator using the built-in television screen. Laser-guided freefall bombs could then be released and guided onto their target with extreme accuracy. Sadly, the squadron's exciting new role was short lived.

During February 1980, a detachment of Buccaneers from No. 15 Squadron was participating in a Red Flag exercise at Nellis AFB in Nevada. Buccaneer S.Mk.2B XV345 was airborne during an exercise mission when the starboard wing structure failed, resulting in a fatal crash over the desert. Investigations revealed that despite the Buccaneer's great structural strength, the front wing spar had failed and much to the RAF's horror, many other Buccaneers were found to be suffering from the same lethal spar fracture. Buccaneer flying ended abruptly and although three of the Buccaneers at Nellis were eventually ferried to the UK, two more were judged to be so badly damaged that they were returned to Hull by sea. It was established that the root cause of the problem was due to a number of factors. There was a basic design deficiency that contributed to the risk of fatigue fractures in a specific area, but the modification of the Buccaneer S.Mk.2's wing tip – a seemingly minor aerodynamic change – had imposed loads on the airframe that had not been fully understood. Additionally, the fatigue test specimen at Brough was a Mk.1 and did not fully represent the Mk.2's structure. However, with the problem finally understood, the Buccaneer fleet was repaired, some aircraft needing only minor fixes while others received replacement parts. A further batch was placed in long-term storage pending eventual repair if the need arose while other aircraft were declared beyond economical repair and assigned to ground duties. While this traumatic process had been unfolding, the RAF's Buccaneer crews were obliged to maintain their flying hours by operating a hastily introduced fleet of Hunters, drawn from storage and from the RAF's TWU, together with FAA examples and aircraft from the RAE. Even so, RAFG's Buccaneers were declared operational and if the need had arisen they would have been flown. Indeed, some aircraft did fly occasionally during the grounding period, but for what purpose remains unclear.

Following this dark period in the Buccaneer's history, plans were underway for the Tornado to be introduced into RAF service and Honington was selected as the home of the new Tornado Weapons Conversion Unit (TWCU). In order to make way for the new unit, the Buccaneers of Nos. 12 and 208 Squadrons and the OCU were transferred north to the Buccaneer's traditional home at Lossiemouth, an airfield that was now in RAF hands. No. 216 Squadron never moved to Lossiemouth as the unit was in the process of acquiring aircraft when the Buccaneer's grounding order had come into effect. Now that less than half of the original RAF Buccaneer fleet had survived the saga, it was no longer practical to equip the unit. Therefore, its handful of aircraft were transferred to 208 Squadron and 216 Squadron disbanded again. Although No. 12 Squadron continued to operate primarily in the maritime attack role, 208 Squadron (and Nos. 15 and 16 Squadrons at Laarbruch) had begun to embrace the Paveway system more and more. However, while 208 Squadron introduced the system as a complete package – designating targets for weapons that were dropped by its own aircraft – the RAFG Buccaneers were also employed as laser designators for the RAFG Jaguar squadrons, although the Paveway system was never a major part of RAFG operations, their main task being the nuclear strike role. The OCU also assumed a reserve wartime role as a laser designator unit for Buccaneer and new Tornado units, much to the distress of the RAF's No. 18 Group that expected the unit to be allocated maritime duties.

However, as the Tornado force slowly built in strength, 208 Squadron was shifted to the maritime attack role and by the time of the unit's move to Lossiemouth, it too had assumed an almost exclusively maritime-orientated role. Operations in Germany continued until the Tornado GR1 was ready for introduction into service, No. 15 Squadron transferring its Buccaneers to No. 16 Squadron from July 1983 followed by the disbandment of 16 Squadron on 1 March 1984, marking the end of RAF Germany's association with the Buccaneer. Nonetheless, this was not the end of the aircraft's service history and it was in its twilight years that the Buccaneer finally went to war. The deteriorating crisis in Lebanon during 1983 persuaded the British Government to send a token for CAS (Close Air Support) aircraft to the region in support of British forces. Six Buccaneers were deployed to RAF Akrotiri, drawn from the Lossiemouth squadrons. Twelve aircraft were modified for the deployment (Operation Pulsator) with AN/ALE-40 chaff dispensers fitted and provision for self-defence AIM-9G or AIM-9L Sidewinder missiles. Although the aircraft were not called into action during their stay in Cyprus, it was decided in September 1983 that a show of force would be appropriate to show that Britain was prepared to take action if necessary and that forces were now in place for this purpose. Two Buccaneers departed from Akrotiri and headed for downtown Beirut, making a series of passes over the city at alarmingly low altitudes. News footage of the sortie was seen across the world and the sight of two Buccaneers wheeling and winding their way around the city, thundering past the clusters of apartment blocks at a mere 100 feet, emphasised Britain's serious preparedness.

The Lossiemouth Buccaneer Wing remained in business long after the Tornado came into RAF service, even though this aircraft had replaced the Buccaneer in the overland strike role. Having been specifically designed to counter the Soviet's surface fleet, there was no other aircraft better equipped to handle this task more than two decades since it was first introduced. The Buccaneer's range, low-level stability, rugged design and excellent radar ensured that the Tornado was hardly any better. It was only the Buccaneer's weapons capability that could have been questioned. The Martel slowly become outdated, especially as Soviet radar detection ranges improved and defensive weapons became more lethal. Despite having anticipated the Buccaneer's retirement as more Tornado GR1s came off the production line, the RAF decided to retain the two maritime squadrons and update the remaining Buccaneers with a new cockpit HUD (Head-Up Display), new ECM (Electronic Counter Measures), and to give the aircraft a formidable new anti-ship weapon. Sea Eagle was designed as a true 'fire and forget' weapon, taking its target information with it at sea level while the launch aircraft flew to safety.

With its own radar seeker that remained inactive until within range of the selected target and a 225 kg warhead – designed to penetrate the hull of even the biggest ship – the missile was built to withstand ECM and to find individual targets within a group. An incredibly effective weapon by any standards, Sea Eagle was ideal for the Buccaneer. Eventually, some twenty Buccaneers were modified at British Aerospace's Woodford factory to carry Sea Eagles, four of which could be carried, two under each wing. The ECM fit was improved on most of the remaining aircraft and a new Inertial Navigation System was also installed, although the proposed HUD refit was dropped in order to save money. The opportunity was also taken to reattach the original Mk.1 wing tip to fifteen of the Buccaneers in an effort to reduce fatigue on the aircraft. Now that they were to remain active far beyond their intended withdrawal date and when the fleet improvement programme was completed, the Martel missile was finally withdrawn during 1989. The Buccaneer was thus equipped to remain at the forefront of NATO's maritime attack force and it was only the eventual inevitability of airframe fatigue that would spell the end for this magnificent aircraft. Various proposals were considered as potential replacements for the Buccaneer but no serious plans were made. It was the eventual reduction in the RAF's Tornado force, caused by governmental spending reductions, that finally presented the RAF with an opportunity to retire the Buccaneer and replace it with an equally capable machine. But even by 1991, the Buccaneer was a vital asset and at the very end of its service life was finally called into action again.

Although the two remaining squadrons had concentrated on maritime operations, the OCU had retained its ability to act as a Paveway designator force for Nos. 15 and 16 Squadrons (now operating the Tornado) and Norway's 311 Squadron. As Britain's commitments in the Gulf as part of Operation Desert Storm grew, it became clear that the Paveway system would be well suited to many of the RAF's attack missions over Iraq, once initial low-level attacks had been completed. With air superiority established, the Tornado force operating in the Gulf could take advantage of this system and press home medium level air attacks with laser-guided bombs and the Buccaneer would be the aircraft to designate each target by laser. During January, six Buccaneers were prepared for deployment and after being fitted with secure radios, a new IFF (Identification Friend/Foe) fit and a coat of 'Desert Sand' camouflage, they departed from gloomy Lossiemouth and headed for Muharraq, far out in the blistering heat of Bahrain.

The first operational mission was flown on 4 February with four Tornado GR1s embarking on a mission over Iraq, accompanied by two Buccaneers acting as laser designators. A vital bridge across the Euphrates River was attacked with pinpoint accuracy and further successful missions followed with only a few sorties being cancelled due to poor visibility that hampered the Paveway system. The Buccaneers had carried self-defence Sidewinder missiles on all flights, but by mid-February, it had become clear that there was no significant air threat and so the Sidewinders were abandoned in favour of two 1,000 lb bombs. On 21 February, the first of these armed missions was launched and it was with great pride that the RAF announced that the illustrious Buccaneer had finally dropped its first bomb in anger against an enemy target. More attacks followed and it was on 27 February that the last of 250 missions was completed, having guided 169 laser-guided bombs onto their targets together with forty-eight dropped from the Buccaneer. During March, the aircraft made their way back to the UK and the crews settled back into routine life at Lossiemouth, although by October, the OCU was stood down in anticipation of the Buccaneer's retirement that was now within sight. No. 12 Squadron remained in business until 30 September of the following year and No. 208 Squadron soldiered on until 31 March 1994.

Just a few days previously, the Buccaneer crews at Lossiemouth had treated friends and families to a spectacular farewell event during which some of the last

Both the FAA (as illustrated) and the RAF embraced the Buccaneer's ability to both receive and donate fuel in flight. The 'buddy-buddy' refuelling pod could be carried by all of the Buccaneer fleet and gave each unit its own degree of flexibility. On operational missions, an external tank was normally carried on the opposing wing both for trim purposes and to provide additional disposable fuel.

surviving Buccaneers made a final simulated attack on the type's much loved home at Lossiemouth. The sight and sound of the dark, smoky monsters streaking across the airfield one last time brought much joy to the countless observers, many of whom had worked on the design and manufacture of the aircraft more than thirty years previously. The last Buccaneer to be seen in British skies was an RAE machine and XW987 earned the distinction of making the final take-off from UK soil on 1 April 1977 after having been sold to a South African owner. After final preparations at St Mawgan – an airfield familiar to many Buccaneer crews as it was a designated forward base for Lossiemouth's operations – the aircraft roared skywards and climbed away over Cornwall and out into international airspace, marking the very end of a spectacularly successful story.

The Buccaneer had enjoyed a long and fascinating service life, becoming a fundamental part of the Royal Navy's offensive capability until the British Government summarily snatched it from the Navy's grasp. It was therefore presented to an air force that patently did not want it, only to realise years later that there was nothing that could match it. By any standards, the Buccaneer was truly magnificent and as the very last all-British bomber, it could be argued that it was also one of the very best.

CHAPTER NINE
Dark Days

It is ironic that Britain's most controversial and influential post-war bomber project was one that ultimately did not produce an operational aircraft. The origins of what became a truly tragic saga can be traced back to the early 1950s when English Electric's Canberra bomber first joined the ranks of the RAF. It was inevitable and vital that with the new Canberra now entering service, attention should be devoted to the long-term future and task of identifying what kind of aircraft should eventually replace it. The Canberra was regarded as an awesome machine. Compared to the slow, heavy and cumbersome Lincoln bombers that preceded it, the Canberra represented a phenomenal leap in capability that gave the RAF an astonishingly agile aircraft that was far in advance of any other bomber design emerging at that time. Not surprisingly, attempting to establish what kind of aircraft might be required to replace the Canberra was an exercise bound by sheer fantasy, even though service chiefs tried their best to visualise what Britain might need a decade later.

A draft requirement for a new 'light bomber' was issued in 1952, but it was in effect nothing more than a discussion document that was intended to generate interest in what was regarded as a fairly long-term goal. The Canberra had been a direct replacement for the magnificent Mosquito, even though in practical terms it ultimately replaced all of the RAF's wartime-era bomber types. Even so, it was regarded by many officials as an 'interim' aircraft that represented only a partial step towards an even more capable offensive structure. The new V-Bombers would give the RAF a true strategic capability and the Canberra could then be reassigned to the tactical and interdiction roles for which it had been designed. But back in the early 1950s, many people within the Air Ministry believed that despite the Canberra's outstanding capabilities, there was every need to create something even more potent: a 'Real Canberra'.

It was not until 1956 that a more serious consideration of the Canberra's replacement got underway. English Electric (designers of the Canberra) were keen to replicate the huge success of the Canberra with a design and by the end of that year, the Air Ministry and the Ministry of Supply had given the company's design team

XR219 thunders into the air at the start of another test flight from Boscombe Down. All of the test flight take-offs were executed with full reheat power. (*Courtesy BAE Systems*)

approval to produce a series of design drawings which would form the basis of a preliminary study process. In typical British fashion, English Electric's chief project engineer, Ollie Heath, opted to avoid complication and created basic sketches on sheets of scrap paper so that the design team had something tangible to discuss. Unusually, the drawings revealed not one basic design concept but a whole series of unusual configurations, some of which looked surprisingly imaginative and ambitious. However, Heath was not suffering from poor judgement or indecisiveness. His ideas reflected the ambiguous nature of the project's requirements. In short, the Air Ministry was now clear that it needed a Canberra replacement, but it was far from clear as to what this replacement should be.

Indeed, the only certainty seemed to be that the RAF would need a 'Supersonic Canberra' and this term was now being used freely around the Air Ministry's corridors. Supersonic flight was now a reality and every military strategist believed that speed would be the key capability that every new fighter and bomber design would strive to attain. It therefore followed that any new British bomber aircraft destined for RAF service from the mid-1960s would have to be supersonic. But all out speed was only one very basic aim. In all other respects, there was no clarity at all and the Air Ministry bravely coined the almost ludicrous term 'Multi-Role Strike Fighter' to neatly embrace every possible requirement for the new design. This kind of all capable aircraft does not seem quite so absurd almost sixty years later, but in the late 1950s, the notion of creating a viable multi-role combat aircraft was, at its best, optimistic.

The Air Ministry began to accept that a clearer requirement was necessary. English Electric were already busy with the development of the legendary Lightning interceptor and for a brief period they had dared to imagine that the RAF's new Canberra replacement could be developed from the existing Lightning design. However, as the Air Ministry slowly clarified what would be required, it was obvious that the need for supersonic performance was only one aspect of a much more ambitious concept. Ollie Heath's drawings had served to illustrate that a much larger and advanced aircraft would be needed – a true 'weapons system' that could give the RAF a supersonic strike capability while performing other tactical roles, not least reconnaissance. Fundamentally, the new aircraft would be a nuclear bomber and all other capabilities would be secondary to this role. Development of atomic and thermonuclear bombs for the RAF's V-Force had enabled British scientists to devise a smaller atomic bomb that could be used 'tactically', i.e. in battlefield scenarios rather than long-range 'strategic' exchanges. This bomb, codenamed 'Red Beard', would be the new aircraft's primary weapon and in many respects the design would be created around this bomb. Additionally, the aircraft would also have to be capable of delivering conventional weapons such as freefall high-explosive bombs and missiles. Also, and largely because of the Army's requirements, the aircraft would have to be capable of conducting effective battlefield reconnaissance.

As a tactical aircraft, it was envisaged that a range of around 350 nautical miles would be ideal, but it was the aircraft's speed that seemingly obsessed the Air Ministry. Russian military technology was undoubtedly developing with disturbing pace, but from Britain's viewpoint it seemed as if the Soviet's capabilities would become even more formidable within a matter of years. One key concern was that Soviet SAM (Surface to Air Missile) technology would soon become so effective that it might become impossible to penetrate Soviet territory unless a new aircraft could be developed. It was hoped that the new bomber could press home an attack at supersonic speed that would be far beyond the capabilities of any defensive missile. This crippling worry was the main reason why the Air Ministry insisted upon supersonic speed and Mach 1.3 was adopted as a goal. This was arguably faster than strictly necessary – a figure of Mach 1.2 was deemed to be far easier to achieve from a technical aspect – but the Air Ministry was unmoved. In fact, they indulged themselves in even more paranoia and swiftly concluded that a speed of Mach 1.5 would be necessary together with a range of 1,000 miles, stretched to more than 2,000 miles for ferry flights. This sudden leap in endurance was indicative of the conflicting requirements that dogged the new design from the very beginning. Although it was to be a tactical aircraft, it was anticipated that the RAF might have to operate the aircraft in various parts of the world which were far beyond the projected European battlefield where conflict with the Soviet Union might take place. Britain's global commitments required military might to back them up and the new strike aircraft might well be needed in the Mediterranean, Far East or Southeast Asia. In essence, this meant that the RAF required a tactical strike aircraft with strategic capability – a classic dichotomy.

Already dogged with conflicting requirements, the Air Ministry then concluded that supersonic capability alone would not ensure that the new strike aircraft could successfully penetrate Soviet airspace. High speed and manoeuvrability would probably be enough to counter the threat from enemy fighters that were expected to be prevalent in many projected theatres of conflict. However, in Europe, it was the Soviet's SAM systems which terrorised British strategists. Battling into the USSR at Mach 1.5 seemed like the only plausible means of achieving 'mission success', but at an altitude of 30,000 feet or more, the bomber would still be vulnerable to missile interception. The only truly reliable way to counter Soviet's defences would be to evade them for as long as possible. Speed would help to achieve this aim, but the key to success would be to avoid enemy radar detection whenever possible so that missile defences could not be brought to bear upon the intruding bomber until it was too late. The only way to avoid radar would be to fly low as physically possible so that the aircraft would remain hidden amongst radar 'clutter' – most notably hills, but also buildings, trees and other topographical features – which effectively destroy most radar pictures at heights of less than a few hundred feet. This meant a fundamental revision of both operational tactics and design philosophy. Traditionally, bomber aircraft had been designed to attain a respectable altitude and it was believed that the higher a bomber could fly, the less vulnerable to interception it would be.

However, SAM technology had changed everything. It would now be necessary to attack at low altitude – astonishingly low altitudes of 100 feet or even less and at high speed in bad weather or at night. Thus, the Air Ministry had clarified what it wanted: a supersonic bomber capable of carrying an atomic weapon over a range of 1,000 miles and able to fly at altitudes of less than 100 feet in bad weather or at night. It would also be able to carry conventional bombs and perform high-speed and low-level reconnaissance. It was undoubtedly the most ambitious requirement that the Air Ministry had ever proposed. It was therefore hardly surprising that it proved to be the most troublesome.

English Electric produced a report entitled 'Possibilities of a Canberra Replacement P17' that defined the fundamental aspects of the projected design as agreed with the Air Ministry's advisors. The new aircraft's radius of action would be fixed at 600 nautical miles at sea level and would have a top speed of Mach 0.9 – a more modest and therefore achievable goal when compared with the ridiculously optimistic aims which had first been proposed. The most suitable engine available would be the Rolls-Royce Conway rated at 2,600 lb thrust with reheat and the aircraft's AUW

XR219 arrives at Warton after completing a long cross-country flight from Boscombe Down. Had the TSR2 programme continued, almost all of the aircraft's test flight schedule would have been conducted from Warton. (*Courtesy BAE Systems*)

(All Up Weight) was expected to be around 80,000 lb. Attention was also given to airfield performance and the estimated take-off and landing distance was required was expected to be around 900 yards. The possibility of providing the aircraft with a STOL (Short Take-Off and Landing) capability was given a great deal of consideration at this stage, even though it was not an issue that had influenced the design of Canberra.

Flexibility was deemed to be the key to the new aircraft's success and reliance upon long concrete runways was no longer expected to be a viable proposition should the aircraft become involved in a conflict where airfields would undoubtedly be priority targets for enemy attack. The Air Ministry believed that fixed runways would inevitably be destroyed or disabled as soon as a European conflict began, therefore it seemed inevitable that the new aircraft would have to operate successfully from small semi-prepared strips. In this respect, the aircraft would build upon the dispersal techniques which were being successfully adopted by the V-Force. However, while the RAF's mighty strategic bombers would require support facilities and an adequate paved runway of at least 6,000 feet, it was agreed that the new tactical strike aircraft would be expected to comfortably operate as a self-sustained system within a site that was far more basic. The Air Ministry stipulated that a landing area no longer than that required to operate a C-47/DC-3 Dakota would be far more representative of the kind of location from which the aircraft would have to operate in wartime. In essence, this would be a simple grass strip of approximately 3,000 feet. Not exactly a generous amount of space for a Dakota, but for a large, heavy nuclear bomber it was, to say the least, an ambitious proposition.

Crucially, this STOL capability was to become a significant factor in the aircraft's design process and one that contributed towards the aircraft's ultimate demise. Other less important potential performance aspirations were also included in the English Electric P.17 report and the possibility of eventually developing the design for use as an interceptor was explored, taking into account the aircraft's projected range and endurance capabilities. Thankfully, this idea was never seriously considered and attention remained directed firmly towards the aircraft's strike and reconnaissance capabilities. (It is probably not coincidental that two decades later the same manufacturer was to design and manufacture an interceptor variant of a strike aircraft design in the shape of the Tornado F2.) The P.17 report enabled the Air Staff to develop their thinking further still and their conclusions came together in Air Staff General Operational Requirement No.GOR.339 – later referred to more simply as OR.339 – that was established and written in March 1957. The report was subsequently circulated to manufacturers on 29 October of the same year.

Although it was clearly stated that the contents of GOR.339 provided only the 'broad, though tentative outlines of the project', it did at least give Britain's aircraft manufacturers, and English Electric in particular, a fairly clear picture of what kind of aircraft would be required. It was enough to generate a number of potentially viable proposals from Britain's aircraft manufacturers. GOR.339 specified the performance of this new tactical strike/reconnaissance aircraft and stipulated that it was to be in RAF service by 1964 or 'as soon thereafter as possible' as a direct replacement for the Canberra bomber. It would incorporate an all-weather capability with a self-contained bombing system, minimum take-off and landing requirements, and would operate mainly at low level at heights of 1,000 feet or less. With a radius of action of 1,000 nm, it would be capable of delivering its weapons by loft manoeuvre from low level or by dive toss attack from medium level. Although there was no clear preference for the type of weapons that would be carried at this stage, it was agreed that the aircraft would be equipped with an atomic weapon.

In order to successfully destroy heavily-defended tactical targets such as industrial complexes and military facilities, a significant degree of weapon delivery accuracy would be vital and the prospect of developing reliable and capable targeting systems for a low-level and high-speed bomber looked like a formidable task. Likewise, the idea of exposing what would surely be a very complex and expensive aircraft to such

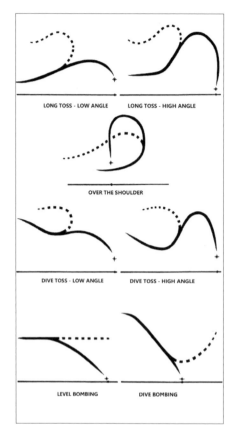

LONG TOSS - LOW ANGLE   LONG TOSS - HIGH ANGLE

OVER THE SHOULDER

DIVE TOSS - LOW ANGLE   DIVE TOSS - HIGH ANGLE

LEVEL BOMBING   DIVE BOMBING

Various attack profiles could be employed to deliver the WE.177 bomb from low level, but three basic profiles became standard procedure. The 'Long Toss" was the preferred option, giving the aircraft's crew plenty of time to escape the effects of the bomb's detonation.

a hostile environment seemed unnecessarily risky, therefore the obvious solution would be to opt for a nuclear capability. The overwhelming destructive power of an atomic bomb would not require extremely precise delivery, nor would it necessarily require the aircraft to be exposed to the most hostile defensive environments for prolonged periods. The destructive power of such a bomb would ensure that whatever target was assigned to the aircraft it would certainly be destroyed. From the very outset of the project, the primary weapon for the new aircraft was to be Red Beard, a surprisingly simple, bulky and temperamental tactical atomic bomb with a nominal 15 kiloton yield that entered service in 1962. This was the weapon that the new aircraft was effectively be built around with its weapons bay dimensions, aerodynamic performance, overall size and layout directly based on the size, weight and delivery requirements of Red Beard.

Interestingly, the GOR.339 specifications clearly indicated that the new aircraft would be designed to operate primarily in the shorter-range tactical role. However, the introductory text that accompanied the issue of GOR.339 also mentioned that despite being a tactical design, a high speed and low flying nuclear bomber had

The Red Beard bomb was the tactical weapon around which the TSR2 was first designed. However, the temperamental bomb was soon replaced by the WE.177, and TSR2 was continually modified to accommodate this weapons. (*Courtesy BAE Systems*)

unexplored potential. The accompanying specification notes mentioned that with the aid of in-flight refuelling, the new aircraft could 'pose a low-level threat to Russia and thus augment the primary deterrent'. This seemingly throwaway comment was possibly intended merely as an indication of the new aircraft's versatility, but by linking the aircraft to a possible strategic capability, the document laid the foundations for more confusion and complication that would eventually lead to the project's downfall.

The Ministry of Supply insisted that a production contract for the new aircraft would only be offered to a company with what they described as 'very large resources', meaning was that the new contract would go to an amalgamated team comprising of two or more companies. The Government believed that Britain's aviation industry was ridiculously oversized and uncompetitive. They preferred to create a streamlined industry comprising of fewer (amalgamated) companies that would be far stronger and efficient. Submissions made in response to GOR.339 included Bristol Aircraft's Type 204, Hawker's P.1129 plus proposals from Fairey, Boulton Paul, Folland and Vickers Supermarine. The latter submitted two versions of their Type 571 design in addition to a separate proposal that came directly from their Weybridge headquarters based on Barnes Wallis' variable-geometry ('swing wing') Swallow project. This revolutionary proposal caused a great deal of interest, but it was undoubtedly ahead of its time.

Handley Page declined to submit a proposal, being set against company amalgamation, and Blackburn submitted the B.103A, a direct development of the NA.39 strike aircraft that was being created for the Royal Navy. Having designed and manufactured the Canberra, English Electric believed that they had expertise in jet bomber design, and with the Lightning now a major part of the company's activity, they also had unique experience of supersonic developments. They devoted considerable time and resources to their embryonic P-17 concept, confident that their experience would give them a major advantage over the competing companies. Understandably, they also firmly believed that the contract for the Canberra's replacement was more than likely to be given to the Canberra's manufacturer. It seemed absurd to imagine otherwise. By now, their design was radically different from the original drawings and in effect had become a completely different aircraft. In order to emphasise this, the project was re-designated accordingly as the P-17A.

Meanwhile, many miles to the south, a very similar project was being created by the Supermarine company at their South Marston offices. Now part of the huge Vickers military manufacturing and design company, Supermarine – and other parts of the Vickers empire – initially produced more than forty concept designs in response to OR.339. Eventually, just two were selected with which to tender for the contract, these being identified as being the most practical and most suitable. They were essentially similar, their differences largely being based on their overall size and corresponding performance with one being a larger, heavier twin-engine derivative of the other, which was smaller and lighter aircraft powered by just one engine. The Supermarine team quickly concluded that in order to undertake the roles specified by GOR.339, the aircraft would have to rely upon a large and complex avionics system. Combined with the necessary range and speed, this would require a fairly large aircraft, and although this was an achievable aim, the team's firm belief in small, compact and inexpensive aircraft convinced them that their smaller design would be a better solution.

However, such systems, particularly digital technology, were still some years away. Supermarine were also keen to explore the design's potential as a naval strike/attack aircraft as they had been encouraged to do so by the Ministry of Supply. The smaller of their two designs was naturally more suitable for this purpose. Powered by a single RB.142 engine, the Conway 11R/3C being identified as an alternative, the larger design also relied upon the same engine, but would require two of these power plants. Both designs would utilise the engine's power to provide additional lift over the full-span trailing edge flaps, this 'wing blowing' system having first been

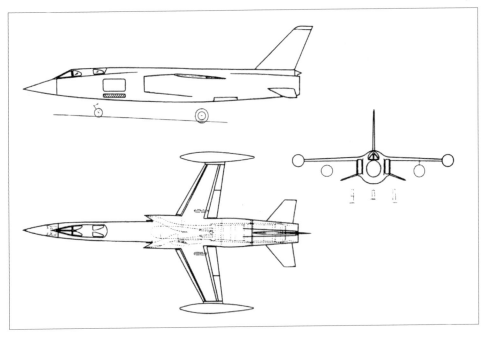

Above and below: These two drawings show the original Supermarine proposals for their Type 571. The basic design was proposed in two versions: one a light single-engine aircraft and the other a more capable twin-engine derivative. The larger design became the basis of the TSR2 concept, and although it was combined with English Electric's proposed design, the aircraft continued to be officially referred to as the Type 571 even up until the time of TSR2's cancellation. TSR2 was in effect the name of the project, not the aircraft.

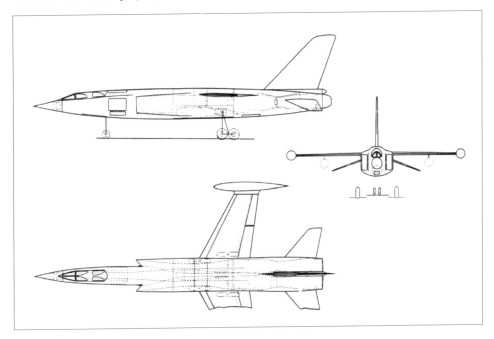

successfully developed for use on their own Scimitar design. It was anticipated that the system would reduce landing speed by almost 20 mph – vital for deck landings if a naval derivative was ultimately produced – but would be equally useful for the projected RAF requirement for short field operations. Both versions of the Type 571 had an estimated top speed of Mach 2.3 above 36,000 feet and would have a maximum range of 1,000 nm, although it was accepted that the single-engine aircraft would require external fuel tanks in order to achieve this.

When Vickers-Supermarine and English Electric finally submitted their proposals, it became clear that they were the two leading designs which showed the greatest promise of success, the P17A's promising aerodynamic performance being matched by the more sophisticated nature of the Type 571's 'weapons system' approach. Although other design proposals were also considered, it was the English Electric and Vickers-Supermarine submissions which emerged as the most suitable.

A simple choice of one or the other might have followed had it not been for two important factors: the Government's insistence that industry rationalisation had to be taken into account and a third design was also on the table. The Navy had the Buccaneer, an aircraft designed and manufactured in response to the Navy's requirements and ideally suited to the low-level maritime strike role that the Navy had specified for it. It was therefore obvious to many people that the Buccaneer had been designed to perform a very similar role to OR.339, and with the design process already completed, it would be logical to simply manufacture Buccaneers for the RAF.

Blackburn duly produced a proposal, the B.103A, for development of the Buccaneer that incorporated increased fuel capacity and more powerful de Havilland Gyron engines to meet the GOR.339 specifications more precisely. With a respectable range of 850 nm and a speed of Mach 0.85, it showed great promise, but it clearly was not as ambitious as the English Electric or Vickers proposals. Also, it failed to match the specified speed and range by quite a margin. A more sophisticated derivative of the Buccaneer, the B.108, was also proposed, but its maximum speed was expected to be subsonic. Blackburn's view was that supersonic performance was not as vitally important for the role as had been implied by the Air Ministry and that the aircraft's delivery date was more important. But the Buccaneer was a naval aircraft and the RAF had no interest in adopting what was regarded by them as an inferior aircraft designed for the Navy's requirements. The RAF maintained a scornful indifference towards the NA.39/Buccaneer programme and had actively lobbied to prevent the Navy from obtaining the Buccaneer, producing a detailed study report that suggested that a modified Scimitar would have been a less expensive and entirely suitable aircraft for the naval requirement. It was a classic case of inter-service politics.

By the summer of 1958, interest had gravitated towards the most promising proposals offered by Vickers and English Electric. The Government was eager to attain the earliest in-service date possible in anticipation of an increasingly capable Soviet threat and the Air Ministry was keen to emphasise that there was no question of needing an 'interim' aircraft, i.e. their much dreaded Buccaneer option. Adopting the English Electric and Vickers designs, merging the two companies, and thereby create a single design to meet the demands of GOR.339 would enable the best elements of the two most promising designs to be combined while accommodating the Government's desire for company amalgamation. The Air Ministry sought the approval of the DRPC (Defence Research Policy Committee) and during a meeting in June, they agreed that GOR.339 should be entered into the Government's Research and Development programme and that some £150,000 should be sought from the Treasury to cover an initial six months of work, subject to successful negotiations with English Electric and Vickers. But even at this significant stage, the project did not have unanimous support.

The Chairman of the DRPC, Sir Frederick Brundrett, expressed concern that although OR.339 would be able to meet the RAF's requirements – specifically referring to Army support which would be provided by the RAF and was obviously not the aircraft's key role – he believed that NA.39 (Buccaneer) could perform the same task perhaps some five years earlier. Effectively, two aircraft were being created to do the same job. It was a repetition of the same argument that had already been thrashed out. Unusually, Brundrett wrote to the Minister of Defence to express his reservations and a copy of his note was forwarded to Chief of the Air Staff. He added a handwritten note stating that he '...would be very glad if you ensured that no quotation is ever made from it nor that its existence is ever known'. In his letter to the minister, he stated that he was 'by no means happy' that the proposed aircraft to meet GOR.339 was 'necessarily the aircraft we ought to have'. And while he accepted that a Canberra replacement was necessary, he had doubts over the thinking behind it. He accepted that the Air Ministry might be obliged to undertake operations in various theatres across the world as part of various existing treaties, but given the proposed in-service date of 1965, he wondered what bases and responsibilities the UK might have by then and whether the Air Staff were therefore 'planning on a realistic basis'. He believed that if they were not, then much of GOR.339's specification was unnecessary and if only an 'Army Support' aircraft was required, it could be acquired much less expensively. The DRPC's endorsement was accepted and while a decision was awaited from the Minister of Defence on whether to proceed, the Air Ministry refined GOR.339 into a final draft, now officially termed as OR.339, and this was circulated to everyone involved with the project.

On 13 November 1958, Sandys informed Secretary of State that '...after very full consideration I am now satisfied that you have made out the case for replacing, in due course, the Canberra with an aircraft which would comply with the general specification defined in OR.339. The way is therefore clear for you to ask the

Ministry of Supply to approach the Treasury for authority to place a development contract for this aircraft.' On 15 December, the Treasury gave approval for a design contract at an estimated £150,000 while requesting that they be informed and '... consulted on measures to control the progress of the programme, to check on the estimates and the costs of the firms engaged on it and to limit the introduction of improvements and modifications'. The Treasury's somewhat reserved attitude indicated that from the outset, the question of costs and project control was an important issue which they had no intention of ignoring. Ominously, just a few months later, the Treasury's initial funding of £150,000 was reluctantly increased to £600,000. Inexplicably, the Air Staff's requirements also continued to increase as the expense of the project began to climb. Still unhappy with the aircraft's top speed that had crept up to Mach 1.7, it was decided that Mach 2.0 would be a superior figure that would ensure invulnerability from Soviet defences.

This may well have been a fair estimation, but it failed to take into account the complexity and cost of creating an aircraft that could routinely operate at such speeds. Not only did it require a huge amount of technical design work – supersonic design was still very much it its early stages – but also required the use of exotic and expensive materials which were suited to the high temperatures and stresses of Mach Two. It was also confirmed that even though a nominal height of 1,000 feet had been selected for the aircraft's low-level performance, a height of just 200 feet would be specified for combat operations. The Air Staff's obsession with rough field operations also reappeared and instead of specifying that the aircraft must operate from suitably cleared concrete surfaces such as motorways, it now stated that it must also be able to fly to and from an unprepared grass field. Of course, this had been implicit from the outset, but no one had ventured to confirm this until now and it had a major influence on the design of the aircraft's landing gear system. This combination of incredibly demanding requirements seemed to be running out of control with more specifications and ambitious figures attached to the Air Staff's requirements every week. No one seemed willing to consider the costs and time delays that would be associated with over-specification, even though it seemed like the Air Ministry were adding increasing capabilities to the specification for the sake of it. With hindsight, it seems far more likely that the Air Staff were ensuring that OR.339 maintained as great a distance from the Buccaneer as was possible and the more complex and capable OR.339 became, the less likely it was that the Government would force the RAF to accept the Buccaneer.

A provisional joint project team comprising of Vickers and English Electric staff was first established in December and detailed design work began the following month, resulting in a new joint specification being produced in just six months. This became the basis for an abandonment of the original OR.339 specifications – which had been constantly revised upwards as described – and their replacement by a completely new specification under OR.343 that was effectively written around the new combined design. Issued by the Air Staff on 8 May 1959, this outlined the requirements for a 'Tactical Strike and Reconnaissance Weapons System'. The original OR.339 document had covered just forty-eight paragraphs, but had now expanded to a staggering 114 paragraphs which outlined in great detail the revised performance specifications as they now stood. The manufacturers, particularly the Vickers-Supermarine team, passively accepted these requirements and were keen to promise more than was strictly necessary, simply to ensure that they retained the Air Ministry's confidence and support. However, the English Electric team were careful to avoid this temptation and their practical and therefore often less ambitious approach was often not what the Air Staff wanted to hear.

Sir Michael Beetham, who had been responsible for the very beginnings of what became the first GOR.339 draft, defended the Air Staff's approach by stating that the Operational Requirements Staff were always obliged to look as far ahead as possible, were reluctant to underestimate potential enemy defences and that the intelligence community were keen to be seen to have not been left behind in their appraisal of potential threats. But when the Air Staff's ambitions were combined with the aircraft manufacturer's natural eagerness to accommodate all of the Air Staff's requirements whenever possible, it was not surprising that the project continued to grow unchecked. Beetham believed that the quest for very high speed combined with a low level and high altitude capability made perfect sense as 'if the enemy had solved the problems of defence at low level, the aircraft might have been driven to operate at higher levels'. Therefore, in his opinion, the Air Staff were right to build in as good a performance as could be achieved, even if this was done with little regard to the costs and delays that would result.

Despite the increasingly ambitious nature of OR.343, the two manufacturers were supremely confident of success. Sir Fredrick Page (English Electric Aviation's Director and Chief Executive) explained in subsequent years that the combined assets of the two companies had the necessary strength and experience to produce the aircraft more cheaply and quickly, but separately they both had significant weaknesses. Vickers had a business that was integrated 'under the control of an able and forceful character, Sir George Edwards, and had got the Valiant into service quickly', but Vickers clearly lacked 'any experience of, and facilities for, the design and testing of supersonic aircraft' and were preoccupied with 'some difficult and unprofitable civil aircraft'. Page also believed that Vickers 'lacked adequate definition of the relationship between project management and specialist departments, particularly finance'. By comparison, he stated that English Electric had the experience of their Canberra programme and 'proven expertise and facilities for the design, development and flight testing of supersonic aircraft plus a clearly defined project management system'. Their weakness was that they had no proper control of the manufacturing

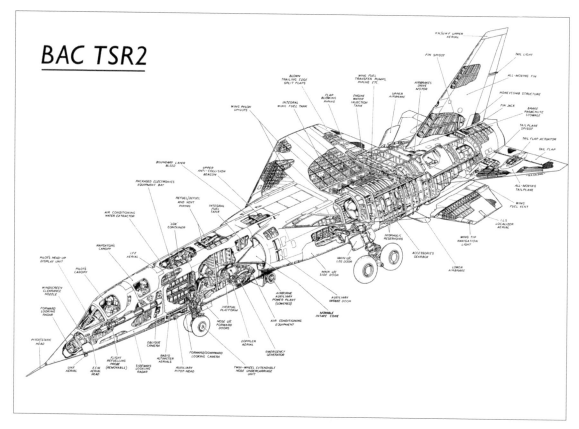

BAC TSR2

TSR2 cutaway diagram. (*Courtesy BAE Systems*)

that had to be subcontracted to the main English Electric parent company and that they were also heavily committed to production of the Lightning interceptor.

Page also claimed that as some of the company's exchanges with the Air Ministry 'challenged the increasingly severe requirements in OR.339, English Electric was possibly seen as being uncooperative' and that the company's geographical distance from Whitehall 'was also a handicap in the intense lobbying'. His comments certainly had foundation and English Electric were undoubtedly both surprised and disappointed when the Air Ministry finally outlined the terms of the initial contract. The Air Ministry expressed a clear preference for the English Electric and Vickers design during the summer of 1958. It had also been evident to English Electric that their P.17A was clearly the most practical and most favoured design. With this fact in mind and the company's supersonic experience established, it was assumed by them that the OR.339 design would be a project shared equally between the two companies, but with English Electric naturally taking the lead. Any other arrangement would be illogical. What emerged was a complete reversal of this assumption and although work share was indeed to be settled on a fifty-fifty basis, the overall control of the project was awarded to Vickers with Sir George Edwards heading the programme. In effect, English Electric would be a subcontractor and all subsequent project contracts connected with OR.343 would be awarded to Vickers, even after the companies had merged. This meant that the programme's definitive decision-making processes would be controlled by Vickers, even though the aircraft would be largely based on an English Electric design. Freddie Page later recalled that 'the Project Director, Chief Project Engineer and all leaders of specialist design, manufacturing, finance and procurement activities were all Vickers men'. Indeed, only the flight test crew were led by English Electric as Vickers had no personnel with substantial supersonic test experience.

No plausible reason was ever offered for the way in which the overall control of the project was handed to Vickers. Handel Davies, who had been responsible for the decision, later commented that his main motivation had been to exploit the capabilities of Sir George Edwards who was an engineer and chairman of the huge Vickers company. He therefore 'had the ideal leadership qualities with which to lead the TSR2 project'. However, he also accepted that with hindsight the decision 'might not have been ideal' as Edwards was clearly preoccupied with the various civil aircraft projects which Vickers were working on, notably the VC10 and BAC-111. Some commentators asserted that awarding the contract to Vickers was a classic symptom of the Government's conservative preferences with Vickers being an important, established and influential player in the corridors of power when compared to the less familiar faces from English Electric's northern industrial base far away in Lancashire. It is certainly true that English Electric's distinctly northern preference for plain speaking did not always win them any favours and even after the project got underway, this attitude still prevailed as Freddie Page subsequently recalled: '...the Vickers project management team accepted all the increased demands spread out over many meetings with officials. At one [meeting] when the design speeds and temperatures were increased, I said "Gentlemen, I hope you realise that what you have done will cost the Earth," but this was dismissed as coming from a disgruntled sub-contractor.'

The resentment that the Government created was never completely forgotten. Despite this less than ideal situation, a press release was issued by the Minister of Supply (Aubrey Jones) on 1 January 1959 stating that subject to satisfactory negotiations a '...new aircraft would be undertaken'. He added that, 'The TSR2 is a tactical support and reconnaissance aircraft. In the course of study, it has been found technically possible to incorporate in the final operational requirement modifications which will greatly increase the usefulness of the aircraft in limited operations and for close support of the Army.' Jones stated that '...while the TSR2 will be capable of performing the roles of all the various marks of Canberra, it will by reason of its

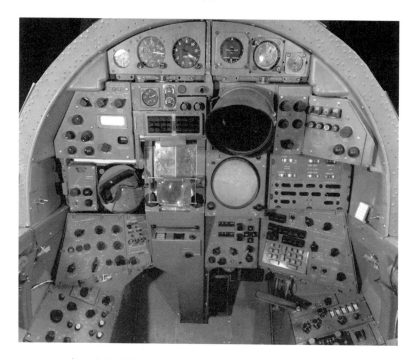

Above left: TSR2's rear cockpit was packed with systems to enable the
aircraft to perform its strike/attack role. As can be seen, little attention was given to the navigator's
forward view (of which there was none) and it seems inevitable that production aircraft would have
had more equipment packed into the rear cockpit. (*Courtesy BAE Systems*)

Above right: Primary navigation was to have been provided by a rolling map printout from the
aircraft's radar. Unfortunately, the map (essentially a 'wet' photographic print) took time to process
and would have required the navigator to retrospectively calculate the aircraft's position – hardly
an ideal solution for a high-speed aeroplane. (*Courtesy BAE Systems*)

greater flexibility and higher general performance be far more versatile and more in
the nature of a general-purpose tactical aircraft'.

This statement was the very first occasion on which the term 'TSR2' was used in
public. It first came into use informally within his own Ministry of Supply rather
than the Air Ministry where it had been expected that a standard bomber designation
– similar to the B.35/46 designation for the V-Bombers – would be given to the
aircraft. Jones incorrectly attributed part of his chosen acronym to denote 'support'
rather than 'strike', the latter term implying nuclear delivery. He had therefore, either
unintentionally or otherwise, downplayed the aircraft's potential capabilities and
there has always been some doubt as to where the use of the term '2' came from.
Various Ministry and industry officials have shared different views on this and it
seems possible that it was a reflection of the aircraft's projected Mach 2 performance.
However, it is also possible that the Canberra was somehow regarded by the MoS

as the 'TSR1' although, sadly, there is no evidence to support either supposition. But regardless of its origins, the term 'TSR2' stuck and became the aircraft's accepted name almost by default.

George Edwards became executive director of the new British Aircraft Corporation – embracing the Vickers and English Electric empires – and as the TSR2's chief guiding figure, he was undoubtedly frustrated by the project's slow progress. He had consistently believed that no matter how the division of design and production work was finally fixed, a single contractor, and preferably the one that he controlled, should retain overall responsibility for the programme. The MoS accepted this viewpoint, indeed Aubrey Jones insisted that the American 'Weapons System' procedure be adopted whereby a prime contractor would agree an overall price and then subcontract work as necessary to other firms, while remaining directly responsible to the MoS for the whole contract.

However, simplicity was never a luxury afforded to TSR2. Vickers, now part of BAC, never managed to establish direct relationships with their suppliers and subcontractors of which there were more than a thousand. In most cases, they had to begin negotiations after the MoS had already discussed terms and cost estimates with them first and these terms were inevitably based on the Ministry's hopelessly biased views as to whether any work or equipment was justified. The MoS was clearly not in a position to judge what work or equipment was strictly necessary and Edwards was unable to convince the MoS that Vickers should be given the freedom to conduct unfettered negotiations with their preferred contractors. The situation was never properly resolved and instead of communicating directly with BAC, many of the contractors continually invited Ministry estimators to 'second guess' their arrangements with BAC, which inevitably wasted more time and money. Perhaps the most damaging example of this process was the choice of engine for the aircraft. Only the aircraft's designer and manufacturer can make an informed decision as to which engine is most appropriate for any given design, but although Vickers were given the opportunity to recommend a choice, they did not have the power to insist upon it.

The Government dictated the final choice that was influenced by political and industrial factors rather than technical ones. Had the situation been different, it is possible that Vickers – based on their own preference and also due to English Electric's traditional employment of Rolls-Royce powerplants – would have opted for the Rolls-Royce Medway turbofan engine. However, the choice was finally made by Government officials who were clearly obsessed by their quest for industry amalgamation. Bristol Aero Engines had already merged with Armstrong Siddeley Motors and were subsequently joined by de Havilland and Blackburn to create what became Bristol-Siddeley Engines. With this merger completed, the choice of engine seemed obvious to the Ministry of Supply. Bristol Siddeley Engines and their all

Various proposals were considered to enable TSR2 to operate from dispersed sites and small 'rough field' locations. Perhaps the most bizarre was this proposal for a jet lift platform, in effect a separate aircraft that could take-off vertically and allow TSR2 to ride piggyback. Perhaps not surprisingly, the idea was never pursued.

new Olympus 22R turbojet would be adopted for the TSR2 and this was a decision that eventually had a major, almost pivotal effect on the project's survival. It was also another graphic illustration of how the TSR2 project was being steered by the Government.

The absurd complexities of the procurement system was matched by the way in which the Ministry maintained an almost suffocating influence on the steering of the project through the introduction of a whole hierarchy of committees, all controlled by the TSR2 Steering Committee. For example, the Development Progress Committee had more than sixty members and met quarterly, producing a written report on each occasion. TSR2 was to be designed, manufactured and procured by committee and although this should not have represented a major hurdle to TSR2's progress – indeed, one of the aims of this vast management structure was ironically to expedite progress – it was the way in which the committees functioned and communicated with each other which caused so many difficulties. Many of the Ministry and RAF officials who sat on these panels did not have the right qualifications for the tasks at hand and generally lacked the technical expertise that ought to have been present. There was no proper structure through which each committee could operate and liaise with their counterparts. Most importantly, there was no firm and decisive overall management, not even from Edwards who inevitably found that whenever he attempted to exercise control, it was taken away from him.

CHAPTER TEN
Project Cancelled

When TSR2's Operational Requirement had first been changed to OR.343, the Treasury was immediately suspicious that the requirement had somehow changed to 'the extent of demanding a whole new weapon system'. In reality, it was simply a refinement of the first OR now that the RAF and the manufacturer were entirely certain of what the new weapons system would be expected to do. Chief of the Air Staff, MRAF Sir Dermot Boyle, was advised that development costs were likely to reach £80 million, a figure which was roughly twice the estimate that had been made back in 1958. By the beginning of 1960, the Ministries of Transport, Civil Aviation and Supply had been replaced by the Ministry of Aviation who drew up a submission for the Research and Development Board. They asked for acceptance of the TSR2's development programme at an estimated cost of £62 million up to CA Release (this is the point at which the aircraft would be officially approved for use).

The R&D Board approved a request that would be made to the Treasury, the estimated cost being subject to an additional amount that might be as much as £25 million. Naturally, The Treasury was horrified by the request and immediate asked the Ministry of Defence on 16 December to reconsider the entire project, including the much discussed possibility of buying the Buccaneer. The Treasury cited the 'enormous increase' in developmental costs, adding that if the latest estimates had 'been before Ministers a year ago' it would seem 'not impossible that the question of meeting the RAF requirement with a version of the NA.39 would have been more strongly pressed'. The Treasury was probably right, and if the potential cost of TSR2 been known from the outset, it seems inevitable that the Buccaneer would have been chosen despite the Air Ministry's objections.

Harold Watkinson, the Minister of Defence, attended an Air Staff presentation on TSR2 in March 1960 and informed the Chiefs of Staff that he was not yet convinced of the need for further development of TSR2 due to its projected cost. The Treasury naturally saw this as a vindication of their reluctance to release further funding. The Chiefs of Staff duly re-examined the project in order to give the Minister of Defence a clear appraisal of the situation and submitted a report in May 1960 entitled 'Aircraft

XR219 high above the clouds during a test flight from Boscombe Down. The aircraft performed brilliantly during the limited test programme that was completed, although it is debatable whether the aircraft's avionics would have performed as well. (*Courtesy BAE Systems*)

Requirements for Tactical Strike, Reconnaissance and Offensive Army Support'. The Minister of Defence announced that he would give the paper the 'earliest possible consideration' but only after he had returned from a trip to the US where he hoped to secure American interest in the aircraft. However, at the same time, Watkinson complicated matters further still by sending a minute to the Chief of the Defence Staff in which he commented that he was 'attracted to the idea' of giving TSR2 'an increased strategic capacity by fitting it with some kind of missile' in order that 'a very high cost aircraft like this' could be given 'all the capacity that we can'.

The eventual loss of both the Blue Streak ICBM and the Skybolt ALGM led to drastic changes in Bomber Command's position. Even though the Polaris submarine-launched missile would provide Britain with a credible deterrent from 1970 onwards, it became increasingly obvious that even by switching to low-level operations, the V-Force would slowly lose its viability as a serious nuclear deterrent. By comparison, the TSR2 was designed for low level and had both high speed and agility. It would therefore be a more viable strategic deterrent than the V-Force if it could be armed with a suitable weapon. Various guided-bomb projects were considered, but the cheapest and fastest solution was eventually identified as a freefall bomb. Fortunately, a bomb was already under development as a long-term replacement for the unreliable and complex Red Beard weapon around which TSR2 had originally been designed. This joint Naval/Air Staff project was described under Operational requirement No.1177 for 'An Improved Kiloton Bomb':

Since the Joint Staff requirement for Red Beard was drawn up in 1953, technical advances have made possible the development of a bomb which will far more closely meet the requirements of the Air Staff for a tactical nuclear weapon. Warhead design improvements now permit the use of a far smaller and lighter warhead in packaged form which will give yields of the order required for the destruction of hard targets (such as bridges, passes, defiles, etc.) In addition, this warhead will be much safer, more robust and have fewer climatic restrictions than existing designs. To take advantage of these improvements in warhead design, it is necessary to develop a new carcass in which to fit it. This carcass must also match the advances in aircraft performances and the developments in unorthodox delivery techniques that have taken place. This requirement supersedes that stated in draft OR.1127 for a Mk.2 version of Red Beard, which can now be regarded as cancelled.

This resulted in another redrafting of TSR2's Operational Requirement:

Because of envisaged enemy countermeasures and the need to change aircraft approach and delivery tactics, the existing British nuclear bombs Yellow Sun, Blue Steel and Red Beard will be unsuitable as primary weapons beyond 1975. Moreover, with the cancellation of Skybolt as the planned replacement for Yellow Sun and the introduction of Polaris unlikely to become fully effective before 1970, and urgent need exists for a new bomb to maintain the United Kingdom independent deterrent during the interim period and as supplementary capability thereafter. By 1966, the manned bomber may survive enemy defences in the European theatre and deliver a successful strike only by flying at high speed at very low level. Yellow Sun and Blue Steel are designed for release at medium/high altitude where the delivery aircraft and/or bomb is vulnerable to interception, while Red Beard cannot stand the low level flight environment, is limited in method of fusing and delivery, and possesses some undesirable safety restrictions when held at readiness in an operational state. Early replacement is essential. The replacement bomb must be multi-purpose by design. It must satisfy joint Naval and Air Staff requirements for carriage and delivery in current medium bomber aircraft and planned high performance aircraft, to exploit fully their low-level strike capability against strategic and tactical, hard and soft targets with corresponding different warhead yields. Research and development studies show clearly that such a bomb can be produced fully within the timescale. However, to maintain an effective United Kingdom nuclear deterrent during development of the Polaris weapon system, priority is to be given to production of the high-yield version for the RAF medium bomber force.

The new high-yield freefall bomb designed to OR.1177 eventually translated into the WE.177B while the thermonuclear warhead was developed by AWRE at Aldermaston. It was stipulated that the Type B version should be ready for service

Oblique lighting illustrates the unique twin condensation vortex generated by TSR2's down-turned wing tips. The wings were designed in this fashion so that the wing did not require overall dihedral that may have affected airflow over the tailplane surfaces. (*Courtesy BAE Systems*)

entry in June 1966 and ultimately the weapon's destructive power was set at 450 kilotons – almost modest when compared to the V-Force's Yellow Sun, but sufficient to give TSR2 an ability to strike hard at strategic targets. Bearing in mind that the American atomic weapons dropped on Japan produced yields of between 15 and 20 kilotons, the TSR2 armed with WE.177B would represent a very serious deterrent. The Government's priority was now to develop and deploy WE.177B as rapidly as possible, so that it could be used to supplement the Vulcan and Victor's freefall bombs and standoff weapons, and to give TSR2 sufficient strike power to represent a credible nuclear deterrent until Polaris entered service. This meant that the original plan to create a smaller tactical bomb to replace Red Beard would have to be put on hold, even though this was effectively the key weapon that TSR2 had first been created to deliver.

TSR2 had now become a strategic bomber and its tactical armament was now a secondary consideration. Development of the tactical weapon, WE.177A, continued as a slower pace, however, and it was envisaged that it would eventually be supplied with different yield options – 50kt, 100kt, 200kt and 300kt – that would enable the RAF to deliver a bomb appropriate to the size of the anticipated tactical target. WE.177B created yet more difficulties that delayed TSR2's progress further still. Having designed the basic structure of TSR2 around the established size of Red Beard, it was anticipated that any subsequent weapon developments would be no larger. Both WE.177A and WE.177B could easily be accommodated in the TSR2's weapons bay as Red Beard's 28-inch diameter was significantly greater than the estimated 16.5 inches of the new bomb. But during 1962, and without explanation fifty years later, a Government decision was made to limit the size of all types of British tactical weapons to a yield of no more than 10 kilotons.

The RAF concluded that it was unable to confidently assure destruction of all types of tactical targets that might be encountered by TSR2 if this 10 kiloton limit was imposed. In order to overcome this limitation, it was proposed that two WE.177As could be carried in tandem within TSR2's bomb bay. It also seemed logical that TSR2's strategic strike capability could also be enhanced by the carriage of two WE.177Bs in a similar fashion, but the 'B' model, being of thermonuclear design, was significantly longer than the tactical 'A' model and a tandem arrangement was impossible without making major structural changes to TSR2's design. Eventually, the BAC design team offered a far easier solution and by modifying the design of the weapons bay doors, recesses could be incorporated into the door's inner faces which would enable two WE.177s to be carried abreast, their tail fins fitting neatly into the door recesses. This arrangement also freed up additional space to the rear of the weapons bay and this could be used to accommodate a fuel tank that would provide TSR2 with additional fuel to extend its strategic capabilities.

The Air Staff were less than happy and further debate ensued until it was finally agreed that the aircraft could also carry a further two WE.177Bs, one under each wing on an external pylon. This would give TSR2 an equivalent combined destructive power of 40 kilotons if the bombs were delivered simultaneously. Repeated bombing of the same target would be impractical – and probably suicidal for the TSR2's crew – and a simultaneous drop of four weapons would adversely affect the detonation mechanisms of the nuclear devices in each bomb. It was therefore agreed that the most suitable method of bomb release would be to drop all four weapons in a rapid succession sequence that would effectively create the same effect as a single 40 kiloton bomb.

By June 1961, BAC had revised their cost estimates from £41.7 million to £48.5 million. Less than a year later, the project's endlessly inflating price was enough to make BAC embark on a serious reappraisal of the programme in an effort to find ways in which it might be brought back under control through the introduction of economies. The Air Ministry, describing costs as 'expensive by any reckoning',

The large and unwieldy undercarriage system designed for TSR2 was intended to give the aircraft an ability to operate from unprepared field strips. Whether this capability would ever have been used is debatable, but the complicated landing gear caused many delays in the flight test programme and contributed to the growing eagerness to abandon the whole project. (*Courtesy BAE Systems*)

informed the Chief of the Air Staff that the Treasury had 'experienced great difficulty in getting any up to date estimates out of the MoA' and that their 'main anxiety' had been generated by various reports that the aircraft would be 'very late into service'.

On 27 March 1962, Peter Thorneycroft, the Minister of Aviation, advised the Minister for Defence that the estimated costs of development for the airframe plus engines and equipment had now reached a staggering £137 million. Some of this figure was attributable to a 'wide variety of equipments' for which design studies had not been completed and for which the projected costs were 'necessarily in some degree uncertain', and also added that there had been a 'serious increase in the engine cost'. Thorneycroft now estimated that TSR2 would enter RAF service in the third quarter of 1966 – in what would effectively be a strategic strike role, with the original tactical operations being assigned later – providing that the aircraft's forward-looking radar development was concluded satisfactorily. At this stage, no decision had been made as to whether proceed with the preferred Ferranti system or if American Texas Instrument equipment would be bought as a substitute.

Thorneycroft had already established that much of the aircraft's electronic equipment was 'lagging behind the aircraft programme'. The Minister of Defence responded by declaring that the project would have to be resubmitted to the Defence Committee as they had originally approved it 'on the basis of much lower estimates of cost'. In May, a decision was finally made to proceed with the Ferranti FLR although the Minister for Defence also agreed that some sort of contractual agreement on performance and delivery dates should be obtained. He also added that despite the rising costs of the overall programme, the Government was 'fully committed to the TSR2' and that it was 'an essential element in our plans for the RAF'. The Defence Committee concurred and requested that the Minister should make a final decision on the aircraft's development and production 'before the summer recess'.

By June 1962, it was disclosed that the first flight of the prototype would now be set for August 1963, delays having been caused by a failure to produce the correct amount of detailed design drawings which had left some aircraft components awaiting manufacture. Efforts were made to address this problem, but by the end of that month, BAC reported that their costs for airframe development had again increased from £48.5 million to £59.7 million. However, further governmental approval was granted in August when it was also decided to cancel BAC's Blue Water missile project, despite an attempt made by the Chief of the Defence Staff to embark upon another full reappraisal of the TSR2 programme. Just four months later, the cost estimates had risen again to an estimated £137 million for the whole programme and an atmosphere of insecurity slowly descended upon Weybridge and Warton.

In January 1963, the Research and Development Board approved continued development at an overall cost of up to £200 million. The Minister of Aviation reported to the Minister of Defence, now Peter Thorneycroft, that as of April 1962, the cost of developing the TSR2 weapons system had been estimated at £137 million with an initial CA release in the third quarter of 1966 and full release late in the following year. After setbacks in airframe and engine progress, it was now envisaged that these release dates had slipped by a whole year and that the airframe costs might be likely to rise to as much as £80 million. The loss of the Vulcan test bed that was destroyed during a ground run and other difficulties would probably increase the estimated engine development costs from £34 million to as much as £45 million. Total costs from the whole programme might now be 'not less than £175 million'. Such astronomical figures, bearing in mind that this was 1963, seem almost incredible, but even they did not provide a complete picture of just how much money had been invested in the project. Research and development costs might now reach £200 million while a projected total

Many of XR219's test flights were made with the air brake doors fixed slightly proud of the fuselage. This was due to a fault in the retraction mechanism that threatened to overextend and cause damage to the aircraft structure. Until repairs could be made, the solution was to fix the airbrakes to only partially close. (*Courtesy BAE Systems*)

production run of 138 aircraft might cost a further £340 million: a total of £540 million. As one ministerial minute recorded, 'the cost increases in this project continue to break all records'.

During February, Thorneycroft suggested that the envisaged production run of 138 aircraft might be reduced to just fifty or sixty, the remainder of the total comprising of Mk.2 variants of the Buccaneer as a cheaper alternative. The Secretary of State for Air and the Minister of Aviation rejected the idea although the Admiralty continued to pursue the concept with some vigour, but despite the increasing costs and increasingly vocal misgivings, the DRPC endorsed continuation of the project. However, late in March, the Chiefs of Staff approved a report on the military implications of replacing a proportion of the TSR2 production batch with Buccaneers. As a result, the Chief Scientific Advisor to the Minister of Defence, Sir Solly Zuckerman, was asked to investigate how the Buccaneer's capabilities might be 'maximised'. In effect, the proposal was to consider whether the Buccaneer – in an improved Mk.2 version – could successfully fulfil TSR2's tactical strike role while a smaller batch of TSR2s could be produced to fulfil the strategic bomber role that was now seen as vital to create a stopgap capability pending the introduction of Polaris.

It was at this stage that the situation was confused further still when Lt-General Sir John Hackett remarked that he had 'serious misgivings about the extent to which it might be possible to meet the Army's needs from manned aircraft resources'. Given that the Army was to rely upon TSR2 for tactical support and reconnaissance, his comments suggested that even they might no longer be quite so convinced that TSR2 was a system that they needed, at least not at the expense of other projects which they had also hoped for. It seems certain that the cancellation of the Blue Water missile destroyed a lot of Army support for TSR2 – their assumption, rightly or wrongly, being that it was probably abandoned in order to find more money for TSR2 – and now that considerable support for the concept of replacing TSR2 with the Buccaneer in the tactical role was emerging, the Chiefs of the Defence Staff were hard-pressed to defend TSR2. The best that they could offer was a conclusion that 'our ability to meet certain essential commitment in our strategy, for which TSR2 is designed, would be seriously prejudiced by TSR2s being replaced by the Buccaneer even with the contemplated improvements'. This rather vague defence of TSR2 probably serves to emphasise that by 1963, the Defence Chiefs were thinking of TSR2 more in terms of strategic bomber capability rather than the key tactical role for which it had first been designed. They were already beginning to envisage a situation in which they might never get the tactical strike aircraft which they had sought for so long.

Thorneycroft stated in a letter dated 3 April that 'the cost of the present planned programme of 138 TSR2s is of the same broad order of magnitude as the aircraft carrier programme or the strategic nuclear deterrent programme', adding that this was 'a remarkable figure for a light bomber replacement'. He said that he had 'from time to time upon professional advice' described TSR2's role as 'anything from a substitute for Blue Water to a substitute for a V-Bomber'. Thorneycroft felt that while some parts of TSR2's proposed roles could not be efficiently undertaken by other aircraft, some roles could undoubtedly be performed by aircraft which possessed capabilities 'far short' of those afforded to TSR2. Even Harold Macmillan, the Prime Minister, was uneasy. In a minute to the Minister of Aviation dated 24 April, he asked, 'Can you give me the latest position about the TSR2? What will it cost? Will it ever fly?' Of course, the Minister, Julian Amery, could say very little with any degree of confidence.

Absurdly, a proposed timescale was pursued on an official level while another was seemingly being implemented from an industrial viewpoint. Treasury approval for continued development was given in October at a cost of £175 million on the understanding that this might rise to £200 million. However, by this stage, the DRPC had agreed to inform the Minister of Defence that the overall cost of the programme

Undercarriage retraction problems dogged the test flight programme. The Vickers-designed gear was undoubtedly overcomplicated and designed for a capability that the RAF would probably have never used. (*Courtesy BAE Systems*)

was now likely to reach £222 million. The target date of October 1966 for Initial CA Release had also slipped again by October and production of the development batch aircraft was estimated to be two months behind schedule. The Treasury authorised production of eleven pre-production aircraft in June and agreed to the announcement being made on production aircraft, but carefully declined to specify how many (the Air Ministry asked for thirty). Eventually, the Chancellor agreed to a statement that outlined 'a development batch order for nine and a pre-production order for eleven aircraft'. But when the announcement was made by the Ministry of Aviation, it was less specific: 'In addition to the orders already placed for TSR2... For development and introductory flying by the RAF, British Aircraft Corporation have now been authorised to acquire long-dated materials to enable production of TSR2s for squadron service to begin.'

On 28 October, the Air Ministry briefed the media in order to 'dispel some current misconceptions in the press about the role and operational uses of TSR2' although the briefing was inevitably dominated by discussion of the cost figures which were being associated with the programme. A few weeks later, *The Times* newspaper ran a long article that examined the TSR2 and a Commons debate discussed the project some days previously. The article claimed that for some time 'the air had been thick with inflated estimates of cost on one side and exaggerated claims of performance on the other'. Of course, the performance claims were not exaggerated at all, but when set against the ever-increasing cost estimates, an atmosphere of 'political spin' was clearly being sensed. *The Times* continued with references to 'dark rumours of cancellation' which had been met with official denials that were 'strenuous enough to spread panic through an arms industry still groping fearfully about in the ruins of Blue Streak and Blue Water'. Surprisingly – as this still was not acknowledged official policy – the report also claimed that TSR2 'was to carry the main weight of the strategic nuclear strike task between the decline of the V-Bomber and the introduction of the Polaris missile' and that the Air Staff had therefore 'contrived an extension of the airborne deterrent by the simple expedient of calling it something else'. With the benefit of hindsight, it is clear that this accusation was technically correct, but it prompted the Air Minister to make an official statement to the effect that the use of TSR2 in a strategic role was 'a bonus – nothing more, nothing less'. Also, the aircraft's design had been frozen 'long before there was any question of cancelling Skybolt'.

This too was technically true, but it failed to explain that no significant design changes, apart from modifications to the weapons bay doors, had been necessary. As the project progressed into 1964, the cost estimates and delays showed little signs of improvement. By the middle of the year, the prospect of getting a prototype aircraft into the air was overshadowed by the gloomy news of a continual postponement of a first flight date that was first estimated to be likely at the end of July, only to be delayed again until August.

Development costs continued to climb and were now pegged at £260 million and the production price of each aircraft was now expected to be £2.8 million. Early in the year, a meeting between the Minister of Aviation and the heads of BAC and BSE concluded by the Secretary of State for Air that the costs were 'uncontrollable'. But against all odds, the first TSR2 finally took to the air on 27 September 1964, just weeks before a new Labour Government came into power. The Conservative Government had undoubtedly supported TSR2 and had continued to do so even at the stage when costs were unacceptably high. Having cancelled twenty-six significant defence projects including Blue Streak and Blue Water in order to save £300 million, it would not have been such a surprise if TSR2 had been added to the list. However, the aircraft's potential had been understood and when a stopgap strategic aircraft had suddenly become an urgent requirement after Skybolt was cancelled, the prospect of abandoning what seemed to be the only available solution must have seemed unthinkable. But as the development and projected production costs spiralled out of control, and the likelihood that TSR2 would come into service only two years before Polaris became clearer, the Conservative Government's appetite for the project started to wane.

For the Labour Party, the issue seemed much clearer. The Labour Party was not an enthusiastic supporter of nuclear armament and many of its most vociferous members were adamant that Britain should rid itself of its stockpile of nuclear weapons together with the machinery with which to deliver them. Although some of the more influential members of the party could at least tolerate the concept of

XR219 ended her days as a static test specimen at the Proof & Experimental Establishment at Shoeburyness. A sad end for an incredibly capable and expensive aeroplane. (*Courtesy BAE Systems*)

a strategic nuclear deterrent, the very idea of producing a nuclear-capable tactical aircraft was rather more difficult to accept. With Polaris firmly on the horizon, the prospect of introducing a new strategic bomber almost by proxy was unacceptable. The country was also on the verge of bankruptcy. With a serious sterling crisis affecting the economy, Wilson's primary objective was to save money wherever possible. As defence expenditure already drained a huge amount of money from the Treasury, it was therefore inevitable that it would face intense scrutiny. But Wilson and his Cabinet also wanted to maintain Britain's international position, both within NATO and on a more global basis. In order to maintain the all important place at the proverbial 'top table', it was vital that Britain maintained a strong influence and this effectively meant maintaining a strong defensive – and therefore offensive – posture that would be heard and understood by America in particular.

It was also essential that from a purely introspective point of view, the country needed to be adequately defended, particularly when East-West tensions were still high and the political situation in the Soviet Union was far from stable. It was with these conflicting interests in mind that Wilson gathered his ministers at Chequers during November. Denis Healey was the new Minister of Defence and countless accounts of TSR2's history have portrayed Healey not only as the person who was ultimately responsible for the cancellation of TSR2, but often dismissively regarding him as an anti-military socialist who was determined to destroy the project at any cost. In fact, it is fairer to say that Healey was very much a pro-military man and earned himself a reputation as a serious, wise and practical man in the corridors of Whitehall. Indeed, some later claimed that he was one of the best defence ministers the country has ever had. At Chequers, the first issue to be raised was the broad question of whether Britain should retain a nuclear capability. Although many rank and file members of the Labour Party were increasingly set against nuclear weapons, the case for unilateral disarmament was not taken particularly seriously within the Cabinet. Little more than lip service was paid to the notion at Chequers, now that Polaris was just a few years away and, at least in terms of proportional costs, was seen to be favourably inexpensive. Some ministers were still unenthusiastic, but with 'heavyweights' such as Healey, James Callaghan and Roy Jenkins set firmly in favour of Polaris and the retention of tactical nuclear weapons, the issue was hardly in doubt before it was discussed.

The Labour Party remained unilateralist by nature, but the Cabinet took a more realistic view. However, the acceptance of a nuclear deterrent did not necessarily imply that TSR2 would be needed in order to deliver it, even as a short-term measure. The new Government appears to have regarded TSR2 as a purely tactical aircraft and a conventional non-nuclear one at that. Both Healey and Wilson made specific public references to the TSR2 as being an aircraft which the Government might still purchase, but primarily, if not exclusively, as a carrier of conventional weapons. Whether this was their honest viewpoint or one which was intended primarily for public consumption is unclear, but almost overnight, the perceived urgent need for a stopgap strategic bomber that had influenced TSR2's progress was dropped and the aircraft was once again regarded as the straightforward Canberra replacement. Healey subsequently stated in Parliament that, 'when we decide the size and pattern of our defences, we must watch with extreme vigilance their impact both on our balance of payments and, even more important, on our productive resources, particularly in scientists and skilled manpower. We must get value for money.' He added that he 'had looked at the books' and that he looked forward to 'discussing some of the skeletons found in the cupboard'. Of course, the biggest of these was TSR2 and with this project no doubt in mind, Healey said, 'unless we are to allow our defence expenditure to rise continually, not only in absolute terms, but also as a percentage of our rising national wealth, we must be prepared to reduce the calls on our military resources.'

Most significantly, Healey was keen to grasp some proverbial nettles which the Conservatives had carefully avoided, tackling projects which should have been examined and acted upon. Like Duncan Sandys, he was willing to take on the fundamental issues of Britain's defence posture as a whole, stating that:

One thing I have already learned from my first five weeks in office is that Britain is spending more on her defence forces than any other country of her size and wealth. We are still trying to sustain three major military roles – to maintain and independent strategic nuclear striking power, to make a major contribution towards the allied

Flight tests at Boscombe Down were conducted from a designated base at the end of Boscombe's secondary runway. For many months, XR219 was a familiar sight to passersby on the adjacent perimeter road as each test flight was prepared for and completed. (*Courtesy BAE Systems*)

defence of Western Europe and to deploy a significant military capacity overseas, from British Guiana through the Mediterranean, Africa and the Middle East to Hong Kong. I put it seriously to the House – and I hope that Right Hon. And Hon. Members will listen seriously because I do not think there is disagreement between those of us who know the facts – that unless we are to impose unacceptable strains on our own economy and to carry a handicap which none of our main competitors in world trade has to bear, Britain too must decide which of these three roles should have priority.

As Chancellor, Callaghan had expressed his view that overall Treasury expenditure should be capped at £200 million. Given that a great deal of existing defence spending was allocated to essentials such as pay, accommodation, pensions and training, it was equipment which faced the closest scrutiny. With a 10 per cent defence budget reduction necessary, it followed that some 40 per cent would have to come from cuts in equipment and aircraft projects were clearly the most expensive projects from where savings could be made. Healey was, according to colleague Lord Carver, 'appalled at the mess he discovered in the aircraft field'. Healey immediately began to investigate ways in which the most expensive projects could be reduced in cost and whether there was any alternative means of providing the RAF with the same capabilities that were cheaper:

> When I asked the Air Force if there was any alternative to the Conservative plans, they were only too glad to tell me. There was a cheaper American equivalent of all three major British Aircraft on order; in at least two cases they would be available much sooner, and of equal or superior performance. I decided to buy them instead, and met the Treasury's concern about their cost in dollars by negotiating an offset agreement, under which the United States would buy British goods to the same value.

Thus, it was Healey who resolved to cancel the P.1154 and HS. As for the TSR2, he was advised that America could provide a viable substitute in the shape of TFX – what was to become the F-111. Although it was slightly inferior to TSR2 in projected performance, it was remarkably similar in most respects and an improved 'Mk.2' version that was under development would meet the RAF's needs. More importantly, it would be available within a similar timescale and be much cheaper. For Healey, while TSR2 would have to be paid for upon delivery, taking a massive chunk out of the defence budget (some £80 million on top of his current projections), the TFX could be purchased up to 1978 which would spread expenditure over a whole decade. The figures could not be disputed: 'At the outset, therefore it would seem that the continuance of TSR2 would automatically rule out any prospect of continuing defence expenditure within £2,000m [1964 prices] by 1969-70.'

In December, the first of a series of fact-finding visits to Washington began to look more closely at the possibility of purchasing TFX. In February1965, the DCAS issued a paper that stated that while these visits were being made, the Ministry of Aviation had been tasked with a re-evaluation of TSR2's progress so that they might 'negotiate a maximum price for it with the British Aircraft Corporation'. In order to achieve this, it would be 'necessary to have an up-to-date specification which took account of actual flight experience with the aircraft so far'. At a subsequent meeting of the Standing Committee, some concern was expressed at an 'apparent degradation in performance represented by the proposed revised specification' and this was also reflected in comments made during a meeting of the Air Force Board. It was stated that if the specification represented 'a realistic assessment of what the aircraft might now be capable of achieving' it could go forward to the MoA as a basis for obtaining a fixed-price quotation from BAC. Precisely how the revised specification suggested any degradation in performance remains unclear and it may well be that this was merely a clouded perception based on the problems that BAC had experienced with engine and undercarriage problems during early flight trials. However, with the F-111 now firmly established as a viable and much cheaper alternative, this may well have been the point at which the Air Staff almost imperceptibly shifted their preference away from TSR2 in favour of the American option.

In late January, Sam Elworthy, Chief of the Air Staff, advised Healey that the Air Staff now preferred TFX to TSR2 on military grounds, rather than only on a politically-driven economic basis. Elworthy had concluded some months previously that TSR2 was a project that was now running a very real risk of ruining other fundamentally important parts of the RAF's expenditure and was no longer their proverbial 'sacred cow' which it had been for so long. It is difficult to pinpoint precisely why the Air Staff had finally relinquished support for what had been such a cherished project, but by this stage in the TSR2 programme, the RAF had clearly accepted that they might never get the TSR2 into service at all and the prospect of a fixed price and fixed delivery alternative was undoubtedly a more attractive proposition. When Healey offered the Air Staff the opportunity to abandon what was now being perceived as a potentially unaffordable and possibly unattainable goal, they seized the chance to accept what Healey assured them what they could have. BAC were still unable, or at least unwilling, to agree to a revised fixed-price contract for TSR2 production and in some ways it is perhaps understandable that BAC maintained this position. Bound by the complexities of the procurement and design process which had been laid down by the Government, so much of the project had been beyond BAC's control that they would have undoubtedly been accepting a major financial risk had they committed themselves to a fixed price. But by refusing to limit the Government's liability, they effectively sealed the project's fate almost as securely as the Air Staff and Healey had done.

A brief on defence expenditure issued late in 1964 outlined the Government's view of the situation with regard to TSR2:

> The US F-111A – the TFX – appears likely to meet the United Kingdom requirement is all significant respects although it is the American custom to build separate versions for strike and reconnaissance. The United States has been very chary of releasing information about this aircraft. There is some reason to believe that there are difficulties about aerodynamics, weight growth and rising cost. Research and development costs of the TSR2 are currently forecast as £272m and production costs for 158 aircraft as £469m. A total of £741m. About £160m has so far been spent or committed. The TFX will cost not less than £2m. 158 aircraft at £2 would, with spare engines, cost £332m. Cancelling the TSR2 and substituting the TFX would therefore save about £250m.

These figures could hardly be dismissed as insignificant. On this basis, the Government would save a huge amount of money and payment could be spread over many years. Also, the RAF would receive a full production order of tactical strike aircraft. Similar savings could be applied to other projects too, and Healey implemented the first

As part of TSR2's short-field performance stipulation, the aircraft's nose gear oleo could be extended in length, giving the aircraft a better rotational ability. The system was tested briefly, but the test pilots doubted the safety and reliability of the concept. When it was established that the aircraft's tailplanes provided very good rotational authority, the nose gear system was abandoned. (*Courtesy BAE Systems*)

of these as swiftly as he could. On 15 January, the Defence and Overseas Policy Committee (DOPC) met and Healey proposed that the TSR2, P.1154 and HS.681 should be cancelled and be replaced by the F-111, F-4 (a developed version of the P.1127 and a less ambitious and expensive VTOL tactical aircraft that would become the Harrier) and the C-130.

The Chancellor accepted this recommendation, but further work was requested to investigate 'measures which might be taken to deal with the difficulties which the aircraft industry might face in the event of a Government decision to cancel certain of the current aircraft projects'. In effect, the ministers were looking at how and when the projects should be cancelled, not whether they should be cancelled at all. At another meeting on 29 January, it was agreed that the P.1154 and HS.681 should finally be cancelled and replaced as had been discussed. The TSR2, however, was to continue for the time being, Harold Wilson in particular believing that the project should be allowed to progress while more information on its cost and performance was determined. It was agreed that development of the P.1127 (Harrier) should go ahead – Healey had pressed vigorously for this particular project – and that forty Phantoms should be ordered with an option for a further 110, together with twenty-four C-130s and an option for a further fifty-eight.

It was also agreed that the Shackleton Anti-Submarine Warfare aircraft should be replaced by development of the Comet airliner (the latter becoming the Nimrod). All of these decisions were confirmed by the Cabinet on 1 February and TSR2 survived, but not with Healey's full blessing. It was only a Cabinet disagreement and Wilson's viewpoint which kept the project alive, prompted by uneasiness over possible industry job losses, lack of confidence in the F-111's capabilities and a general sense that cancelling three projects simultaneously would be a difficult task to defend both within Parliament and across the country. Disposing of the projects that were defended less fiercely seemed like a preferable option. Healey commented that he 'had to keep development going purely for political reasons at a cost of £4 million a week until April 6th. I was deeply conscious of what could have been done with the £40 million for more useful purposes.' The deadline of 6 April was when Callaghan would introduce his first budget and he had made it very clear to Wilson and Healey that he would prefer to incorporate the TSR2's cancellation into his budget speech. Roy Jenkins later commented that he believed Callaghan had 'evolved a tactic of announcing the cancellation in April in order to provide a boost for sterling at what was bound to be a difficult time'. In other words, Callaghan thought there would be some advantage in presenting the cancellation as an example of financial prudence rather than military policy. Meanwhile, the Ministry of Aviation looked at ways in which TSR2's costs might be brought down by reducing the aircraft's capabilities and/or the roles it would undertake. The exercise was largely fruitless as the aircraft was designed, undergoing flight testing and could not be altered unless even more money was spent on it.

BAC were only too aware that a final decision would come in April and they were under no illusions as to what the outcome would probably be, although Roy Jenkins continued to assure BAC that the project was not yet completely dead. Jenkins also firmly believed that although Healey had been given assurances by his US counterpart Robert McNamara that Britain could exercise an option on purchasing the F-111 – but would have the right to subsequently cancel it if it was decided that the aircraft was no longer required – it was important to maintain a strong bargaining position with America. Prematurely cancelling TSR2 would leave Britain with no other option than to buy the F-111 or have nothing which was hardly a strong position from which to strike a favourable deal.

It was hardly the most encouraging basis on which to keep TSR2 alive, but it was better than nothing. Indeed, he had proposed to Healey that purchasing a smaller batch of TSR2s might be acceptable (probably no more than fifty) but Healey saw no logic in this, although he did look at the possibility of reducing the number of F-111s which might be ordered, suggesting that eighty might be sufficient. However, CAS Sam Elworthy insisted that the RAF could not fulfil its tasks with anything less than 110 aircraft, be they F-111s or TSR2s, and that substituting the Phantom or Buccaneer for some roles was not acceptable in his opinion. Of course, the two aircraft did eventually assume some of TSR2's roles and Elworthy had undoubtedly been dismissive of the Buccaneer and Phantom in order to justify a substantial F-

111 order. Having abandoned interest in TSR2, the RAF was desperate not to allow the F-111 to slip away and Healey assured Elworthy that they would get what they wanted.

When Jenkins was briefed in March, he was advised that TSR2 should be replaced by the Buccaneer, but after having given his assurances to the RAF, Healey's response was that he found it 'difficult to conceive of any future military role for this country which would enable us to do without any aircraft of the TSR-2/F-111A class'. The idea of opting for the Buccaneer was finally dropped for good or so it seemed at the time. Of course, the whole issue re-emerged some years later following the cancellation of F-111 and the Buccaneer eventually entered RAF service. The notion that the RAF could not successfully function without a TSR2/F-111 aircraft was almost entirely based on the premise that Britain was to maintain a significant presence east of Suez and this was by no means a certainty now that the Labour Party was governing the country. Healey was unashamedly in favour of Britain's military commitments far beyond Europe and so was Wilson, but many others within the Government were set firmly against what they regarded as an outdated and unaffordable relic of imperialism. Healey's support for Britain's east of Suez roles was undoubtedly fostered by his relationship with America and in particular Robert McNamara who made no secret of the fact that he wanted Britain to maintain its overseas commitments, not only in order to avoid the responsibilities being handed to America, but in order to ensure that Britain was seen to be effectively endorsing America's international position.

With the east of Suez commitments came the requirement for a long-range tactical bomber. Without these roles, the F-111 or TSR2 were unnecessarily over-specified and therefore hugely overpriced, given that the prospect of using either aircraft as a stopgap strategic bomber was not a priority for the Labour Government who were never entirely comfortable with the prospect of an overtly overabundance of nuclear capability. Polaris was on the way and this was grudgingly accepted, but there was no appetite to create an additional strategic capability even as a short-term fix. Despite advocates such as Wilson and Healey, there was a growing appetite to abandon Britain's global presence and this, together with the aircraft's diminishing pseudo-strategic role, was one of the key reasons why TSR2 had slowly become less important to both the Government and the RAF. It was being pursued at huge costs in order to fulfil a role that no longer existed.

Finally, the Cabinet met on 1 April to make a binding decision ahead of the Chancellor's budget speech. In such situations it was, according to Jenkins, 'Wilson's practice to let everyone talk themselves out'. In his typical style, the Prime Minister allowed discussion to flow, avoiding expressing any firm view on TSR2 himself and it was other members of the Cabinet who argued long and hard through a meeting that began at 10 a.m. The meeting commenced once more after 10 p.m. after Healey had

TSR2's cockpit illustrating the conventional layout and logical placement of controls, all of which had been designed with the direct input of project test pilots. (*Courtesy BAE Systems*)

insisted on a second meeting to reach a firm conclusion on this divisive matter that was in effect the Government's first 'Cabinet crisis'. While Healey was convinced that TSR2 was no longer sustainable, he remained resolutely in favour of giving the RAF what they wanted: a fleet of F-111s in the shape of an initial order of ten F-111As to be followed by a more advanced F-111K version. He bombarded his colleagues with figures which indicated that purchasing F-111 would save £280 million over thirteen years and that orders for the Mk.2 F-111 would not have to be placed until 1967, by which time the Government would have had time to establish precisely what, if any, role Britain was to maintain east of Suez.

Some Cabinet ministers were reluctant to formally abandon TSR2 immediately, preferring to wait until a full Defence Review could be completed. Others, including Roy Jenkins, were still unconvinced that purchasing the F-111 would be a wise move. Jenkins commented that by purchasing an initial batch of ten Mk.1 aircraft, it would be difficult not to justify purchasing the larger batch of Mk.2 aircraft and given the choice, he would probably have preferred to buy Buccaneers. Callaghan, driven by financial considerations, was happy to cancel both TSR2 and F-111, and

Healey's position was shared by only a few, most notably Michael Stewart, the Foreign Secretary, who advocated a continuing east of Suez presence. Ironically, despite having often being branded as a 'butcher' responsible for the TSR2's demise, Healey was firmly on the RAF's side and he fought long and hard against a Cabinet that was largely in favour of abandoning both aircraft.

When the second evening meeting began, Healey had again spoken to McNamara, largely upon the insistence of Jenkins. Healey reported that providing a firm order for F-111As was placed in 1966 and that Britain ordered at least seventy Mark 2s in 1967, the US would not only keep the current favourable terms on the table, but would also fix the price of the Mk.2 at the level of the F-111A. McNamara could hardly have done any more, short of almost giving the F-111s to Britain for free. But the same arguments bounced back and forth: how would cancelling TSR2 affect BAC and its workforce? Would the Buccaneer be suitable if Britain was to remain east of Suez? What effect would an F-111 purchase have on foreign exchange? Would Britain's aircraft industry survive? As midnight passed, Wilson concluded that the Cabinet effectively had three options: postpone a decision on TSR-2 even longer; cancel the aircraft without an F-111 option; or cancel it and take the American offer.

This presented the ministers with a situation that Wilson later described as '... difficult – indeed, I think, in all our time, a unique situation'. Ten of the twenty-four ministers remained convinced that the TSR2 should be retained, if only because its abandonment would leave Britain with no other option than to buy American should a tactical strike aircraft still be needed. But with a small majority of ministers now in favour of accepting Healey's proposal to take up a non-committal option on the F-111 and no appetite for allowing the Government to be seen as indecisive on this issue any longer, it was finally accepted that Healey's solution was the only politically acceptable route that made sense. And so, at around 12.30 a.m. on the morning of 2 April, the Cabinet agreed to formally cancel the TSR2.

The full story of the TSR2 project is more complicated and absurd than this concise account might indicate. But the story is an important one as it represented a seminal moment in the history of Britain's military history. TSR2 was the very last aircraft to be created within an industrial structure that had barely changed since the First World War. Conversely, it was the first aircraft to be developed as part of a more 'hands on' procurement system. TSR2 was undoubtedly the last British aircraft that could be described as a pure 'bomber' even though the Buccaneer, designed before TSR2, ultimately succeeded it. The Wilson Government has always been held responsible for what is inevitably described as the TSR2's 'untimely demise', but this flies in the face of the true facts. It is true that the Labour Cabinet did take the final decision to abandon the project, but by 1965, the TSR2 project should already have been dumped. With hindsight, the many deficiencies of TSR2's procurement history can be seen, but even with the best of motives in mind, the ludicrous procedure through which the aircraft was designed and manufactured ought to have been halted long before 1965.

Fundamentally, it is also vitally important to understand that it was the RAF that ultimately abandoned TSR2 before the Government did. The Air Staff clearly expressed their willingness to dismiss TSR2 in favour of TFX and by 1965, the Government was presented with the prospect of buying a hideously expensive strategic bomber that would be redundant within a couple of years. Little wonder that when a cheaper alternative was on offer they took it. TSR2 was a magnificent mistake. It was undoubtedly a truly superb flying machine, but it was the wrong aircraft at the wrong time. It was created by a ridiculous bureaucratic structure designed to exercise control, but one that ultimately allowed the project to spiral completely out of control. It was designed to fulfil a requirement that constantly shifted and fell victim to a political battle between the armed services. It was undoubtedly ahead of its time, relying on technology that was often in its infancy. It was inevitable that TSR2 would eventually be abandoned, but it is remarkable that it survived for so long. TSR2 influenced everything that followed. It affected Bomber Command's future policies and had a huge effect upon Britain's aerospace industry. It also provided a technical legacy that enabled its systems to live on in future aircraft such as the Harrier, Jaguar, Nimrod and Tornado. TSR2 was a hugely important part of the RAF's post-war history, sometimes for all the wrong reasons, but its significance cannot be overstated.

CHAPTER ELEVEN
Reaping the Whirlwind

Although the Panavia Tornado is often regarded as a 'new generation' aircraft that sits firmly within the current range of contemporary warplanes in service around the world, one might be surprised to realise that it is now slowly approaching the end of its operational life. Even more surprising to many is that even as a 'Child of the Eighties', the Tornado programme's roots are to be found way back in the 1960s and that the Tornado represents the end product of a long and sometimes painful story. In simple terms, the Tornado came into being because of the TSR2. The long, monstrously expensive and often bitter TSR2 saga came to an end in 1965 when the new Labour Government axed the aircraft and the RAF tried to forget the painful years of mismanagement, confusion and clouded thinking that left the RAF without any kind of credible tactical bombing capability.

Back in 1965, the Canberra had progressively moved out of the medium- and high-altitude bombing business in order to make way for the Valiants, Vulcans and Victors which had given the United Kingdom a powerful strategic and decisive nuclear and conventional attack capability. Good though the Canberra undoubtedly was, it had never been expected to remain assigned to its primary role for long. By 1965, the Canberra could still function as a very effective short-range tactical bomber, but it was undoubtedly a creation of the 1950s, and as new Soviet defensive systems emerged, the Canberra gradually looked increasingly obsolescent. The TSR2 had been the solution to the Canberra's inevitable decline, but even the RAF who had fought so hard to get the aircraft into service, finally accepted that the TSR2 was a machine that the country simply could not afford. More importantly, it was also a machine that the RAF no longer needed.

The TSR2's final abandonment was made possible by the availability of a very suitable alternative. The American F-111 had come along at just the right time. Designed for virtually the same role, it matched TSR2's predicted performance, but promised to deliver it at a much lower price and to the delight of the British Government, could be purchased on very reasonable payment terms that avoided making a huge one-off cost for the Treasury. For the RAF, the opportunity to adopt the F-111 was a 'no brainer' and for the Government, buying an aircraft 'on credit' made perfect sense. When Defence Minister Denis Healey succeeded in getting TSR2 replaced by this more affordable alternative, the longer-term future for Bomber Command's structure looked secure. However, defence procurement is inextricably linked to politics and as the Government's appetite for withdrawal from its 'East of Suez' commitments grew stronger, the very idea of buying any sort of long-range strike aircraft suddenly seemed open to question. Clearly, if Britain was not going to find itself embroiled in a Middle East or Far East conflict, the F-111's long-range strike capabilities had a distinct feeling of 'overkill' about them.

To some extent, this growing political unease about F-111 was moderated by the Government's decision to join France on a programme to design and build the AFVG – the Anglo French Variable Geometry aircraft that promised give the UK and France a smaller strike aircraft than F-111 with a nominal range of around 600 miles. A force of around 175 AFVGs for the RAF was anticipated, combined with perhaps only fifty of the long-range F-111 aircraft. Together, the two aircraft would in theory create an effective and affordable strike/attack force that would satisfy the Government's appetite for international (particularly European) collaboration and also enable far fewer of the expensive F-111 aircraft to be purchased. The AFVG came into being as part of an ongoing dialogue between Britain and France, concerning a future requirement for both an advanced trainer and a light attack aircraft. The RAF had been looking for a potential replacement for the Gnat and Hunter trainers for some time while France had been looking for something similar, albeit with a combat capability. France's primary interest in the aircraft's combat capabilities conflicted with the RAF's preoccupation with the trainer specification, but when the TSR2 was finally dumped, the RAF began to show more interest in the concept of creating not only an advanced trainer, but a more combat-capable machine along the lines required by France. Ultimately, the RAF clearly needed something rather more sophisticated than France was envisioning, but after a great deal of negotiation, a solution was found and it was agreed that two different designs would be pursued. One would be the advanced trainer based on Breguet's existing Br.121 studies and the other an advanced combat aircraft based on BAC's P.45 studies.

France would take leadership of the trainer programme while BAC would have authority over the design of the combat aircraft. This agreement made perfect sense, especially when BAC had so much relevant experience from the years of TSR2 development. BAC also knew a lot about variable geometry (swing wings), indeed the original concept had been proposed by Barnes Wallis of the Dambusters fame. He had developed the principle of variable geometry wings during the 1940s, and the idea had been considered when the TSR2 programme first began; however, even though Vickers-Armstrong had done a great deal of research into the concept, there was not sufficient confidence to justify introducing it into a project as important as

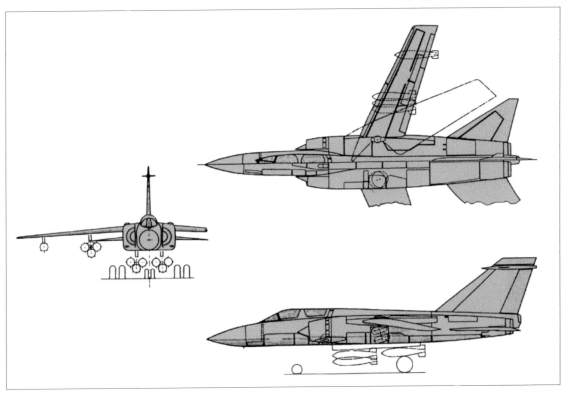

The Anglo-French Variable Geometry aircraft was a direct result of TSR2's cancellation. Designed to complement the long-range F-111K that was to enter RAF service, the AFVG was remarkably similar to the Tornado that followed it. France's self-interest in their indigenous aircraft designs led to the project's downfall.

TSR2. However, by 1965, the situation was very different and continuing research had now confirmed the practicality of the swing-wing concept, not least in the shape of America's F-111 that demonstrated only too clearly that Wallis' idea was a good one. Consequently, BAC believed that variable geometry was the way forward and France, influenced by research being conducted by Dassault, agreed.

Like the Anglo-French combat trainer, which eventually emerged as the Jaguar, the AFVG was envisaged as a multi-role aircraft. Just a few weeks before TSR2 was cancelled, Denis Healey had agreed to purchase F-4M Phantoms for the RAF in order to compensate for the cancellation of the P.1154. The new Phantoms would be assigned to the ground-attack role as a replacement for the Hunter fleet and in Germany they would also be equipped for the nuclear strike role so that the Canberra could be withdrawn. But when the Jaguar and AFVG were ready for introduction into service, the Phantom would be reassigned to the air defence role, allowing the Lightning interceptor fleet to be retired. AFVG would therefore be designed to perform well as both a fighter and bomber. Although no detailed plans emerged, it was expected that the same basic AFVG airframe would be used for both roles with new avionics fitted to the aircraft when it eventually switched from a bomber to a fighter. This was probably a slightly naïve supposition, but in 1967, it all seemed to make perfect sense even though in practical terms AFVG never made much sense at all.

The basic idea was sound, but it was also obvious that meeting the conflicting demands of two countries would never be easy, even with two very different designs. Early in 1967, the editor of *Flight International* commented:

> The French now say that the agreed design will not meet their interceptor requirements. This has come rather tiresomely late in the day, making it even more difficult to produce one basic aeroplane that will be all things to all men – from a 36,000 lb French naval interceptor to a British Canberra replacement. There has always been a certain technical improbability about a 36,000 lb aeroplane performing the heavy-strike task of a 60,000 lb Canberra, even with variable geometry. Desirable though such a common aeroplane is politically, the new French requirements appear to make it impossible – even if funds and the ability of designers to perform miracles were unlimited, which they are not.

Perhaps it is fortunate that the project was soon killed off by France, leaving only the Jaguar programme to continue. With typical French national interest firmly in mind, AFVG had soon become a far less attractive proposition to the French Government when Dassault announced its intention to create a remarkably similar aircraft itself. Having studied the concept of variable geometry wings for some time, and having now learned even more from Britain, Dassault became confident that it could produce an aircraft better suited to France's requirements than AFVG ever would be. Consequently, the French Government immediately recognised the national value of pursuing an indigenous project and resolved to dump AFVG as swiftly as possible. This they did, ostensibly on the grounds of cost. Technically speaking at least, they were not lying. Defence Minister Healey was clearly wounded by the news of France's withdrawal, but he was equally satisfied that F-111 was on the way and so he believed that the RAF would be getting the aircraft that it had really wanted, regardless of the abandonment of AFVG. But Britain's economic state was deteriorating badly and it was therefore inevitable that the increasingly expensive F-111 would be subject to even closer scrutiny. After just a few more months it became clear that like the TSR2, it too could not survive. In January 1968, Prime Minister Wilson announced:

> We have decided to cancel the order for 50 F-111 aircraft. Further study is being given to the consequences of this decision on the future equipment of the Royal Air Force. Leaving

out of account the results of this study, the cancellation of the F-111 is estimated to yield total savings on the Defence Budget of about £400 million between now and 1977-78. This figure allows for likely cancellation charges. The saving in dollar expenditure over the period, again allowing for likely cancellation charges, will be well over $700 million. Because of the credit arrangements, these savings will mature over a period of years. We are discussing with the United States Government future arrangements for offset orders and credit for the Phantom and Hercules aircraft. The reduction in our overseas commitments will make it possible to cut down the RAF transport force.

Remarkably, despite huge resources, time and money that had been poured into TSR2, F-111 and AFVG, the RAF was now approaching the 1970s with no sign of the elusive Canberra replacement that had been sought for so long. The complicated saga continued and some six months passed before the Government agreed to purchase a batch of Buccaneers for the RAF as direct replacements for the cancelled F-111 and AFVG. Having battled against the Buccaneer for so many years during the TSR2 programme, the RAF was, to say the least, reluctant to accept the Buccaneer, but it was now clear that it was the only suitable aircraft on offer. The Government inevitably reverted to its long held belief that the Buccaneer was perfectly capable of undertaking the RAF's strike/attack role, especially if the RAF's projected theatre of operations would be within Europe. But the RAF's lack of faith in the Buccaneer's suitability meant that even before the aircraft had entered service, RAF's chiefs were already looking for an aircraft to replace it.

Across the Channel, France elected to leave NATO in pursuit of a more independent military posture. Having destroyed any hopes of developing the AFVG project into a viable warplane, the RAF had been forced to accept an aircraft that it had bitterly opposed for years. Likewise, it is arguable whether the Jaguar was an aircraft that the RAF really wanted, especially when it was not the advanced trainer that had been sought in the first place. As a light attack aircraft, it was hardly better than the Phantom that it would swiftly replace and for the RAF it was yet another less than ideal solution. Indeed, had the British Government known just how eager the French were in abandoning the AFVG when it no longer suited them, it is quite likely that the Jaguar would also never have been produced. This would have been reinforced had it been known how France would eventually dissuade potential export customers from buying Jaguar so that their own indigenous aircraft could be sold instead.

International co-operation seemed like a poisonous recipe and in the wake of the AFVG cancellation, BAC's Preston Division continued to work on the projected design as a purely private venture, albeit with the tentative and discrete support of the RAF. The British Variable Geometry (BVG) aircraft and British Advanced Combat Aircraft (BACA) were both direct derivatives of the still-born AFVG, but with the Buccaneer now on order for the RAF, the Treasury did not want to hear about anything that was perceived as an attempt to resurrect the AFVG, F-111 or TSR2 saga. It was obvious to BAC and the RAF that the only way forward was, despite its evident risks, international co-operation. The same conclusion had been reached in Europe where NATO members were looking at potential designs that might eventually replace the ubiquitous F-104G Starfighter. In January 1968, the Air Force Chiefs of Germany, Belgium, Italy and the Netherlands agreed to establish a working group to develop a joint requirement for a new strike/attack aircraft that could replace the Starfighter. Initially referred to as the Multi-Role Aircraft (MRA), it was soon known as the MRCA: the Multi-Role Combat Aircraft.

By July, the British Air Staff had joined the working group as had Canada. Basic design proposals were duly submitted by BAC, MBB (Messerschmitt Blokow Blohm) and also from Canada as the basis for further study. Canada and Belgium decided to pull out of the project, claiming that changes to their national defence strategies meant that the MRCA would not be suitable for their needs. In fact, it was more likely that when the complex and advanced nature of MRCA was laid before them, the anticipated cost probably persuaded both countries to abandon any interest in MRCA and pursue closer ties with the US from where 'off the shelf' purchases could be made far more cheaply.

By the end of 1969, the group had agreed that the BAC and MBB proposals were suitable for the requirements of all four nations and work began on combining the assets of both designs to create one coherent project. In effect, it was the British (BAC) design that formed the core of the MRCA design – essentially a refinement of the earlier AFVG aircraft – and with this process at a satisfactory stage, the four countries came together to establish a joint company to share the management, design and production of the MRCA. Panavia Aircraft GmbH was the result but in July 1969, the Netherlands decided to leave the project having become influenced by the same thinking that had persuaded Canada and Belgium to leave previously. Germany opted to purchase a huge fleet of some 700 aircraft while the British Government finally agreed that some 385 aircraft should be ordered on the basis that by the time MRCA was translated into an operational warplane, it would meet the right timescale to begin replacement of both the Vulcan bomber and Buccaneer that were committed to the overland strike role in Germany. Germany also appreciated the likelihood of a long development programme and rather than soldier on with its fleet of Starfighters for longer than necessary, the Luftwaffe opted to purchase the F-4E and F-4F Phantom as a short-term partial replacement and reduced its order to 324 MRCA as a result.

Test Pilot Paul Millett was involved in both the Buccaneer and Jaguar test programmes and as his fascinating account recalls, he was also to play a pivotal part in the Tornado project:

The first Multi-Role Combat Aircraft prototype pictured at Manching in Germany. British test pilot Paul Millett made the aircraft's first flight on 14 August 1974. (*Courtesy BAE Systems*)

During the negotiating stage of the programme, the Germans had been insistent that the first flight should be made in Germany on the grounds that they were buying more aircraft than either Britain or Italy. Sir Frederick Page (BAC) reluctantly agreed to this argument, but cannily insisted that the flight should be made by a British pilot, so it came about that in early 1974, I moved to Bavaria to prepare for the occasion. I found that I was well received there and I was never made to feel that I was taking a first flight away from a German pilot, just that I was one of the team. While the first MRCA prototype was being completed in the hangar at Manching, the aircrew busied themselves with operating the various ground systems test rigs at the Ottobrun MBB factory, talking to the systems designers and attending the innumerable meetings that a multi-national programme of this sort seems to generate. The usual routine for testing engines on an aircraft was that the engine company engineers would do all the long-winded running-in tests, but Neils Meister (the MBB project pilot) and I decided that we would do all of the ground engine running ourselves, which would get us thoroughly at home in the cockpit and familiar with operating the systems.

When P01 (the prototype) had its first engines fitted, we put this plan into action and spent many hours of useful work in the cockpits. We alternated between the front and rear cockpits, despite there being no controls in the rear cockpit of P01, because it was very useful to be able to talk to each other about the tests and it also helped to consolidate the already good team spirit. Taxiing trials came up in due course and it was a great boost to everyone to get the aircraft moving under its own power. This also provided the opportunity to check out the telemetry system that was to be used to monitor all of the early test flying. High speed taxi trials followed, along with testing of the reverse thrust system. There was an inevitable temptation when checking the nose wheel lifting speed on the long runway at Manching to lift the aircraft clear of the ground for a short hop, but the aircraft was a political hot potato and the engines were not flight cleared so I resisted the temptation and put the nose wheel back down again!

The first flight-cleared engines arrived and were fitted to P01. With thoughts of an imminent flight, Neils Meister and I went out to do our final pre-flight engine run. When the left engine was opened up to full dry (non-reheated) power, it wound up as usual to full rpm at which point the compressor exploded with an impressive noise. I returned to Warton to await further developments and Turbo-Union went back to Munich to find out what they had done wrong.

After a pause of some four months, a pair of flight modified engines were ready for the aircraft and on 14 August 1974, we went back into flight preparation mode. All went well this time, right up to the attempt to start engines for the actual flight. The Tornado engines are started from an internal auxiliary power unit. The drive from the APU to the engine gearbox contains a small, necked shaft to act as a weak link in case of gearbox seizure. This shaft had failed and there was no spare shaft at Manching. Undaunted, the aircraft crew chief asked me to stay in the cockpit and disappeared, clutching the pieces of the shaft in his leather gloves. When he reappeared with a look of triumph on his face, he showed me the shaft that he had taken to the workshop and brazed together so expertly that the join barely showed. The shaft was refitted and the APU restarted; the engines then started perfectly. Despite the rather uncertain start, the flight went perfectly from then on. Tornado was the first aircraft in Europe to be designed as a fly-by-wire machine without direct mechanical connection from the stick to the control surfaces, but from the time it left the ground it flew so beautifully that the thought of this did not occur to me. As planned, I left the aircraft in the take-off configuration and climbed to 10,000 feet before cleaning up and carrying out a pre-planned series of handling tests. Aircraft handling was delightful, as anticipated – much better than the simulator – and all the aircraft systems behaved perfectly, with the possible exception of an occasional howl from the air conditioning system, which was easily cured after flight and never recurred. I checked the low speed handling in the landing configuration and found the aircraft to be very responsive in pitch, but nothing that worried me about the landing approach to come. I went back to the Manching airfield circuit and made a low approach and overshoot, followed by a very easily made landing. I had practiced the first flight so often by this time in simulators, and even by flying around the projected route in the company HS125 jet, and the actual flight went so smoothly that I did begin to wonder whether this was not yet another simulation.

The second flight was used to extend the handling envelope up to the initial limits of 3g and 300 knots. The wings were swept for the first time with virtually no trim changes or change in handling characteristics, which showed that the aerodynamicists had done their job well. The excellent handling found on the first flight was fully confirmed and the air conditioning noise experienced on that flight had been cured. After landing there were no faults to be reported. The initial flight test programme had stipulated that I should make the first three flights, then hand the aircraft over to the MBB pilots. Since the first two flights had gone so well, I could see no reason for not getting the German pilots in on the flying of their aircraft right away, so on flight three I sat in the back of Po1 with Neils Meister at the controls and he confirmed the delightful aircraft handling. I was quite content to leave the subsequent flying of Po1 to the MBB aircrews, but I was delighted to be invited to return to Manching to make Flight No. 8, which was to be a demonstration of the aircraft for the benefit of the Defence Ministries and Air Staffs of the three countries as well as introducing it to the aviation press. To show our confidence in the aircraft, I had the aircraft parked in front of the VIP grandstand, and did away with all the usual paraphernalia of equipment and ground crew that surround most military aircraft before flight. The only person outside the aircraft was Herr Herrold, the crew chief. I started the APU on the aircraft internal battery and did a quick run through of the pre-start checks (I had previously checked everything necessary in slow time). I then started the engines, checked the controls and taxied out. It was also hoped that this demonstrated how the Tornado could operate, if necessary, from a remote base without the need for extensive back-up facilities. The flight demonstration consisted of a run through the full cleared flight envelope, showing as much manoeuvrability as possible, the full range of wing sweep, rapid roll capability, acceleration in full reheat and a short landing run using reverse thrust. From the post-flight comments, this was all well received.

The second prototype was close behind Po1 in construction at Warton. Dave Eagles and I operated the same routine that had been established at Manching and we did all the engine running and ground systems testing ourselves. For the first flight, it was considered to be a valuable gesture of solidarity to invite Pietro Trevisan, the Aeritalia chief test pilot to fly in the back seat, so I had the pleasure of his company on this flight on 30th October. There had been considerable problems in setting up the flight control system on Po2, so we decided to make the first flight in 'direct link'. What this meant was that the pilot control inputs would he signalled directly to the control actuators, without any computer generated inputs. In other words, without autostabilisation. The aircraft Command and Stability Augmentation System (CSAS) has three modes: full CSAS; direct link; and manual, which clutches in a mechanical connection between the control column and the all-moving tailplane. The flight was a good one in which we went around the full initially cleared flight envelope, including a short supersonic run and found that the basic aircraft without autostabilisation still flew pretty well. Full marks again to the aerodynamicists. We did have an unexplained engine problem on this flight, however. When I opened the throttles to full power before releasing the brakes, the left engine surged with an almighty bang. I throttled back and discussed the situation with a 'boffin' on the telemetry desk. They did not know what had caused the engine stall, so I rechecked full power on the left engine with no further problems. The engines looked OK from the cockpit indications and telemetry, with many more read-outs, could see nothing wrong, which caused the boffin to say 'We don't know what the problem was. It is up to you whether you go or not.' So I went! Much later on, it was found that the early engines needed warming up at high rpm before going to full power, apparently because the internal tolerances were very tight and parts of the engine warmed up faster than other bits, causing unwanted airflow disturbances and compressor stalls.

The first flight of P02 took-off before the majority of the Warton workforce had arrived for work. When I came back to the airfield, I found that word had rapidly spread that P02 was airborne and, instead of going to their offices and workshops, it appeared that everyone had come out to the airfield to watch their new aircraft. I found this a very heart warming sight, so I cheered them all up by making a couple of low level rolls down the runway before landing. P02's primary task was to extend the clean aircraft flight envelope. All nine prototypes were allocated different tasks in order to clear the aircraft for use in their respective services, although there was some inevitable overlap and changes of task as time went by. P02 was fitted with 'bonkers', small explosive charges on the wings, which could be fired to excite an oscillation in the control surfaces. The damping of this oscillation could then be assessed to ensure that the aircraft was well clear of any potential flutter problems and the aircraft could then go on to make further 'bonker' tests at a higher speeds. On one of these envelope expansion flights on P02, the engine oil temperature and oil low pressure warning lights illuminated on the right engine. I throttled that engine back and the warning lights went out. Discussion with the boffin confirmed no engine problems on telemetry, so I decided to discontinue the high speed tests on that flight and revert to a secondary task, which consisted of flypasts of the control tower at the airfield with kinetheodolites recording height and speed to check cockpit instrument pressure errors. I left the right engine throttled back to idle for these tests in case of further engine oil problems. On one of these flypasts at slow speed with wheels and flaps down a seagull appeared too late for me to avoid it and it was ingested by the left engine, terminally damaging both the seagull and the engine. All the cockpit warning lights and alarms came on as I shut down the left engine and hopefully slammed the right engine throttle from idle to maximum reheat, at the same time raising the wheels and starting to bring the flaps up. The aircraft was at this time slowly sinking from its already low height down towards the ground, so I warned Dave Eagles to prepare to eject. The aircraft should have been able to climb away on one engine, but this just happened to be the first time that reheat had failed to light on selection! As a result, the reheat nozzle was fully open without reheat being lit, which caused a considerable reduction in the dry power thrust. Luckily, the engine did not like being treated like this, so it surged and the reheat nozzle closed, producing enough thrust to allow us to climb up out of the weeds and turn around for a thankful landing. On inspecting the engine with the oil problem after flight, it was found that the oil system was full of carbon. One of the engine seals which had been exposed to dynamic air pressure as the aircraft speed increased, had allowed this pressure into the engine oil system and, like a diesel engine, the oil had actually caught fire. On a later envelope expansion flight, after rectification of the oil seal defect, a frighteningly loud noise appeared abruptly and disappeared just as quickly as I throttled back and slowed down. As there was no obvious cause for this noise, I tentatively increased speed again and the noise reappeared at the same speed. Several more attempts were made to pinpoint the source of this very loud noise when Ray Woollett, Warton's chief navigator, said from the rear seat, 'I've got it. As we accelerate, I can see the rubber canopy seal stretching higher and higher until at the point where the noise starts, it becomes invisible.' After flight, the canopy seal was trimmed back and the noise did not recur.

It is of interest that prior to Tornado flying, some noise experts from Farnborough had predicted that the cockpit would be very noisy and that this noise would become limiting at high speeds. In fact, the cockpit environment was very pleasant and comfortable, both for temperature and lack of excessive noise. The Farnborough team asked if they could measure the cockpit noise levels and wired up the cockpit and ourselves with microphones and recorders to be turned on at appropriate speeds. Nothing more was heard of these tests and when I made enquiries many months later, I was told that the noise levels recorded were so low that Farnborough had concluded that they had a problem with their recorders. We then turned our attention to extending the supersonic flight envelope clearance. The early flight engines were a long way short of their required thrust so supersonic acceleration was very slow and fuel was being used up very quickly. A solution was to use in-flight refuelling so the IFR probe was fitted and checked and the flight refuelling clearance was brought forward to much earlier in the programme than had been envisaged. The Royal Air Force was extremely co-operative over the use of their tanker aircraft and clearance to flight refuel was very expeditious. Tornado handles so well and is so stable a platform that flight refuelling is easier with her than with any other aircraft that I have flight refuelled with. After the initial dry contacts with the flight refuelling basket at varying speeds and altitudes, I filled up the tanks to full and set off south down the Irish Sea from the Mull of Galloway without any fuel worries. After that, it seemed that whenever we wanted to make another supersonic clearance flight, there just happened to be a tanker aircraft exercising in the Irish Sea with some fuel to spare for us. By this time, the third prototype was flying from Warton. This was the first dual-control aircraft and was tasked with flying with heavy loads under the wings and fuselage. P02 had already cleared the wing tanks for flutter and progressive clearances were made on the whole range of external stores to be carried. P04 flew shortly after

Aircrew training on the Tornado was conducted on an international basis at RAF Cottesmore. Aircraft, instructors and students came together as the Tri-national Tornado Training Establishment (TTTE), with aircraft from all three nations being used as required.

P03 in September 1975 from Manching. This was the first aircraft with the full Tornado avionics system and was tasked with clearing the navigation, autopilot and ground mapping systems.

The first Italian prototype, P05, flew from Caselle in December 1975. Like P02, the CSAS had been troublesome to get ready for flight, so it also flew in direct link mode. By Flight No. 5, the CSAS was ready for flight. Pietro Trevisan switched it on in flight for a brief check and pronounced it satisfactory. While on the landing approach at the end of the flight, it was suggested that Trevisan should switch to full CSAS again. The CSAS approach mode was the very responsive mode mentioned previously and Trevisan was using the larger stick inputs required in direct link mode. The result was a divergent pilot induced pitch oscillation. At the bottom of one of these oscillations the aircraft contacted the runway, suffering considerable damage. Happily, the pilot was unhurt, but P05 was then out of the development programme for just over two years. P06, the third British prototype also flew in December 1975. This aircraft was fitted with two Mauser guns and the flight test instrumentation, which was fitted in the ammunition bays on other prototypes was placed in the rear cockpit, so P06 could only be flown solo.

Very few airframe modifications were required to be made during the development programme. In the transonic flight regime, a shock wave at the base of the fin reduced the fin effectiveness and caused a reduction in directional stability. Fitting a row of vortex generators on either side of the lower fin cured this problem. Some buffet and increased drag were also noted at high subsonic speeds and an improved fillet between the base of the fin and the fuselage was devised by filling in this area with a foam plastic shape that could be carved to a new shape between flights. A short intensive flying programme produced the optimum profile for this fillet that was subsequently retrofitted to all aircraft. The position of the reverse thrust buckets behind the engine tailpipes at the very aft end of the aircraft was destabilising during reverse thrust deceleration on the landing run. This sometimes called for some fast footwork on the runway and this problem became critical when P03 ran off the runway onto soft ground when landing in heavy rain and a strong crosswind. It was also reported that one of the MBB aircraft had made an inadvertent 360 degree turn on its landing run. We had heard that SAAB had had similar problems with the Viggen in reverse thrust, so we requested a visit to Linköping to discuss it with them. Dave Eagles and I flew a small team of designers over there in the company HS125 and found the Swedish design team very helpful and open in explaining their problems and solutions. The outcome for Tornado was that, in effect, the aircraft yaw damper was connected to the nose wheel steering system. Once this had been done it was possible to land the aircraft, select full reverse thrust and run straight down the runway without touching the rudder pedals at all.

When manoeuvring at Mach 0.6-0.7 at high incidence, the left engine was prone to surge with loud machine-gun-like noises and impressive sheets of flame from the tailpipe. Embarrassingly, this was just the area of flight in which we needed to be for displaying Tornado to VIPs and at air displays. After some heated discussion between the intake designers and the engine manufacturers as to whether the problem was one of intake distortion or the engine's being too sensitive to small airflow disturbances, a small fillet was fitted onto an intake lower corner and the problem was cured. Another intake problem was discovered at a later date during the supersonic envelope expansion on P02. Just as we were close to reaching the clearance of the significant figure of Mach 2, it was found to be impossible to get past Mach 0.92 without encountering violent intake bangs and engine stalls. This problem was put down to an unwanted shock wave generated in an intake upper corner and was cured by fitting a vortex generator in the offending corner. On post-flight inspection after many development flights, one or more turbine blades were found to be missing, but it is interesting that the loss of these blades was never noticed by the pilots.

Tornado prototypes P07 and P08 flew for the first time in 1976 at Manching and Warton respectively. These aircraft were fully up to date with their avionics and, since a large part of the aircraft flight envelope, both with and without external stores, had by then been cleared, the emphasis began to focus on testing the aircraft as a complete weapons system. Aircraft handling with a variety of external stores remained as good as with the clean aircraft and an intensive programme of weapon aiming and releases, gun firing, avionics and radar testing got into full swing. Automatic terrain following tests were made over northern England and Scotland. Because the emphasis for these tests was on flight safety, the early terrain following flights were made in clear weather. Even so, they could be quite harrowing for the pilot as the system was configured such that, if any of the in-built checking system detected an anomaly, an automatic pull-up was triggered.

The terrain following system was designed to extremely tight tolerances, which detected many spurious errors, so on the initial flight tests the pilot had to undergo numerous unexpected sudden 3g pull-ups. I happily left this testing to our avionics specialist, John Cockburn. Production of the prototypes was completed by the first flight of P09 in Italy in February 1977. Later the same day, P11, the first of six pre-series aircraft also flew. These aircraft were used to back-up the development programme and subsequently to go either to the respective service test flying units for evaluation or direct to the Services after conversion to full production standard. Tornado development flying continued at a high rate through 1977 and 1978 with so many aircraft in the programme. A number of Service VIPs were introduced to Tornado, and were all suitably impressed. A Canadian Air Force team also came to Warton to evaluate the aircraft, although nothing was heard subsequently from Canada. Tornado P02 was fitted with an anti-spin parachute and an emergency power unit (EPU) and commenced a series of handling tests at high incidence preparatory to full spinning trials. P02 recommenced high speed flight envelope tests in early 1979 and this time it had no problems in reaching the Mach 2 test point. After hitting Mach 2 in March 1979, I dived the aircraft, holding the Mach number constant, aiming for a flutter check at the corner point of Mach 2 and 800 knots IAS. P02 had never been fitted with a head-up display, so I was using the standard head-down cockpit flight instruments.

Despite steepening the dive considerably, I was unable to get the airspeed indicator to go far past about 780 knots when the 'boffin' said with some alarm in his voice, 'Slow down! You are going too fast!' It turned out that the airspeed indicator had a stop at 800 knots, but this was a compressible stop acting from about 775 knots. The ground telemetry indications had gone off the clock also and it was estimated that the actual IAS had been between 820 and 830 knots. Later that month, I flew P15 to check the 1.8M/800 kt point and, using the head-up display digital readout, I was proudly holding what I thought was a superbly accurate 800 knots, when I was once again told that I was going too fast. The head-up display specification calls for it to read up to 800 knots and that is what it does – and no more. Tragically, P08 and its crew were lost in an accident in June 1979 and similarly P04 and its crew were lost in an accident in Germany in May 1980. Inevitably, these losses caused some delays to the test programme, but the test aircraft were designed to be able to carry out multiple tasks, so the disruption was minimised.

Full spinning trials started with P02 in January 1980. Modern military aircraft do not possess a conventional stall, they usually reach an angle of incidence where directional

The Tornado is expected to be withdrawn from the RAF's inventory as more Typhoon aircraft come into service. It seems likely that the very last examples will be phased out of service by 2020 at the latest, marking the end of a hugely successful operational career of more than thirty years. Some of the earliest examples have already been withdrawn, their forlorn carcasses acting as spares sources for active aircraft.

control is lost and the aircraft yaws into a fully developed spin. Because it was expected that the engines would not be able to cope with air coming into the intakes at up to 90 degrees from straight ahead, a hydrazine emergency power unit was fitted to P02 and connected to the gearboxes supplying hydraulic and electrical power to the aircraft. This EPU was switched on just before each individual spin test. Tests were made at all wing sweep positions and in every case it was found that the aircraft did depart into a fully developed spin, but also that the engines would be forced into a silent stall and would overheat if not shut down immediately. The spin was quite oscillatory and it was an interesting exercise for the pilot to evaluate what was happening in the spin, watch the engine temperatures and shut the engines down when necessary, apply spin recovery action, check that the spin was fully recovered, relight the engines, shut down the EPU and then climb back up to 40,000 feet for the next test. The first spin tests were made from standard straight slowdowns, but later in the trials we pulled the aircraft to high angles of incidence in dynamic tests from higher airspeeds. In one of these tests, I had pulled full back stick and reached an angle of incidence of 45 degrees when 'boffin' told me to recover because the EPU had failed. My cockpit indications were all normal, but it was found after flight that the drive shaft connecting the EPU to the gearbox had failed. Happily, this was one occasion in which the aircraft did *not* yaw off into a spin. Naturally, we did not recommend that service aircraft should be cleared for spinning.

The first British production Tornado, BT001, made its first flight in July 1979 and was subsequently taken to Boscombe Down for weapons trials. BT002 flew in December 1979 and on 1 July 1979, I was delighted to take the aircraft with Ollie Heath in the rear seat on its delivery flight to the TTTE at Cottesmore to be handed over to the services. We believed that we were giving the air forces an excellent product, which would serve them well.

There was perhaps a hint of irony in the arrival of Ollie Heath at Cottesmore in the RAF's first Tornado. He had been TSR2's project manager and the overall head of the TSR2 design team. Having been so heavily involved in the TSR2's creation, he was also involved in the projects that succeeded it, including the Tornado. It had taken twenty years to translate the RAF's order for a Canberra replacement into the delivery of the RAF's first Tornado, the aircraft that finally emerged from this almost incredible story.

CHAPTER TWELVE
The End Game

The Eurofighter Typhoon is inevitably regarded as a high-tech contemporary fighter and the latest in a long line of manned fighters that have equipped the RAF. But the Typhoon is much more than a fighter, and like many of the RAF's post-war combat aircraft, it is capable of performing the role of a bomber and attack aircraft. Unlike many of its predecessors, it was designed with this dual-role capability firmly in mind from the outset.

With the mighty V-Force long gone and the tactical Tornado reaching the end of its operational life, the Typhoon is destined to take on the mantle of both an offensive and defensive aircraft, sharing the RAF's future Order of Battle with the new F-35. But even though the Typhoon is very much an aircraft of the present and future, its origins are to be found in the 1960s. It was during this era that Germany first looked at possible replacement programmes for their fleet of Lockheed F-104G Starfighters. The F-104 had already proved to be a highly versatile fighter-bomber and even though Germany experienced many operational difficulties with the aircraft – largely due to their own inadequate training system that simply was not geared towards high-performance jets – the F-104G looked set to remain in service for at least another decade at this stage. However, it was necessary to sow the seeds of an eventual replacement and this became the Neue Kampfflugzeug (NKF) programme. This was a purely national project and was not pursued with any great vigour, but it eventually re-emerged years later as a foundation of the Typhoon's developmental history. Nevertheless, Germany's search for a new fighter-bomber was embroiled in politics from the very start and it would be another thirty years before the ultimate result of this aspiration would finally be achieved. What emerged was an aircraft quite different to the one that might have been envisaged back in the 1960s, but the result was an aircraft that achieved everything that Germany had wanted, plus a great deal more.

While Germany contemplated its future combat aircraft requirements, Britain's RAF had a rather different agenda. Air defence of the United Kingdom was the responsibility of the Lightning squadrons and this legendary interceptor was scheduled to remain at the forefront of the RAF's air defence force until the mid-1970s, at which stage it would be replaced by Phantoms. The Phantoms had been purchased during the 1960s when the Government had finally abandoned the much troubled P.1154 that had been scheduled to replace the Royal Navy's Sea Vixen fighters and the RAF's Hunter ground attack aircraft. The supersonic, vertical take-off P.1154 promised a great deal, but designing an aircraft to fulfil two different roles for two different customers was a difficult task that was probably doomed to failure from the outset. The Navy wanted a single-seat fighter and the RAF a twin-seat attack aircraft, and although there was no reason why one aircraft could not perform both roles, it became clear that the requirements of the RAF and Fleet Air Arm conflicted. More importantly, American manufacturer McDonnell Douglas became aware of the emerging requirement and with its new F-4 Phantom available for export, the Royal Navy was an obvious potential customer.

The Navy was immediately attracted to the Phantom, not only because it was a relatively inexpensive and extremely capable aircraft, but it also required a conventional aircraft carrier from which to operate. The Navy, ever keen to protect its global presence and national importance, believed that the P.1154's vertical take-off capability might encourage the British Government to abandon plans for new aircraft carriers in favour of smaller vessels that could accommodate an aircraft like the P.1154. Consequently, the Phantom became almost irresistible and it was agreed that the Navy would get its Phantoms while the RAF would get the P.1154. However, when a new Labour Government assumed power, they were prepared to tackle many of the defence procurement issues. Of course, the most famous outcome of this reappraisal was the cancellation of the TSR2, but the P.1154 was also swiftly cancelled when Defence Minister Healey learned that the RAF was happy to settle for the Phantom. It was proposed that in addition to Phantoms for the Navy, further aircraft would be delivered to the RAF as ground-attack aircraft, suitable as partial replacements for the RAF's Hunters. Healey also proposed that a more simple derivative of the P.1154 should be developed as a light ground-attack aircraft to act as a more direct replacement for the Hunters. This was be the iconic and world-famous Harrier.

The story was complicated further still by the decision to purchase the Jaguar. It is debatable whether the Jaguar would ever have been built had it not been for the politics that created and drove it. The Jaguar was a direct result of a desire for co-operation between France and Britain and was based on a slightly dubious military requirement from the very start. The RAF had no real need for the aircraft and the Jaguar was originally planned as an advanced trainer aircraft, even though France required a more capable light-attack platform. The two requirements could be reconciled, but eventually the RAF agreed to pursue the Jaguar as a combat aircraft rather than a trainer. With the Phantom due to enter RAF service around 1969-70, it was proposed that the Phantom should first be assigned to the ground attack and reconnaissance role and supplemented by the Harrier. It would also be assigned to RAF Germany as a strike/attack aircraft armed with American Mk.28 nuclear bombs in order to supplement the Canberra strike force already established there. When the Jaguar was ready to enter RAF service a few years later, the Phantom could be released from the attack role. It would then be replaced by the Jaguar and the Phantom reassigned to air defence enabling the Lightning interceptor force to be retired.

This was what was proposed and what happened, although the story of the Phantom, Jaguar, Harrier and Lightning was slightly more complex than this overview might suggest. But while these programmes were being pursued, there was little interest in anything else and it was not until the 1970s that the British Aircraft Corporation – BAC that became British Aerospace in 1977 – began to look more seriously at new aircraft designs. They were particularly interested in a small and inexpensive aircraft designed as a potential export replacement for the hugely successful Hawker Hunter that had been sold around the world. However, while the concept was being considered, it became clear that a more capable aircraft might also be required for the RAF. The emergence of America's F-16 fighter and the more advanced F-15 Eagle emphasised how fighter-bomber capabilities were rapidly developing. The Soviet Union's MiG-29 'Fulcrum' and Su-27 'Flanker' illustrated only too clearly how the RAF's Lightnings, Phantoms, Harriers and Jaguars would soon be outclassed by these new, high-performance warplanes. Clearly, a new tactical fighter would be necessary that would be capable of meeting or exceeding the performance of these new generation aircraft.

By 1977, the German, British and French Governments had come together to look at this issue and to consider the possibility of working together on a new programme. Germany required a replacement for its F-104 Starfighter interceptors while Britain and France were interesting in creating a replacement for the Jaguar ground-attack aircraft that had by now entered service. Britain in particular felt that a multi-role aircraft would be a perfect solution, possibly being influenced by the new F/A-18 Hornet that America was developing. In typical political fashion, a great deal of discussion took place but very little concrete action resulted and it was only in Britain that any practical steps were taken.

British Aerospace eventually initiated a series of twelve Technology Demonstrator Programmes (TDPs) that would enable the foundations of a new attack fighter to be established. This move was certainly bold, eventually costing BAE some £190 million, although these costs were translated into huge savings when the Typhoon project got underway. Jaguars, Tornados and both BAC-111 and Airbus test aircraft were assigned to the TDPs, exploring and developing a wide range of subjects including radar, avionics, cockpit displays, flight control systems, engines

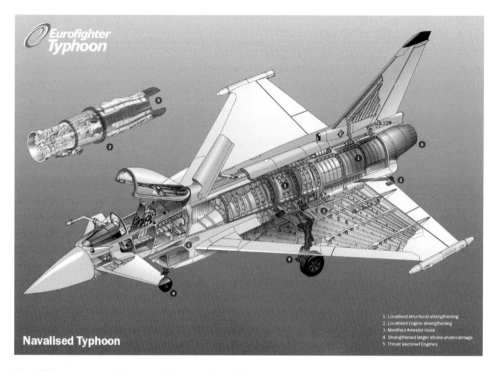

Eurofighter cutaway diagram. (*Courtesy Eurofighter*)

and construction techniques. Ferranti, GEC and Smiths Industries also became involved, and although the TDPs produced a huge amount of vital knowledge and data, it also became increasingly clear that the different requirements and projected development time scales required by Britain, France and Germany would make any joint programme impossible.

It was France's position that effectively blocked any further progress as Dassault was producing the Mirage 2000 and the prospect of working on a joint project with Britain and Germany was therefore of little interest to them. When France eventually refused to participate in any joint programme unless it was under their leadership, it became obvious that Britain and Germany would have to abandon the concept and Governmental discussions were abandoned in 1980. Britain began to look more seriously at its own requirements. The RAF's Lightings were now nearing the end of their useful lives, but the Phantom had assumed the air defence task after having been withdrawn from the strike/attack role. The Phantom fighters would eventually be replaced by an interceptor version of the emerging MRCA – Multi-Role Combat Aircraft that became the Tornado – tailored to suit the RAF's requirement for BVR (Beyond Visual Range) defence. There was no significant requirement for a smaller, lighter 'dogfighter' at this stage and the RAF was far more interested in a suitable replacement for its Jaguars and Harriers in the attack role. Air Staff Target 396 was created to produce what was envisaged as a STOL (Short Take-Off and Landing) or STOVL (Short Take-Off and Vertical Landing) aircraft, somewhat similar to the Tornado but with a single seat. This AST was eventually abandoned in favour of two separate ASTs, one of these being AST 409 for a direct replacement of the Harrier (to become the Harrier GR5-9 series) while AST 403 was intended as a replacement for the Jaguar and remaining RAF Germany Phantom squadrons.

The RAF's all important presence in Germany required both strike/attack and fighter aircraft, therefore AST 403 was very much a multi-role requirement, returning to the earlier aims of the tri-national studies. Although primarily a ground attack aircraft, AST 403 would also require a good defensive capability that matched or bettered the capabilities of the Phantom. Unfettered by the complicated and expensive need for VTOL or STOVL, now only required by AST 409, the AST 403 design emerged as a series of exciting and futuristic designs. The first of these was for an aircraft that looked remarkably similar to today's Gripen, although BAE's Kingston department produced a more conventional design that shared some similarities with the F-16. Meanwhile, the Warton department created an unusual design that shared some similarity with France's Vautor from the 1960s, but with an advanced wing design and a forward fuselage similar to the Tornado air defence variant. The various designs were undoubtedly influenced by BAE's contact with their counterparts at MBB (Messerschmitt Bolkow Blohm) where Germany's future requirements were also being developed into potential designs.

By this stage, Germany's requirement for a Starfighter replacement had developed into a more capable aircraft that could also replace the Luftwaffe's F-4F and RF-4E Phantoms which were assigned to the air defence and reconnaissance roles. Like the RAF, the Luftwaffe needed a multi-role aircraft that could function effectively as both a fighter and attack aircraft. It soon became obvious that Britain's and Germany's requirements were now remarkably similar and it was logical that co-operation between the national manufacturers would make good sense. MBB had by now established a clear preference for a delta-wing aircraft with foreplanes and either a single fin or a twin-fin arrangement as being developed on America's F/A-18. Also clear by this stage was the adoption of an under-fuselage air intake, similar to that being employed on the F-16. This was a basic design configuration that France had also considered and proposed during the early tri-national talks. But when France eventually withdrew in favour of its own national design programmes, their design concept was no longer open to scrutiny. It did, of course, re-emerge many years later as the Dassault Rafale. However, the new co-operation between BAE and MBB suffered a major setback when the British Government cancelled AST 403 in 1981. Likewise, MBB suffered similar problems with Germany's Government and funding for TKF 90 (Taktisches Kamppfflugzeug) was cut, but both companies continued to work together on a private basis, confident that Governmental interest would inevitably resurface.

BAE pursued what became the P.110, a lightweight fighter design intended primarily for export. With the now familiar cranked delta wing and foreplanes (plus twin fins), the aircraft showed great promise, but without any Governmental support it never proceeded beyond the mock-up stage. Progress was effectively stifled without any firm interest from the Government. By 1982, the Panavia companies – BAE, MBB and Aeritalia that had created the Tornado – had made an agreement to pursue a joint design on a private basis in the hope that Government funding would be attracted to it. The Agile Combat Aircraft (ACA) design bore a strong resemblance to Germany's TKF 90 proposal, although it was a merger of the British and German fighter-bomber designs. France remained resolutely indifferent to the programme, opting to pursue its own ACX (Avion de Combate Experimentale) that became the Rafale. Germany was undoubtedly frustrated that its neighbour and senior European partner would not join the ACA project, but Britain was somewhat relieved. Having born the trauma of the abortive AFVG project that France effectively killed off, the Jaguar programme had also suffered at the hands of the French with many potential exports being systematically lost in favour of France's Mirage F1.

With a new tri-national project finally established, it was decided that a couple of flying technology demonstrators should be built, not only to explore and develop the technologies required for the new advanced aircraft, but to demonstrate to potential customers that the project would translate into an effective aircraft. One German-built and one British-built aircraft would be manufactured as part of the Experimental Aircraft Programme (EAP). A contract for the British demonstrator was signed between BAE, Aeritalia and the British Ministry of Defence Procurement Executive on 26 May 1983.

Unfortunately, the German demonstrator was not to follow. Before work on the British aircraft commenced, MBB announced that it was withdrawing from the project, the German Government having refused to provide any funding. MBB was undoubtedly reluctant to pull out, but without any funding or any promise of an eventual German interest in the ACA, there was little point in remaining within the programme. ACA was therefore dead and with it the newly contracted EAP demonstrator. Remarkably, British Aerospace took a particularly bold step and opted to continue manufacturing the demonstrator as a private venture. Without the support of MBB, it seemed inevitable that EAP and therefore ACA would be abandoned, but thanks to BAE's determination, the project survived. The demonstrator was constructed as an indigenous Warton-based project, utilising components from BAE, MBB and Aeritalia, and one wing built in Italy. In order to simplify the aircraft, thereby saving both time and money, a Tornado rear fuselage and tail were adopted to which the new composite aluminium, lithium and titanium structure was attached.

The rear fuselage was to have incorporated new manufacturing techniques such as carbon-fibre composites and superplastic-formed and diffusion-bonded titanium. As these technologies were incorporated into other parts of the airframe, the standard light alloy Tornado rear fuselage was a much simpler alternative that merely added weight to the airframe and did not affect the EAP's value as a technology demonstrator. The ACA was to have featured twin tail fins similar to the F/A-18 Hornet. Twin fins were deemed to be more suitable as they are less susceptible to aerodynamic blanking at high angles of attack when air flow from the fuselage and wing can mask the fin's effectiveness. By 'toeing-in' the twin rudders on take-off, the fins can increase the aircraft's rotational capability, acting as a pseudo tailplane. However, a single fin can provide space for additional fuel capacity and requires fewer mechanical linkages and driving mechanisms and is therefore lighter. The Tornado's large fin was judged to be more than adequate for control of lateral stability and so BAE retained this as part of the rear fuselage structure. It therefore became part of the eventual ACA and Typhoon design almost by default.

It might have been imagined that the EAP demonstrator was in essence only an aerodynamic test bed destined to explore the capabilities of the cranked delta wing and foreplane configuration. The EAP was much more than this and was a true technology demonstrator. Designed to be aerodynamically unstable, it employed fly-by-wire systems which had first been tested in a specially-modified Jaguar. This unstable design made the aircraft extremely agile and manoeuvrable and created an airframe with lower drag, thereby increasing speed and/or range capability. The EAP did not incorporate any weapons systems nor did it have radar, but it did introduce a new 'glass' cockpit layout with MFD (Multi-Function Display) screens developed by Smiths Industries and a wide-angle holographic Head-Up Display (HUD) designed by GEC that was originally intended for the F-16. It also incorporated a voice warning system. As a technology demonstrator, the EAP was not a prototype of a projected combat aircraft and on this basis the British Government funded 50 per cent of the project, clearly indicating that financial support was not indicative of any future purchase of an operational standard aircraft.

Some 15 per cent of funding came from Italy while MBB provided a token one per cent in order to maintain close contact with the programme. The remainder was funded by BAE. Although the EAP was not a prototype for any future aircraft, it was designed to test and demonstrate the technology and aerodynamics that would be put into it and so influence what eventually became the Typhoon. Apart from the adoption of a single fin, the EAP was also designed as a single-seat aircraft from the outset. A twin-seat configuration could have been used, spreading the cockpit workload between the pilot and a navigator/weapons systems operator in the rear cockpit. This configuration had worked well for the Phantom, but Britain wanted a new fighter-bomber that incorporated a great deal of automation for routine cockpit tasks. A great deal of emphasis was placed on the creation of a Man-Machine Interface (MMI) that was both simple and intuitive. It would enable the pilot to manage the cockpit workload easily so he could concentrate on the all important task of aerial combat or weapons delivery. The EAP was therefore a weapons system concept and was a single-seat aircraft from the very start. These became further key aspects of the Typhoon many years later.

The EAP demonstrator (ZF534) was completed during the early summer of 1986 in No. 2 Hangar at British Aerospace's Warton factory and comprised of three major fuselage structures: front, centre and rear. The front fuselage contained many innovative structures in carbon-fibre composites and aluminium lithium alloy. The centre and rear fuselage structures being more conventional with the modified Tornado fin being used while the right-hand wing assembly, manufactured at the Samlesbury plant, was a co-bonded carbon-fibre composite assembly proving new tooling and manufacturing techniques which were put to good use on the Eurofighter programme. The left-hand wing assembly was manufactured at the Corso Marche facility of Alenia in Turin. The foreplanes were manufactured in carbon composite at Preston and Samlesbury, and detail design and manufacture of the windscreen and canopy assemblies was completed by Aerostructures Hamble on the south coast. The aircraft's first flight took place on 8 August and it proved to be a remarkably agile and impressive machine. Fitted with a pair of RB.199 turbofans – standard powerplants fitted to the Tornado – and with a considerable amount of conventional alloy structure, which made the aircraft heavier than it needed to be, ZF534 was a sprightly performer, capable of reaching its take-off speed of 150 knots in only nine seconds. At transonic speeds, the aircraft regularly left its Lightning chase aircraft behind and eventually the aircraft attained Mach 2.0 during its relatively short test programme.

Test pilot Dave Eagles commented that he judged the demonstrator to be 'remarkably agile and very easy to fly' and that he believed it to be 'ideal' and 'just what any fighter pilot would want'. He also added that he wished British Aerospace was 'making 800 of them rather than just one'. Indeed, it is interesting to speculate whether the EAP demonstrator could have formed the basis of a new fighter aircraft without any significant further development. Certainly, the aircraft had the necessary agility and with developed engines, a direct voice system and helmet sight for the cockpit, respected author Jon Lake concluded that the RAF could have had a fourth generation fighter 'more than ten years before it will eventually introduce the definitive Eurofighter'. As it was, ZF534 completed its test programme and was retired to an engineering college in Loughborough before moving to the RAF Museum at Cosford. By the time that the aircraft reached the end of its useful life in May 1991, ZF534 had flown some 259 sorties.

Even though it would have been possible for British Aerospace to develop the EAP into an operational fighter-bomber, Britain's Government was keen to ensure that any future programme was a multi-national one, both for financial reasons – sharing and spreading costs – and political ones. The brave decision to 'go it alone' with the EAP demonstrator was the most important step in persuading Europe to come back onboard and re-examine the possibility of creating a new-generation fighter. Italy and Spain soon expressed their enthusiasm and both German and France returned to discussions, having now seen the potential demonstrated by ZF534. Together, they created an Outline European Staff Target that was issued on 16 December 1983, calling for a single-seat cranked-delta aircraft with canard foreplanes and a projected empty weight of 9.75 tonnes, designed for service entry around the mid-1990s. Additionally, the new multi-national group also initiated further feasibility studies which were completed in 1984 and on 11 October of that year, a definitive European Staff Target was issued. Finally, a new European fighter-bomber was going ahead. Two basic design concepts soon emerged, both of which were generally similar to earlier proposals (and, of course, the EAP demonstrator) but also varying in important details.

Although one of the designs was agreed to be suitable by four nations, France favoured a smaller and lighter design that perhaps not surprisingly resembled their emerging Rafale aircraft. France also continued to insist that the new programme should be under France's leadership on the basis that Dassault had experience in designing and building delta-winged aircraft. This stance neglected to mention that France's delta experience had initially been gleaned from the British, but there was undoubtedly some merit in France's assertion. Far less reasonable was France's insistence that prototype construction and all flight testing should also be undertaken in France and that 50 per cent work share of the programme should be theirs. In effect, France was proposing a French aircraft built for French requirements, but funded by other countries. One commentator remarked that he wondered 'what France would have demanded had it not been interested in collaboration and had wanted to put us off the idea!' It was clear that France's participation would not only be impractical, but that it would be utterly poisonous to the programme. It was at this stage that France left the project for good, even though there was a short-lived suggestion by the US that a true NATO-wide project could be developed to encourage co-operation between European countries and the US. However, the idea went no further and France went off to pursue the Rafale, while the remaining countries – Britain, Germany, Spain and Italy – moved towards Project Definition during June 1985.

On 1 August, the countries agreed to proceed with the established design that was essentially a direct development of the EAP. Work share was agreed with 38 per cent for Britain, 38 per cent for Germany, and 24 per cent for Italy, changed to 33, 33 and 21 per cent in September so that Spain could come onboard with a 13 per cent share. Comically, France occasionally expressed interest in the programme, even offering at one stage to settle for design leadership and a 31 per cent work share. However, by this stage, the foundations of a combat aircraft programme had been laid and France's ludicrous attitude was ignored.

Finally, the participating nations were able to fix a common design that catered for the needs of each country. For the RAF, the requirements for the new aircraft had shifted slightly since the project was first considered. There was still a need to replace the Jaguar squadrons based in Germany and the UK, but by this stage there was also a pressing issue to replace the air defence Phantoms based in Germany. Although the Tornado Air Defence Variant was destined to replace both the Phantom and Lightning in the UK air defence role, the Tornado was a long-range interceptor designed to operate in the BVR (Beyond Visual Range) role, launching 'fire and forget' missiles against incoming targets. The Phantoms in Germany were tasked with the air defence of a more local region and would need to have an effective close-in defence capability both in terms of weapons and manoeuvrability. In essence, this meant a classic 'dogfighter', but the RAF was keen to ensure that the new aircraft would also be able to handle the Jaguar's ground-attack tasks and also be capable of operating from improvised sites such as motorways and cleared fields. The RAF stipulated that the new aircraft should be capable of operating from a 500 m (1,640 feet) landing strip. This contrasted with some of the requirements set by the other participating countries. Italy needed to replace its Starfighters – an aircraft that certainly did not have a short-field capability – primarily in the air defence role, while Spain was primarily interested in a multi-role aircraft with a good ground-attack capability. Germany was looking for a Phantom replacement, having replaced its Starfighter attack squadrons with Tornado IDS (Interdictor Strike) aircraft. In essence, this meant an agile fighter with a secondary reconnaissance capability.

These combined requirements could be seen as contradictory, but the basic aim of creating a multi-role aircraft meant that the fighter and attack roles could be handled by one generic design. By December 1985, a European Staff Requirement for a European Fighter Aircraft was issued and a Project Definition study was completed by September the following year. The study revealed some potential difficulties, not least the realisation that the aircraft would have to be bigger and heavier than envisaged. The RAF's requirements dictated that an aircraft with an empty weight of around 11 tonnes (10.8 tons) would be necessary in order to provide the necessary weapons load and range capability. This was not a popular move as a heavy aircraft was unlikely to be potentially exportable and the RAF eventually relaxed its requirements in order to settle on a common design.

There were many other disagreements such as Germany's original insistence that an American AN/APG-65 radar should be used and that General Electric engines should be installed in the initial pre-production aircraft, rather than the RB.199 that was being developed specifically for the EFA. There was also much debate over the work share figures and whether these should be proportionally based on projected orders for each country or based on the need for avionics commonality. A great deal of time was also devoted to negotiations with Belgium that expressed interest in joining the programme in August 1986. The discussions were ultimately fruitless and it was perhaps not surprising that France's interest in the programme also re-emerged, the suggestion being made that their Rafale and the new EFA could share a variety of common avionics and equipment items. It was also not surprising that the concept was soon abandoned.

The programme continued, but it was not an easy progression. Eurofighter Jagdflugzeug GmbH was created to manage the joint programme, but Germany's politicians became increasingly reluctant to allow the EFA programme to continue unchecked. Germany's Defence Minister called for a DM2 billion reduction in the EFA research and development costs, based on his projections of Germany's financial status and military capabilities. MBB endeavoured to co-operate with Defence Minister Woerner by studying alternatives to the EFA, including a notionally cheaper Hornet derivative and an advanced F-16, but neither aircraft offered the same capability and any significant reduction in cost. Once again, Britain tried to kick-start the floundering programme and confirmed its commitment to EFA's full-scale development phase on 25 April 1988 in the hope this would encourage the other nations to do likewise. A Memorandum of Understanding was signed by Britain, Germany and Italy on 16 May and was endorsed by Spain in November. The Full Scale Development contract was finally signed on 23 November 1988 based on the approved design that had slowly matured to incorporate the large, square-shaped intakes under the fuselage and removal of the radar warning receiver fairings on the fin. The empty weight had now been fixed at 9.75 tonnes – a further 250 kg allocated to national equipment fits – although and with some irony, the weight figure was revised upwards to incorporate convergent-divergent exhaust nozzles that were stipulated by Germany in order to improve supersonic performance.

Germany's requirements caused many other headaches and delays. Perhaps the most serious was their clear preference for an American radar for the EFA. The Luftwaffe wanted the AN/APG-65, much to the surprise of Britain who naturally assumed that Germany would adopt a pro-European stance. Perversely, Germany was openly criticising Britain for allowing an American company to effectively takeover Westland Helicopters – instead of adopting a European solution – while advocating the use of American radar in the new EFA, even though an all-European radar would be more effective and a better deal for European manufacturing. Germany's excuse was that an American radar could be introduced far more swiftly than an all-new European solution. However, Germany's preference for an American radar was simply a case of self interest: their F-4 Phantoms were fitted with American radars. It soon became clear that the advantages of a new European radar were hard to resist, but it was also clear that the adoption of American radar would result in restrictions on potential exports, thanks to the restrictions placed on technology transfer by the US. In any case, the choice of radar was non-negotiable as far as Britain was concerned. Apart from replacing RAFG's Phantoms, the new EFA would also be assigned to UK air defence and would require a good BVR capability – something that the American radar did not possess.

The EFA's engines were another source of contention. It seemed logical to adopt the RB.199 turbofan to power the pre-production EFA aircraft and the first twenty production machines chiefly because Britain, Germany and Italy were familiar with the engine that powered the Tornado IDS and ADV variants in service with these nations. The new Rolls-Royce EJ2000 projected for EFA offered great potential and it seemed logical that it could be retrofitted to the Tornado fleet as part of update programmes if required. But for reasons that have never been made clear, Germany proposed the use of the General Electric F404 even though Spain was the only participating country that used this engine. Spain also admitted that the RB.199 was a superior solution. Eventually, Germany accepted the view of the other three nations and RB.199 was finally adopted to power the first EFAs with installation commonality with the EJ200 so this engine could be retrofitted at a later stage. Even more difficult was the establishment of work share between the participating countries with many decisions being based on rigid percentage agreements or simple political considerations.

The most difficult of these issues was the development of EFA's flight control system. British Aerospace was given leadership of the avionics integration programme and it was therefore inevitable that the FCS development would be awarded to Germany's DASA. This company did have some experience with flight control system development, having operated the F-104CCV aircraft, a neutrally stable machine designed to explore digital fly-by-wire control systems. However, DASA's experience was almost insignificant when compared to British Aerospace's and GEC's where the ACT/FBW Jaguar had demonstrated a far more relevant quadruplex fly-by-wire system that was almost ideal for EFA. Of course, Britain had also designed, built and operated the EAP demonstrator. Therefore, it was obvious that GEC should have handled the task. GEC claimed that it could have designed the EFA's Flight Control System for one-third of the cost projected by DASA. Eventually, both BAE and GEC did takeover EFA's FCS after DASA proved to be incapable of solving various software problems. Eurofighter hid this move as a shift on work share allocation in response to a reduction in German orders, but in reality it was simply a shift to the logical solution that should have been adopted in the first place.

Construction of the first EFA began in 1989 and in May 1992, the first prototype was transferred from DASA's Ottobrunn facility to Maching where it made the first installed engine runs on 6 June. Sadly, the programme suffered more delays, largely due to FCS software problems, but also because of more German politics. Having signed to the Maastricht Treaty, Germany was obliged to maintain tight fiscal control in order to establish monetary union throughout Europe, and having already become severely strained by the reunification with East Germany, it was inevitable that the Eurofighter would be a political Aunt Sally. Portrayed by German politicians as a relic of the Cold War, there was an easy political advantage to be made by openly opposing the EFA. Matters reached almost absurd proportions when the Chief Executive of the State of Brandenburg, sponsors of the ILA 92 air show, refused to attend the event because a Eurofighter mock-up was on show. The situation reached crisis proportions in the summer of 1992 after Germany announced withdrawal from the project. British Prime Minister John Major met Chancellor Kohl in Germany to discuss the project. In August, Germany agreed to continue support of development, but did not make any commitment to financing production.

Having originally agreed to purchase 250 aircraft – which were in many ways designed specifically to meet Germany's requirements – the projected purchase had now dwindled to eighty aircraft, a figure that the Luftwaffe regarded as unviable. This impasse prompted Germany, Italy and Spain to look at alternative aircraft, and although there was no change in Britain's position, it seemed likely that a potential purchase of either the F-15 or F/A-18 must have been examined. Germany eventually concluded that EFA was by far the least expensive and most effective solution. However, this was a bitter pill to swallow for many German politicians, many of whom referred to the Eurofighter as 'Das Englische Flugzeug' (The English Aeroplane). This was totally at odds with reality as the EFA was geared towards German requirements as much as Britain's. All four participating nations accepted that the EFA was by far the most suitable aircraft even though by its very nature it was a compromise solution.

German pressure eventually resulted in the EFA becoming a more austere machine. Renamed 'Eurofighter 2000', the aircraft was presented as a baseline airframe that customers could elect to equip with high-cost systems depending on what was required or what could be afforded. Some reports suggest that the aircraft's short-field capability was relaxed somewhat, but in essence there was little that could be done to make any substantial reductions in the aircraft's overall cost. It was expensive, but it represented far better value for money than any other competing programme. Meanwhile, Italy maintained a fairly stoic position, even though they had the most urgent need for the Eurofighter. Italy's fleet of F-104G/S Starfighters was undoubtedly obsolete. Magnificent though the Starfighter was, it had to be replaced. One commentator described the F-104 as a 'treasured vintage Ferrari' that Italian pilots occasionally took out for a drive on the autostrada. Italy finally concluded that it could not wait for the Eurofighter and an interim solution was found in the shape of a fleet of RAF Tornado F3 interceptors, which were supplied to Italy on a lease basis, agreed in November 1993. Spain remained patient while Britain continued to push for progress.

When the ongoing FCS problems were finally solved, the first prototype (DA1) finally made its maiden flight from Manching on 27 March 1994, a staggering two years later than had first been planned. Ironically, despite so much British expertise and support – without which the programme would undoubtedly have collapsed – the first flight was conducted from a German airfield using an aircraft sporting German markings and flown by Peter Weger, a German test pilot. There were many observers who felt it was ironic, if not offensive, that Germany was somehow being rewarded for its reluctant participation in the programme, although more diplomatic observers believed that a perceived German leadership was a small price to pay if it ensured that Germany stayed with the programme.

DA1's first flight was a great success. Accompanied by an Alpha Jet and Phantom chase aircraft, the aircraft (serial 98+29) climbed to 10,000 feet and attained 300 knots, and although the first flight was a low-key affair, DA1 was soon attaining 450 knots and altitudes of up to 36,000 feet, performing manoeuvres up to 5g. In England, the second prototype (DA2) was prepared for flight at Warton and after delays caused by poor weather, Chris Yeo took ZH588 on a fifty-minute flight on 6 April. It seems likely that weather was not the only cause of ZH588's delayed first flight: the recent loss of Lockheed's YF-22 and Saab's JAS39 Gripen was sufficient to cause a great deal of worry within Eurofighter. Although confident in the EFA's Flight Control System, Warton's team may well have thoroughly checked and double-checked the FCS before allowing ZH588 to get airborne. DA1 and DA1 proceeded to each complete fifteen hours of test flying before being temporarily grounded. There was speculation that the programme had encountered serious technical problems, but the aircraft were simply being refitted with more developed avionics and an improved Flight Control System.

The real delays were caused by Germany's continual reluctance to fully support the programme. Funding was slow and often insufficient and Germany continued to insist that they retained a 30 per cent work share on the aircraft, even though Germany was now proposing to buy 25 per cent of the planned production. Their expectation that they should be the prime contractor for production was illogical. Even more ludicrous was the proposal to merge Eurofighter with Panavia under the leadership of a German managing director. But stoic acceptance of Germany's position continued and even though their attitude contributed to further costs, the increasingly austere aircraft that Germany wanted was ultimately little different to those ordered by Britain, Italy and Spain. The adoption of the title 'Eurofighter 2000' for EFA did little to change the direction of the programme that effectively stalled while Germany's politicians wrestled with the issue. Britain insisted that further slippage in the commencement of production would be 'unacceptable', but this did little to push Germany into action.

Likewise, Britain's unilateral agreement to begin production in September 1996 achieved nothing. By the beginning of 1997, the situation was a bleak as it ever had been and Germany's politicians attempted to stall progress further still when it became clear that Britain would soon be ruled by a new Labour Government. Their belief was that the new Government based on its historical dislike for military spending would presumably abandon British interest in Eurofighter, thereby enabling Germany to neatly escape from the programme by default. Remarkably, the Shadow Defence Secretary informed Germany that despite plans for defence cuts, Eurofighter would be excluded from this process and that Britain would procure the planned 232 aircraft under the new Government. This news came as something of a blow to many German politicians and with no other obvious way forward, Germany finally signed a production investment MoD (Memorandum of Understanding).

The third development aircraft (DA3) made its first flight on 4 June 1995. This aircraft (MM-X-602) was completed and flown from Alenia's Caselle airfield by test pilot Napoleone Bragnolo. With initial-standard EJ.200 engines, the aircraft was fitted with production-standard engines by the end of 1997. Initial experience with the new engines was satisfactory and the engine's performance was as good as or better than expected. On one early test flight, DA3's test pilot accelerated to supersonic speed at 40,000 feet at which stage the engine afterburners were deselected. Much to the pilot's surprise, DA3 continued to accelerate in 'dry' (unreheated) power. Just two months after DA3's first flight, the very first dual-control EFA took to the air from Spain's Getafe facility on 31 August.

The twin-seat trainer version of EFA was an important part of the design programme from the outset with all four participating nations anticipating a requirement for a dual-control variant that could be used for conversion and continuation training. Designed as a minimal-change version of the standard airframe, the twin-seater is slightly heavier than its single-seat counterpart and carries slightly less internal fuel – despite an additional fuel tank in the enlarged dorsal spine – but in all other respects it maintains the same performance characteristics. Although the dual-control variant will inevitably be allocated to training duties, it will be used in an operational role if necessary and seems likely that specialised versions of the twin-seater may well emerge in the future designed for specific missions. The first production contract was signed on 30 January 1998 between Eurofighter GmbH, Eurojet and NETMA. The procurement totals were set as follows: UK (232), Germany (180), Italy (121) and Spain (87). Production was again allotted according to projected procurement: British Aerospace (37.42 per cent), DASA (29.03 per cent), Aeritalia (19.52 per cent) and CASA (14.03 per cent).

In September 1998, the EFA enjoyed a particularly high profile at that year's SBAC Farnborough show. During the event, the aircraft was finally relieved of its unwieldy and unimaginative name and a more appropriate title for projected export versions was bestowed upon it: Typhoon. A great deal of thought had gone into the naming process as the tastes of four nations were and are often very different. There was significant British enthusiasm for naming the aircraft the Spitfire II, but with Germany as a major partner in the programme, this would have been less than tactful to say the least. Finding a name that translated into each country's language was not easy, but eventually it was accepted that Typhoon was a good compromise, having been applicable to a rather less than successful RAF fighter-bomber, but also to the German Bf 108 Taifun decades previously. It was proposed that all export versions would be referred to as Typhoons, but when the first aircraft were delivered to the RAF, they swiftly adopted the name. Although Germany, Italy and Spain claimed that their aircraft would still be known as EFAs or Eurofighters, the name Typhoon has now effectively become adopted by each country.

Further development aircraft soon joined the programme, the last of the initial seven aircraft being – thanks to a change in the delivery schedule – the British DA4, the second twin-seater aircraft to be completed, which took to the air on 14 March 1997. The first IPA (Instrumented Production Aircraft) were next to emerge with IPA2 making its first flight from Turin on 5 April 2002. Just a few days later, IPA3 made its maiden flight from Manching and finally on 15 April, IPA1 got airborne from Warton. After a long and sometime precarious journey, the Typhoon was finally ready to enter service. Final German approval to purchase Typhoon came in October 1997 and the first series production aircraft for Germany took to the air on 13 February 2003. It was the first of 180 aircraft destined to join the Luftwaffe as a replacement for F-4 Phantoms and MiG-29s, and as a partial replacement for some of the service's Tornado aircraft. As with so much of the Typhoon programme, Germany was allowed to believe it was leading and so it was the next day that the first British (BT001) and Italian (IT001) aircraft made their first flights, followed by Spain's ST001 three days later. On 30 June, 'Type Acceptance' was signed to mark the formal delivery of the first aircraft to each of the Eurofighter nations.

The RAF established its first Typhoon unit on 1 September 2002 when the Typhoon Operational Evaluation Unit (OEU) was created at BAE's Warton factory. This unit was responsible for evaluating the new aircraft, examining its capabilities and the ways in which it could be integrated into regular squadron service. The OEU moved to Coningsby on 1 April 2005 and became No. 17(R) Squadron tasked with evaluation of the Typhoon, particularly its weapons capabilities and tactical use. Formal activation of this first Typhoon Squadron at RAF Coningsby occurred on 1 July 2005. No. 29(R) Squadron then reformed as the Typhoon OCU (Operational Conversion Unit), tasked with the training of the RAF's Typhoon aircrew. The first regular squadron to equip with the Typhoon was No. 3 Squadron, having exchanged its Harriers for Typhoons and reformed at Coningsby on 31 March 2006. The Typhoon then embarked upon the progressive replacement of the RAF's Tornado F3 fleet and eventually took over responsibility for UK QRA (Quick Reaction Alert) on 29 June 2007, becoming formally declared as an advanced air defence platform on 1 January 2008.

Initial production aircraft of the Tranche 1 standard (Typhoon F.Mk.2) were capable of air-to-air roles only and were the first Typhoons to hold UK QRA duties. In order to fulfil a potential requirement for the RAF's Typhoons to deploy to Operation Herrick – Britain's deployment to Afghanistan – urgent single nation work was conducted on the Tranche 1 fleet to develop Typhoon's air-to-ground capability in 2008. Tranche 1 aircraft were thus declared as multi-role in July 2008, gaining the designation FGR.Mk.4 – the twin-seat variant re-designated as the T.Mk.3 – fielding the Litening Laser Designator Pod and Paveway 2, Enhanced Paveway 2 (both being laser-guided bombs) and 1,000 lb freefall class of weapons. Only a handful of F.Mk.2 and T.Mk.1 aircraft now remain in RAF service and these will be upgraded to the FGR.Mk.4 and T.Mk.3 standard probably by the end of 2013. Tranche 2 aircraft, the second batch of British aircraft, deliveries commenced under the four-nation contract in 2008 and were all completed to undertake the air-to-air role only. Some of these aircraft were deployed to the Falkland Islands to take over air defence duties from the Tornado F3s based there in September 2009 and the Tranche 2 fleet continues to be slowly brought up to a common standard with full air-to-ground capability.

A total of fifty-three Tranche 1 aircraft were delivered to the RAF with Tranche 2 contract provisioning for ninety-one aircraft. Some twenty-four of these were diverted from delivery in order to meet an urgent export requirement for Saudi Arabia, leaving sixty-seven Tranche 2 aircraft due for delivery to the RAF. The Tranche 3 contract has been signed and this will deliver a further forty aircraft. It then seems likely that the early Tranche 1 aircraft fleet will be retired over the period around 2018 and this will leave 107 Typhoon aircraft in RAF service until the currently projected withdrawal date in 2030. Germany's Luftwaffe began taking deliveries of Typhoons in May 2004 and in Italy the first operational-standard Typhoon was handed over on 20 February 2004 at Cameri.

Typhoon is also enjoying some export success although overseas sales have not been as plentiful as Eurofighter might have hoped for. Austria opted to purchase the aircraft in July 2002 as a new fighter aircraft destined to replace a fleet of aged Drakens. A fleet of eighteen aircraft was agreed although by June 2007, this order had been reduced to fifteen. The first delivery was made on 12 July 2007 and the Typhoon has now settled into operational service although not without controversy. Allegations persist that political lobbying influenced Austria's order and claims that sums of up to 100 million euros being used to support this lobbying have tainted what was Eurofighter's first export order.

Equally controversial was the sale of seventy-two Typhoons to Saudi Arabia. The order that was placed in August 2006 was won after a fierce battle with France who was all too keen to sell Saudi Arabia the Rafale. Continuing allegations in the UK over the Al Yamamah arms deal that was secured in the 1980s undoubtedly troubled negotiations between the Eurofighter nations and Saudi Arabia, but eventually some twenty-four aircraft were delivered from 2009. The first handover took place on 11 June, these being diverted from the production order for the RAF. A further forty-eight aircraft will be assembled in Saudi Arabia. Sadly, attempts to sell Typhoon to India failed after a long and intensive campaign that was ultimately thwarted by France and a lower bid for a fleet of Rafales. Likewise, attempts to export Typhoon to Japan looked promising, but US pressure to buy the F-35 – dubiously on the basis of its advanced stealth characteristics – led to the abandonment of its sales campaign. Other orders seem likely, although uncertain. Greece certainly has a requirement for the Typhoon, but with a crippled economy, it seems certain that an obsolete fleet of F-4 Phantoms and A-7 Corsairs will remain in use for some time. Qatar is also considering a Typhoon order and other countries may also eventually emerge. Amongst the most likely are Denmark, Norway, Romania, Switzerland and Turkey.

The Typhoon emerged from a long and often precarious gestation period. For many years, it seemed likely that the Eurofighter concept would never be translated into reality, and when more concrete plans were finally made to produce the new combat aircraft, it became a political football that rarely received the proper financial backing that it required. But despite this troubled history, the Typhoon has emerged as an outstanding warplane. The programme did suffer some setbacks thanks to a variety of technical glitches, but most of the Eurofighter's delays were undoubtedly caused by politics. By 1998, the British National Audit Office had estimated Typhoon's unit price cost at some £40.2 million per aircraft. If development costs are added into the equation, it puts each Typhoon at a total cost of £61 million. This is an astonishing figure for a small fighter aircraft, but when compared to its counterparts, it is a surprisingly competitive one. The Dassault Rafale can be calculated to a unit cost of £72 million per aircraft for a design that is less capable than the Typhoon. The sophisticated F-22 Raptor weighs in at a staggering £122 million per aircraft and although developments of designs such as the F-15 and F/A-18, plus the F-16 and the MiG-29, can be regarded as competitors in terms of overall cost, they do not match the capabilities of the Typhoon. It is fair to say therefore, that Typhoon represents excellent value for money. However, it would also be fair to state that the programme could have been completed much more inexpensively had politics not intervened.

The creation of a single final assembly line and a single flight test centre would undoubtedly have saved a great deal of money. As it was, the utilisation of four was wasteful, but necessary in order to satisfy the political demands of each participating nation. This inevitably made the programme artificially expensive, but this was a price that each nation was prepared to pay in order to achieve a political aim. However, the very act of creating a multi-national programme did result in a very capable warplane that would have been far more expensive to design and manufacture had the project been tackled by just one country. Another important point to consider is that there are projected costs which will be incurred throughout the Typhoon's life span and these costs were factored into the design. Low maintenance and reliability were key design aims and Eurofighter ensured that in terms of potential technical problems, Typhoon would be capable of having at least 50 per cent of any such defects rectified within forty-five minutes and 95 per cent within three hours. It was also stipulated that each engine could, if necessary, be replaced within forty-five minutes and that overall ease of maintenance is catered for. This has ensured that Typhoon is a remarkably reliable machine and one that can be maintained with relative ease in stark contrast to older combat aircraft, such as the Lightning interceptor, which were regarded as logistical nightmares. This design approach means that the Typhoon will be cheaper to operate than its counterparts and the reliability of the aircraft means that fewer aircraft need to be maintained in operational condition at any given time.

The most important issue to consider is whether the Typhoon delivers everything that was expected of it. Initial speculation suggested that the aircraft was not as manoeuvrable as its potential adversaries such as the Su-27 and MiG-29 in particular. Much of this speculation was undoubtedly nonsense and it was probably the initial public demonstrations of the Typhoon that led to such premature conclusions. Eurofighter deliberately kept Typhoon's display flights within very conservative limits during the programme's early days in order to avoid stretching the known performance envelope ahead of the development process. This inevitably encouraged uninformed observers to conclude that the Typhoon was not an agile 'turn and burn' dogfighter. Nothing could have been further from the truth. Typhoon is more than capable of engaging in combat with its contemporaries and adversaries. It can outturn all of its contemporaries and above supersonic speeds. It can outmanoeuvre the Su-27 and MiG-29. At high-subsonic speeds, only the F-22 and thrust-vectoring Su-27 can offer a better sustained turn rate and it is unlikely that Typhoon will be required to engage either of these aircraft in combat.

Indeed, it could be argued that Typhoon is a superior aircraft to every other comparable type other than the somewhat over-specified and monstrously expensive F-22. Typhoon does not have thrust-vectoring nor does it seem likely that it ever will, but the capability is there and a great deal of research and development has been conducted on potential thrust vectoring systems for the Typhoon. The aircraft's rear bulkhead is capable of being retrofitted and if a suitable engine derivative is produced, only new software would be required to enable the Typhoon to embrace thrust vectoring. The Typhoon could also be utilised as a very useful seaborne multi-role aircraft and various studies have been completed that suggest the Typhoon could be modified for carrier operations without significant difficulties. The sorry

Inside Typhoon's cockpit, illustrating the simple and uncluttered layout dominated by three MFD (Multi-Function Display) units on which all of the aircraft's systems can be displayed. (*Courtesy Eurofighter*)

tale of Britain's new carrier programme often included the possibility of modifying Typhoons to operate at sea and this would undoubtedly have been a far more logical and less expensive solution than the F-35 order that is currently being pursued. But once again, it seems that politics have prevailed over common sense.

Another much discussed issue is Typhoon's stealth capabilities. When compared to the impressive F-22, it is clear that Typhoon is not a true 'stealthy' aircraft. However, it is important to consider the Typhoon's multi-role capabilities and the scenarios in which the aircraft is expected to operate. Designed as an agile interceptor-fighter, the aircraft only requires a low radar signature from a head-on aspect as most fighter engagements start from a head-to-head position, particularly in the all important BVR (Beyond Visual Range) scenario that is the Typhoon's key role. Typhoon's rather ungainly square intakes certainly do not give the impression that stealth technology has been incorporated into them, but first impressions can be deceptive. Throughout the Typhoon's development and initial operational use, a great deal of effort has been employed in dissuading photographers from capturing clear images of the Typhoon's internal air intake design structure. The intake incorporates some carefully designed curves which shield the engine compressor blades from radar detection and it seems likely that the intake is far more stealthy than initial impressions might suggest.

The Typhoon was subjected to a great deal of RCS (Radar Cross Section) testing, much of which was observed on a special range at BAE's Warton site. Eurofighter admit that an all aspect stealth capability was never an aspiration – it would have been far too expensive – but they also claim that only the F-22 has a lower frontal RCS. Eurofighter claim that Typhoon's frontal RCS is probably only one-seventh of the Su-27's and one-fifth of the F/A-18 Hornet's. Even the elegant design of the Rafale does not compare well with Typhoon's frontal RCS being only one-third of the Rafale's. This is quite an achievement, although there is always the possibility that Eurofighter's very overt RCS testing and the restrictions on intake photography might be an elaborate bluff to compensate for a RCS that is not as good as Eurofighter claim.

What is certain, however, is that the Typhoon is a very agile and manoeuvrable aircraft. It is also capable of carrying a very varied and weighty ordnance load. It is efficient and is capable of 'supercruise' performance where the aircraft maintains supersonic speed without the use of engine reheat (afterburners). This means that Typhoon does not necessarily have to accelerate into a missile interception and enables the aircraft to enter and escape from hostile zones much more swiftly and economically than its counterparts. During test flights, the Typhoon was routinely observed to lose speed when reheat was deselected at speeds of Mach 1.4 or more, but the aircraft settles into supercruise without reheat at around Mach 1.1 and can sustain this speed as required.

Although the Typhoon is now firmly established in operational service with the RAF, Luftwaffe and the air forces of Italy, Spain, Austria and Saudi Arabia, it is inevitable that the aircraft will eventually become a part of other air forces. Also, the aircraft will be developed further to increase its already impressive capabilities and to enable the aircraft to take on new tasks. Its weapons capabilities are highly remarkable and these will be improved ensuring that the Typhoon continues to be a very potent warplane for at least another two decades. Its troubled and precarious development programme was unnecessarily long and complicated, but the participating Eurofighter nations can be justifiably proud of the magnificent warplane that emerged.

Britain and British Aerospace can be particularly proud of the support and investment that was put into the Eurofighter when other countries were all too keen to walk away. Britain's persistence and belief in the aircraft resulted in a truly impressive warplane and one that is undoubtedly the most capable fighter-bomber to have ever served with the RAF. Many of Britain's and Europe's combat aircraft designs have often suffered from political indecision, lack of finance, design requirement shifts and all manner of problems which inevitably compromise the capabilities of the final product. It might have seemed inevitable that a complicated four-nation European aircraft would suffer more than most. But even though the project was certainly not without its difficulties, it is clear that the result was an outstanding machine that was not compromised in any way by its complex development and history. Britain, Germany and Italy got the aeroplane that they wanted and in the world of military aircraft procurement and politics, this was quite an achievement. The Typhoon will remain in service with the RAF for many years to come and it might still be in business in 2040 or beyond. But by then, the RAF will undoubtedly have changed dramatically and it is impossible to predict what political, technological, financial and military developments might have influenced the RAF's direction.

By 2040, the Typhoon's offensive capabilities will almost certainly have been surpassed by new weapons systems and it may well be that UAV (Unmanned Aerial Vehicle) technology may have reached a stage that enables the RAF to finally relinquish the role of the manned bomber entirely. Unmanned attack aircraft are already part of the modern military scene and it is therefore inevitable that they will become an increasingly capable resource that will eventually render the very notion of manned aircraft obsolete. Whether the Typhoon and the F-35 will prove to be the very end of the manned bomber concept remains to be seen, but it seems more than likely that they probably will.